Practicing Multiculturalism

Practicing Multiculturalism

Affirming Diversity in Counseling and Psychology

Edited by
Timothy B. Smith

Brigham Young University

PEARSON

Boston • New York • San Francisco
Mexico City • Montreal • Toronto • London • Madrid • Munich • Paris
Hong Kong • Singapore • Tokyo • Cape Town • Sydney

Series Editor: *Kelly May*
Editorial Assistant: *Marlana Voerster*
Marketing Manager: *Wendy Gordon*
Production Administrator: *Michael Granger*
Editorial-Production Service: *Omegatype Typography, Inc.*
Composition and Prepress Buyer: *Linda Cox*
Manufacturing Buyer: *JoAnne Sweeney*
Cover Administrator: *Kristina Mose-Libon*
Electronic Composition: *Omegatype Typography, Inc.*

For related titles and support materials, visit our online catalog at www.ablongman.com

Between the time Website information is gathered and then published, it is not unusual for some sites to have closed. Also, the transcription of URLs can result in typographical errors. The publisher would appreciate notification where these errors occur so that they may be corrected in subsequent editions.

Library of Congress Cataloging-in-Publication Data

Practicing multiculturalism : affirming diversity in counseling and psychology / edited by
   Timothy B. Smith.
      p.   cm.
   Includes bibliographical references and index.
   ISBN 0-205-33640-X
      1. Cross-cultural counseling.   I. Smith, Timothy B.

   BF637.C6P7 2004
   158'.3–dc21

                                                                    2003040433

Printed in the United States of America

10   9   8   7   6   5   4   3   08   07   06   05

Contents

6 A Contextual Approach to Assessment   97

PART THREE • Considerations for Multicultural Practice with Specific Populations   121

7 Effective Interventions with Children of Color and Their Families: A Contextual Developmental Approach   123

8 Counseling and Psychotherapy with African American Clients   145

Preface

This book is about change. It is about context, power, and improving relationships. It is about enhancing the efficacy of prevention and treatment initiatives. It is an invitation to readers to practice multiculturalism in counseling and therapy.

As emphasized in the first chapter, the notion of "practicing multiculturalism" simply means putting the ideas contained within this book into practice. It means being genuinely committed to multiculturalism and acting accordingly ("walking the walk"). This book aims to improve the skills of the reader by helping the reader *internalize* the principles of multiculturalism.

A compilation of works by multiple authors, this book represents a variety of individuals and perspectives within the field. The first section describes the context of multiculturalism within mental health disciplines. It provides an overview of the key ideas and controversies represented in the current literature. The second section focuses on the development of multicultural competencies, including awareness, communication, and assessment. The third section presents specific information relevant to the mental health treatment of five racial-cultural groups and covers issues specific to four other aspects of sociocultural diversity. The final section emphasizes the importance of contextual approaches to mental health treatment and describes the usefulness of a relational perspective for effective multicultural practice.

Taking a contextual approach to multicultural mental health treatment and prevention, this book attempts to integrate multiple aspects of diversity within each chapter. Issues related to gender, sexual orientation, family dynamics, acculturation, and age therefore receive attention across several chapters.

Particularly unique is the integration of spiritual and religious issues with other aspects of diversity. Many authors have indicated that spirituality is a fundamental aspect of multiculturalism, and this volume accords it that status. Other notable features of this book include an overview of the history of the multicultural movement and discussion of philosophical tensions within the field (Chapter 2); coverage of multicultural organizational development and activism (Chapter 5); description of Arab American culture (Chapter 12); and content specific to social class and classism (Chapter 15). Chapters on children and families, international students and immigrants, and religious diversity also provide a breadth of coverage useful to practitioners and students alike.

A limitation of this book, and any book on multiculturalism, is the tension between describing characteristics of a particular group and the tendency to stereotype individual group members. For that and other reasons, several chapters emphasize the necessity of accurate contextual understanding of individuals. Seeing individuals in their context informs and enhances effective counseling and therapy, whereas only seeing contexts (race, gender, sexual orientation, age, etc.) obscures the individual and ironically prevents accurate contextual understanding. Thus, although this book presents information that may generalize from one situation and from one individual to another, it also emphasizes the essential skill of addressing each individual contextually.

Acknowledgments

The author expresses appreciation to the pioneers of the multicultural revolution in counseling and psychology. Special thanks to Sharon Black for her help with technical editing, to the students of my classes for their invaluable feedback, and to the external reviewers: Jose Abreu, University of Southern California; Daisuke Akiba, Queens College of the City University of New York; Madonna G. Constantine, Teachers College at Columbia University; Arpana Inman, Lehigh University; and Bryan S. K. Kim, University of Maryland at College Park.

About the Contributors

Timothy B. Smith is an associate professor of counseling psychology at Brigham Young University, editor of the *Journal of College Counseling,* and author of several publications on multiculturalism and spirituality.

Daisuke Akiba is an assistant professor at Queens College of the City University of New York, and adjunct professor at Brown University. He has written several publications on the development of children of color and children from immigrant families.

Nada R. Al-Timimi is a counselor at Temple University's Counseling Services Center and conducts research on multicultural counseling and sexual orientation.

Patricia Arredondo is an associate professor of counseling psychology at Arizona State University, author of many publications on multiculturalism, and a recognized leader in the field of multicultural counseling.

Leonie J. Brooks is an assistant professor of psychology at Towson University.

Elisa M. Castillo is a staff psychologist and multicultural specialist at Northeastern University in Boston. She received her doctoral degree from the University of Wisconsin–Madison, and she has published chapters on cultural competence in assessment and therapy with children, adolescents, and adults.

June Chu is a graduate student in the Department of Psychology, University of California, Davis.

Matthew Draper is an assistant professor of counseling psychology at Indiana State University and the author of several publications on counseling and philosophical issues relative to mental health treatment.

Chris D. Erickson is an assistant professor of counseling at George Washington University and the author of several publications on multicultural issues and vocational counseling.

Cynthia Garcia Coll is a professor of education, psychology, and pediatrics; chair of the Education Department at Brown University; and director of the Center for the Study of Human

Development at Brown University. She is the author of many publications on the development of children of color and is a recognized leader in the field.

Alberta M. Gloria is an associate professor of counseling psychology at the University of Wisconsin–Madison. Her research interests include psychosociocultural factors for Chicano/a and Latino/a students in higher education. She has served as the secretary, membership chair, and chair of the Section for Ethnic and Racial Diversity for Division 17 of APA and as the secretary for the National Latino/a Psychological Association. She was awarded the Women of Color Psychologies Award from Division 35 in 1999 and the Emerging Professional Award from Division 45 in 2002.

Deborah G. Haskins is an assistant professor and director of master's education at Loyola College in Maryland.

Aaron P. Jackson is an assistant professor of counseling psychology at Brigham Young University and the author of several publications on career and Native American issues.

Judith V. Kehe is a faculty member at the Community College of Baltimore County Essex Campus and an adjunct faculty member at Loyola College in Maryland.

Roger R. Keller is a professor of religion at Brigham Young University and the author of many publications on comparative world religions.

Nancy Lin is a graduate student in the Department of Psychology, University of Massachusetts, Boston.

William M. Liu is an assistant professor of counseling psychology at the University of Iowa and author of several publications on multiculturalism and social class issues.

Heath Mac Granley is a practicing psychologist at the Center for Change in Orem, Utah.

Teru Morton is a professor at the California School of Professional Psychology, Alliant International University, San Diego.

Festus Obiakor is a professor of exceptional education at the University of Wisconsin-Milwaukee and is the author of over 100 publications on multicultural education.

Paul B. Pedersen is a professor at the University of Alabama at Birmingham, author of many books and other professional publications, and a recognized leader in the field of multicultural counseling and psychology.

Donald B. Pope-Davis is a professor of counseling psychology at Notre Dame University, editor of the *Journal of Multicultural Counseling and Development,* author of many publications on multiculturalism, and a recognized leader in the field of multicultural counseling.

Tiffany Rice is a doctoral student in the Counseling/Counseling Psychology Program at Arizona State University.

P. Scott Richards is a professor of counseling psychology at Brigham Young University, fellow of APA Division 36, and author of *A Spiritual Strategy for Counseling and Psychotherapy* and the *Handbook of Psychotherapy and Religious Diversity.*

Gargi Roysircar is a professor of psychology at Antioch New England Graduate School (ANE), founding director of the ANE Multicultural Center for Research and Practice, fellow of the American Psychological Association (Divisions 17 and 45), former president of the Association for Multicultural Counseling and Development (AMCD), and a recognized leader in the field of multicultural counseling.

Ester L. Ruiz is an associate professor at Arizona State University where she teaches counseling skills to psychiatric nurse practitioner students. She is a consulting editor for *Professional Psychology: Research and Practice,* and her research interests include health, mental health, and psychotherapy issues for Latinos and other racial/ethnic populations.

Chalmer E. Thompson is an associate professor and director of training at Indiana University, Bloomington, and is the author of several publications on racial identity and psychotherapy processes related to oppression and social change.

Sherri Turner is an assistant professor of counseling psychology at the University of Minnesota and the author of several publications on career and Native American issues.

Billy E. Vaughn is the president of Diversity Training University International and the director of the Psychology Doctoral Program in Culture and Human Behavior at the California School for Professional Psychology, San Diego.

Nolan Zane is an associate professor of psychology at the University of California, Davis, and the director of the National Research Center on Asian American Mental Health.

Practicing Multiculturalism

Part I

Overview: Understanding Multicultural Contexts

1

Practicing Multiculturalism

An Introduction

**Timothy B. Smith, P. Scott Richards,
and Heath Mac Granley**
Brigham Young University

Festus Obiakor
University of Wisconsin, Milwaukee

In North America, no President has ever been White. Up until the past century, men could not vote. Nearly all public officials and corporate executives are lesbian or gay. Television images, movies, and glamour magazines promote the elderly as role models. Inner cities and rural areas enjoy abundant wealth and educational opportunities. Buddhism is the predominant religion. As part of ongoing reparations to the descendents of European Americans traded as slaves until the 1800s, English was recently made an official language. All North America has remained sovereign Native American land.

Culture is invisible without contrast. Just as a fish may be oblivious to the water in which it swims, mental health professionals often fail to recognize the multicultural contexts in which we practice. If we contrast our perspective with that of any other person or group of persons in the world, we will see the need for multiculturalism.

Power and reward structures in any given society, organization, or relationship are also often invisible without contrast. Individuals or groups who have the power to influence social interactions, social structures, and environmental contexts often take that power for granted, but those denied access to such power notice its absence. Most of us can remember a time when we felt completely unable to change a harmful, unjust situation. And we can compare our many privileges as English-speaking professionals (or future professionals) with the opportunities available to people with little education. Both experiences show us the need to recognize context, status, and power in all human interactions.

Culture and power are omnipresent at multiple levels in every human interaction. They are therefore fundamental to the dynamics of every therapeutic relationship, whether or not the therapist or client acknowledges them. Optimally, culture and power should be recognized in *all* therapeutic relationships, but it is usually the contrasts in inter-racial or inter-gender relationships, for example, that heighten awareness of cultural and power dynamics that impact treatment. Therefore, as defined in this book *multicultural counseling and psychology* refers not merely to working with diverse populations, but to an approach that accounts for the influences of culture and power in any therapeutic relationship. Thus this chapter and all of those that follow seek to increase the efficacy of treatment by calling attention to the pervasive yet often implicit multicultural contexts in which we work as mental health professionals.

Why Practice Multiculturalism?

Anisah was a devout Muslim who had heard that counseling and psychotherapy were to be avoided. When Anisah began experiencing panic attacks, she first sought medical help, believing that she was having heart attacks. After two trips to the hospital emergency room, along with a complete cardiac workup, Anisah was reassured by her physician that there was nothing wrong with her heart. Her doctor explained that she seemed to be experiencing panic attacks, and she recommended that Anisah seek mental health assistance. After enduring many more severe panic attacks, Anisah finally became so desperate that she made an appointment with a therapist she found listed in the phone book. In the first session with the therapist, Anisah was nervous and disclosed that she had not wanted to attend therapy that day. Anisah asked the therapist if he could refer her to a female Muslim therapist. The therapist told her that he didn't know of any therapists who met that description and went on to explain how religious beliefs were irrelevant to panic attacks. Confused and upset, Anisah returned to her physician, who prescribed medication and who located a therapist who had a good reputation for working with a variety of clients. Although the therapist was agnostic, she was familiar with basic Islamic beliefs, and she encouraged Anisah to rely upon Allah for help and to share her concerns with older women she knew and trusted. The therapist validated Anisah's concerns about her physical health by explaining the close association of physical health and anxiety, and she instructed her in relaxation techniques. Sensing her hesitation to practice the techniques at home, the therapist offered to travel to meet with her family and religious leaders to resolve concerns she still had. Although Anisah declined the invitation, she did discuss the therapist's recommendations with two women at her mosque and with her husband before returning for seven more sessions.

As is evident in this case example, practicing multiculturalism in counseling and psychotherapy is essential for a number of reasons, including client retention and enhanced treatment outcomes. Research demonstrates that when multiculturalism is practiced, clients feel more understood and respected, and positive treatment outcomes improve significantly (e.g., Obiakor & Schwenn, 1995; Zang & Dixon, 2001). More people are provided access to mental health services, and disadvantaged groups utilize mental health treatment more frequently and with fewer early terminations than when multicultural issues are ignored (Atkinson & Hackett, 1995; Pedersen, 1991; Ponterotto, Casas, Suzuki, & Alexander, 2000).

Practical observation also supports multiculturalism as essential to effective practice. Because every human is in many ways unique from any other, no single approach or technique will work with every person or group (Obiakor, 1994; Sue & Sue, 1999). This problem of generalizability has not yet been adequately addressed in mental health research (Sue, 1999). In our theories, and in our training, we attempt to generalize from one client to the next, but in the real world, attentive professionals are often surprised by something a client says or does. Tailoring treatment to each individual is facilitated when a counselor or therapist considers the client's uniqueness along with the contexts in which the individual lives and functions.

Another benefit of multiculturalism is that it allows for a variety of valid approaches to healing. Because all cultures have developed means for enhancing mental health, the efficacy of counseling and psychotherapy may be enhanced by integrating other traditions and insights into contemporary therapeutic practices, which are almost exclusively based on European and North American healing traditions (e.g., Atkinson & Hackett, 1995; Sue & Sue, 1999). Moreover, contemporary practitioners can learn from the past. From a historical perspective, psychology and counseling are recent developments, yet the prevalence of mental illness has at least remained stable over time, if not increased. The weekly 50-minute session with each individual client is not the only way to treat mental illness. For example, even though cognitive therapy was not practiced in times past, similar effects have been achieved through community teachings and traditions such as spiritual rituals that increased hope, meaning, and pro-social thoughts. Researchers are now recognizing the wisdom in traditional cultural and religious practices and values that for generations have been effective in enhancing mental health and preventing mental illness (Koenig, McCullough, & Larson, 2001; Pargament, 1997; Richards & Bergin, 1997, 2000).

Finally, it is ethically and even morally "best practice" to incorporate cultural values and symbols when working with people who are culturally diverse (Obiakor, 2001a, 2001b). To adapt practices to suit the characteristics and needs of those who seek mental health assessment or treatment is a professional responsibility. For this reason, among others, ethical standards of the American Psychological Association (APA, 1992) and American Counseling Association (ACA, 1995) emphasize the importance of multicultural practice.

Despite the research evidence, logical arguments, and ethical guidelines that support a multicultural perspective, some counselors or therapists may resist the ideas presented in this book. Others may openly acknowledge the benefits of multicultural principles, particularly in public, but then fail to apply them in their own work. Still others may affirm the need for diversity but then attack anyone who challenges their own way of thinking. Counselors or therapists with such attitudes must address a critical question: "In a society that is incredibly diverse at multiple levels, what are the aims and potential consequences of any alternative to practicing multiculturalism?"

The Aim of Multiculturalism

Although contrast helps to identify difference, recognition of people's differences is not a desirable outcome in and of itself. Mere awareness or even tolerance of others' differences does not make for effective therapy or for an optimal society. To do that, an understanding of differences must foster unity: *not* unity through similarity, but unity through mutual enrichment. *Mutual enrichment* in interpersonal relationships, in organizations, and in societies is the essential aim of multiculturalism.

Differences will always exist among individuals in relationships, organizations, and societies. The goal of multiculturalism is to benefit from those differences. Other perspectives end up dismissing or glossing over differences ("we're all the same"), pitting groups against one another in competition ("X group scores higher than Y group on Z test"), emphasizing divisive labels and perceptions ("X group is better than Y group"), patronizing differences ("Y group needs our help"), overemphasizing and reifying differences ("X group and Y group are incompatible and will never get along"), or exploiting differences ("X group deserves more than Y group"). Multiculturalism simply acknowledges the reality that differences do exist and can contribute to unity and mutual enrichment when power differences and social equity are also addressed.

Consider this example of multiculturalism:

> In a graduate program where mutual cultural enrichment was a primary goal, both faculty and students appropriately struggled to maintain open forums for dialogue. Problems would become a focus of group discussion, with all students and faculty present. Often these discussions would follow a similar pattern. They began with a tense uncertainty and sometimes remained tense for quite some time, but often validation and understanding led to a resolution to do better. Even then, misunderstanding often continued, and another group meeting was usually called some time later to deal with a new variant of an old problem. Some students openly resented having to attend the meetings, and a few others harbored mistrust. Although they faced major difficulties, participants in this training program continued to struggle with difficult issues and received national recognition for their efforts to practice multiculturalism.

Reality is rarely optimal. In fact, real situations often disappoint people by failing to match the ideal, or falling short of some expectations. In a group striving toward mutual cultural enrichment, the differences will be as real as the points of unity. The difficult work of multiculturalism is establishing contexts of equitable, constructive use of power. As in the above example, unity is enhanced not when differences disappear but when people remain committed to one another and use structures and resources to maintain open and ongoing relationships.

In reality, open and ongoing relationships necessitate personal change. To achieve mutual enrichment, people must be appreciated and "enriched" (changed for the better) by others, as new perspectives are formed and old expectations are questioned or replaced as a result of the new relationship. We cannot have effective relationships with individuals who are different without expecting to be changed ourselves through the process.

Making the Implicit Explicit: Addressing Power and Culture

We all have expectations that we seek to validate in our interactions with others. When expectations must be changed, this adjustment is facilitated when we (1) realize that expectations are often based on assumptions, not facts, (2) value the experiences of others, and (3) have sufficient self-worth to minimize defensiveness when our expectations are challenged (Obiakor, 1999).

Assumptions That Shape Expectations and Perceptions of Reality

Legend recounts that when the French princess Marie Antoinette was informed that her country was in deep turmoil because the people had no bread, she replied, "Let them eat cake." A similar narrow perspective is reflected in expressions such as "let them work harder" from those who have never been denied employment or "let them get over slavery" from those whose ancestors were free. Privilege taken for granted is one example of how assumptions may lead to expectations that blind us to the experiences of others.

Assumptions based on privilege are maintained and perpetuated because they are rarely challenged. When left unchallenged, assumptions become reality. For example, unchallenged beliefs in Germany during the mid-1930s led directly to the events of the subsequent decade. Millions of Jews, Gypsies, and gays were killed in the minds of the Nazis before the first concentration camp was ever built.

Multiculturalism challenges our own assumptions, informs us of the experiences of others, and thereby helps us relate more effectively with one another (Obiakor, 2001a). In the earlier example, working harder and forgetting past injustices are indeed fine solutions in many contexts. Eating cake satisfies hunger as much as eating bread. The problem is that assumptions (and solutions, perceptions, and behaviors) that work well in one context may not work at all when applied in other contexts.

Even the common assumption "let them seek individual weekly 50-minute sessions" only makes sense in a context where individualism and symptom reduction are valued over approaches that emphasize prevention, familial dynamics, or long-term healing and change. Multiculturalism challenges assumptions about effective treatment, encouraging mental health practitioners to adapt their practices to fit the experiences of the client (e.g.,

Atkinson & Hackett, 1995). When therapists' assumptions and expectations prevent them from seeing clients' needs and experiences, therapy may prove harmful (Sue & Sue, 1999), as shown in the following example.

> A 27-year-old international student from India sought treatment for symptoms of severe depression. When the therapist learned that part of the student's dilemma was that his parents insisted that he pursue a career in medicine, even though he would prefer to study journalism, the therapist changed the focus of treatment to address dependency and appropriate assertiveness with others. The client did not return for future sessions or for classes the following semester.

Good Intentions and Valuing Others

Many people who enter the mental health professions do so out of a desire to help others. It therefore comes as a surprise and disappointment when good intentions may not lead to positive results. As demonstrated above in the case of the student from India, good intentions are simply not enough. Applied without heed to the differences in context, typically "good" solutions can produce bad outcomes. Unintentional awkwardness, misunderstanding, and other negative outcomes occur in therapy to the extent that expectations based on one's own culture and privileges are valued more than the actual experiences of the client.

The following adaptation of the Indian student's story alters the therapist's behavior to be more effective.

> Though the international student's depression seemed to be related to his career interests, the therapist sought to understand the context of the problem by spending another session discussing the client's family and his current academic and social situation. The therapist learned that in the client's culture, children traditionally follow their parents, and in this particular case, both the client's parents were physicians. The therapist also learned that the client's only friend at the university studied journalism and that they spent many hours discussing current events. Focusing on the perceptions and experiences of the client, the therapist facilitated the client's social involvement (including participation in a campus journalism group) and the client's insights on how best to communicate with his parents. The client began sending his parents articles that he had written for newspapers on new medical technology. Although his desire to study medicine did not increase, the young man felt more confident in his relationship with his parents, and his symptoms of depression improved as he developed new friendships on campus. He continued studying medicine.

In this example, therapy did not need to be drastically modified to effectively work with the client (although sometimes it does). What benefited the treatment outcome was the therapist's willingness to hear and value the client's context.

Listening to and valuing others are skills that are so overdiscussed that their effect is often overlooked. For example, at a recent national convention on multicultural psychology, a session designed to enhance participant dialogue concerning difficult issues broke down in part because some participants did not respectfully listen to the group's facilitators. Open dialogue proved difficult even for people apparently committed to multiculturalism! Listening to and valuing others are foundations for constructive relationships and for change, as shown in the following example.

> A recently hired European American psychologist got to know the support staff in his new organization. Over time, he began to hear from them evidence of discrimination within the organization. In individual and group meetings with others in the organization, he raised the issues that the staff had struggled with but had not yet articulated openly. Organizational policies that had been thought to be helpful but were actually problematic were revised to the satisfaction of all members of the organization.

As shown in this example, valuing others often requires making changes as individuals and as organizations. Without a willingness to make these changes, there is little value in valuing others.

However, this does not mean that mental health professionals need to alter all of their own beliefs to agree with those of others. Relativism is problematic and logically inconsistent (Bergin, 1980; Richards & Bergin, 1997). We assert that some values are "better than others because they do more to promote spirituality, mental health, and harmonious interpersonal relations" (Richards & Bergin, 1997, p. 131), even and especially when cultural and power contexts are addressed accurately. For example, certain values or behaviors have harmful consequences (e.g., female circumcision, substance abuse, physical violence, sexual abuse), even though these values and behaviors may have been strongly influenced by a given culture and/or power structure. In such cases, the principle of "valuing others" requires that therapists inform clients of the consequences of values and behaviors that may compromise their own health or the well-being of others (Richards & Bergin, 1997; Richards et al., 1999). Because what is considered "unhealthy" values/behaviors may differ greatly from one context to another, therapists who value others will never impose their own ideas about what is "healthy," but will help clients examine for themselves the consequences of their cultural assumptions and values. After doing so, therapists must ultimately respect clients' right to pursue values that may be unhealthy from the perspective of the therapist, except where ethical and/or legal responsibility exists to intervene (e.g., potential suicide, threats to harm others, abuse of children or the elderly). In sum, effective multicultural work requires listening to others, valuing others, and making changes at the personal and institutional levels to enhance mental health. A willingness to listen, value, and then change accordingly develops as therapists minimize their own defensiveness and act genuinely in the service of others.

Defensiveness versus Genuineness

Fear of saying the "wrong thing" is a common reaction among counselors or therapists who perceive a client to be different from themselves. It is also common for therapists to feel frustration at not being understood or accepted by a client who apparently sees the therapist as being different. Differences are often perceived as threatening by both the therapist and the client. Fear and anger are natural responses to perceived threat. Defensiveness, fear, and anger further limit the ability to perceive others accurately. Hence, the admonition to listen and value others is repeated often in the mental health professions. It is the common tendency for inattention to defensive reactions that makes the repetition necessary.

Genuineness enables effective multicultural communication. It is harder to feel frightened of or angry with another person if one is at peace with oneself. It is easier to accept others and adapt to their differences if one is focused on building relationships, rather than focused on one's own anxiety or discomfort. The field of psychology has taught the world many things, but the wisdom to simply be at peace, to be fully present, to be real, etc., are lessons seldom heard in the classroom, perhaps because they are the hardest lessons to learn.

This is not to say that conflict should be avoided. Conflict is unavoidable when people are genuine. But as research in interpersonal relationships has shown, it is defensiveness and hostility, not confrontation over differences, that destroy relationships (Gottman, 1993). Confrontation may be helpful if it is proactive and focused on strengthening the relationship rather than reactive and characterized by contempt, retribution, withdrawal, and demands. Thus, multiculturalism has more to do with the *process* of handling differences and unity than with the actual content of the differences and points of unity.

In the example of the newly hired European American psychologist whose proactive confrontation of discriminatory organizational policies led to positive organizational change, such change would not have been likely had there not been confrontation by a person in a position of power. However, when the confrontation is reactive and characterized by contempt, retribution, or withdrawal, positive outcomes are also unlikely, as shown in the following continuation of that example.

> Over time, the new psychologist became disgruntled by the amount of work expected by his organization relative to the amount of pay. When he complained, the administration was able to do little. He spent more and more time socializing with the support staff, who empathized with his situation. In organizational meetings, he became very vocal in defending their interests and in pointing out evidences of discrimination within the organization, including many issues that the support staff had not previously considered. He distanced himself from the other professional personnel, including the psychologists of color, who he felt perpetuated aspects of institutional racism. He stopped attending organizational meetings, which had become quite volatile and hurtful. Suspicion and tension heightened as members of the organization clustered into separate camps, and many support staff began to look for positions elsewhere.

As with therapy, content is important, but process is key. When the content of multiculturalism (e.g., group traits) becomes more important than the process of multiculturalism (e.g., effective communication across group differences), mutual enrichment rarely occurs. Although much of this book addresses important issues of multicultural content, the foundation for each chapter is multicultural process, sometimes referred to as *multicultural competency,* the effective application of multicultural content in therapeutic relationships.

Multicultural Competencies

At a simplistic level, practicing multiculturalism involves challenging assumptions, valuing others, and being genuine in all interactions. These and other principles have been distilled into specific guidelines for the profession, referred to as multicultural competencies. Because traditional counseling and psychotherapy have been based exclusively on European and North American culture, the needs of diverse client populations are often unmet (Richardson & Molinaro, 1996). To more effectively work with all clients, several theorists and researchers have proposed specific models of multicultural competence (e.g., Arredondo et al., 1996; Sue, 1981). Multicultural competencies provide a framework for therapy that recognizes the client's context, including race, gender, socioeconomic status, sexual orientation, abilities, age, religion, national origin, and power (e.g., Sue, Arredondo, & McDavis, 1992).

Most authors delineate multicultural competence into three general areas: awareness, knowledge, and skills (e.g., Arredondo et al., 1996). *Awareness* refers to therapists' personal self-awareness: awareness of their worldview, values, assumptions, expectations, privileges, biases, theoretical orientation, and so on. *Knowledge* refers to therapists' understanding and knowledge of human diversity in all its forms: racial, cultural, religious, gender, sexual orientation, and so on. *Skills* refers to therapists' ability to use their personal awareness and knowledge of client culture and diversity in a therapeutic manner during the treatment process.

Each of the three areas of multicultural competence—awareness, knowledge, and skills—is interrelated with the other two. For example, it is impossible to have a truly effective relationship without being knowledgeable about the other person and aware of how each impacts the relationship; it is also impossible to be fully aware of one's own assumptions and biases without interacting with others and learning from the differences. As has been noted, "awareness and knowledge competencies are essential prerequisites to developing adequate multicultural skills" (Hansen, Pepitone-Arreola-Rockwell, & Greene, 2000, p. 654). Although the following sections describe basic elements of multicultural awareness, knowledge, and skills, it should be kept in mind that these content areas overlap significantly and are more complex than the following lists may suggest. More thorough descriptions and greater specificity regarding multicultural competencies are provided in other chapters of this book and in related articles on this topic (APA, 2002; Arredondo et al., 1996; Axelson, 1985; Constantine & Ladany, 2001; Hansen et al., 2000; Sue, 1981; Sue et al., 1992).

Therapist Self-Awareness

A personal self-awareness including one's own worldview, values, biases, theoretical orientation, and privileges is essential in working effectively with clients. Specifically, therapists must be aware of the following:

1. Their own worldview, values, and racial-cultural heritage and ways that these may influence their perceptions of clients and their work in therapy.
2. Their stereotypes, biases, and assumptions about races, cultures, genders, sexual orientations, religions, age groups, abilities, etc.

3. Their theoretical orientation and treatment approach, with its possible limitations in working with clients from diverse backgrounds.
4. Their communication style and the social impact it has on clients.
5. Their unearned privileges, particularly those that perpetuate inequality and discrimination.
6. Their level of efficacy, self-confidence, anxiety, and defensiveness when working with others.
7. Their actions (not just intentions) designed to increase multicultural knowledge, skills, and self-efficacy.

Knowledge of Culture and Diversity

In addition to developing multicultural awareness about themselves, it is critical for therapists to acquire detailed knowledge regarding the background, worldview, and contexts of others. When they acquire and utilize accurate multicultural knowledge, mental health professionals can be more aware of structural and interpersonal dynamics, and thus they are more skilled in their interventions. Among other topics, therapists must gain knowledge and understanding of the following:

1. Multicultural theory and research addressing the mental health issues faced by their clients.
2. The historical background, cultural heritage, and life experiences of their clients.
3. Clients' family and community structures and dynamics, including roles and responsibilities.
4. Institutional barriers and sociopolitical influences that may be affecting a client's welfare (e.g., racism, sexism, poverty).
5. Social and cultural resources that may be available to clients.
6. Perceptions of the client concerning mental health, helping, and healing.

Therapeutic Skills

Grounded in the awareness and knowledge components just described, multiculturally competent mental health professionals should develop certain therapeutic skills:

1. To monitor their own attitudes, beliefs, and reactions to clients.
2. To engage in honest and nondefensive self-analysis and personal reflection as they work with clients.
3. To communicate effectively with clients by sending and receiving verbal and non-verbal messages accurately and by clarifying content whenever a message appears to have been inaccurately interpreted.
4. To reduce client mistrust and develop an effective working alliance with clients.
5. To demonstrate respect for clients whose beliefs and values are different from their own.
6. To apply assessment methods and interventions in a contextually sensitive and relevant manner.

7. To apply relevant multicultural theory and research to address mental health issues of clients.
8. To work to reduce the effects of institutional barriers and discrimination practices on clients.
9. To actively consult with clients' support networks, including traditional healers or religious leaders when appropriate.
10. To openly share and discuss with clients the expectations, assessment procedures, therapeutic interventions, and legal rights that are relevant to the situation.
11. To anticipate and plan for difficulties.

Assessing Multicultural Competence

Assessment of multicultural competence is essential for practitioners and for trainees enrolled in courses on the topic (e.g., Tomlinson-Clarke, 2000). To facilitate valid and reliable assessment of multicultural competencies, several measures have been developed for personal and programmatic use. Self-report measures include (1) *Multicultural Awareness/Knowledge/Skills Survey* (MAKSS) (D'Andrea, Daniels, & Heck, 1991), an instrument which has been used primarily to assess the effectiveness of multicultural training, which is composed of three subscales that measure awareness, knowledge, and skills; (2) *Multicultural Counseling Inventory* (MCI) (Sodowsky, Taffe, Gutkin, & Wise, 1994), an instrument designed to operationalize some of the proposed constructs of multicultural competence, consisting of four subscales that assess multicultural awareness, knowledge, skills, and relationships; (3) *Multicultural Counseling Knowledge and Awareness Scale* (MCKAS) (Ponterotto, Gretchen, Utsey, Rieger, & Austin, 2000), which is a measure of general knowledge related to multicultural practice and subtle Eurocentric worldview bias; and (4) *Cross-Cultural Counseling Inventory-Revised* (CCCI-R) (LaFromboise, Coleman, & Hernandez, 1991). Measures that assess the overall effectiveness of training programs are the *Multicultural Competency Checklist* (MCC) (Ponterotto, Alexander, & Grieger, 1995) and the *Diversity Mission Evaluation Questionnaire* (DMEQ) (Ducker & Tori, 2001). Finally, Coleman (1997) and Constantine and Ladany (2001) have suggested a portfolio approach to assessment, wherein examples of an individual's work demonstrate multicultural awareness, knowledge, and skills across various treatment modalities.

The Secret to Successful Multicultural Practice: Practicing Multiculturalism

Therapists who become anxious or frustrated when working with someone who is very different from themselves often seek to learn the quickest and easiest step-by-step formula or special technique that will allow them to feel confident in their work. But multicultural competence and self-efficacy entail more than following a checklist. The secret to successful multicultural relationships is that there is no secret. There is no "quick and easy" formula or technique. The guidelines and principles listed in the previous section can certainly help, but there are no shortcuts to positive relationships. All helping relationships require effort, adaptation, and more than a little humility.

Unlike many other areas of learning where memorizing and intellectualizing are valued, multiculturalism demands engagement with the subject on a personal level. Multiculturalism is not just a set of lists, facts, guidelines, or principles—*multiculturalism must be practiced to be understood.* Action must precede and accompany real learning. Although reading books and observing expert models can help, there is simply no substitute for personal experience, such as immersion in another culture (e.g., Pope-Davis, Breaux, & Lui, 1997).

Therefore, the responsibility to not only understand but *internalize* principles of multiculturalism rests with each individual. No one else can "teach" what individuals must experience for themselves. While others may facilitate learning, all people must first look to themselves as the source of change.

As encouragement for professionals engaged in the difficult process of personal change that multiculturalism requires, Thomas Parham (2001) has provided five recommendations, summarized here:

1. Have courage. Dare to confront your own limitations and to face public condemnation for your stance against intolerance.
2. Become a risk-taker. Be willing to stretch your ways of thinking, speaking, and acting. Do things differently.
3. Inform yourself through new relationships. Meet others from different backgrounds and learn by deepening those associations.
4. Rediscover the capacity to trust. Accepting others requires that you trust yourself and are willing to risk trusting others without requiring them to meet your own standards.
5. Renew your faith. Believe that overcoming intolerance is possible and that progress will come as you work toward it. Hold yourself and others accountable for that progress, and practice what you preach. (pp. 878–879)

It should be clear that each of Parham's (2001) recommendations requires internal, emotional work. As mental health professionals work toward multicultural self-efficacy and as they truly engage with others who are different, they may not be able to avoid feeling frightened, angry, surprised, humiliated, justifiably indignant, and even ambivalent as defenses against feeling anything else. Recognizing and working with emotions can facilitate the growth and change required to become more effective in working with others. Defenses such as ambivalence are normal, but that is why having courage to face limitations and take risks, etc., is so central to multiculturalism. A professional who works toward enhancing multicultural awareness, knowledge, and skills can expect to be enriched (changed for the better) by taking those risks. Real growth comes in extending the trust and acceptance that can strengthen a relationship and in working to overcome intolerance—especially outside of one's comfort zone.

Conclusion

Power and culture are invisible without contrast. This implies that mental health professionals may be blind to their own values and assumptions that can negatively impact those with whom they work. Multiculturalism offers a perspective informed by contrast, such that the implicit dynamics of power and culture are made explicit. Mental health professionals who practice multiculturalism are therefore attuned to privileges, inequities, needs, and biases, enabling them to respond more effectively to the contexts in which they work. They value others, listen attentively, and work hard to minimize their own defensiveness, reactivity, and prejudice. Multiculturally competent therapists are *aware* of their own assumptions, *knowledgeable* about clients' contexts, and *skillful* in their efforts to promote positive change.

Practicing multiculturalism means *internalizing* the principles of multicultural competency and acting accordingly. A therapist may attempt to fake genuineness or respect, but one who does this cannot be competent in multicultural contexts. Genuineness and respect are spontaneous ways of responding to others, habits developed through repeated experience.

In sum, it is impossible to separate multicultural competence from the character and personality of the therapist. One's personality, assumptions, values, defenses, and genuineness are inseparable from therapeutic work. A book or class cannot provide for multicultural competence (Parham, 2001) because multiculturalism is not just a set of facts, guidelines, or principles. It is a way of life.

References

American Counseling Association (ACA). (1995). *Code of ethics and standards of practice*. Alexandria, VA: Author.

American Psychological Association (APA). (2002). *Guidelines on multicultural education, training, research, practice, and organizational change in psychology*. Washington, DC: American Psychological Association.

American Psychological Association (APA). (1992). Ethical principles of psychologists and code of conduct. *American Psychologist, 47,* 1597–1611.

Arredondo, P., Toporek, R., Brown, S. P., Jones, J., Locke, D. C., Sanchez, J., & Stadler, H. (1996). Operationalization of the multicultural counseling competencies. *Journal of Multicultural Counseling and Development, 24,* 42–78.

Atkinson, D. R., & Hackett, G. (1995). *Counseling diverse populations*. Madison, WI: WCB Brown & Benchmark.

Axelson, J. A. (1985). *Counseling and development in a multicultural society*. Monterey, CA: Brooks/Cole.

Coleman, H. (1997). Portfolio assessment of multicultural counseling competence. In D. Pope-Davis and H. Coleman (Eds.), *Multicultural counseling competencies: Assessment, education and training, and supervision* (pp. 43–59). Thousand Oaks, CA: Sage.

Constantine, M. G., & Ladany, N. (2001). New visions for defining and assessing multicultural counseling competence. In J. G Ponterotto, J. M. Casas, L. A. Suzuki, & C. M. Alexander (Eds.), *Handbook of Multicultural Counseling* (2nd ed., pp. 482–498). Thousand Oaks, CA: Sage Publications, Inc.

D'Andrea, M., Daniels, J., & Heck, R. (1991). Evaluating the impact of multicultural counseling training. *Journal of Counseling & Development, 70,* 143–150.

Ducker, C., & Tori, D. (2001). The reliability and validity of a multicultural assessment instrument developed for a graduate program in psychology. *Professional Psychology: Research & Practice, 32,* 425–432.

Gottman, J. M. (1993). The roles of conflict engagement, escalation, and avoidance in marital interaction: A longitudinal view of five types of couples. *Journal of Consulting and Clinical Psychology, 61,* 6–15.

Hansen, N. D., Pepitone-Arreola-Rockwell, F., & Greene, A. F. (2000). Multicultural competence: Criteria and case examples. *Professional Psychology: Research and Practice, 31*(6), 652–660.

Koenig, H. G., McCullough, M. E., & Larson, D. B. (2001). *Handbook of religion and health*. New York: Oxford Press.

Obiakor, F. E. (1994). *The eight-step multicultural approach: Learning and teaching with a smile*. Dubuque, IA: Kendall/Hunt.

Obiakor, F. E. (1999). Teacher expectations of minority exceptional learners: Impact on "accuracy" of self-concepts. *Exceptional Children, 66,* 39–53.

Obiakor, F. E. (2001a). Multicultural education: Powerful tool for preparing future general and special educators. *Teacher Education and Special Education, 24,* 241–255.

Obiakor, F. E. (2001b). *It even happens in "good" schools: Responding to cultural diversity in today's schools.* Thousand Oaks, CA: Corwin Press.

Obiakor, F. E., & Schwenn, J. O. (1995). Enhancing self-concepts of culturally diverse students: The role of the counselor. In A. F. Rotatori, J. O. Schwenn, & F. W. Littan (Eds.), *Advances in special education: Counseling special populations: Research and practice.* (vol. 8, pp. 191–206). Greenwich, CT: JAI Press.

Pargament, K. I. (1997). *The psychology of religion and coping.* New York: Guilford.

Parham, T. (2001). Afterword: Beyond intolerance: Bridging the gap between imposition and acceptance. In J. G. Ponterotto, J. M. Casas, L. A. Suzuki, & C. M. Alexander (Eds.), *Handbook of multicultural counseling* (2nd ed.). Thousand Oaks, CA: Sage.

Pedersen, P. (1991). Multiculturalism as a generic approach to counseling. *Journal of Counseling & Development, 70,* 6–12.

Ponterotto, J. G., Alexander, C. M., & Grieger, I. (1995). A multicultural competency checklist for counseling training programs. *Journal of Multicultural Counseling and Development, 23,* 11–20.

Ponterotto, J. G., Casas, J. M., Suzuki, L. A., & Alexander, C. M. (Eds.) (2000). *Handbook of Multicultural Counseling* (2nd ed.). Thousand Oaks, CA: Sage.

Ponterotto, J. G., Gretchen, D., Utsey, S. O., Rieger, B. P., & Austin, R. (2000). *A construct validity study of the multicultural counseling awareness scale (MCAS).* Unpublished manuscript.

Pope-Davis, D., Breaux, C., & Lui, W. (1997). A multicultural immersion experience: Filling a void in multicultural training. In D. Pope-Davis and H. Coleman (Eds.), *Multicultural counseling competencies: Assessment, education and training, and supervision.* (pp. 227–241). Thousand Oaks, CA: Sage.

Richards, P. S., & Bergin, A. E. (1997). *A spiritual strategy for counseling and psychotherapy.* Washington, D.C.: American Psychological Association.

Richards, P. S., & Bergin, A. E. (Eds.). (2000). *Handbook of psychotherapy and religious diversity.* Washington, D.C.: American Psychological Association.

Richards, P. S., Rector, J. M., & Tjeltveit, A. C. (1999). Values, spirituality and psychotherapy. In W. R. Miller (Ed.), *Integrating spirituality into treatment: Resources for practitioners* (pp. 133–160). Washington, DC: American Psychological Association.

Richardson, T. Q., & Molinaro, K. L. (1996). White counselor self-awareness: A prerequisite for developing multicultural competence. *Journal of Counseling & Development, 74,* 238–242.

Sodowsky, G. R. (1996). The multicultural counseling inventory: Psychometric properties and some uses in counseling training. In G. R. Sodowsky & J. C. Impara (Eds.), *Multicultural assessment in counseling and clinical psychology* (pp. 283–324). Lincoln, NE: Buros Institute of Mental Measurements.

Sue, D. W. (1981). *Counseling the culturally different.* New York: Wiley.

Sue, D. W., Arredondo, P., & McDavis, R. J. (1992). Multicultural counseling competencies and standards: A call to the profession. *Journal of Counseling and Development, 70,* 477–486.

Sue, D. W., Bingham, R., Porche-Burke, L., & Vasquez, M. (1999). The diversification of psychology: A multicultural revolution. *American Psychologist, 54,* 1061–1069.

Sue, D. W., & Sue, D. (1999). *Counseling the culturally different: Theory and practice* (3rd ed.). New York: Wiley.

Sue, S. (1999). Science, ethnicity, and bias: Where have we gone wrong? *American Psychologist, 54,* 1070–1077.

Tomlinson-Clarke, S. (2000). Assessing outcomes in a multicultural training course: A qualitative study. *Counseling Psychology Quarterly, 13,* 221–231.

Zang, N., & Dixon, D. N. (2001). Muticulturally responsive counseling: Effect on Asian students' ratings of counselors. *Journal of Multicultural Counseling and Development, 29,* 253–262.

2

The Multicultural Context of Mental Health

Paul B. Pedersen

University of Alabama at Birmingham

Change is painful, but without change there is no learning, and without learning there is no change. The field of mental health is changing in ways we cannot foresee and at an accelerated rate that will leave many, if not most, of us behind. We are only now beginning to appreciate the ways that our understanding of mental health is being changed (Mahoney & Patterson, 1992). The strength of multicultural controversies in mental health is in itself an indication of the centrality of culture to these changes in mental health services. While most agree that change is taking place, there is a great deal of disagreement about the exact direction, nature, and rate of that change.

My view is that the change is from a *monocultural* perspective, dominated by what is currently the most powerful system of cultural values, toward a *multicultural* perspective, which combines many different value systems. As the field of mental health responds to the many different culturally defined special interest groups around us and cultural identities within us, the rules will need to be changed, causing still more controversy and confusion. Even when we recognize that the old rules are not working, it is not easy to replace them with new culturally different rules. The old rules of psychology focused on reduction of dissonance. The new rules focus on tolerance of ambiguity (Pedersen, 2001).

The Historical Context of Culture and Mental Health

The monocultural perspective has historically served the purposes of a "dominant culture" in specific ways (Pedersen, 1997). The motivation for studying cultural similarities and differences has changed or evolved from a defense for colonization, to a demonstration of political activism, to the development of affirmative action and/or the justification of elitism, toward a more interdependent global perspective. To the extent that mental health has neglected the complex and dynamic context of human behavior by imposing a "one-size-fits-all" perspective, mental health has been culturally encapsulated. The spread of multiculturalism as a generic perspective has escaped notice because it is a bottom-up movement, in contrast to the top-down leader-generated way that traditional mental health theories have emerged from Freud, Rogers, and Skinner. As special interest groups—culturally defined by demographics, status, affiliation, and ethnographic boundaries—have demanded recognition and equity, multiculturalism has become politically controversial. The perspective of dominant culture taught that only those who make use of their opportunities and develop special skills can be assured of earning their fair share. The minority's perspective became characterized and defined by oppression as minorities competed in the same context (Atkinson, Morton, & Sue, 1998). Currently there is even a controversy over the use of the term *minority* as being potentially offensive, because of the pejorative criteria with which that term is associated.

A comprehensive review of multicultural theory would need to go back to the beginning of recorded societies. We know relatively little about the role of culture in "prehistoric" Asia, Africa, and other ancient civilizations. The social construct of culture has evolved from academic disciplines in Europe and areas colonized by Euro-Anglo powers. In many cases the study of cultural differences has been motivated by a defense of and rationale for social, economic, and political colonization of less industrialized societies (Miles, 1989). Europe in the Middle Ages was concerned with the preservation of "civilization" against "primitive" peoples outside the European context. European colonial powers sent scholars, philosophers, naturalists, and physicians on scientific expeditions to study the cultural and physiological differences among peoples partly to rationalize their social, economic, and political colonization. By the twentieth century, German scholars had taken the lead in studying the mentality of "primitive peoples", along with their folk psychology (Segall, Dasen, Berry, & Poortinga, 1990). The disciplines of psychology, anthropology, and sociology that began to emerge were influenced by the monocultural political and economic values of the "civilized" world.

The psychological study of cultures assumed that there was a fixed ideal state of mind and that cultural differences were distortions. All behavior was evaluated by a single universal definition of "normal behavior," whatever the person's cultural background. A contrasting anthropological position assumed that cultural differences were clues to divergent attitudes, values, or perspectives that distinguished one culture from another. The anthropological perspective assumed that different groups or individuals had somewhat different definitions of "normal behavior" as a result of their own cultural contexts. Anthropologists have taken a relativist position when classifying and interpreting behavior across cultures. Psychologists, by contrast, have described social characteristics and psychological phenomena with minimum attention to the different cultural contexts, in a more absolutist perspective. Only recently has there been a serious attempt to bridge these polarized alternatives by cross-cultural and cultural psychology (Pedersen, in press).

Two contrasting definitions of culture emerge from this historical context. One views culture as the values, beliefs, norms, rationalizations, and mental products which provide descriptive categories. The other views culture as the total way of life of a people, including their interpersonal relations and attitudes. The broad and more inclusive perspective of culture is emerging as the preferred perspective (Thomson, Ellis, & Wildavsky, 1990). Berry, Poortinga, Segall, and Dasen (1992) point out the implications of a broad and inclusive perspective in an interdisciplinary study of behavior from multiple cultures.

> Thus, in our frame of reference, we need to avoid reducing culture to the level of psychological explanations, of psychological phenomena to biological explanations, biological to chemical, and so on. That is, we must recognize that there are, for example, cultural phenomena that exist and can be studied at their own level. (p. 6)

There are many reasons why a broadly defined multicultural perspective has become more globally popular and controversial in recent years (Sloan, 1990), related to the economic, political, and military shifts in power and influence. Much of the controversy surrounding culture in the last century has focused on race. The tendency to differentiate races according to inherited characteristics and to rank them hierarchically according to presumed ability or potential dates back to European imperialism of the Middle Ages. Two centuries ago Carl Linnaeus classified "Homo sapiens" into four races based on phenotypic traits, resulting in as few as 3 and as many as 37 races (Molnar, 1992). The biological concept of race has become more and more controversial as evidence discrediting race as a scientific construct—but emphasizing the political importance of racial identities—has increased (Yee, Fairchild, Weizmann, & Wyatt, 1993).

Race as a socially constructed term continues to have a profound effect, especially through theories of racial identity development (Cross & Fhagen-Smith, 1996), which build a multidimensional scale of identity that integrates the stages of Nigresence (Cross, 1995) with the stages of adolescent-identity development.

> Racial identity theory evolves out of the tradition of treating race as a sociopolitical and, to a lesser extent, a cultural construction. In such theories, racial classifications are assumed to be not biological realities, but rather sociopolitical and economic conveniences, membership in which is determined by socially defined inclusion criteria (e.g., skin color) that are commonly (mistakenly) considered to be racial in nature. (Helms, 1995, p. 181)

Theories of racial identity development have been applied to both White and non-White populations with regard to their mental health. The process of "White" racial identity development is described as a series of interactive states rather than one-directional, sequential, stage-based categories that move from a limited awareness of race (contact status) to a complex appreciation for one's own race and the race of others (autonomy status). The non-White status sequence moves from unquestioning acceptance of societal norms (conformity status) through stages of dissonance and immersion to a similar complex appreciation of one's own race and the race of others (integrative-awareness status) (Helms, 1995). A variety of scales have been validated to measure racial identity development of different ethnocultural groups (Sodowski & Impara, 1996).

In sum, contemporary multicultural counseling and psychology continue to struggle with issues of race that are rooted in historical contexts. Having traced the controversial evolution of culture and mental health as a psychological construct, it is now important to identify contemporary theories that take a more culture-centered perspective.

Multicultural Mental Health Theory

A multicultural theory (Sue, Ivey, & Pedersen, 1996) provides a conceptual framework that values both the complicated cultural diversity of a plural society and the basic shared concerns. Multicultural mental health is not an exotic perspective, but rather the necessary perspective for competence in delivering mental health services. Atkinson, Kim, and Caldwell (1998), for example, cite multicultural theories that have empirical validation. The ultimate multicultural theory requires understanding of every behavior in the context in which that behavior was learned and is displayed. Multicultural theory is the underlying basis of mental health services.

> There may well come a time when we will no longer speak of cross-cultural psychology as such. The basic premise of this field—that to understand human behavior, we must study it in its sociocultural context—may become so widely accepted that all psychology will be inherently cultural. (Segall et al., 1990, p. 352)

Sue, Ivey, and Pedersen (1996) have attempted to describe a multicultural counseling theory (MCT) based on six propositions to demonstrate this culture-centered perspective. These propositions are as follows: (1) Each Western or non-Western theory represents a different worldview. (2) The totality and interrelationship of client-counselor experiences and contexts must be the focus of treatment. (3) A counselor or client's racial/cultural identity will influence ways that problems are defined and dictate or define appropriate counseling goals or processes. (4) The ultimate goal of a culture-centered approach is to expand the repertoire of helping responses available to counselors. (5) Conventional roles of counseling are only some of many alternative helping roles available from other cultural contexts. (6) MCT emphasizes the importance of expanding personal, family, group, and organizational consciousness in a contextual orientation. These six propositions lead to new questions about a comprehensive multicultural understanding of mental health.

To the extent that psychological analysis is monocultural, it will result in incomplete data and misunderstanding. Multicultural theory has raised the possibility of an "orthogonal" (Oetting & Beauvais, 1991) identity, based on belonging to many different cultural affiliations at the same time. Belonging to one group does not exclude belonging to many other groups simultaneously. Each individual is a complex adaptive system for which a salient identity is both complicated and dynamic in its cultural context. Lifton (1993) describes multicultural persons as "shape-shifters." Those shape-shifters are flexible enough to change with each changing cultural context, maintaining multiple identities as a source of their strength. Lifton contrasts the shape-shifting self with a traditional "fundamentalist self." Those who follow the notion of the fundamentalist self maintain the same rigid position regardless of the different cultural contexts to avoid fragmentation by being consistent, whatever the consequences. In the postmodern world, discontinuous change seems to be a permanent feature, but this need not result in confusion or in abandonment of conventional rules for thinking. Rosenau (1992) distinguishes between "skeptical post-modernists," who react against any quest for certainty and unitary truth, and "affirmative post-modernists," who react against modernism but reject a world without meaning and recognize the importance of plural identities, ambiguous truth, and multiplicities of identities, even without having all the answers.

This social constructivist perspective is also based on the premise that we do not have direct access to a singular stable and fully knowable external reality, but rather we depend on culturally embedded, interpersonally connected, and necessarily limited notions of reality. This emphasis on personal reality and constructed meaning provides a subjective understanding of knowledge. Rather than define the self as self-contained, self-reliant, independent, individual, egocentric, and selfish, Hermans, Kempen, and Van Loon (1993) promote a dialogical view of self, beyond rationalism and individualism, based on the stories, patterns, or dialogues by which people understand themselves and construct their notion of reality.

Hermans et al. (1993) contend that "the embodied nature of the self contrasts with conceptions of the self found in mainstream psychology, which are based on the assumption of a disembodied or rationalistic mind" (p. 23). We each perceive the same situation in different ways. Reality, according to the contextual and constructivist view, is not based on absolute truth but on an understanding of complex and dynamic relationships learned in and perceived from each cultural context. Life is a narrative of culturally learned stories and rules that locate the self in its cultural context. Culture is made up of the stories we live by and have learned in our lifetime. A life becomes meaningful when one sees her- or himself as an actor within the context of a story. Early in life we choose what life story we will inhabit as our own (Howard, 1991).

Our cultural identity grows out of what we have learned and are learning in each multicultural context central to our understanding of our own and others' behavior. This perspective can be structured in a list of multicultural hypotheses for testing and for developing theory.

1. If all behavior is learned in a cultural context, culture controls our lives and defines reality, making all theories of human behavior dependent on understanding the cultural context of the behavior in question.

2. When we make culture central rather than marginal to our understanding, behavior otherwise labeled as a mental health problem may be perceived to serve a useful function.

3. Values and worldviews are not synonymous with the culture, but have been constructed to help us better understand ourselves; however, once constructed those values will shape behavior.

4. Attempts to measure, understand or change a behavior without regard for the cultural context will fail.

5. The same cultural context is experienced differently by each individual at each separate time, causing two people to sometimes disagree without either one necessarily being wrong.

6. We can best understand the cultural context of others by studying the patterns, rules and stories through which they have constructed meaning.

7. Group similarities are generalized from how members present their culture, whereas within-group differences reflect how members present the culture to themselves.
8. Attempts to change or shape a culturally learned behavior are only effective when they reframe, change, or shape the cultural context.
9. Only when the cultural context has been changed will individual members change accordingly.
10. In defining culture, the more we depend on abstract or aggregate data, the less useful that definition will be for individuals seeking to construct meaning in their own cultural context.
11. The more we limit our analysis to each individual's unique perspective, the less useful those data are to understanding the group.

As multicultural theory becomes more accepted and generic to psychology in general and psychotherapy and counseling in particular, we will be led to ask new questions leading to a more comprehensive culture-centered understanding of counseling as basic to the discussion of "outcomes" resulting from appropriate or inappropriate therapy. Under what circumstances and in which culturally circumscribed situations does a given psychological theory or methodology provide valid explanations for the origins and maintenance of behavior? What cultural boundary conditions potentially limit the generalizability of psychological theories and methodologies? Which psychological phenomena are culturally robust, and which phenomena appear only under specified cultural conditions? (Gielen, 1994). The basis for a multicultural or culture-centered theory has been established and is gaining increased recognition in the literature about counseling and psychotherapy. The next task is moving from theory to practice.

Multicultural Counseling Skills

Appropriate multicultural counseling skills are based on accurate awareness and meaningful knowledge, as outlined in the literature about multicultural competencies (Sue et al. 1982; Sue et al. 1998; Pedersen, 2000a). These skills are internalized through teaching and training to help the counselor or therapist "hear" what a culturally different client is thinking but not saying. This definition of skill makes several assumptions. First, messages are encoded before sending and decoded after receiving, so communication is primarily intrapersonal rather than interpersonal. Second, the rules for encoding and decoding messages are culturally learned. Third, the more cultural differences there are between people (ethnographic, demographic, status, and affiliation), the more likely that the messages will be misunderstood. Internal dialogue, therefore, becomes very important to the competent use of multicultural counseling skills.

The importance of internal dialogue was emphasized by Ellis (1962) in his discussion of self-talk and by Meichenbaum (1977) in his discussion of self-instruction, but the concept goes back at least as far as Plato, where thinking is described as a discourse the mind carries on with itself by talking to itself. Internal dialogue, which is well grounded in the psychological literature, also has a tradition in Eastern cultures, such as the mystery of

Taoism or the remembered sayings of Confucius as a basis of psychological support. To the extent that thought is conducted in words, thinking may be characterized as talking to one's self, usually in terms of a two-sided or positive versus negative discussion. McCall and Simmons (1982) combine the "I" and the "me" in what G. H. Mead (1934) called an inner forum of continuous internal conversation, which he developed through symbolic interactionalist theory. Herz-Lazarowitz and Miller (1995) describe four types of inner speech that occur during problem solving: task related, self-related, other related, and task relevant. McKay (1992) reviews data on four fundamental issues addressed by theories of inner speech: (1) What is the nature of inner speech? (2) What are the perceptual and generative aspects of inner speech, and where do they come from? (3) How are internal and overt speech related? (4) What role does internal speech play in cognition such as visualization and memory? Vygotsky (1934/1986) used the term *inner speech* both as self-dialogue and as a process of thought being realized in words, where internal dialogue was considered a part of our developmental process and of the internalization of social interaction (Daniels, 1996).

In discussing orthogonal cultural self-identity, implications of belonging to many different cultures at the same time were brought out. Mead's idea of an inner forum fits with this orthogonal identity model.

> The me is best thought of not as the antagonist in a dialogue with the I but as an audience, all the people in a multipersonal discussion who are temporarily silent while the I holds the floor. But though they are politely silent, they are evaluating and criticizing all the while that the I is talking. Each has a somewhat different reaction, corresponding to his different perspective, and when the I has finished and relinquished the floor, so to speak, every member of this metaphorical audience strives to inform him of his own personal reaction to what was said. (McCall & Simmons, 1982, pp. 53–54)

The interaction of thinking and culture produces a different notion of self for each individual. The metaphorical voices that have created culture are internalized in "inner speech," through which all external communication is processed. The intrapersonal dialogue is where our interpersonal communication is rehearsed and behavior competence is developed. Pedersen (2000b) has developed a model to train counselors and therapists to hear the internal dialogue of culturally different clients, called the Triad Training Model, which matches a counselor with a coached team of clients, procounselor and anticounselor, all from the same contrasting culture.

Even when clients cannot articulate their own positive and negative thoughts, they readily admit to having them. The thoughts, which are not necessarily rational or coherent self-statements, may be less articulate than emotional associations. It is as though the client is "hearing" anticounselor and procounselor voices during the interview. These self-statements influence behavior in the same way that statements by others do. While we cannot know the client's internal dialogue with accuracy, we can assume that some of these messages are negative or anticounselor, while other messages are positive and procounselor. The Triad Training Model simulates cross-cultural interviews in which the anticounselor explicates the negative messages a client from a particular culture might be thinking but not saying, while a procounselor seeks to explicate positive messages.

In the Triad Training Model the anticounselor is deliberately subversive, attacking both the client and the counselor and exaggerating barriers in the interview. The anticounselor encourages the counselor trainee to become more aware of the client's cultural perspective by articulating the embarrassing and impolite comments a client might not otherwise say. This process raises the counselor's threshold for being nondefensive, identifies resistance in specific terms, and provides the opportunity to rehearse recovery skills. The procounselor is deliberately facilitative, encouraging both the client and the counselor by identifying common ground throughout the interview. The procounselor facilitates the counselor's effective responses. The culturally similar procounselor understands the client better than the culturally different counselor and is thus able to provide relevant background information to the counselor during the interview. The procounselor is not a co-therapist, but an intermediate resource person who can guide the counselor through suggesting specific strategies and insights that the client might otherwise be reluctant to volunteer. The procounselor reinforces the counselor's more successful strategies, both verbally and non-verbally.

Research on the Triad Training Model (Pedersen, 2000b), while incomplete and largely anecdotal, suggests that it increases counselor awareness, knowledge, and skill. The evidence of increased awareness is reported in the positive evaluation of in-service training, favorable comparisons with Interpersonal Process Repertoire (IPR) training on awareness, and self-reports of increased awareness of negative thoughts in counseling and therapy. The evidence of increased knowledge includes increased receptivity to additional multicultural information about clients, a more articulate description of values, self-reports of increased sensitivity to different populations, and increased knowledge about the client's host culture. The evidence of increased skills includes increased frequency of good verbal counseling statements, increased confidence for working with client populations unfamiliar with counseling, self-reports of greater effectiveness in family therapy, and more favorable feedback from Black students working with White counselors.

The Triad Training Model provides one way of increasing multicultural counseling skill by recruiting resource persons from the community as coached clients, procounselors, and anticounselors. These resource persons provide immediate and continuous positive and negative feedback to counselor trainees who are otherwise unfamiliar with the client's culture. The more sociocultural differences are revealed in the interview, the more difficult it will be for the counselor to accurately anticipate what the culturally different client is thinking but not saying. Through role playing, the counselor learns to internalize the voices of an anticounselor and a procounselor to better estimate the internal dialogue of a culturally different client.

Increased attention to the cultural context of counseling will increase the accuracy of assessment, the depth of understanding, and the appropriateness of intervention in the practical application of multicultural counseling skills. First of all, accurate assessment requires that we evaluate behavior in the sociocultural context where that behavior was learned and is being displayed, without deconstructing the complexity and ambiguity inherent in that cultural context. Second, a meaningful understanding or comprehension of the client's behavior requires that instead of a "self-reference-criterion" we seek to understand the behavior from the client's own perspective, which might be quite different from the perspective from which we would experience the same event. Third, the appropriateness of an intervention requires that the culture-centered counselor focus on the expectations and values behind the behavior rather than attempting to interpret a behavior out of context. The same behavior may have different meanings, and different behaviors might have the same meaning, depending on the culturally learned expectations and values behind that behavior.

Multiculturalism as a "Fourth Force"

Transpersonal psychology (Tart, 1975) was the first to claim a "Fourth Force" status, based on the spiritual revolution in modern society. Many of the principles of transpersonal psychology have been accepted by the larger and more diffuse multicultural movement. Mahoney and Patterson (1992) described the fourth force as a cognitive revolution with an interdisciplinary perspective in which human behavior is described as reciprocal and interactive rather than linear and unidirectional. Wrightsman (1992) likewise described the fourth alternative to textbook psychology based on George Kelly's personal construct theory.

A culture-centered perspective implies that multiculturalism will become a "Fourth Force" in the mental health fields (Pedersen, 1999, 1990), contributing added meaning to the three psychological forces of psychodynamism, behaviorism, and humanism much as the fourth dimension of time gives meaning to three-dimensional space. Culture, for example, is central to the psychodynamic definitions of the unconscious, the reinforcing contingencies of behaviorism, and the personhood of the individual in humanism. Conventional theories of mental health are strengthened, not weakened, by a culture-centered perspective.

In the shift from a culture-exclusive to a culture-inclusive science, mental health in the future will include competing and contradictory cultural perspectives just as naturally as mental health up to now has disregarded them. We will be asking questions such as which psychological theory works best in each cultural context, what cultural boundaries exist for each psychological theory, or which psychological phenomena are more likely to occur in most cultures (Gielen, 1994). We will no longer talk about cross-cultural mental health, but will rather understand all human behavior in the cultural context in which that behavior was learned and is displayed.

Smith, Harre, and Van Langenhove (1995) compare the old paradigms of the past with new rules for the future. These new paradigms emphasize understanding and describing more than just measuring; predicting consequences more than fixing causation; social significance more than establishing statistical significance. They consider language, narrative, and discourse more than numerical reductionism; holistic perspectives more than atomistic trivia; complex interacting particulars more than simplistic universals; and subjective derived meaning more than objectively imposed interpretations.

Pedersen (1999) reviews the arguments supporting multiculturalism as a Fourth Force. First, we know that fundamental changes are taking place in the social sciences and particularly in the applied areas such as mental health. Some sort of paradigm shift is occurring; more than a continuation of historical patterns, it changes the rules by which mental health has been guided. While there is disagreement about the nature of these changes, the metaphor of culture or "multiculture" is gaining increased attention as an explanatory principle. Second, we know there is a necessary distinction between the processes of multicultural contact—including the behaviors, attitudes, perceptions, and feelings of participants—and the institutional structures that characterize, support, or hinder intercultural contact. Multicultural processes have had a great impact within culturally heterogeneous societies, but as yet multiculturalism has not become a significantly global Fourth Force across national boundaries. Third, each society has had a different interpretation of multiculturalism: for example, in South Africa arguments based on multiculturalism were used to defend apartheid. Fourth, it may be premature to describe multiculturalism as a Fourth Force when so many mental health textbooks continue to present culturally biased perspectives. Fifth, much of the literature about multiculturalism has been written from a dominant culture perspective, with individualistic values of individual autonomy, individual goals, and individual human rights that minimize the collectivist perspective of the global majority. Sixth, multiculturalism is being broadly defined to include both within-group and between-group similarities and differences beyond nationality and ethnicity, based on age, socioeconomic status, gender, and lifestyle. Seventh, we know that cultural similarity among youth across cultures, based on psychosocial development processes, separate youth from previous generations in their national or ethnic group. Eighth, we know that multiculturalism is changing the process as well as the content of our ways of thinking about ourselves and others. Ninth, we know that all behaviors are learned and displayed in a cultural context, making that context essential to mental health assessment, interpretation, and intervention.

Sue (1998) has identified resistance to the designation *multiculturalism* as a Fourth Force. First, some view multiculturalism as competing with already established psychological theories. Second, the term *multiculturalism* is closely associated with controversial topics such as affirmative action, quotas, civil rights, discrimination, racism, sexism, political correctness and other political matters. Third, to the extent that multiculturalism is connected with postmodernism the arguments against postmodernism would apply. Fourth, those favoring a universalist perspective contend that the same practice of mental health applies across cultures. Fifth, there are no accepted standards for describing multiculturalism as a theory or as a practice. Sixth, there is no database of measurable competencies for multicultural applications of mental health in practice. Seventh, multiculturalism is too complicated and unrealistic in its demands. Eighth, more research is needed on multiculturalism. Ninth, multicultural standards cannot be incorporated into mental health until or unless all possible cultural groups are included. Tenth, multiculturalism represents reverse racism, being "anti-White." While the arguments against multiculturalism as a Fourth Force are persuasive, the reality of our culture-centered experiences is perhaps even more persuasive. We are faced with a complex problem to which there are no easy answers.

Multicultural Issues and Controversies

To the extent that counseling and psychotherapy have moved from a monocultural to a multicultural perspective, there have been many issues of controversy that need to be addressed by professionals in the field. There are no final answers to these controversies, but it is important for counselors and therapists to be informed on the issues being debated (Ponterotto, Casas, Suzuki, & Alexander, 1995, 2001).

The first controversy is whether or not mental health services are culturally encapsulated, as defined by Wrenn (1962, 1985). Cultural encapsulation refers to the tendency of humans to simplify the complexities of life by building a "capsule" around themselves and pretending that only those factors inside the capsule are real. George Albee (1994), former President of the American Psychological Association, asserts that psychology has been seriously encapsulated in the past 100 years.

> Most of the early leaders in psychology embraced ideological views that stressed the natural superiority of a white male patriarchy, the acceptance of Social Darwinism, the inferiority of women and of the brunette races. Calvinism stressed economic success as the hallmark of salvation and psychology concurred. Anti-semitism and homophobia were standard. Eugenics spokesmen urged the elimination of the unfit and inferior and opposed welfare programs, decent wages and safe working conditions. (p. 22)

Pedersen (2000a) describes nine examples of cultural encapsulation in the definitions of "normal" behavior: preferences for individualism, narrowly defined professional boundaries, disregard for contextual factors, devaluation of dependency, ignorance of support systems, linear thinking, status-quo conformity, minimalization of history, and presumption of self-insight. Ponterotto (1988) summarizes other examples of cultural encapsulation in the research literature, while LaFromboise and Foster (1989) identify examples of bias in the literature about psychological ethics. Counseling and psychology have bad reputations in many minority communities for protecting the status quo regarding racism, even when that racism is unintentional (Sue & Sue, 1999; Ridley, 1995). Sampson (1988) identified core cultural values for freedom, responsibility, and achievement as part of the individualistic perspective of modern psychology. Miller (1999) has further examined the self-interest motive and the self-conforming role of assuming self-interest in textbook psychology. The research support documenting the cultural encapsulation of psychology is overwhelming (Sampson, 1993).

The second controversy concerns whether or not "standardized" measures and assessments are culturally biased. Lonner and Ibrahim (1989; in press) point out how assessment measures used in counseling have indeed been culturally biased. Any accurate assessment across cultures must be sensitive to the client's worldview, beliefs, values, and culturally unique assumptions, as well as the client's specific norm grouping, and it must provide a combination of approaches using clinical judgment along with standardized or appropriate objective measures. These criteria would be nearly impossible for any single assessment to meet.

Samuda (1998) reviews the issues and consequences of cultural bias in testing American minorities. Dana (1998) takes an even broader perspective in reviewing the controversies of cultural identity in the process of accurate assessment of clients from different cultural groups using different approaches. Paniagua (2001) reviews the problems of diagnosis in a multicultural context, with particular emphasis on the accurate and appropriate use of the *Diagnostic and Statistical Manual of Mental Disorders* (DSM-IV) with a series of case examples. The considerable problems presented by multiculturalism continue to diminish the accuracy of the DSM-IV as it is now written.

Cultural bias in assessment results in overdiagnosis, underdiagnosis, or misdiagnosis unless counselors and therapists are trained to interpret biased test data in ways appropriate to culturally different populations. The search for culture-free or culture-fair tests has failed. Such a test would need to demonstrate equivalence in content, semantics, technical concepts, and criteria across cultures, which is an impossible demand (Escobar, 1993). However, mental health professionals can still be trained to compensate for cultural bias in their interpretation of test data.

A third controversy is whether *culture* should be broadly or narrowly defined. The broad definition presumes that potentially salient aspects of cultural identity will include ethnographic, demographic, status, and affiliation variables. According to the broad definition, all counseling is multicultural, given the complexity of the counseling relationship. A narrow definition of *culture* limited to ethnic and racial membership would be less generic to all counseling relationships and more specialized in its focus. Differences of power, prestige and money coincide with socioeconomic differences in both how people are perceived and how they perceive themselves. Gender provides another example of a potentially salient perspective in the broad definition of cultures.

Triandis (Triandis, Botempo, Leung, & Hui, 1990) argues against the broad definition of culture. Cultural constructs, as defined by Triandis, are shared by persons with the same dialect, from the same geographic region, who have norms, roles, values, and associations in common to explain their experiences. Demographic constructs deal with the same topic but only within a select group, such as the old and young. Lee and Richardson (1991) are critical of the broad definition because it waters down the term *culture* and takes away its meaning. Locke (1992) agrees that the broad definition "has been increasingly stretched to include virtually any group of people who consider themselves different" (p. 6).

While Sue (1998) favors a more culture-specific approach, he acknowledges the dangers of a narrow definition of *culture* in counseling because it may foster technique-oriented definitions of counseling without regard to a conceptual framework and thus be contrary to the goals of good counseling. Counselors could limit their effectiveness by focusing too narrowly on a particular ethnic group.

A fourth controversy is whether the profession should emphasize similarities or differences. Pike (1966) has borrowed from the linguistic term *phonemics* (emic) referring to sounds unique in a particular language and the linguistic term *phonetics* (etic) or universal language sounds. The emic/etic distinction has led some counselors to focus only on cultural similarities while others focus only on cultural differences, ignoring the essential complementarity of the two. The emic approach has been associated with relativism and the etic approaches with universalism. Neither view by itself gives an accurate or complete picture.

Brewer (1991) describes social identity as deriving from a tension between similarity and unique individuation in what she calls "uniqueness theory." A counselor begins with an "imposed etic," applying one's own cultural assumptions "as though" they were universally true, while refining and adapting those assumptions to fit the cultural context. As a result the two cultures are distinguished by their differences, resulting in a "derived etic" in the process of adapting to the client's cultural context. Some models of multicultural counseling emphasize culture-general features; others emphasize culture-specific ones. Ideally, multicultural counseling will emphasize both similarities and differences. Both similarities and differences must be understood to clearly assess the client's cultural context. Understanding differences contributes an identity; understanding similarities defines common ground.

A fifth controversy is whether professional ethical guidelines are adequate to guide effective multicultural practice (Meara, Schmidt, & Day, 1996). The culture-centered counselor too often has to choose between following professional ethical guidelines and acting in an ethical manner. Professional associations emphasize the responsibility of counselors and therapists to know a client's cultural values before delivering a mental health service, but professional guidelines continue to assume the value perspective of the dominant culture, sometimes requiring the counselor to demonstrate "responsible disobedience" to those guidelines (Pedersen & Marsella, 1982). The trend toward ethical consciousness in culture-centered counseling is credited to demographic changes favoring minority groups, increased visibility of alternative value perspectives, pressure by civil rights and human rights groups worldwide, and economic incentives to attract minority clients (Casas, 1984).

Dana (1998) distinguishes between "principle ethics," by which judgments are based on value systems, and "virtue ethics," by which ideas are based on historic content and purpose linking individuals and their community.

> As a minimum requirement, cultural competence should include (a) assessment of the client as a cultural entity; (b) culture-specific delivery styles, including different cultural rules for dual roles and physical contact; (c) cultural belief systems of health and illness, values and identification of legitimate providers; (d) use of the client's first language for services and (e) familiarity with general principles, procedural details and local examples of culture-specific assessment. (p. 351)

The ethical imperative has been overshadowed by the need to fix blame. The orientation to polarize society into majority versus minority has resulted in moral exclusion demonstrated by distancing psychologically, displacing responsibility, expressing group loyalty, and normalizing violence, any of which can occur through overt and malicious action or through covert support and passive disregard (Opotow, 1990). Most of the criticism of professional ethical guidelines presumes that the principles are valid but poorly implemented due to inadequate training and inappropriate mental health interventions. As a result, professional ethics reflect a consistent cultural bias (Axelson, 1999; Ponterotto & Casas, 1991). We need to move toward pluralistic contextually sensitive ethical guidelines that accommodate different culturally learned assumptions for counselors and their clients.

There are many controversies surrounding the interface between culture and counseling to stimulate field research and classroom teaching. The controversies discussed in this chapter are only some of the issues that promote discussion and debate. It is important to go beyond these selected examples of controversy in adapting the counseling process to a multicultural reality.

Conclusion

Understanding the context of multiculturalism in mental health is difficult. The most vivid weakness of mental health services for multicultural client populations as they are currently taught and practiced is our inability or reluctance to identify the underlying culturally learned assumptions on which those teachings and practices are based. Counseling and psychology are experiencing a revolutionary change, although the ultimate direction of that change remains unclear.

Multiculturalism may provide a "Fourth Force" in psychologically based sciences that gives meaning to the psychodynamic, behavioral, and humanist perspectives, much as the fourth dimension of time gives meaning to three-dimensional space. Since all behaviors are learned and displayed in a cultural context the generic applicability of multiculturalism for psychology seems clear. The absence of a clear and coherent theory of multicultural practice has been a significant barrier. There has been considerable disagreement about the theoretical relation between counseling and culture, but some of the foundation premises for a theory of multiculturalism seem to be in place. The criteria for multicultural counseling skill competencies are also being developed. There are many different approaches to developing multicultural skill, but the one reviewed in this chapter has focused on the intrapersonal dimension. Finally, several of the many controversies surrounding multicultural counseling have been identified for discussion.

This chapter has probably raised more questions than it has answered in the complex and dynamic perspective of multicultural counseling. Other chapters in this book are designed to target some of the questions raised by this chapter. Readings cited in this chapter discuss these questions in much greater depth, and the reader is encouraged to follow up those references of interest. The context of multicultural mental health is both complex and dynamic. Beware of simple solutions to complex problems.

References

Albee, G. W. (1994). The sins of the fathers: Sexism, racism and ethnocentrism in psychology. *International Psychologist, 35*(1), 22.

Atkinson D. R., Kim, B. S. K., & Caldwell, R. (1998). Ratios of helper roles by multicultural psychological and Asian American students: Initial support for a three dimensional model of multicultural counseling. *Journal of Counseling Psychology, 45,* 414–423.

Atkinson, D. R., Morton, G., & Sue, D. W. (1998). *Counseling American minorities: A cross-cultural perspective* (5th ed.). New York: McGraw-Hill.

Axelson, J. A. (1999). *Counseling and development in a multicultural society* (3rd ed.). Pacific Grove, CA: Brooks/Cole.

Berry, J. W., Poortinga, Y. H., Segall, M. H., & Dasen, P. J. (1992). *Cross-cultural psychology: Research and applications.* Cambridge, England: Cambridge University Press.

Brewer, M. B. (1991). The social self: On being the same and different at the same time. *Personality and Social Psychology Bulletin, 17,* 475–482.

Casas, J. J. (1984). Policy training and research in counseling psychology: The racial ethnic minority perspective. In S. Brown & R. Lent (Eds.), *Handbook of counseling psychology* (pp. 785–831). New York: Wiley.

Cross W. E. (1995). The psychology of Nigrescence: Revisiting the Cross model. In J. G. Ponterotto, J. M. Casas, L. A. Suzuki, & C. M. Alexander (Eds.), *Handbook of multicultural counseling* (pp. 93–122). Thousand Oaks, CA: Sage.

Cross, W. E., & Fhagen-Smith, P. (1996). Nigrescence and ego identity development: Accounting for differential Black identity patterns. In P. B. Pedersen, J. G. Draguns, W. J. Lonner, & J. E. Trimble (Eds.), *Counseling across cultures* (4th ed., pp. 108–123). Thousand Oaks, CA: Sage.

Dana, R. H. (1998). *Understanding cultural identity in intervention and assessment.* Thousand Oaks, CA: Sage.

Daniels, H. (Ed.). (1996). *An introduction to Vygotsky.* London: Routledge.

Ellis, A. (1962). *Reason and emotion in psychotherapy.* New York: Lyle Stuart.

Escobar, J. I. (1993). Psychiatric epidemiology. In A. C. Gaw (Ed.), *Culture, ethnicity and mental illness* (pp. 43–73). Washington, DC: American Psychiatric Press.

Gielen, U. P. (1994). American mainstream psychology and its relationship to international and cross-cultural psychology. In A. L. Comunian & U. P. Gielen (Eds.), *Advancing psychology and its applications:*

International perspectives (pp. 26–40). Milan, Italy: Franco Angeli.

Helms, J. (1995). An update of Helms' White and People of Color Racial Identity models. In J. Ponterotto, J. M. Casas, L. A. Suzuki, & C. M. Alexander (Eds.), *Handbook of multicultural counseling* (181–198). Thousand Oaks, CA: Sage.

Hermans, H. J. M., Kempen, H. J. G., & Van Loon, R. J. P. (1993). The ideological self: Beyond individualism and rationalism. *American Psychologist, 47*(1), 23–33.

Herz-Lazarowitz, R., & Miller, N. (1995). *Interaction in cooperative groups: The theoretical anatomy of group learning*. New York: Cambridge University Press.

Howard, G. S. (1991). Culture tales: A narrative approach to thinking, cross cultural psychology and psychotherapy. *American Psychologist, 46*, 187–197.

LaFromboise, T. D., & Foster, S. L. (1989). Ethics in multicultural counseling. In P. Pedersen, J. Draguns, W. Lonner, & J. Trimble (Eds.), *Counseling across cultures* (3rd ed., pp. 115–136). Honolulu: University of Hawaii Press.

Lee C. C., & Richardson, B. L. (1991). *Multicultural issues in counseling: New approaches to diversity*. Alexandria, VA: ACA.

Lifton, R. J. (1993). *The protean self*. New York: Basic Books.

Locke, D. C. (1992). *Increasing multicultural understanding: A comprehensive model*. Newbury Park, CA: Sage.

Lonner, W. J., & Ibrahim, F. A. (1989). Assessment in cross-cultural counseling. In P. Pedersen, J. Draguns, W. Lonner, & J. Trimble (Eds.), *Counseling across cultures* (3rd ed., pp. 229–334). Honolulu: University of Hawaii Press.

Mahoney, M. J., & Patterson K. M. (1992). Changing theories of changes: Recent developments in counseling. In S. D. Brown, & R. W. Lent (Eds.), *Handbook of counseling and psychology* (2nd ed., pp. 665–689). New York: John Wiley & Sons.

McCall, G. J., & Simmons J. L. (1982). *Social psychology: A sociological approach*. New York: Free Press.

McKay, D. G. (1992). *Constraints on theories of inner speech*. In D. Reisberg (Ed.), *Auditory imagery* (pp. 121–149). Hillsdale, NJ: Lawrence Erlbaum Association.

Mead, G. H. (1934). *Mind, self and society: From the standpoint of a social behaviorist*. (C. W. Morris, Ed.). Chicago: University of Chicago Press.

Meara, N. M., Schmidt L. D., & Day, J. D. (1996) Principles and virtues: A foundation for ethical decisions, policies and character. *The Counseling Psychologist, 24*, 4–77.

Meichenbaum, D. (1977). *Cognitive behavior modification: An integrative approach*. New York: Plenum.

Miles, R. (1989). *Racism*. New York: Routledge.

Miller D. T. (1999). The norm of self interest. *American Psychologist, 54*(12), 1053–1060.

Molnar, S. (1992). *Human variation* (3rd ed.). Englewood Cliffs, NJ: Prentice Hall.

Oetting, E. R., & Beauvais, F. (1991). Orthogonal cultural identification theory: The cultural identification of minority adolescents. *International Journal of the Addictions, 25*(5A–6A), 655–685.

Opotow, S. (1990). Moral exclusion and injustice: An introduction. *Journal of Social Issues 46*(1), 1–20.

Paniagua F. A. (2001). *Diagnosis in a multicultural context: A casebook for mental health professionals*. Thousand Oaks, CA: Sage.

Pedersen, P. (1990). The multicultural perspective as a fourth force in counseling. *Journal of Mental Health Counseling, 12*(1), 93–95.

Pedersen, P. (1997). *Culture-centered counseling interventions: Striving for accuracy*. Thousand Oaks, CA: Sage.

Pedersen, P. (1999). *Multiculturalism as a Fourth Force*. Philadelphia, PA: Brunner/Mazel.

Pedersen, P. (2000a). *A handbook for developing multicultural awareness* (3rd ed.). Alexandria, VA: ACA.

Pedersen, P. (2000b). *Hidden messages in culture-centered counseling: A triad training model*. Thousand Oaks, CA: Sage.

Pedersen, P. (2001). The cultural context of peacemaking. In D. J. Christie, R. V. Wagner, & D. D. N. Winter (Eds.), *Peace, conflict and violence: Peace psychology for the 21st century* (pp. 183–192). Upper Saddle River, NJ: Prentice Hall.

Pedersen, P. (in press). The importance of cultural theory for multicultural counselors. In R. Carter (Ed.), *Handbook of racial and cultural psychology*. New York: Wiley.

Pedersen, P., & Marsella A. J. (1982). The ethical crisis for cross-cultural counseling and therapy. *Professional Psychology, 13*, 492–500.

Pike, R. (1966). *Language in relation to a united theory of the structure of human behavior*. The Hague, The Netherlands: Mouton.

Ponterotto, J. G. (1988). Racial/ethnic minority research: A content analysis and methodological critique. *Journal of Counseling Psychology, 3*, 410–418.

Ponterotto J. G., & Casas, J. M. (1991). *Handbook of racial/ethnic minority counseling research*. Springfield, IL: Charles C. Thomas.

Ponterotto, J. G., Casas, J. M., Suzuki, L. A., & Alexander, C. M. (1995). *Handbook of multicultural counseling*. Thousand Oaks, CA: Sage.

Ponterotto, J. G., Casas, J. M., Suzuki, L. A., & Alexander, C. M. (2001). *Handbook of multicultural counseling* (2nd ed.). Thousand Oaks, CA: Sage.

Ridley, C. (1995). *Overcoming unintentional racism in counseling: A practitioner's guide to intentional intervention.* Thousand Oaks, CA: Sage.

Rosenau, P. M. (1992). *Post-modernism and the social sciences.* Princeton, NJ: Princeton University Press.

Sampson, E. E. (1988). The debate on individualism: Indigenous psychologies of the individual and their role in personal and societal functioning. *American Psychologist 43,* 15–22.

Sampson, E. E. (1993). Identity politics: Challenges to psychology's understanding. *American Psychologist 48,* 1219–1230.

Samuda, R. J. (1998). *Psychological testing of American minorities: Issues and consequences* (2nd ed.). Thousand Oaks, CA: Sage.

Segall, M. H., Dasen, P. R., Berry, J. W., & Poortinga, Y. H. (1990). *Human behavior in global perspective: An introduction to cross-cultural context* (pp. 281–286). Beverly Hills, CA: Sage.

Sloan, T. S. (1990). Psychology for the Third World? *Journal of Social Issues 46*(3), 1–20.

Smith J. A., Harre, R., & Van Langenhove, L. (1995). *Rethinking psychology.* London: Sage.

Sodowski, G. R., & Impara, J. (Eds.) (1996). *Multicultural assessment in counseling and clinical psychology.* Lincoln, NE: Buros Institute of Mental Measurement.

Sue, D. W., Bernier, J. E., Durran, A., Feinberg, L., Pedersen, P., Smith, C. J., & Vasquez-Nuttall, G. (1982). Cross-cultural counseling competencies. *The Counseling Psychologist 19*(2), 45–52.

Sue, D. W., Carter, R. T., Casas, J. M., Fouad, N. A., Ivey, A. E., Jensen, M., LaFromboise, T., Manese, J. E., Ponterotto, J. G., & Vasquez-Nuttall, G. (1998). *Multicultural counseling competencies.* Thousand Oaks, CA: Sage.

Sue, D. W., Ivey, A. E., & Pedersen, P. B. (1996). *A multicultural theory of counseling and psychotherapy.* Pacific Grove, CA: Brooks Cole.

Sue, D. W., & Sue, D. (1999). *Counseling the culturally different: Theory and practice* (3rd ed.). New York: Wiley & Sons.

Sue, S. (1998). In search of cultural competencies in psychology and counseling. *American Psychologist, 53,* 440–448.

Tart, C. T. (1975). Some assumptions of orthodox Western psychology. In C. T. Tart (Ed.), *Transpersonal psychologies* (pp. 59–112). New York: Harper & Row.

Thompson, M., Ellis, R., & Wildavsky, A. (1990). *Cultural theory.* San Francisco: Westview Press.

Triandis, H. C., Botempo, R., Leung, K., & Hui, C. H., (1990). A method for determining cultural, demographic and personal constructs. *Journal of Cross-Cultural Psychology, 21,* 302–318.

Vygotsky, L. S. (1934/1986). *Thought and language.* (A. Kozulin, Trans.). Cambridge, MA: MIT Press.

Wrenn, C. G. (1962). The culturally encapsulated counselor. *Harvard Educational Review, 32,* 444–449.

Wrenn, C. G. (1985). Afterword: The culturally encapsulated counselor revisited. In P. Pedersen (Ed.), *Handbook of cross-cultural counseling and therapy* (pp. 323–329). Westport, CT: Greenwood Press.

Wrightsman, L. S. (1992). *Assumptions about human nature: Implications for researchers and practitioners.* Newbury Park, CA: Sage.

Yee, A. H., Fairchild, H. H., Weizmann, F., & Wyatt, G. E. (1993). Addressing psychology's problems with race. *American Psychologist, 48,* 1132–1140.

Part II

Multicultural Skill Development

3

Awareness and Identity

Foundational Principles of Multicultural Practice

Chalmer E. Thompson

Indiana University, Bloomington

> Excising the political from the life of the mind is a sacrifice that has proven costly. I think of this erasure as a kind of trembling hypochondria always curing itself with unnecessary surgery. A [literary] criticism that needs to insist that literature is not only "universal" but also "race-free" risks lobotomizing that literature, and diminishes both the art and the artist.
>
> —Toni Morrison (1992, p. 23)

Nobel Prize Laureate Toni Morrison makes a sage observation about the practice of many literary critics who dismiss sociopolitical issues from their interpretations of literature. This same observation can be made about the work of mental health professionals. Spanning beyond race and to all issues concerning social stratification (like sexism and socioeconomic status), one can argue that the extraction of "the political" is even costlier to the practice of counseling and psychotherapy. With professional credentialing, practitioners are sanctioned to deliver competent mental health services to a diverse public. Yet evidence suggests that theorists, researchers, and practitioners generally harbor resistance toward and a lack of understanding about the relevance of structures of disadvantage to psychological functioning, assessment, and treatment (e.g., Helms, 1994; Prilleltensky, 1997; Yee, Fairchild, Weizmann, & Wyatt, 1993).

In this chapter, I examine why this erasure of sociopolitical forces occurs. Elaborating on the work of racial identity theorists, I propose that people are exposed to an implicit conditioning that supresses and distorts their knowledge about these forces in society. This conditioning is comprised of a system of rewards and adverse consequences that influences psychological development. I also propose that therapists who become aware of this conditioning will likely respond initially by holding onto their distorted views about reality.

In effect, people are likely to resist disrupting the conditioning. Many people experience negative emotions, like rage and shame, when they are exposed to aspects of reality that counter their perceptions about the world and about themselves. Fortunately, many people avail themselves of opportunities to integrate these aspects of reality into their personal and professional lives and thus better serve their clients.

Because of space limitations, I focus largely on the phenomenon of racism. However, many of the principles presented here can also apply to sexism, heterosexism, class exploitation, and, notably, to their intersection. *Racism* is defined as "whatever acts or institutional procedures that help create or perpetuate sets of privileges for Whites and exclusions and deprivations for minority groups" (Chesler, 1976, p. 22). I hope to demonstrate that a careful examination of racism can reveal pervasive pathologies in society. These pathologies recursively influence macro- and micro-systems levels. Hence, efforts to end racism will require that people recognize its complexity and counter it at various ecological levels. One especially difficult level to pierce is the individual's engagement in a system of racism. Using case illustrations, I eventually enfold information about the *self* that relates not only to race, but to additional aspects that synergistically influence the ways in which people form perceptions of themselves and others around them. Parenthetically, the self as described in these pages refers to the individual as dynamically shaped by factors that are biological (e.g., maturation, genotype, predisposing disorders) and environmental (e.g., race, culture, child-rearing practices, formal educational practices). I also use the terms *structure* or *system of disadvantage* to refer to the systemic nature of such phenomena as racism, sexism, heterosexism, and class exploitation (see Thompson & Neville, 1999a).

As an example of how the suppression of the reality of racism can lead to unresolved dilemmas of the self, I have interspersed passages from Morrison's (1992) *Playing in the Dark: Whiteness and the Literary Imagination*. In this richly insightful book, Morrison addresses the role of the "Africanist presence"—depictions of African and African-descended people—in the unfolding of several literary works, and in deriving understanding about the White authors themselves. Morrison analyzes the treatment of African-descended characters in these works and identifies clues to the authors' struggles with feelings of vulnerability, repressed sexuality, low self-worth, and racial privilege. I try to draw parallels between these passages and the psychological effects that suppressed sociopolitical awareness can have on psychological and interpersonal functioning and thus, on the promotion of positive mental health.

Psychological Blindness

The alertness to a slave population did not confine itself to the personal encounters these writers may have had. Slave narratives were a nineteenth-century publication boom. The press, the political campaigns, and the policy of various parties and elected officials were rife with the discourse of slavery and freedom.... How could one speak of profit, economy, labor, suffragism, Christianity, the frontier, the formation of new states, the acquisition of new lands, education, transportation (freight and passengers), neighborhoods, the military—of almost anything a country concerns itself with—without having as a referent, at the heart of the discourse, at the heart of definition, the presence of Africans and their descendants?… It was not possible. And it did not happen. (Morrison, 1992, p. 50)

Psychological blindness is a useful term for describing the relative inability of people to understand the impact of a sociopolitical context on society and, by implication, on their everyday lives. It can be stated, based on interdisciplinary writings, that people in contemporary American society generally hold vague and unexplored ideas of how various issues pertain to racism. Meanwhile, issues of racial inequity and inequality are intimately related to such topics as education (e.g., Berlak & Mozenda, 2001; Weis, 1990), health care access and reform (e.g., Dula & Goering, 1994; Lillie-Blanton, Leigh, & Alfaro-Carera, 1996), the judicial process (e.g., Carter & Gesmer, 1997; Crenshaw, Gotanda, Peller, & Thomas, 1995), labor and employment (e.g., McCall, 2001; Roediger, 1990), the mass media (Campbell, 1995; hooks, 1996), environmental policy and practice (Bullard, 2000; Westa & Wenz, 1995), the economy (Betancur & Gills, 2000; Tuan, 1998), humanitarianism (Shields, 1995; Witt, 1999), and, as Morrison states in her passage, virtually anything a society concerns itself with. Reading some of these works is a good beginning for those just exploring these issues.

How can people who live in a society replete with racism *not* perceive fully its existence and relevance to their lives? I believe a more pointed question asks how people can manage a reality of racial injustice *and simultaneously maintain their expressed beliefs about equality and fairness for all people.* In order for a structure to both nurture racism *and* establish racism as anathema to its core, it must erect a *Zeitgeist* that tolerates these ostensibly contradictory agendas. The American legal system is one institutional manifestation of this structure, claiming "color-blindness" and "equal justice" as established givens while simultaneously sanctioning legal practices and decisions that have been unfair to millions of Americans by virtue of their race, social class, and gender (e.g., Carter & Gesmer, 1997; Crenshaw et al., 1995; Guinier, 1994).

Why do these institutional practices continue? Institutional, group, and individual practices share certain common elements as they perpetuate oppression. In a racist society, people learn to tolerate the dissonance because of a two-pronged process of socialization or conditioning. This is a process in which people in American society learn to (1) diminish, appropriate, or cast as negative or inferior the perspectives and worldviews of historically marginalized people, like people of color, and (2) establish as "standard," credible, superior, or even innocent the perspectives and worldviews of dominant groups, like Whites. I'll start with a quick example of how this conditioning manifests by anticipating the reactions of some readers to the last sentence of the previous paragraph. Some readers may react by stating that any evidence of unfairness is probably grossly exaggerated and, therefore, needs to be dismissed. They may simultaneously accept what they have already been conditioned to accept: that the American legal system, though obviously with its share of faults, is basically fair to everyone. The way in which this conclusion reflects the two-pronged process is that the perspectives of literally millions of people throughout the history of the United States are patently dismissed with the conclusion of over-exaggeration. The "standard" conclusion is that the American legal system is fair, but little is reflected in this statement about the fact that this conclusion has been amply conveyed and influenced by Whites.

As shown in the example, much of this conditioning is implicit though not entirely undetectable. For example, at a macro-systems level, this socialization is manifest at the first prong in portrayals of people of color in stereotypical or ancillary roles in the media, the practice of erasing or minimizing historical events or figures that include the contributions of people of color to the contemporary society, and the tendency of normalizing discursive practices that equate "race" primarily with people of color and with negative connotations (e.g., "playing the race card"). The second prong is evident in efforts to focus inordinate attention on the achievements of Whites and to condone discursive practices that disengage Whites from racial issues, unless the displays are overt (as in the practices of White hate groups). These practices converge into an implication of innocence or neutrality within a system of racism (see Gotanda, 1995; Lipsitz, 1998; Roediger, 1990). Together, these prongs increase divisions, not only between people of different races, but also among people of similar races (see below under Racial Identity Theory). These divisions are not always obvious: People can engage in relationships in which they believe they have broken barriers to racial divisions, but these relationships may not necessarily involve meaningful discussions about this aspect of their identity. Indeed, people who talk about their personal experiences with race may find that they can only talk with racially similar others. Some may find that they need to keep silent altogether because of the anger, disbelief, and powerlessness these expressions can provoke in themselves and in the people to whom they reveal these experiences. Others may talk in codes, thereby avoiding meaningful discussions about race (see Fine, 1994 and Morrison, 1992 for discussions on racial codification). These are different forms of avoidance that probably results from not having the means to discuss race meaningfully and not feeling comfortable about the direction that such discussions may lead. But as Freud (1921) postulated in his construct of defense mechanisms, the avoidance of problems does not translate into their disappearance. These problems reappear in different ways, often taking on obscured manifestations. Below are two examples of defensive strategies that people use to maintain a certain view on reality that is based on the two-pronged process of socialization.

The first example is the *universalizing* strategy. Consider the following statement: "I don't see any racism. And even if it does exist, people of all walks of life have to accept the hardships that go along with life, even if that means having to deal with difficult people who judge you on some quality of your physicality. I deal with a client's experience with racism the same way I deal with anyone who might run into problems simply because he or she is human." Note that this statement can be made by anyone irrespective of race (as in the other examples in this section), although the implications are different for people of color than for Whites, as will be explained below in the section on racial identity theory. The *universalizing* strategy minimizes a reality of racism by perceiving it merely as individual acts of bigotry and discrimination and additionally as not necessarily distinct from prejudice, bullying, and so forth. The individual who makes this statement may also believe that people of color are preoccupied with racism and therefore care little about other types of hardships that "others" (presumably Whites) experience. Thus the statement, the attendant belief structure, and the overriding purpose inherent in the structure of racism diminish the experiences of people of color who have been and continue to be targets of a phenomenon that is historically embedded and distinguishable from prejudice (see Baker, 1998; Brodkin, 1998; Gaines & Reed, 1999; Smedley, 1993). The person casts the perspectives of those who talk about racism negatively (as preoccupied and exaggerating). What the person may also believe implicitly (and not voiced in the statement) is that Whites are no better off than people of color. The distorted nature of this statement is that many people may automatically come to understand that the person is referring to "them versus us" when, naturally, hardships happen to all people. In other words, the person seems to imply that he or she is speaking on behalf of those who are not targets of racism—that is, Whites—when, in fact, the dichotomy is a false one because all people experience hardships. One can find such falsely dichotomized statements in other discursive samples (e.g., see Ancis & Syzmanski, 2001). With the universalizing strategy, the person deflects a reality of racism and thereby attempts to level the playing field by reasserting the privilege and deservedness of those who occupy the highest rungs of the economic, social, and political ladders. Although the person may not intend to perpetuate racist ideology, he has engaged the two-pronged process by diminishing the perspectives of (and therefore, diminishing the humanity of) people of color and reinforcing the fictive innocence of Whites.

Perhaps a more troubling defensive strategy is when the individual ascribes equal or more power to people who are at the lower rungs of the social hierarchy than to those at the higher rungs. I label this the *reversal of power* strategy. A person may state, "My boss is Hispanic. Everyone I work with at my job as a bank teller in El Paso, Texas, is Hispanic. Black basketball players make a great deal of money. No, it's these people who have the power and privilege, not Whites." The "them versus us" angle is more apparent, but more troubling is the possibility that the person may believe that those occupying the "them" category need to be reigned in or, worse, controlled violently. There is a definite tone of competition, implying one group may be winning or losing. The statement also seems to be a reaction to some stimulus about the existence of racism. The person may wish to shrug off or minimize the meaning of the stimulus because of the personal feelings it has invoked in her. The reader now may begin to see how invested people can be personally in contributing to the two-pronged process. For example, this person may feel disempowered on a personal level and may resort to this defense in order to project blame onto a convenient group of "others" for any feelings of guilt or shame she is experiencing about racial injustice. Taken to the extreme, when this individual feels that "others" are invading her sense of entitlement (e.g., as a White person or as a White-identified Japanese American), she may strike out aggressively, rally together other like-minded people who perceive Whites as being overly generous or innocent and who need to re-invest energy to preserve their entitlement, or commit acts of violence. Key to both of these defenses is that the implicit conditioning builds a foundation from which the individual can perpetuate racism. This foundation is antithetical to a worldview in which people are perceived and treated as human and as part of a common humanity. This foundation also can breed personal dilemmas and affect interpersonal functioning and psychological development.

I present two cases to further illustrate manifestations of the two-pronged process; later I will re-examine them in the context of mental health promotion.

Two Case Illustrations

Mr. Sol

Mr. Sol recently emigrated from Korea to America to seek a better life for his family. With the boom in technology over the past 40 years, Mr. Sol and his family had been increasingly exposed to images of African Americans while they lived in Korea. These negative images have been reinforced since they have been living in Los Angeles where the majority of Mr. Sol's customers are Black and poor or working-class. When asked, Mr. Sol explained that he believes that Affirmative Action is unfair because it grants undeserved favors to Africans and Native Americans who are undeserving and lazy. He also states that "hard work" is what made America great, and that the absence of African Americans and Native Americans in the upper socioeconomic strata in society is evidence that they do not have what it takes to succeed in society. Asian Americans, on the other hand, are the model minority because they possess the stamina, diligence, and motivation to succeed.

This illustration is admittedly oversimplified because it presents a very narrow aspect of Mr. Sol's life. However, I want to single out early on in the chapter how "acceptable" language translates into personal expressions of racist ideologies. For example, we learn in this passage some of Mr. Sol's attitudes about African Americans, Native Americans, and Asian Americans. His attitudes are apparently built on an absence of knowledge or on selective attention to or memory about the extent of exploitation and oppression that these groups have experienced historically and continue to experience in contemporary American society (e.g., Franklin & Moss, 2000; Hu-DeHart, 2000; Takaki, 1990, 1993). He accepts what he has learned from mainstream culture and may not raise doubts about media portrayals of different racial groups. He considers the sociopolitical hierarchies in American society as troubling, but blames African Americans and Native Americans as being responsible for their position on the lower rungs. He also views members from these groups as somehow possessing some biological or cultural endowment that predisposes them to be disproportionately represented in prisons, on the welfare system, and in low-paying and low-status occupations. Mr. Sol believes that Asian Americans are making their way up their ladder because they *do* possess the biological and cultural endowment to succeed.

With regard to the second prong of socialization, Mr. Sol is exposed to ample knowledge about the experiences of Europeans and Whites as architects of the United States and other nations (e.g., Hu-DeHart, 2000). Contrariwise, little or distorted attention is directed to how Europeans and Whites enslaved, colonized, raped, terrorized, broke promises with, exploited, or enacted restrictive legislation against people of color (e.g., Brown, 1970; Gonzales, 2000; Zia, 2000). In brief, we can conclude that Mr. Sol's attitudes are based on a distorted account of reality.

Yet another important feature of this example is Mr. Sol's unexpressed, but still present, attitudes toward White Americans. Note the italicized words in the passage below that were excluded yet inferred from the original scenario:

Affirmative action is unfair *to Whites;* hard work *by Whites* is what made America great; the absence of African Americans and Native Americans in the upper socioeconomic strata in society *and concomitant presence of Whites* is evidence that People of Color do not have what it takes to succeed in society *whereas Whites do have what it takes.*

Mr. Sol adopts a language that allows Whites to be invisible and, therefore, disengaged from an active system of racial stratification. We move now to our next case illustration.

Ms. Hopkins

Ms. Hopkins, a White woman from the U.S. rural Midwest, moved to the beach community of Ensenada, Mexico, when she was 22 years of age to start a new life. She considered the Whites in her town to be "redneck" and felt ashamed of her parents and hometown community. She moved to Mexico because of her considerable interest and appreciation in Mexican art, music, jewelry, and culture. She came to know the people in her new community well, and they seemed to take a liking to her. As her parents were aging and she was experiencing some guilt about leaving them, Ms. Hopkins moved to a U.S. college town with a large international population that was about two hours from her hometown. As the owner of a Mexican clothing and jewelry store, she was instantly drawn to the international community and to Whites who lauded her for being "worldly" and "racially tolerant." She admits freely to her White and international friends that she has "nothing in common" with American racial/ ethnic groups (save other worldly Whites), yet has a slight affinity to Mexican Americans whom she believes can benefit from her knowledge about Mexico and Mexican culture. She believes that the problems that Mexican Americans experience—in crime, substandard housing, and relative low achievement compared to Whites—are due primarily to their not having an appreciation for their heritage and to their reluctance to learn English. She believes that Whites need to expose themselves to Mexican culture as a way to spice up their "boring, bland lives."

Like the illustration of Mr. Sol, this characterization is overly simplified. But what I hope is apparent in this case illustration is the observation that Ms. Hopkins' relationships are influenced to some degree by her need to perceive herself as non-racist and, therefore, as distinct from those in her family and community who have undoubtedly influenced her development. At least some part of her interest in Mexico is linked to her need to escape an unwanted aspect of her identity as a White. In essence, she "uses" Mexicans and Mexican culture to meet her own needs and to resolve her desire to escape identification with Whites and with racism. She objectifies and exoticizes Mexican-descended people to fill her need to feel worthy. Moreover, by perceiving Mexican Americans as needing to know more about Mexican culture—a need for which she believes can provide—she projects an arrogance and condescension that fuels racism. Stated another way, Ms. Hopkins is perpetuating racism by appropriating people of color to help her overcome some guilt or shame about her upbringing.

Ms. Hopkins' treatment of Whites is also condescending. She believes that something is missing in the lives of White people. She perceives Whites as being bland and unexotic, which contrasts her view of Mexicans and Mexican culture. She is also blinded to a reality of racial disparities between Whites and Mexican Americans that were apparent in her hometown. Although poverty was shared among people in her community across racial groups, virtually all the Whites distanced themselves from the Mexican Americans. Ms. Hopkins also grew to detest the wealthier Chicano/as for being "misguided and uncaring toward their own people." Without recognizing these deep-seated issues, Ms. Hopkins' manner of coping with her feelings about Mexican people is to invest her attentions to issues of culture as distinguished from race. Her focus on encouraging Whites to appreciate Mexican culture is narrow and avoids issues pertaining to structural disadvantage. To heighten her status with Whites, she recommends with wanton arrogance that Whites similarly appropriate Mexican culture for selfish reasons. Against a reality of (denied) racism, Ms. Hopkins deploys the second prong of socialization by ignoring or making innocent the role of Whites in contributing to racial disparities.

Parenthetically, Ms. Hopkins' suggestion that both Whites and Mexican Americans can benefit from learning about Mexican culture is not without merit. For everyone affected by the racism *Zeitgeist,* achieving an appreciation of cultures that are too often dismissed or romanticized is an extremely important aspect in learning about racism (e.g., Thompson, in press). However, Ms. Hopkins' suggestion of heritage learning is limited if she fails to teach thorough approaches that encourage her students to explore why and how this learning is rarely conveyed in media or in many learning environments. This aspect of learning, called critical pedagogy (Beauboeuf-Lafontant & Augustine, 1996; Freire, 1970; Shor, 1992), is important in inoculating students against the two-pronged process of socialization.

Helms' Racial Identity Theory (1990, 1995a) is a conceptual frame for developing assessments of and treatment for Mr. Sol and Ms. Hopkins when their strategies for offsetting reality and aspects of themselves fail and they seek the help of mental health practitioners. I turn now to a description of this theory.

Racial Identity Theory

Racial identity "involves an individual's continual, and at times highly conflicted assessment of the people who comprise his or her externally ascribed reference group as well as the people who comprise other racial groups" (Thompson & Carter, 1997 p. 15). Research on racial identity theory is still unfolding, yet relatively substantive. A cross-section of these studies have shown factors predicted by racial identity attitudes: Blacks' attitudes toward counseling and therapy (Austin, Carter, & Vaux, 1990); Whites' expression of racism (Carter, 1990); Blacks' psychological functioning (Carter, 1991); Whites' adherence to traditional work values (Carter, Gushue, & Weitzman, 1994), Blacks' life role domains (Carter & Constantine, 2000), Blacks' levels of self-esteem (Parham & Helms, 1985a) and self-actualization (Parham & Helms, 1985b), and White's susceptibility to the influence of racial stereotypes as they process information (Gushue & Carter, 2000). Within the scope of counseling relationships, some of the research to date has shown the following: Cross-racial therapy interactions are of better quality when the counselors have resolved more of their own racial concerns than has the client (Carter & Helms, 1992); Black surrogate male clients' emotional reactions to dyads comprised of a therapist and client with similar racial identity statuses were predicted by racial identity attitudes (Richardson & Helms, 1994); counselor trainees' working alliance perceptions of same- and cross-racial dyads were predicted by racial identity attitudes (Burkard, 1997); and racial identity attitudes predicted White-counselor preferences for Whites and Black-male counselor preferences for Blacks (Helms & Carter, 1991).

In actuality, racial identity theory subsumes three theories, also termed models: The People of Color (POC) Identity Model, the White Identity Model, and the Racial, or People of Color (POC)–White, Interaction Model (Helms & Cook, 1999). The first two models are described in this section. The Racial Interaction Model is discussed in the next section.

The People of Color (POC) Identity Model

The POC Identity Model consists of five statuses, each representing assessments of the racial self and racial others. Accompanying each status are one or more types of information processing strategies (IPS) that people *primarily* use when coping with racial stimuli. I emphasize "primarily" because theoretically no person operates solely in one status. According to the concept of epigenesis, people need to resolve earlier status conflicts before they fully proceed to the next status. Moreover, higher status IPS can be used even when the individual operates primarily in a lower status. Consequently, the construct of epigenesis is helpful in explaining how people are able to show variation in how they respond to racial stimuli.

The statuses of the POC Identity Model are *conformity, dissonance, immersion-emersion, internalization, and integrative awareness.* People who operate primarily in the *conformity* status assume that they and racially similar others occupy the lower rungs of the strata due to what are presumed as their own biological or cultural insufficiencies. Whites are perceived as occupying the upper rungs because of presumed superior biological or cultural endowments. Other racial groups may be hierarchically arranged according to their relative similarity or dissimilarity with Whites. This hierarchy may also be arranged within racial groups. For example, lighter-skinned Mexicans may be perceived as being superior to darker-skinned Mexicans because of their apparent link to European lineage. Second generation Chinese may perceive themselves as being superior to recent Chinese immigrants because they have had more opportunities to associate with Whites and White culture or to intermarry with Whites. The IPSs in the conformity status include the tendency to deny or be oblivious.

Through a series of events sparked positively or negatively by interpersonal encounters, increased exposure to non-mainstream histories, and critical reflections on the self, a person can move to other statuses. Each racial identity status is characterized by differentiations of the self and others against the backdrop of societal racism. The person can experience general confusion about racism (*dissonance*) and about his levels of conformity in perceiving people within imposed hierarchies. This status is called *dissonance* and is primarily transitional. This status is followed by a sense of rage and mistrust toward Whites and, simultaneously, a tendency to reify people of similar races. This is called the *immersion-emersion.* In the next status, *internalization,* the person begins a process of perceiving people more humanly and individually after working through some of the reality of racism. At this penultimate status, people of color gradually recognize that their lingering tendency to idealize racially similar others—and, by implication, themselves—is short-sighted, merely a reaction to a divisive and hostile environment. They also recognize that their portrayals of Whites are stereotyped. They have generalized negative qualities onto all Whites and have avoided approaching Whites as individuals. In the first four statuses, the IPSs of selective attention, hyperviligence, and dichotomous thinking are variously employed to cope with racial stimuli.

Probably as a means of dualistically defining the self one way (e.g., a Latina or "old money" African American) and as something that is not another thing (e.g., White or "not-old money" African American), the person who operates in the first four statuses is caught up in trying to define the self within the structures that society has imposed and to which people generally adhere. She does not define the self from *within* but rather from *without.* The person deals with the pathologies that exist within this structure by being in lockstep with the distortions that are encrypted to maintain the hierarchies of lesser-than versus greater-than. This becomes especially daunting when the person also harbors beliefs about fairness and equal justice among humans. The individual may believe that the best approach to dealing with racism is to accept and treat everyone equally, but without a concomitant quest to deal with the segmentation that affects the people, he or she is still strapped within a system of oppression.

Racial pride is considered a key factor in moving the person of color to the advanced statuses. This pride acknowledges the significance of the past and recognizes the generations of people of color who have worked to endure the oppressive structures and make inroads for future populations. Indeed, this aspect suggests that in order for people of color to develop healthy racial identities in a society that demoralizes people of color, they must develop love and appreciation of racially similar others (Thompson, in press). Conversely, people of color need to develop a love of Whites—not as superior or inferior, but as human. They need to see people of all walks of life as humans rather than as flat, biased images.

The final status, *integrative awareness,* is characterized by a self that is internally defined. The person fully recognizes that society is systemically oppressive and acknowledges that she and *everybody else, racially similar and dissimilar,* suffer as a result of the oppression. People of color whose status schema is primarily *integrative awareness* come to learn that race is a social construction that imposes an unfair hierarchy on people, and that the stereotypes that cast people into unfair categories, positive or otherwise, deflate individuality and humanity. They also know that by continually working through a reality of racism and other structures of oppression, they can optimally overcome the fragmentation that once prevented the political self from becoming integrated into other aspects of the self. As she develops a more synergistic understanding of the whole self, the person of color who uses *integrative awareness* approaches rather than avoids reality. She approaches people of all backgrounds rather than avoiding certain groups and overcomes any discomfort such contacts have formerly elicited in her. By increasing her exposure to people, irrespective of background, the person with *integrative awareness* comes to learn that her definition of self does not have to be determined by stratification factors; she accepts not only that these factors exist but also that they must be dismantled. She now knows that racism and all structures of disadvantage limit her own and others' ability to forge relationships and to form collective, harmonious communities. She is also determined to invest time and effort in practices that help eradicate the various structures of oppression that obstruct human relations and cohesion across groups, throughout organizations, and in communities around the world.

The White Identity Model

The White racial identity model is composed of six statuses: *contact, disintegration, reintegration, pseudo-independence, immersion-emersion, and autonomy.* At the *contact*, the White person learns of his or her whiteness. Before this contact, the person believed that he or she merely "existed." Thompson and Carter (1997) have described an example of how this socialization might occur:

> The parent or adult may explain to the [White] child that the Black person or Person of Color is "different" and may encourage the child to touch the person's hair or skin, thereby indulging him or her in the fascination of the other person's "difference." In either case [whether promoting fascination or fear, as in the parent who scolds the child for noticing], there lacks any or little acknowledgement that the child is White, that his or her characteristics are reflective of being White, and that people vary in appearance as a result of their race. Instead, the Black or Brown is perceived as the exotic, the other (hooks, 1993), while no examination of the child's difference is acknowledged. (p. 23)

At the *contact* status, Whites conform to a status quo in which racial groups assume different positions along the hierarchy, and they consider themselves to have little role in the construction or maintenance of it. When Whites experience a single event or series of events that jar this distortion of reality (*disintegration* status), they experience anxiety, confusion, and/or anger. Some experience anger toward other Whites, and still others experience anger toward both people of color and Whites. Those who blame other Whites feel duped, misinformed, and potentially powerless. In the progression of racial identity, they variously feel a sense of rightful privilege about themselves as Whites and irritation or rage toward people of color for not trying hard enough (*reintegration*). In this *reintegration* status, Whites re-invest in beliefs about their superiority as White people. When faced with the fallacy of these beliefs, and with re-surfaced concerns about equality and fairness, Whites move to the *pseudo-independent* status. Although they continue to have lingering beliefs about the deservedness of Whites, they also believe that People of Color can ascend the racial hierarchy given the proper skills or tools. Denial, selective attention, dichotomous thinking, and obliviousness are IPSs that operate in the first five statuses of the White Identity model. The latter two statuses of White Identity theory, *immersion-emersion* and *autonomy,* are characterized by a gradual liberation from the perspective that Whites are the standard, the universal, and the superior and that the other is inferior, exotic, pitiable, or undeserving. The twofold struggle for Whites in proceeding along this course of development is first to recognize and overcome their role in the perpetuation of racism and second, to discover a positive White identity. This latter struggle primarily surfaces in the last two statuses.

If the feature of racial-ethnic pride is important to the development of People of Color, then it can be argued that a particular challenge for Whites in their racial identity development is the relative absence in their lives or in history of White people who have engaged in the formidable struggle against racism *as* White people. This is not to state that White people have not been engaged in the struggle against racial oppression, but rather that their stories have been largely diminished or distorted. Therefore, in order for Whites to advance through this sequence of racial identity development, it is important that they develop a love and appreciation for racially similar others—those Whites who have used their privilege in the service of eradicating racial oppression. They must also develop a love and appreciation for People of Color, *not* for the purpose of meeting their own needs or purposes but for realizing their morality. Whites also need to recognize the often-subtle ways in which the "Africanist presence," or rather any symbolic presence of marginalized others, has been adopted to imply self-contamination (e.g., "dirty blonde hair").

The two final statuses of the two racial identity models are similar in that both People of Color and Whites make use of complex and flexible IPSs to cope with racial stimuli. Whites with *autonomy,* like People of Color with *integrative awareness,* seek out relationships and strive to forge meaningful connections with people of all backgrounds. They become fully aware of how superficial politeness and physical distancing between certain populations are artifacts of the various structures of disadvantage. This awareness helps them to anticipate and continue the struggle to overcome problems in communicating with others. They come to understand that their efforts to forge meaningful relationships with people across races, genders, and social classes will be met with suspicion, anger, or even enamored eagerness because of their association with Whiteness. Both Whites and People of Color at the final statuses also learn to anticipate and cope with the ascription of labels like "bleeding heart liberal" or "racially preoccupied." They understand that name-calling represents one effort to sway them back in step with conformist practices and attitudes. Like People of Color with primarily *integrative awareness* status schemata, Whites with primarily *autonomy* status schemata are committed to dismantling societal oppression on all fronts because they recognize that their relationships with people across all backgrounds are convoluted as a result of these structures. Whites with *autonomy* want to pierce these structures and can best do so when their actions reflect manifestations of themselves absent of the strategies that were employed to deflect their undeserved privilege.

Racial Identity Assessments: The Cases of Mr. Sol and Ms. Hopkins

> Freedom (to move, to earn, to learn, to be allied with a powerful center, to narrate the world) can be relished more deeply in a check-by-jowl existence with the bound and unfree, the economically oppressed, the marginalized, the silenced. (Morrison, 1992, p. 64)

A key definitional feature of racial identity assessment is the interdependence of the racial self and racial others. It assumes at a fundamental level that there is a communal component of the person's development of self. Stated another way, people appraise themselves in juxtaposition to others (e.g., Erikson, 1968). Hence to assess a Native American child as having a "poor racial identity" is incomplete. This assessment must acknowledge the child's perceptions of herself and her perceptions of those who are racially similar and dissimilar to her. This assessment of others' perceptions is taken into account because the child's sense of herself racially is shaped by her interactions with and perceptions of racial others.

Therapists' reluctance to make complete assessments may be yet another by-product of social conditioning. Because of the social conditioning that separates and diminishes the sociopolitical context of reality, it becomes difficult for many people to competently conduct this sort of assessment because to do so is to acknowledge racism and, by implication, its originating and sustaining association with White people. It may be easier for some people to concentrate on the first-prong of socialization in making racial identity assessments because, especially for Whites, it imposes some distance in explaining the phenomenon of internalized racism. However, to integrate the second prong is to surface a reality in which Whites contribute to the construction of unhealthy racial identities among People of Color.

Consistent with the integration of the two prongs in conducting assessments, it is important to point out ways in which People of Color attempt to elevate themselves because of their relatively inferior status on the racial hierarchy. For example, the Native American child described earlier may decide to dilute her heritage by "becoming" European and therefore engage in "passing" as a way to avoid racism (see Harris, 1995). As an important aspect of her assessment, the therapist would need to look for indications not only of the manner in which she tries to re-create herself racially, but also of the strategies she uses to make herself appear or be like Whites and to reject other Native Americans. Within the two-pronged socialization process, the child attempts to elevate her "standing" to become more human in a society where she is racially marginalized.

I'll elaborate on these points relative to the characterization of Ms. Hopkins as a White person. Ms. Hopkins believes that the vast beauty of nature is a testament of her values concerning a shared humankind among equals. Despite these beliefs, her parents' constant vocalizations about Mexicans have instilled in her a sense of fear of Mexican Americans. This fear prevents her from being comfortable with Mexican Americans and perceiving them as humans. In order to overcome her fear, she develops a fascination with artifacts by Mexicans, which eventually leads to her move to Ensenada. But this fascination does not address her fear of Mexican Americans in general, whom she vaguely recognizes as being different from those she knew in Ensenada. Moreover, by learning about Mexican culture she has an opportunity to be with Mexican Americans, but in a way that feels most comfortable to her—in the role of their teacher. Any efforts she makes to provide courses to Mexican Americans in the community may involve solely teacher-student relationships which, because of her preferred teaching approaches, turn out to be formal and relatively distant.

Ms. Hopkins unconsciously attempts to resolve her fear of Mexican Americans not by acknowledging the reality of societal racism and the concomitant source of her fear, but by asserting greater privilege in relating to them. By not working through racism, Ms. Hopkins is bound to commit further acts of dehumanization, even though she perceives herself as compassionate and non-racist. She has some characteristics of Pseudo-Independence, recognizing at least on some level that Whites need to learn more about People of Color, but she has not resolved earlier status schemata. To resolve these levels, Ms. Hopkins needs to realize that her life is confining and is designed to bring her comfort in thinking about herself in positive ways. She also needs to realize that she attends selectively to reality in order to preserve her entitlement and her sense of self as worthy and compassionate.

Mr. Sol considers himself a devout Christian. He experiences dissonance when he faces the contradictions between his Christian religious beliefs—the belief in people's worth and their equality in the eyes of God—and his highly varied interactions with the people who patronize his store. Though he may seek uniformity in the stereotypes he conveys, he cannot find it. Mr. Sol's customers are obviously not all the same, nor are his interactions with them. He occasionally chats with some of his clients in a friendly way.

By harboring negative stereotypical images of certain groups and relatively positive images of others, Mr. Sol crafts two or more separate belief systems about humankind, countering his religious beliefs of a shared humanity. His stereotypes about several populations—Africans, Native Americans, Whites, and Asian Americans—serve to diminish the human qualities of these groups of people by casting them into faceless, unfair categories. Even though he constantly witnesses necessarily nuanced images of people across racial groups, he generally holds firm to his beliefs, perhaps assimilating disconfirming evidence to create further divisions (e.g., better-educated Blacks are better than less-educated Blacks because they better emulate Whites; Cambodians are inferior to Koreans because of their cultural upbringing, etc.). But in these rationalizations Mr. Sol avoids recognizing the reality of structural oppression and its effects on the lives of these racial groups. These rationalizations are in keeping with the two-pronged socialization process. They serve to affirm Mr. Sol's sense of worth *relative to others* and may help him justify his perception of higher standing in comparison to Blacks within the racial hierarchy. His investment in racism, therefore, has to do with the popular notion that Asian Americans are "proof" that hard work and stamina lead to success. This belief simultaneously acknowledges that "Asianness" is not representative of the entitled group and fuels distortions about certain populations of color (including non-Chinese or non-Japanese Asian ethnic groups) as not trying as hard as Asians; thus it is rooted in the suppressed conditioning of racism. As hopefully is evident, Mr. Sol has to commit energy to maintaining the fiction of a "deserved" and immutable racial hierarchy.

By assuming that Whites are deserving, unfairly treated, and successful, Mr. Sol portrays this racial group flatly, without regard for human differences. To *dehumanize* is to "divest of human qualities" (*Webster's New Collegiate Dictionary,* 1980); consequently, Mr. Sol is also dehumanizing Whites. Yet the demoralizing component of dehumanization is experienced quite differently for Whites than for People of Color. Racism provides that structure that casts Whites in flattering and benevolent ways but characterizes People of Color negatively, even as subhuman (e.g., as objects or as inherently criminal, unclean, or morally bereft: Baker, 1998; Smedley, 1993; Thompson & Neville, 1999). Whites can and do feel demoralized within a structure of racism, but this occurs when they are confronted as being visibly White and associated as the beneficiaries of this structure.

Although Mr. Sol's dealings with Whites are primarily in purchasing merchandise to sell in his store, his contacts are typically pleasant, which confirms his perceptions of Whites as decent, deserving people. When Mr. Sol witnesses exceptions to his view of Whites as deserving or successful, he may develop rationalizations to accommodate the new data into his worldview on race. He may treat poor Whites with sympathy, perceive Whites who commit crimes as products of unfortunate circumstances and, therefore, more deserving of restitution or compassion than Blacks who commit crimes. He may also propose that White people who behave rudely are stoic and, therefore, deserving of his admiration.

Mr. Sol's beliefs about fairness and equality reflect vestiges of advanced racial identity statuses (*integrative awareness*). However, he needs to resolve earlier statuses to continue his racial identity development and to relate more authentically to people of diverse backgrounds. In order for Mr. Sol to resolve the dilemmas of his earlier statuses, he must realize that his perspectives have been fallacious, and he must develop more realistic assessments of society and of himself as a by-product of structural disadvantage.

Spiritual Identity and Awareness

People who believe in a higher power are capable of perpetuating and conforming to the structures of disadvantage. Like Mr. Sol, they can create exceptions to their beliefs about human equality and justice, propose that personal responsibility outweighs all else, and in *self*-righteous ways work to save the less fortunate by working in or contributing to charities or by trying to teach "the other" about how to be more like they are. These efforts can sometimes occur as a result of racial privilege, whereby Whites practice these behaviors relative to the racial/ethnic "other." Similar effects can occur with the efforts to splinter oppression, such as when Blacks in corporate America may informally encourage Black neophytes to act White so that they "prevent" themselves from being pigeon-holed or stereotyped by White managers. Irrespective of the type of entitlement, people with spiritual beliefs may also be caught up in feeling indifferent toward the "other" because they can readily and successfully dispel the dissonance, ensconce themselves in privileged lifestyles, and reliably repress the realization of the interdependence of humanity.

Myers (1988) proposed that people who have dismissed the spiritual component of themselves lead fragmented lives. They fail to see themselves and others as interdependent because they do not recognize themselves and others as manifestations of God or Goddess. Instead, they equate worth with aspects of material reality; consequently, their valuation of human worth is determined through the five senses. Because this suboptimal reality strips away the spiritual component of people's lives, assessments of worth are dictated by how one appears: e.g., phenotypes, suggestions of racial designations, effeminate or masculine behavior in accordance to societal norms, wealth, and so forth. This fragmentary reality allows people to believe that their strivings for "things" will garner more favorable assessments from others and thus elevate or affirm their worth within the political structures. Again, these assessments are founded primarily on perceptions of reality based on five senses, not on the knowledge that people are manifestations of God or Goddess.

Perceiving people and the self as being better than or inferior to others while recognizing, at some level, that these formulations go against one's faith or belief in a shared humanity is a dilemma that is decidedly moral. Perhaps a more fundamental dilemma is having knowledge about the impact that such beliefs have on those who are consigned socially to the inferior category and yet doing nothing or little to help dissipate these structures of disadvantage. Being aware of these structures and coming to recognize their reality-deflecting elements are essential conditions for motivating people to learn about the self. I believe that the moral problems that constitute the fabric of racism can be resolved through racial identity development.

People who experience this development enter into a series of transformations that gradually leads them to realize more fully their fairly vague yet persistent beliefs about equality and fairness. They recognize that society offers people moral challenges. To overcome these challenges, the individual must think and behave in ways that are consistent with the ideal of a shared humanity. More significant, people who take risks that help chip away at the structures of oppression can find that their interactions with others take on new and more profound meaning. They learn to avoid being at odds with people in ways that demean, fear, or exoticize, and they learn instead to better align themselves with the forces that unite humankind. They engage with others, in spite of the structures that divide people across and among different groups, for the purpose of fostering appreciation among those with whom they have contact. The individual who now *approaches* reality is able to better expose himself more fully to various people. He also is informed of the convergence of forces that shape people's lives. His blinders are gradually fading.

Racial identity development and its concomitant moral and spiritual development are difficult. Alice Miller (1990) wrote about the tremendously difficult quest to act on behalf of what one believes is good and just, rather than on what society expects one to do. Her passage, which refers to the experiences of people living in Nazi Germany, addresses the relationship between moral actions and the development of self:

> Individuals who refuse to adapt to a totalitarian regime are not doing so out of a sense of duty or because of naivete but because they cannot help but be true to themselves.... Rejection, ostracism, loss of love, and name calling will not fail to affect them; they will suffer as a result...but once they have found their authentic self they will not lose it. (pp. 84–85)

Discovering the authentic self requires exposure to a diversity of perspectives and people, self-other reflection, time, and critical inquiry. By tapping into the moral core, racial identity development will allow the spiritual self to be increasingly and harmoniously aligned with other aspects of the self.

Racial Interaction Model: The Facilitation of Awareness in Counseling and Psychotherapy

> The fabrication of an Africanist persona is reflexive; an extraordinary meditation of the self; a powerful exploration of the fears and desires that reside in the writerly conscious. It

is an astonishing revelation of longing, of terror, or perplexity, of shame, or magnanimity. It requires hard work *not* to see it. (Morrison, 1992, p. 17)

The development of racial identity is not linear; rather, it is a fluid process that is theorized as occurring in cycles, with each "return" to an earlier status manifesting differently than previously experienced (see Parham, 1989). The different statuses likewise are not static and mutually exclusive. Consequently, given the vast complexity that characterizes us humans, we have the capacity to think in complex and flexible ways about racial stimuli, take bold stands on racial matters and, conversely, commit errors that reflect our fears, longing, shame, or perplexity. Furthermore, the recursive interaction between individuals with the environment is important to the cultivation of growth. Changes within the person are prompted by environmental events. These events are influenced by individuals. The changes that individuals experience will influence their interactions with others, and others will too react. These reactions can be positive and negative. As these cyclical changes occur, interjected by instances of fixation of statuses and by a recycling of statuses, the person's worldview takes on new dimensions.

The crown jewel of Helms' racial identity theory is the Racial Interaction Model (see Helms & Cook, 1999 for update). This model presents a framework for facilitating racial identity development. In a context of counseling and psychotherapy, therapists who employ advanced racial identity IPSs are able to assist clients by assessing their levels of racial identity development and determining how the impact of racism and other structures of disadvantage have influenced the individual's construction of self and percieved ways of being in the world. It is my belief that therapists who are able to successfully employ complex and flexible IPSs in their work have also successfully tapped the moral or spiritual core. They are apt to perceive and appreciate humanity to its fullest. Although the model describes the qualities of interaction in therapist-client dyads based on similar racial identity schemata (termed *parallel* interactions) or on counterproductive matching (termed *regressive* interactions), I focus on those interactions that facilitate racial identity development. These interactions are termed *progressive* interactions.

In facilitating racial identity development, therapists strive to encourage their clients to take a hard look at reality and to make disturbing discoveries about a world they may have once considered to be good and just, however vague or perplexing this formative worldview may be. Consequently, strategies to end racism or internalized racism require that clients perceive as credible and important the expressions of people who experience racism and suffer as a result of it. Even when these expressions are perceived in complex terms (perhaps in some cases as exaggerations of unfair practices presumed to be due to race), the person needs to understand the context in which some exaggerations are made. For a Person of Color, this encouragement to see racism would mean helping the person recognize racism when he is inclined not to see it as such or, conversely, when he interprets all harmful acts to be the result of racism. For all clients, the therapist must help unravel the socialization process and replace it with healthier and more flexible ways of relating and being. Ultimately, clients can no longer assume or treat Whites as being more deserving or worthy than People of Color merely because they are White. People of Color cannot be viewed in demonized or exotic ways, minimized or exploited for the purpose of promoting

White superiority. Conversely, reactive racism should not make one see Whites as uniformly evil. People of Color cannot be perceived as ideal or superior to Whites.

Piercing the conditioning requires more than attention to a reality outside of the self. As a reality of racism is perceived with increasing accuracy, psychological processes are spurred. Cognitive, affective, and conative factors converge to spur questions about the self. People who experience this process gradually recognize that they have ranks within the hierarchy and that their ranking depends on the ranking of others. How have they participated in ensuring their positions within the hierarchy and, by implication, positioned others outside it? Can they forgive themselves and others, endure movement beyond their formative worldviews, and develop more internal definitions of themselves?

These are the sorts of questions that therapists must continually ask themselves. Therapists need to be keenly aware of their own racial identity profiles and of ways that they perpetuate and collude in racism. These self-assessments will also reveal the extent to which the therapist has access to advanced status sensibilities. Consequently, assessments of therapists' profiles should include not only the facets that represent areas to resolve and improve upon, but also those existing resources that promote their racial identity development along with their moral and spiritual growth.

Elsewhere (Thompson, 1997), I have identified six approaches for therapists to apply in facilitating racial identity development with their clients. First, the therapist must set a climate for talking about race, in itself a daring move given the silence and codification that occurs with the racism *Zeitgeist*. However, the therapist's attempt to establish this climate is important because it provides clients with the opportunity to discuss aspects of reality that are too often unexpressed yet vaguely important to their lives. Second, the therapist must be able to assess the racial identity of the client. I stress again that this assessment is complete only when it includes the client's perception of self as well as racial others who have informed her way of being in the world.

The third approach is to constantly maintain a focus on the relationship. People learn optimally when they feel safe and regarded as human and worthy. Additionally, therapists need to be aware of the power their clients ascribe to them as raced, gendered, classed, abled people. Older therapists may invoke in younger clients a sense of deference when other elements are taken into account: For example, older White male counselors who are presumed non-gay and whose office setting suggests a degree of affluence may need to consider the likelihood that clients who are working-class, White, and admittedly bisexual will respond in ways that are embedded in stratification factors. Therapists too can respond to clients based on stratification factors and need thus to anticipate and work through some of the dynamics that are brought to bear in these interactions.

The final three approaches relate to helping clients work through the strategies they use that reinforce the two-pronged socialization process. Therapists need to confront the dissonance in their clients' thinking and encourage them to use complex and flexible IPSs in resolving the dilemmas that frustrate them. The fifth, a didactic approach, is advised when the therapist can illuminate situations or lead the client to readings or other media that will promote learning about societal disadvantage and can surface suppressed knowledge about the "other." The final approach is corrective socialization, which involves helping the client understand what went wrong in his or her socialization and, more specifically, what messages or practices contributed to the problem or pathology.

I return to the case illustrations but this time, focus attention on Ms. Hopkins and Mr. Sol in a clinical context. Imagine that Ms. Hopkins learns that her parents both have been diagnosed with cancer and have only a few months to live. She has chided them constantly about their lack of sophistication and now feels deeply remorseful and depressed and seeks the help of a therapist. In the therapy, Ms. Hopkins's therapist will encourage her to address her feelings about her family and about other Whites she knows who perpetuate racism. As her therapist explores family dynamics, he will need to surface other factors that might contribute to her shame regarding her family, such as social class status, history of abuse in the home, gender stratification forces, and so forth.

The therapist will also eventually help Ms. Hopkins discover in her healing that she needs to take risks to forge authentic relationships with Mexicans and Mexican Americans without asserting authority over them. The therapist will reinforce and encourage her complex IPSs and help her understand how best to resolve her deep-seated fears toward Mexican-descended people. He will warn her that her interactions will not always be pleasant, but rather than resigning herself to avoiding Mexican Americans or other people who spur her feelings of vulnerability and inadequacy she needs to take risks and confront the discomfort. The therapist will applaud her for the desire to effect change within her community, but help her reframe her current way of perceiving problems. He will help her recognize that in her teaching she can be less distant and most effective when she is capable of talking with her students about White culture and about being White instead of conveying implicitly that her culture is somehow neutral or bland.

Mr. Sol has been robbed on three separate occasions and is increasingly fearful of his rage. He wants to purchase a handgun, but is terrified at the thought of using it. He seeks the advice of his minister at the church he belongs to. He hopes, secretly, that his minister will condone his having a gun and, therefore, help relieve his guilt about the prospect of using it. With the help of his minister, Mr. Sol can be invited to talk openly about the conflict between his belief in the Golden Rule and his beliefs about the inferiority and superiority of certain groups. His minister will also help him distinguish between immediate solutions to protect himself and his business and longer term solutions that relate to criminal behavior and social disenfranchisement. Mr. Sol's minister will also help him see the linkage between both types of solutions and the futility of violent measures to resolve problems.

Mr. Sol will need the support of his friends and family, and his minister may assist in these efforts by calling for collective action not only among Koreans, but also among other marginalized groups in the community. Establishing community watches and making efforts to discover the reasons the robberies occur can pave the way to the kinds of action that lead to help for those who tend to rob (e.g., drug users). Mr. Sol's minister may also work to help Mr. Sol eventually discover that his beliefs about humanity are rooted in history and context and that Mr. Sol behaves in ways that counter his beliefs. For example, because of his vague and unexplored sense of guilt about his attitudes toward African Americans, he has sometimes given away items without charging certain customers or has excused patrons' debts and paid them himself. As racial identity development is facilitated, Mr. Sol will recognize that he may have done these things so that he could be seen as "kind" and "fair"—a reflection of how he believes he ought to be and behave, given his rearing. With changes in his worldview, Mr. Sol will discover that his interactions may not always be pleasant, but he can feel released from maladaptive attempts to settle his dissonance. He can treat his customers honestly and avoid incurring problems that result from failing to resolve earlier racial identity status conflicts.

With further counseling, Mr. Sol can learn to approach persons and situations with greater freedom. His minister may need to help him realize that the notion of Asian Americans as the model minority is a myth constructed within the bounds of racist ideology. In addition, as he learns about the endurance that many Asians have demonstrated in the face of oppression and exploitation (Takaki, 1993; Zia, 2000), he can learn how to experience racial pride that is reality-based and thereby disentangled from sinister racial hierarchies.

The suggestions for clinical treatment of these case illustrations have hopefully demonstrated that counseling can be more than the erasure of symptoms or immediate relief of clients' distress. Realistically, it is often the short-term outcomes that clients seek. Psychotherapy that encourages moral dialogue and community action can be seen as merely an ideal. However, I urge readers to consider seriously the impact of psychological theory to the practice of counseling and psychotherapy, as well as to prevention. With collective effort, mental health professionals can create change in a society so desperately in need of purposeful and humanistic intervention.

References

Ancis, J. R., & Szymanski, D. M. (2001). Awareness of White privilege among White counseling trainees. *The Counseling Psychologist, 29*(4), 548–569.

Apple, M. W. (1993). *Official knowledge: Democratic education in a conservative age.* New York: Routledge.

Austin, N. L., Carter, R. T., & Vaux, A. (1990). The role of racial identity in Black students' attitudes toward counseling and counseling centers. *Journal of College Student Development, 31*(3), 237–244.

Baker, L. D. (1998). *From savage to Negro: Anthropology and the construction of race, 1896–1954.* Los Angeles, CA: University of California.

Beauboeuf-Lafontant, T., & Augustine, D. S. (1996) (Eds.). *Facing racism in education* (2nd ed.). Cambridge, MA: Harvard Educational Review. (Reprint Series No. 21).

Berlak, A., & Mozenda, S. (2001). *Taking it personally: Racism in the classroom from kindergarten to college.* Philadelphia, PA: Temple University.

Betancur, J., & Gills, D. (2000) (Eds.). *The collaborative city: Opportunity and struggles for Blacks and Latinos in U.S. cities.* New York: Garland.

Brodkin, K. (1998). *How Jews became White folks and what that says about racism in America.* New Brunswick, NJ: Rutgers University.

Brown, D. (1970). *Bury my heart at Wounded Knee: An Indian history of the American West.* New York: Bantam.

Bullard, R. D. (2000). *Dumping in Dixie: Race, class, and environmental quality* (3rd ed.). Boulder, CO: Westview.

Burkard, A. (1997). *The impact of counselor trainees' racial identity upon working alliance perceptions in same- and cross-racial dyads.* Doctoral Dissertation, Fordham University, 1997. Dissertation Abstracts International: 57 (10-B): 6559.

Campbell, C. P. (1995). *Race, myth, and the news.* Thousand Oaks, CA: Sage.

Carter, R. T. (1990). The relationship between racism and racial identity among White Americans: An exploratory investigation. *Journal of Counseling and Development, 69,* 46–50.

Carter, R. T. (1991). Racial identity attitudes and psychological functioning. *Journal of Multicultural Counseling and Development, 19,* 105–114.

Carter, R. T., & Constantine, M. G. (2000). Career maturity, life role salience, and racial/ethnic identity among Black and Asian American college students. *Journal of Career Assessment, 8,* 173–187.

Carter, R. T., & Gesmer, E. (1997). Applying racial identity theory to the legal system: The case of family law. In C. E. Thompson & R. T. Carter (Eds.), *Racial identity theory: Applications to individual, group, and organizational interventions* (pp. 219–235). Mahwah, NJ: Lawrence Erlbaum.

Carter, R. T., Gushue, G. V., & Weitzman, L. M. (1994). White racial identity development and work values. *Journal of Vocational Behavior, 44,* 185–197.

Carter, R. T., & Helms, J. E. (1992). The counseling process as defined by relationship types: A test of

Helms' interactional model. *Journal of Multicultural Counseling and Development, 20,* 181–201.

Chesler, M. A. (1976). Contemporary sociological theories of racism. In P. A. Katz (Ed.), *Towards the elimination of racism* (pp. 21–72). New York: Pergamon.

Crenshaw, K., Gotanda, N., Peller, G., & Thomas, K. (1995). *Critical race theory: The key writings that formed the movement.* New York: New Press.

D'Augelli, A. R. (1994). Identity development and sexual orientation: Toward a model of lesbian, gay, and bisexual development. In E. J. Trickett, R. J. Watts, & D. Birman (Eds.), *Human diversity: Perspectives on people in context* (pp. 312–333). San Francisco, CA: Jossey-Bass.

Dula, A., & Goering, S. (1994). *"It just ain't fair": The ethics of health care for African Americans.* Westport, CT: Peter Lanz.

Erikson, E. (1968). *Identity, youth and crisis.* New York: W. W. Norton.

Fine, M. (1994). Working the hyphen: Reinventing self and other in qualitative research. In N. K. Denzin and U. S. Lincoln (Eds.), *Handbook of qualitative research* (pp. 70–82). Thousand Oaks, CA: Sage.

Forbes, J. D. (1990). The manipulation of race, caste and identity: Classifying AfroAmericans, Native Americans and Red-Black people. *The Journal of Ethnic Studies, 17,* 1–51.

Franklin, J. H., & Moss, A. A. (2000). *From slavery to freedom: A history of African Americans,* (8th ed.). Boston: MacGraw-Hill.

Freire, P. (1970). *Pedagogy of the oppressed.* New York: Seabury.

Freud, S. (1921). *Group psychology and the analysis of the ego.* W. W. Norton & Co.

Gaines, S. O., Jr., & Reed, E. S. (1999). Prejudice: From Allport to Du Bois. *American Psychologist, 50,* 96–103.

Gonzales, M. G. (2000). *Mexicanos: A history of Mexicans in the United States.* Bloomington, IN: Indiana University.

Gotanda, N. (1995). A critique of "Our Constitution Is Color-Blind." In K. Crenshaw, N. Gotanda, G. Peller, & K. Thomas (Eds.), *Critical race theory: The key writings that formed the movement* (pp. 257–275). New York: New Press.

Guinier, L. (1994). *The tyranny of the majority: Fundamental fairness and representative democracy.* New York: Free Press.

Gushue, G. W., & Carter, R. T. (2000). Remembering race: White racial identity attitudes and two aspects of social memory. *Journal of Counseling Psychology, 47,* 199–210.

Harris, C. I. (1995). Whiteness as property. In K. Crenshaw, N. Gotanda, G. Peller, & K. Thomas (Eds.),

Critical race theory: The key writings that formed the movement (pp. 276–291). New York: New Press.

Helms, J. E. (1990). *Black and White racial identity: Theory, research, and practice.* Westport, CT: Greenwood.

Helms, J. E. (1994). The conceptualization of racial identity and other "racial" constructs. In E. J. Trickett, R. J. Watts, & D. Birman (Eds.), *Human diversity: Perspectives on people in context* (pp. 285–311). San Francisco, CA: Jossey-Bass.

Helms, J. E. (1995a). An update of Helms's White and People of Color racial identity models. In J. Ponterotto, J. M. Casas, L. A. Suzuki, & C. M. Alexander (Eds.), *Handbook of Multicultural Counseling* (pp. 181–198). Thousand Oaks, CA: Sage.

Helms, J. E. (1995b). Why is there no study of cultural equivalence in standardized cognitive ability testing? In N. W. Goldberger & J. B. Veroff (Eds.), *The culture and psychology reader* (pp. 674–719). New York: New York University.

Helms, J. E., & Carter, R. T. (1991). Relationships of White and Black racial identity attitudes and demographic similarity to counselor preferences. *Journal of Counseling Psychology, 38,* 446–457.

Helms, J. E., & Cook, D. A. (1999). *Using race and culture in counseling and psychotherapy: Theory and process.* Needham Heights, MA: Allyn & Bacon.

hooks, b. (1993). *Sisters of the yam: Black women and self-recovery.* Boston: South End.

hooks, b. (1996). *Reel to reel: Race, sex, and class at the movies.* New York: Routledge.

Hu-DeHart, E. (2000). Rethinking America. In V. Cyrus (Ed.), *Experiencing race, class, and gender in the United States* (3rd ed., pp. 168–171). Mountain View, CA: Mayfield.

Jones, J. (1988). Psychological models of race: What have they been and what should they be? In J. D. Goodchilds (Ed.), *Psychological perspectives on human diversity in America* (pp. 7–46). Washington, DC: American Psychological Association.

Kozol, J. (1991). *Savage inequalities: Children in America's schools.* New York: Crown.

Lillie-Blanton, M., Leigh, W., & Alfaro-Carera, A. (1996). *Barriers to care: Assessing access to health care for Hispanics and African Americans.* Lanham, MD: Joint Center for Political and Economic Studies.

Lipsitz, G. (1998). *The possessive investment in whiteness: How white people profit from identity politics.* Philadelphia, PA: Temple University.

McCall, L. (2001). *Complex inequality: Gender, race, and class in the new economy.* New York: Routledge.

Miller, A. (1990). *For your own good: Hidden cruelty in child-rearing and the roots of violence.* New York: Farrar, Straus, & Giroux.

Morrison, T. (1992). *Playing in the dark: Whiteness and the literary imagination.* Cambridge, MA: Harvard University.

Myers, L. J. (1988). *Understanding an Afrocentric world view: Introduction to an optimal psychology.* Dubuque, IA: Kendall/Hunt.

Parham, T. A., & Helms, J. E. (1985a). Attitudes of racial identity and self-esteem by Black students: An exploratory investigation. *Journal of College Student Personnel, 20,* 143–147.

Parham, T. A., & Helms, J. E. (1985b). Relation of racial identity attitudes to self-actualization and affective states of Black students. *Journal of Counseling Psychology, 32,* 431–440.

Parham, T. A. (1989). Cycles of psychological nigrescence. *The Counseling Psychologist, 17,* 187–220.

Prilleltensky, I. (1997). Values, assumptions, and practices: Assessing the moral implications of psychological discourse and action. *American Psychologist, 52,* 517–535.

Richardson, T. Q., & Helms, J. E. (1994). The relationship of the racial identity attitudes of Black men to perceptions of "parallel" counseling dyads. *Journal of Counseling and Development, 73,* 172–177.

Roediger, D. R. (1990). *The wages of whiteness: Race and the making of the American working class.* New York: Verso.

Shields, D. (1995) (Ed.). *The color of hunger: Race and hunger in national and international perspective.* Lanham, MD: Rowman & Littlefield.

Shor, I. (1992). *Empowering education: Critical teaching for social change.* Chicago, IL: University of Chicago.

Smedley, A. (1993). *Race in North America: Origin and evolution of a worldview.* Boulder, CO: Westview.

Takaki, R. (1990). *Iron cages: Race and culture in 19th century America.* New York: Oxford University.

Takaki, R. (1993). *A different mirror: A history of multicultural America.* Boston: Little, Brown.

Thompson, C. E. (1997). Facilitating racial identity development in the professional context. In C. E. Thompson & R. T. Carter (Eds.), *Racial identity theory: Applications to individual, group, and organizational interventions* (pp. 33–48). Hillsdale, NJ: Lawrence Erlbaum.

Thompson, C. E. (in press). *Applying racial identity theory to peace education: Tools for the teacher in all of us.* Interchange.

Thompson, C. E., & Carter, R. T. (1997). *Racial identity theory: Applications to individual, group, and organizational interventions.* Hillsdale, NJ: Lawrence Erlbaum.

Thompson, C. E., & Neville, H. A. (1999). Racism, mental health, and mental health practice. *The Counseling Psychologist, 27,* 155–223.

Tuan, M. (1998). *Forever foreigners or honorary whites? The Asian ethnic experience today.* New Brunswick, NJ: Rutgers University.

Weis, L. (1990). *Working class without work: High school students in a deindustrializing economy.* New York: Routledge.

Westa, L., & Wenz, P. S. (1995). *Faces of environmental racism: Confronting issues of global justice.* Lanham, MD: Rowman & Littlefield.

Witt, D. (1999). *Black hunger: Food and the politics of U.S. identity.* New York: Oxford University.

Yee, A. H., Fairchild, H. H., Weizmann, F., & Wyatt, G. E. (1993). Addressing psychology's problems with race. *American Psychologist, 48,* 1132–1140.

Zia, H. (2000). *Asian American history: The emergence of an American people.* New York: Farrar, Straus, and Giroux.

4

Intercultural Communication as Contexts for Mindful Achievement

Billy E. Vaughn

Alliant International University
Diversity Training University International

A high-ranking California state official used the word "nigger" instead of Negro in his speech at an annual awards dinner for the Coalition of Black Trade Unionists. He later referred to his foible as an embarrassing slip of the tongue (The Associated Press, 2001). One member of the audience told a reporter that she was appalled, as she felt that the speaker would not have made such a slip unless it were something he normally said. The state official, a Democrat, was clearly embarrassed: "I know it came out of my mouth, but it is not how I was taught. It is not how I teach my children." He will undoubtedly feel for a long time the guilt, shame, and political repercussions of using the word. The real-life incident demonstrates the power of words in intercultural contact, the consequences of intercultural blunders, and the importance of intercultural competence.

Intercultural competence refers, in part, to the awareness, knowledge, and skills needed to engage effectively in cross-cultural interactions. Without specialized training or experience, most of us are anxious about saying or doing the wrong thing in intercultural interactions because we have been socialized to value openness to people of different social groups (Devine & Monteith, 1993). However, social science studies demonstrate that we tend to reproduce the divisions among groups within society when we talk honestly about other groups, even when we are trying to be egalitarian (van Dijk, 1987).

Our best efforts to talk about the relationship between intelligence and race, for example, often result in supporting the view that different groups are not equally capable of learning or of taking care of themselves without public assistance. A major barrier is that we are overly anxious about saying something that will offend our audience (Vaughn, 1998), even those of us who are low in prejudice (Devine, 1996; Devine & Monteith, 1993). The politician was undoubtedly nervous about making a social foible, but he did not possess the intercultural competence to avoid it.

This chapter is based on four assumptions about intercultural communication. One assumption is that intercultural communication, like all other communication, involves efforts to construct meaningful, goal-directed social interactions. A second is that even though a therapist may be low in overt prejudice, he or she may lack knowledge and skills needed to support his or her egalitarian ideals. A third assumption is that insufficient knowledge and skills result in reproducing, rather than overcoming, intercultural barriers. Finally, it is assumed that the intercultural competence needed to effectively construct meaningful, goal-oriented intercultural contexts requires *mindfulness* to produce culturally sensitive behaviors. A mindful person is so keenly aware of personal intercultural interactions that modifying behavior in order to improve effectiveness occurs instantaneously (Gudykunst, 1991). Mindfulness overcomes anxiety toward intercultural contact by redirecting the competent communicator's attention to the moment of constructing the communication context. A mindful therapist reads both verbal and nonverbal cues in an effort to heighten cultural sensitivity in serving the client's needs.

In the sections that follow, this chapter will provide a working definition of intercultural communication and a detailed discussion of each assumption just listed. The chapter will conclude with a description of two intercultural skills: powerful questions and compassionate communication. Examples of each will be offered. The major argument presented is that intercultural communication competence involves understanding those who are different through consciously creating an effective social context in the moment.

Intercultural Communication and Its Obstacles

Intercultural communication refers to communication between people based on both the shared and distinct cultural perceptions and symbol systems that influence communicative contexts (Samovar & Porter, 1995). Poor intercultural communication is the result of differences in cultural perceptions and symbol systems of the interlocutors. In the previous example, the state official did not believe his behavior reflected his attitude about Black people, but many Blacks believe that those who make such slips merely reflect their true beliefs. The considerable research indicating that contemporary racism is more indirect and symbolic than in times past, when racism was more overt, supports such suspicions that "slips of the tongue" are not merely accidental (e.g., McConahay, 1986). An important point is that intercultural competence is crucial in a society in which race relations remain tenuous at best. Competent intercultural communication requires self-awareness of personal barriers, knowledge of how to negotiate cross-cultural interactions, and practice in using those skills.

Different cultural perceptions, along with the words and gestures associated with them, can create obstacles to effective intercultural communication. Moreover, these obstacles and differences are reinforced by a history of clashes in cultural practices. The intergenerational pain that African Americans share, for example, is closely connected with a history of slavery from which unresolved bitterness haunts efforts to achieve harmonious relations today. Many intercultural difficulties can therefore result from attempts to move forward in therapy without adequately addressing issues of suffering and oppression. A therapist who chooses a color-blind approach in working with clients of a different race or culture cannot competently diagnose and treat them as a group because such a therapist will not accurately understand their context. By ignoring the influence of oppression, socioeconomic class, group identity, and power in psychotherapy, the therapist avoids the challenges that must be addressed to effectively serve the clients' needs.

The need for effective intercultural communication is as great today as it has ever been, in part because of the increasing diversity characteristic of North American society but also because the consequences of ineffective intercultural communication are more serious than ever. Legislation and public policies that protect the interests of identity groups are prevalent, as is an emphasis in the popular media to expose intercultural tension. Therefore, the fact that organizations and individuals can be legally prosecuted or, more commonly, singled out in public for saying or doing the wrong thing makes the egalitarian but interculturally incompetent person anxious. People fear unintentionally saying or doing something insensitive. This fear of making mistakes adds to the complexity and difficulty of intercultural communication, even in superficial conversations—let alone in therapy sessions. Counselors and therapists particularly understand that connecting with clients is the key to successful outcomes in general practice. Developing intercultural skills, therefore, empowers therapists to minimize stepping on toes in the dance of effective communication.

Assumptions about Intercultural Communication Contexts

Effective Communication Creates Meaningful, Goal-Directed Interactions

Four assumptions about intercultural communication underlie the views offered here. One assumption is that the ability to co-construct a communicative context determines the extent that intercultural communication goes smoothly. A communicative context is more than the physical space in which people are interacting. More importantly, it involves what the participants are doing and what assumptions they make in deciphering what is being jointly shared (Erickson & Schultz, 1997). The co-construction of a shared context is like a dance between participants, who use whatever shared knowledge they can muster and any other useful resources to achieve their objectives. Intercultural communication creates a particular challenge because the rules of constructing joint meaning are likely to be dissimilar across participants. The more intercultural competence each participant possesses, the less likely someone will step on multicultural toes. However, even one competent person can reduce the occurrence of foibles and general misunderstanding.

An intercultural communication context is marked by styles of speaking, listening, and coordinating with others that require characteristically different skills from those used by those who share culture. The popular educational video *The Color of Fear*[1] (Lee Mun Wah, 1994) is a good example of co-constructing an intercultural context, showing the inherent challenges of doing so. Lee Mun Wah facilitates a dialogue about racial and ethnic group relationships among eight American men who were essentially strangers to each other. The group has an equal representation of Asian Americans, Latino Americans, African Americans, and European or White Americans. One important lesson from the edited video is that establishing an intercultural communication context is difficult, even for the most skilled and committed. In the video the men struggle in their communication, even though each is clearly interested in working together and has volunteered to spend concentrated time doing so.

The following excerpt of dialogue from the video demonstrates how cultural differences can create communication barriers. The people of color in the group have been sharing their individual stories about being treated unfairly and inequitably in American society. David, a White American participant, reacts to their claims by honestly sharing what he considers to be an important distinction between White Americans and people of color. The subsequent dialogue goes as follows:

> **David (White American):**   I never considered myself, as you do, a part of an ethnic group. I think that's what you are looking for, and you are not going to find that amongst us because we don't look at ourselves as an ethnic group.
>
> **Victor (African American):**   Do you know that that means something?
>
> **David:**   I don't know what it means, I mean—(interrupted)
>
> **Victor:**   I'm telling you that that means something—(interrupted)
>
> **David:**   I am trying to answer your question, Victor, and as you were asking that question, I am saying, "Well, gosh. I have never seen myself as part of a White group."
>
> **Victor:**   I just wonder that…Doesn't that seem kinda deep to you that you don't have an answer to that question? That…Do you have any notion that the fact that you have no answer to that could be a source of deep meaning, experience, or knowledge?
>
> **David:**   The opposite is how I feel about you, Victor. That you have no comprehension that the world is open to you. You think that the White man is a block and a dam to your progress, and he is not. I think you have put up that dam and that block yourself in your regard to the White man.
>
> **Loren (African American):**   See, I think that is one of the major problems with racism. I think he [David] did answer the question. As a White male, he doesn't have to think about his position in life, his place in the world. The history books tell him, as they are written, that this world is his. He doesn't have to think about, um, you know, where he is, what he does. He doesn't have to think like a White person. The way the world has been set up—America in particular—America is human…That does not enter a White person's mind.

---

[1]Copyright 1994 by Stir Fry Seminars and Consulting. Used with permission.

As the excerpt demonstrates, the participants quickly create an intercultural context filled with communication barriers. The major barrier to building an effective intercultural context is the different points of view about equality. David openly shares his view that America is a society of equal opportunity for all of its citizens. The other participants try over and again to make David see that his view is one of privilege, which creates a problem for people of color.

No matter what any of the other participants say, even the other White male, David continues his attempts to express his points about individual responsibility. David soon becomes frustrated with the bantering of the others because he feels they ignore the good intentions underlying his claims. The more he tries, the more the others try to get him to see their points of view. Soon the others grow tired and frustrated, and a couple of them reach the point of overt anger. The outcome is a classic reminder of why people avoid talking about topics such as race, gender roles, affirmative action, and other divisive social topics.

No one wins in intercultural encounters that go wrong because the different perspectives are not shared. The people of color think they understand David, but their reactions to him are as marred by their unwillingness to connect with him, unless it can be on their terms, as his naïve attempt to get them to appreciate his views. The group mutually creates a communication context filled with barriers.

Emotions run high in intercultural discussions of controversial social topics because different sides tend to lack empathy for the other's perspective, which is needed to co-construct an effective communication context. Instead, hurt feelings, frustration, and anger emerge as efforts to connect result in stepping on multicultural toes. Such barriers make communication more difficult, if not impossible. In the video, an effective communication context begins to emerge among the men only with Lee Mun Wah's excellent intervention as a facilitator, which will be discussed in more detail later.

What we have learned about symbol systems and about constructing contexts can influence our ability to communicate with others. Inevitably, we will encounter people who do not share our history and symbolic meaning system. The result is intercultural encounters that are filled with land mines. David does not understand why his emphasis on "individual responsibility" should be such a problem for the other participants, even if his views are different from the others. He thinks that everyone is there to listen to each other, but their reactions indicate that his views are unacceptable. The other participants also believe in equality and individual responsibility, but they do not believe that American society allows every person an equal opportunity to gain from individual effort.

David's perspective, as a White American male, comes from the belief that considerable progress in social equality has been made in society, and, as a result, individuals are treated according to character rather than according to social group identity. The participants of color share a perspective that comes from a history of subordination, insensitive treatment, and intergenerational pain passed down initially from the generation that endured the greatest indignity. The two realities are difficult to negotiate.

Intercultural Knowledge and Skills Are Needed

A second assumption is that most people in the Western World believe they are egalitarian, but they typically lack the intercultural knowledge and skills needed to support their egalitarian attitude. Many parents teach their children that they should treat people with respect and accept those who are different. However, parents' actions seldom model the moral imperative they maintain for their children. The church pastor, schoolteacher, and neighborhood hair stylist rarely do better. Few people model the tools to help us live by their words. Instead, they complain to other adults in front of their children about how poor people or people of color cause problems in society, steer their children away from dating people of other backgrounds, and raise their families in segregated neighborhoods. Confronted with such hypocrisy, many attempt to explain their behavior by claiming that although *society* may be racist, classist, and sexist, they themselves are not. Research provides little support for such reductionism (Devine et al., 1991).

In one set of studies, Devine et al. (1991) had White American undergraduate participants in a large psychology course complete a prejudice survey. They then selected both high- and low-prejudice participants for their research studies. Participants were presented vignettes of interracial encounters in which a dilemma concerning intercultural contact would be solved. First, participants were required to rate the extent that they *should* react to the imagined racial encounter based on societal norms (e.g., feeling comfortable sitting next to an African American on a bus). They were then instructed to re-rate the same vignettes to indicate the extent to which they *would* feel comfortable in each situation. The majority of the participants' ratings, regardless of prejudice level, showed a discrepancy between their personal standards (i.e., *should*s) and actual behaviors (i.e., *would*s). Results also indicated that the high-prejudice participants tolerated more prejudice, as evidenced by significantly higher *should* ratings (i.e., they believe prejudice toward a Black person in contact situations is justified). Low-prejudice participants were more egalitarian in their *should* ratings, but their higher *would* responses revealed more prejudiced behaviors than their personal standards would indicate.

Devine and colleagues (1991) used an affective measure to investigate the extent that the participants' awareness of discrepancies between personal standards and behavior created dissonance. Participants received response feedback informing them of the extent to which their ratings were consistent and were asked how they felt about the results. Those who were made aware of their inconsistencies indicated emotional consequences that varied as a function of prejudice level and amount of discrepancy. Statistical analysis isolated six factors that accounted for the differences: negative self, discomfort, positive feelings, negative other, threatened, and depressed. High-prejudice participants tended to support their prejudiced views and behaviors and to manage their dissonance by pointing out the problems people of color cause for society (i.e., negative other and threatened). Low-prejudice participants tended to experience guilt and shame when they learned that they were not as liberal-minded as they would like to be (i.e., negative self, threatened, or depressed). The overall results support the claims that most White Americans (about 71 percent of the total participants) harbor inconsistent racial attitudes. They are unconscious of this inconsistency, and they experience discomfort when they become aware of it. Similar results were found when the vignettes focused on encounters with gays or lesbians (Devine, Monteith, Zuwerink, & Elliot, 1991).

A promising outcome of this set of studies is that the researchers determined that although providing most people with information showing a discrepancy between their intercultural beliefs and behaviors caused anxiety, the awareness motivated participants to do things to bring their attitudes into alignment (Devine & Monteith, 1993). Low-prejudice participants tended to seek ways to make their behaviors more egalitarian to fit their self-image.

Anxiety over and Misunderstanding about Differences Raise Barriers to Communication

The third assumption is that our best efforts to communicate competently across cultures can be disastrous. Different groups of people experience different socialization, even within the same society. One of the most striking examples is the difference in socialization across gender. A male and female living in Western society can be raised by the same parents, yet learn different communication strategies for achieving interpersonal goals. Deborah Tannen (1990) is one of the first social scientists to bring this to our attention. She demonstrated that women tend to communicate their requests indirectly as a relationship-building strategy, while men tend to communicate directly in their efforts to meet goals competitively. The result is that men and women in the workplace may make trouble for each other by using different communication strategies. The differences in cultural realities Tannen observed across gender are similar to those we experience across race, socioeconomic status, age, sexual orientation, etc.

In our efforts to achieve a multicultural reality, we have been taught more about derogatory ethnic labels (kike, spick, Jap, etc.) and off-color ethnic jokes than about defeating stereotypes when talking about people who are different (van Dijk, 1987). There are few people who are competent in the ways they talk about and treat members of other cultures to serve as models (Vaughn, 1994a, 1994b). While we tend to overlook the need to work out gender differences, we sense the gap between our intercultural beliefs and behaviors, even if we are not conscious of doing so. The result is that we feel anxious when we have to be on our very best behavior.

The most salient information about an individual's cultural group is often based on negative stereotypes, which enter into consciousness automatically. Our goal is to engage in the most socially appropriate behavior so that we will be viewed as tolerant and accepting. In focusing more attention on avoiding mistakes in intercultural situations than making positive contribution, we have fewer mental resources to monitor our actions. The result is that a derogatory word or deed surfaces that we have been trying to repress. Once the damage is done, we do not have the social-repair skills needed to resolve the matter effectively. Lack of intercultural competence makes some of us so anxious about intercultural encounters that we prefer to avoid them, and we refuse to acknowledge that cultural differences are important when we do.

Effective Communication Requires Mindfulness

A final assumption is that competently doing the "intercultural thing" means mindfully meeting the demands of constructing a communicative context in interactions with people from a different culture. We can overcome the shortcomings of not being sufficiently prepared for intercultural encounters by developing adequate skills. Gudykunst (1991) relates intercultural competence to awareness, or what he refers to as *mindfulness.* In contrast, *mindlessness* is automatic, unconscious social information processing which results from well-ingrained ways of knowing and learning. Gudykunst assumed that a major intercultural communication barrier is our tendency to automatically use knowledge of our own experiences in interpreting the behaviors of those we know little about. We also tend to be unaware of the intercultural barriers mindlessness often creates.

Mindfulness, for the present purposes, refers to consciously focusing on learning new information in unfamiliar social situations. It requires (a) focusing more on the process than the outcome (Gudykunst, 1991), (b) drawing new distinctions from novel information to remain situated in the present (Langer & Moldoveanu, 2000), and (c) thinking less about making mistakes in order to enjoy and appreciate what is being shared in the moment (Hanh, 1991). A mindful person seeks out, is open to, and appreciates complexity in intercultural encounters.

Adults have well-learned ways of meeting new people and interacting with them. It is more efficient to treat everyone the same when meeting them for the first time, rather than to put effort into treating each person uniquely. However, these ingrained social strategies can create problems in intercultural encounters because the social practices shared by members of one group may prove inadequate for connecting with those of a different culture. Awareness of our tendency to perceive others from our biased perspective tends to force us to rely on more distinctions in learning about others. This expanded perspective, in turn, leads to (1) greater sensitivity to the social context, (2) more openness to differences, (3) opportunities to learn new information that can alter our perceptions, and (4) awareness of how taking multiple perspectives can promote problem solving (Langer & Moldoveanu, 2000). The heightened state of being involved in the interaction in the moment, of the potential to use inappropriate strategies, and of the need to be open to learning novel behaviors are results of mindfulness.

A good example of what one needs to do in order to improve mindfulness is to consider how Americans categorize people. Americans tend to view the world from a dualist perspective, the result of a Puritan heritage. Instead of viewing groups, such as race, on a continuum, we tend to think of them as distinct social categories. The result is that we share the negative stereotypes associated with the superficial social categories. Viewing differences, such as skin color, on a continuum (e.g., they are all Americans, but some happen to be darker in skin color than others) has different consequences in terms of inclusion than assuming that the superficial differences represent meaningful, distinct human traits (differences in intelligence, trustworthiness, work ethic, etc.). The racial categories serve a particular social, political, and economic function in the United States; thus the change from treating race as categorical to viewing it as continuous would hinge on redefining this contrived human characteristic. Therapists must understand the sociopolitical bases of skin color in western society to effectively treat and retain clients of color.

Thich Nhat Hanh (1991), a Buddhist Zen master, teaches that mindfulness is the key to human compassion. His work is not grounded in Western research approaches, but in the much longer history of practicing Buddhist doctrine. His philosophy views training focused on the goal of reaching a state of inner peace as the foundation for self-development and social responsibility. Practicing meditation and compassionate mantras helps one become fully present in the moment, which is key to achieving inner peace.

Inner peace promotes mindfulness, which in turn promotes human compassion. Anger, for example, is considered an unpleasant feeling that is harmful to the self and others. Awareness complements anger by making us mindful of our emotional state and reactions. The awareness alone does not change the anger, but being aware is crucial to bringing about understanding and resolve. Mindfulness is nonjudgmental and serves primarily to sooth anguish, which helps return the self to a pleasant state.

The person who does something that appears prejudiced toward people with physical challenges can be viewed differently. We move from thinking about the person as acting with malice to understanding the individual as someone who lacks awareness and is struggling within the self to understand those who are different. A mind without anger is happy, a state which is the foundation for love and compassion (Hanh, 1991). Treating people compassionately requires taking their point of view and discovering how they prefer to be treated. One may not agree with their views or support their behavior, but understanding them will empower the compassionate individual in making him or herself understood. This is the basis of mindful interactions with people who are difficult to communicate with, and those who may not share similar cultural symbols.

The mindful therapist is not color blind. While a color-blind approach enables the counselor to consider the client's needs from a monocultural perspective, the mindful therapist is sufficiently present in the interaction that both individual differences and group patterns are likely to emerge in diagnosis and treatment. In contrast, the therapist who assumes that cultural differences are of central importance in intercultural counseling will not be mindful of the uniqueness that individuals bring to such encounters. A mindful therapist is simultaneously aware of uniqueness and group patterns in counseling interactions. The result is a flow from treatment focused on group membership to individual needs across and within sessions. Mindfulness shapes and is shaped by the intercultural context. Thus the intercultural context is a mindful achievement.

While the mindful individual in interaction with people who are different can replace anxiety with pleasure, curiosity, and a sense of purpose (i.e., connecting compassionately with others), mindfulness alone is insufficient as an intercultural communication skill. It allows us to decrease the automatic behaviors that can lead to social foibles or conflict, but it does not automatically provide skills to produce the desired goal. We must also learn to engage in planned, creative, strategic, reason-based (in contrast to emotional), and flexible communication to be competent (Burgoon, Berger, & Waldron, 2000). Burgoon et al. (2000) offer the following list of intercultural communication strategies that are influenced by mindfulness:

- Entertaining multiple interpretations of information being shared
- Using questioning strategies to clarify information
- Tactfully encouraging the communication partner to self-disclose in culturally appropriate ways
- Anticipating possible responses to remarks, along with creative response planning
- Integrating information shared by the partner in an earlier part of the conversation into planned remarks

The above techniques can help us to interact mindfully with people who are different. Practicing them will allow for intercultural communication that manages the unexpected situational exigencies that tend to arise. Responding to intercultural challenges requires sufficiently quick, fluent, and effective communication strategies. Overall, the literature indicates that being mindful benefits all parties involved, even in situations where only one party has developed the necessary skills.

Intercultural competence is about modeling how to effectively engage people who are different from oneself in meaningful interactions. The ability to engage in mindful intercultural interactions is the result of first accepting that we lack intercultural competence and then doing what is needed to develop it. Mindful communication leads to more effective intercultural context building because the anxiety of dealing with differences is arrested, and the words that cause negative emotional reactions are reduced. Even if one person in the interaction lacks the competence, the competent person can support joint construction of an effective intercultural context.

The Roles of Emotion Management and Confrontation in Intercultural Communication

While mindfulness relates to regulating the self, the ability to effectively engage others relates to social competence. Social competence plays an important role in helping one do one's part in constructing effective intercultural communication contexts. The more one has the ability to empathize, listen, ask questions, and be genuine, the more likely that a productive context will be constructed. Recent research indicates that emotional intelligence is a major social competence characteristic (Goleman, 1995). As we now accept that academic intelligence is culturally mediated, we become increasingly aware that the same is true of emotional competence. Emotions are intimately connected to social activities motivated by human goal-oriented action, which relies on shared symbolic meaning (Ratner, 2000). In the video *The Color of Fear*, David's perspective would not have been a problem had he and the other participants shared assumptions about such phrases as "the world is open to you" and "you think that the White man is a block and a dam to your progress." David's words make the others feel misunderstood, which eventually leads to their frustration and anger. How we control our emotions, display them, and derive meaning from others' emotional expressions determines our intercultural competence.

Certain social topics readily activate strong emotional reactions due to the intergenerational pain connected with them. Intergenerational pain[2] refers to the shared emotional trauma that has been passed down from one generation to another rooted in a history of human suffering. Internment of Japanese Americans during World War II continues to be a source of pain for Japanese who were born decades afterward. Enslavement of early African Americans is relived in modern-day discrimination because the pain associated with the suffering has not changed significantly over time. Today, intercultural encounters between White and African Americans retain at least a hint of this historical tension. Engag-

---

[2]I credit a graduate student in the Culture and Human Behavior doctoral program for teaching me this word.

ing in mindless interactions with members of groups with historic conflicts can easily lead to social injury that resurfaces the intergenerational pain. All intercultural interactions are potentially volatile due to the lack of awareness and poor intercultural skills that members of each side bring to the social interaction. Diversity training is an effort to help people work directly through many of the barriers that reproduce intergenerational pain and human misunderstanding. However, a facilitator with poor understanding of the relationship between emotional and attitudinal change can make the training itself part of the problem.

Ideally, diversity training would provide the knowledge and skills needed to make one aware of one's personal intercultural challenges, empathize with those who are different, communicate across cultures with the least amount of misunderstanding, and increase one's knowledge about cultural differences. However, the reality is that too many trainers do not have sufficient knowledge and skills to support intercultural competency development. One reason is that many have not adequately dealt with their own biases and personal intercultural limitations, as evidenced in poor emotional self-control.

Diversity trainers with limited competency often interpret negative emotional reactions to training as either (a) a form of resistance they need to overcome in order to achieve multicultural competency (Brislin & Yoshida, 1994; Gay, 1984), (b) an aversive reaction to intrapsychic conflict about race (Kovel, 1970), or (c) a lack of racial identity awareness (Helms, 1990). Some believe that emotion is a healthy and necessary part of intercultural competency development, while others believe that emotion retards learning and, therefore, should be avoided or controlled as much as possible. Between the extremes is the assumption that emotional discharge is inevitable in such training because we lack intercultural competence (Brislin & Yoshida, 1994) and that emotion can be used effectively for training purposes (Vaughn, 1998).

Efforts by the American military to improve intercultural relations among its recruits provide specific examples of how diversity training practices that exploit human emotions for intercultural competency development can be unsuccessful. A broad and vigorous training program was required of all recruits in an attempt to integrate a large, diverse, and racially segregated organization during the 1970s (Day, 1983). Basic training included at least two weeks of race relations instruction using an experiential learning format.

Confrontational techniques were common in experiential training (Day, 1983). It was assumed that confrontation is useful for getting recruits emotionally involved in healing racism, especially White American recruits. The technique involved putting the recruits on the "hot seat" and challenging them to admit that they were prejudiced and to make amends for it. Often the facilitators did not feel that it was their responsibility to help the participants manage the trauma resulting from the exercise. Many White recruits dealt with the experience by becoming more open to close contact with racial minorities. Others either did not change noticeably or became more prejudiced. A few changed to the extent that they became crusaders against all forms of racism and discrimination, which resulted in adjustment problems with peers and family members. Others were more apprehensive about interracial contact.

Little research existed at the time to provide insight into the influence of emotional reactions to diversity training on the recruits' learning, but research by Devine et al. (1991) indicates that confronting intercultural beliefs is discomforting and that awareness of discrepancies between beliefs and behaviors promotes attitude change. Over time, military officials grew concerned about many recruits' reactions to the training, particularly to the confrontational techniques associated with it. This led to a shift toward discouraging the use of confrontational techniques (Day, 1983). Confrontational techniques activate emotions by making people aware of their beliefs and values, but fall short when used alone as an approach to closing the gap. Those who advocate the use of confrontation will need to consider the technique's limitations.

Developing Intercultural Competence through Emotion Management and Mindful Communication

An ability to manage one's emotional reactions to human differences is considered a critical social competence in modern life (Vaughn, 2002). One cannot be mindful when emotionally charged. High negative affect tends to take resources away from the conscious effort needed to make novel distinctions in stressful situations. The result is that we tend to resort to well-learned behaviors in an effort to cope. We are simply too upset to engage in productive problem solving. For example, many students react negatively to required courses in multicultural counseling and psychology, believing that they are not prejudiced and feeling that a required course in learning about how to navigate cultural differences is a waste of time (Vaughn, 1994a, 1994b, 2000). Willingness to take the course depends on one's assumptions about the course (Vaughn, 1998). High-prejudice participants become resistant, while most low-prejudice participants either experience ambivalence toward taking the class or are excited about the opportunity. The ambivalent participants feel inadequate in their ability to demonstrate their liberal beliefs, unlike other low-prejudice people who see value in learning more knowledge and skills. Everyone is at least a bit anxious about exposure to the course content in a group, which can affect the construction of a context conducive to learning.

Mindfulness enables participants to seek value in the course by attending to the factors that offer a unique experience to learning about the self and others. Counselors and psychologists in training can use mindfulness to increase their capacity to manage the self in situations in which they perceive lack of control; and learning to do so can serve them well in professional practice. Being open to learning about differences is an important part of learning to be mindful as a multicultural or cultural mental health professional.

However, mindfulness is not easily self-taught. Ironically, few counseling or psychology training programs include direct training in these skills. Counselors and psychologists in training can certainly benefit from learning intercultural competence. Their work involves modeling for others, helping clients overcome desperate situations, and supporting clients in learning new, more effective behaviors. Intercultural competency can increase the effectiveness of this work. A considerable amount of the professional work of counselors and psychologists includes managing emotions, so training their capacity to be mindful will be helpful. The remainder of this chapter describes the benefits of training professionals in two intercultural communication competency skills that support mindful intercultural interactions: asking powerful questions and engaging in compassionate communication.

Asking Powerful Questions

An ability to ask questions that engage clients in the critical thinking needed to solve problems is crucial in mental health treatment. Therapeutic discourse involves asking clients questions to elicit understanding of their predicament and to seek possible solutions. The personal coaching professional uses questions to assist clients to fulfill personal goals, similar to a consultant helping an entrepreneur. Skillfully asking questions supports the client in becoming aware of the self and in dealing with the personal blocks that need to be addressed in order to achieve some goal. Asking questions in intercultural settings can make the difference between successfully meeting social goals and feeling the sting of making a social faux pas.

Asking powerful questions in intercultural interactions brings the participants' attention to the moment and to the barriers that must be overcome to achieve joint goals. Another excerpt from the *Color of Fear* video provides an example. The facilitator, Lee Mun Wah, intervenes by asking David, the White American, several questions in an effort to help move the dialogue along once everyone is frustrated by the differences in points of view. Lee Mun Wah uses powerful questions, as evidenced by the participants' shift from resistance to willingness to work together. In the following excerpt the powerful questions are in bold and italicized, for the reader's convenience.

> **David (White American):**   I know my feelings are very opposed to some of yours, and I don't understand why you have this intense anger and emotions.... Why it is so difficult for you to just be yourself and make your place? I think that's the big difference here. We White men don't have this camaraderie, if you want, that you coloreds have. (snickering sounds from other participants) We, we have.... We don't go out and organize,...we don't,...and have discussions. We just do our stuff. Whatever our stuff is, I guess.

> **Victor (African American):**   I see that we are living in two completely different consciousnesses, and I think I get yours and I have to be able to understand yours in order to survive. You live in a world where it is not necessary for you, in most instances, to understand my consciousness and my experience. It's like one of those parking garages with the spikes coming up. You live in the world where, when you drive your car past, the spikes are down. I live in a world where, and the men of color here, live in a world where, when we come up to the spikes, man, they are facing right at us.

> **David:**   The thought comes to me, Victor, that you are going the wrong direction, if the spikes are opposing you. ***Does that ever occur to you that you are going the wrong direction?***

> **Victor:**   That's a beautiful statement to me—that I am going the wrong direction. It's a marvelous illustration of the consciousness of White supremacy.

> **David:**   Well, let's not say White supremacy—

> **Victor:**   That's, that's what I want to say—

> **David:**   This is where...As you speak this analogy, and I am thinking to myself, golly, why does it always have to be in opposition to the way things are structured? And I constantly sit here and think, Why is he taking this direction? Why

don't they as a group…? Why don't you with your people look for something within yourselves that can make you feel equal to us? Because what I hear is that you are not equal, and I do not feel that.

Lee Mun Wah (Chinese American):   *So what's keeping you from believing that that's happening to Victor?…Just believing. Not to know why that is happening to him, but what is keeping you from believing that that's happening to Victor?*

David: Because that seems like that is such a harsh life. And I just don't want to believe…. I would assume, Victor, that your life isn't really that hard, difficult, and unpleasant.

Lee Mun Wah (Chinese American):   *What would it mean, David, then, if the life was really that harsh? What would it mean in your life? If it really was that harsh for them?*

David: (emotionally) That would be a travesty of life…. You have here something that shouldn't exist.

Lee Mun Wah: *And so what if it does? What if the world were not as you thought…? That it actually is happening to lots of human beings on this earth? What if it actually were, and you didn't know about it? What would that mean to you?*

David: Well, that's very saddening. (trembling voice and tearful eyes) You don't want to believe that man can be so cruel to himself or his own kind. I do not want to accept that it has to be that way, but maybe it is. And it must be because you express it (looking toward Victor), and the others in the group express that it is.

Victor: From here I can work with you. (Others nod their heads in agreement.)

Mun Wah's questions were powerful because they helped David uncover a source of his resistance to empathizing with the participants of color. The questions helped him connect with their experiences. They felt that his tearful account of their plight was evidence of his willingness to empathize with them. This was sufficient to get them to continue the work they had come together to do. The confrontational strategies the individuals used to create a meaningful context, such as shouting in angry voices, pleading, and making accusations, were inadequate to include David. Confrontation fell short of promoting the critical thinking David needed to make what the others shared relevant to himself. Powerful questioning as a strategy is excellent for facilitation because it can get individuals to engage in meaningful intercultural dialogue.

Given that both confrontation and powerful questioning coexisted in the example, one may argue that confronting David had been, at least in part, responsible for his subsequent empathic behaviors. The rationale could be suggested that David needed to be confronted repeatedly before his resistance wore down sufficiently to hear what the other participants were trying to convey. However, throughout the video each time the participants use confrontation to get David to empathize with them, he tries to get them to see how they may be hampering their own progress. In contrast, Lee Mun Wah's powerful questions increase David's empathy every time. This confrontation-resistance and powerful question-empathy pattern occurs several times throughout the video, resulting in a pattern similar to an ABCBC behavior modification treatment design, with David's behavior becoming more resistant each time confrontation is used and becoming more empathetic every time a powerful question is used.

The argument being made here is that aggressive confrontation causes David to become resistant, and he becomes empathetic only after Mun Wah asked powerful questions. The powerful questions also alleviate the resistance caused by using the confrontation strategy. The implication is that techniques that engage individuals in critical thinking and self-reflection about the impact of their values and beliefs are useful in helping others empathize with those who are different.

It should be noted that powerful questions and the other techniques outlined in this chapter strengthen rather than silence the voice of oppressed peoples. Shouting and confrontation, which would seem to be the opposite of silence, too often result in a breakdown of communication and ultimately silence. Shouting is too often labeled as pathological and dismissed; confrontation too often leads to resistance, defensiveness, and reprisal. Clearly, the men of color in the educational video needed to say what they said to David and to each other. However, their voices were not truly heard by David until Mun Wah cut to the core issues that fed into David's resistance. Similarly, any participant in intercultural learning interactions may find that her or his words are not honored by one or more people in the audience, and powerful questions are one way to create the space for those who are unheard or unappreciated to communicate their needs and intentions clearly.

Training therapists and counselors to use powerful questions does not require considerable change in the training models. The emphasis on training the use of powerful questions to engage the client in critical thinking about the self is consistent with the clinical interviewing and counseling techniques common in talk therapy. The powerful question technique fits nicely with the traditional training models for nondirective therapy and counseling. Trainees synthesize what they learn about therapeutic encounters with the specialized technology designed to help clients with intercultural challenges. Use of videotaped examples of powerful question competencies, along with written vignettes to test the competencies, can help trainees learn to how to help clients address intercultural barriers.

Engaging in Compassionate Communication

Another strategy, compassionate communication, empowers us to work toward achieving social contexts through sharing information about our needs and resolving differences nonviolently (Rosenberg, 1999). Specifically, compassionate communication involves identifying the issues, considering the needs/beliefs of others, and articulating one's own reactions and needs back to the other person. The following basic principles apply: (1) listening carefully, (2) leaning into the discomfort of hearing beliefs/issues that one disagrees with, (3) empathizing with others, and (4) learning about oneself and others through the interaction. The following demonstration of compassionate communication strategy is a paraphrase of a facilitated classroom discussion that took place in one university course the author was teaching. Indications of a compassionate communication strategy are in bold italics for the reader's convenience.

Jill (White American student):   I think affirmative action is a form of reverse discrimination. Giving anybody an unequal advantage over others solely on the basis of race is discriminatory. We will never get along as a society if people are not treated equally.

Reginald[3](African American student):   That was a racist thing to say. It shows that you don't understand that the playing field is not equal for everyone, even with affirmative action. Affirmative action merely gives us the possibility of being considered for a job. If we get it, it is because we are qualified. That's what you don't get.

[Dead silence in the classroom]

Instructor (African American):   Talking about race in America often leaves us at odds with one another. The idea is to keep the dialogue going. The more we talk, the more we have the possibility of understanding where the other person is coming from. Can anyone help us by using what we learned about compassionate communication while taking Jill's or Reginald's point of view?

Linda (White American student):   *When you* (Jill) refer to affirmative action as reverse racism, *I feel* frustrated, disappointed, and angry. *I value* affirmative action because it provides people of color with the opportunity to compete, when they would otherwise not be considered as an applicant. I am frustrated because I get tired of hearing White people misinterpret affirmative action. I am disappointed because I want to believe that my fellow students are more aware of the true spirit of affirmative action than those in the larger society. I believe that *you value* equality and want everyone to be treated fairly. Affirmative action is a symbol of inequality for you, but not for me. *I request* that you consider how being White offers you a point of view about affirmative action that may be very different if you were a woman of color. I believe that doing so will help you understand my reactions better and perhaps allow us to remain committed to our classroom dialogues.

The reader's initial reaction may be that Linda is using a lot of words to get her point across. Compassionate communication initially offers a lot of information to promote the co-construction of a mindful intercultural context. Articulating what one's reactions are and how they reflect one's values (i.e., When you…, I feel…, I need…, I request…), while considering the reactions and related values of the interlocutor helps everyone compassionately reflect upon the immediate experience. In the long run, however, more words and energy are saved compared to a circular dialogue, which leads to anger and verbal sparring, exemplified in the *Color of Fear* video. On the other hand, the silence brought about by different points of view tends to result in individuals becoming hardened in their positions instead of empathizing with the other person's point of view.

The compassionate response to Jill strategically disarms defensiveness and promotes dialogue that penetrates the differences she has with Reginald. First, Linda's response is

---

[3]The example is used merely to demonstrate the approach. Reginald's response is considered legitimate and has merit in its own right, given that it captures the predicament that people of color (or anyone in a position with less power than the person to whom they are speaking) often find themselves in when talking about race with White people (or anyone in a position with greater social power). This implies a challenge that is discussed in this chapter.

mindful in that it points out (1) what she believes Reginald heard Jill say (what he observed that was a problem for him), (2) his possible reactions to Jill's words (his feelings), (3) how the reactions may be related to his personal values (what personal values are being challenged), and (4) a direct request of Jill for the two of them to communicate more effectively. Implicit in this example is the fact that Linda actively listened to both Jill and Reginald and leaned into her own discomfort about the situation, taking the risk to openly express her own reactions. Compassionate communication, also known as nonviolent communication, focuses attention on what is happening to us internally in the moment, while we simultaneously make inferences about what those who we are communicating with might be experiencing.

Teaching counselors and psychologists in training how to focus on internal dialogue and make empathetic inferences about others' inner states can increase their capacity to react compassionately instead of habitually. Because our cultural conditioning causes us to focus on what we want at the cost of considering the needs of others, compassionate communication offers a way to increase the probability of getting our needs met in collaboration with others getting theirs.

As with any technique, compassionate communication has its limitations. One challenge is that it is primarily based on Western communication practices. For example, it is unlikely that this strategy, as presented, will succeed with people from a collectivist society who are expressing their needs to others. Another limitation is that intercultural interactions often involve people with unequal social status, which can create communication barriers. For example, people of color may feel limited in expressing their perspectives and pain within the constraints of compassionate communication.[4] However, that need not limit the cross-cultural benefits of compassionate communication. The main point is *to learn about one's own internal process and make empathic inferences about the internal processes of others.* Though one may need to consider how to strategically express needs and requests in order to fit compassionate communication into the specific cultural practices of a particular group, the practice of mindfulness has global utility.

In summary, this section presented two approaches to intercultural communication, powerful questions and compassionate communication, to demonstrate how to engage strategically in the construction of effective intercultural interactions. Each strategy demonstrates how focusing attention on the present moment can lead to more empathic and rewarding intercultural communication. The methods are useful because they overcome common communication barriers caused by differences in points of view, contrasting communication styles, and lack of empathy. An example from the *Color of Fear* video demonstrated that powerful questions serve better than confrontation in the joint construction of communicative contexts. Generalizing the use of compassionate communication to an excerpt from a classroom dialogue provided an example of how the strategy reduces the frustration and anger that often surfaces in difficult intercultural encounters.

---

[4]Related to this idea is the fact that many people of color have grown tired of being nice to White people and operating within the pleasantries of White communication rules. They resent having to talk in ways that do not give full justice to the real intercultural differences, especially those that can make their lives better if responsibly addressed.

Conclusion

Many therapists suffer from the same problem as the government official mentioned in the introduction to this chapter—an inability to control anxiety in crucial intercultural encounters. Many people believe themselves to be fair, tolerant, and liberal-minded, but they often have not been taught how to do the intercultural thing. They know that one mistake can be costly when the stakes are high in intercultural encounters. The result is that they try to be extra careful. However, anxiety may overwhelm them to the point of turning their fear of an unfortunate outcome into a self-fulfilling prophecy.

This chapter focused on intercultural communication barriers and on two skills that can be used to overcome them. Effective intercultural communication is assumed to be a function of strategically engaging in dialogue that aims to achieve mindful social information processing. Competent intercultural communication involves awareness of one's own internal state, along with an ability to empathically make inferences about others. Training counselors and psychologists to conduct their work mindfully will offer models and teachers for society at large. Hopefully, the politician who made the offensive remark will have grandchildren who grow up to serve as interculturally competent role models.

References

Brislin, R., & Yoshida, T. (1994). *Intercultural communication training: An introduction*. Thousand Oaks, CA: Sage.

Burgoon, J. K., Berger, C. R., & Waldron, V. R. (2000). Mindfulness and interpersonal communication. In E. J. Langer & M. Moldoveanu (Eds.), *Mindfulness theory and social issues. Journal of Social Issues, 56*(1), 105–127.

Day, H. R. (1983). Race relations training in the military. In D. Landis & R. Brislin (Eds.), *Handbook of intercultural training, Vol. II: Issues in training methodology* pp. 241–289. New York: Pergamon Press.

Devine, P. G. (1996). Breaking the prejudice habit. *Psychological Science Agenda Science Briefs*. Washington, DC: APA Science Directorate.

Devine, P. G., & Monteith, M. J. (1993). The role of discrepancy-associated affect in prejudice reduction. In D. Mackie & D. Hamilton (Eds.), *Affect, cognition, and stereotyping: Interactive processes in group perception* (pp. 137–166). San Diego: Harcourt, Brace, & Jovanovich.

Devine, P. G., Monteith, M. J., Zuwerink, J. R., & Elliot, A. J. (1991). Prejudice with and without compunction. *Journal of Personality and Social Psychology, 60,* 817–830.

Erickson, F., & Schultz, J. (1997). When is a context? Some issues and methods in the analysis of social competence. In M. Cole, Y. Engeström, & O.

Vesquez (Eds.), *Mind, culture & activity*. Cambridge, UK: Cambridge Press.

Gay, G. (1984). Implications of selected models of ethnic identity development for educators. *The Journal of Negro Education, 54*(1), pp. 43–52.

Goleman, D. (1995). *Emotional intelligence: Why it can matter more than IQ*. New York: Bantam.

Gudykunst, W. B. (1991). *Bridging differences: Effective intergroup communication*. Newbury Park, CA: Sage.

Hanh, T. N. (1991). *Peace is every step of the way: The path of mindfulness in everyday life*. New York: Bantam Books.

Helms, J. E. (1990). *Black and White identity: Theory, research, and practice*. Westport, CT: Praeger.

Kovel, J. (1970). *White racism: A psychohistory*. New York: Pantheon.

Langer, E. J., & Moldoveanu, M. (2000). The construct of mindfulness. *Journal of Social Issues, 56,* 1–9.

McConahay, J. B. (1986). Modern racism, ambivalence, and the modern racism scale. In J. F. Dovidio & S. L. Gaertner (Eds.), *Prejudice, discrimination, and racism* (pp. 91–126). New York: Academic Press.

Mun Wah, L. (Producer) (1994). *Color of fear* [video]. (Available from Stir Fry Seminars and Consulting, 154 Santa Clara Avenue, Oakland, CA, 94610.)

Ratner, C. (2000). A cultural-psychological analysis of emotions. *Culture & Psychology, 6,* 5–39.

Rosenberg, M. B. (1999). *Nonviolent communication: A language of compassion.* Del Mar, CA: Puddle-Dancer Press.

Samovar, L., & Porter, R. (1995). *Communication between cultures* (2nd ed.). Belmont, CA: Wadsworth.

Tannen, D. (1990). *You just don't understand: Women and men in conversation.* New York: Ballantine Books.

The Associated Press (2001, February 13). Lt. Gov. Cruz Bustamante uses a racial slur. *New York Times* (Online). Retrieved March 2, 2001 from www.nytimes.com/aponline/national/AP-BRF-Racial-Slur.html.

van Dijk, T. A. (1987). *Communicating racism: Ethnic prejudice in thought and talk.* Newbury Park, CA: Sage.

Vaughn, B. E. (2002). A heuristic model of managing emotions in race relations training. In E. Davis-Russell (Ed.), *Multicultural Education, Research, Intervention, & Training* (pp. 296–318). San Francisco: Jossey-Bass.

Vaughn, B. E. (2000). Managing emotion in race relations instruction. In Carl Grant (Ed.), *Proceedings of the National Association for Multicultural Education 7th Annual Conference.* Albuquerque, New Mexico, October 29–November 2 (pp. 159–175). Mahwah, New Jersey: Lawrence Erlbaum Associates.

Vaughn, B. E. (1998). *A heuristic model of emotion in contemporary psychology race relations training.* Unpublished manuscript, Alliant University.

Vaughn, B. E. (1994a, Fall). Harnessing the multicultural debate in the classroom. *Thought and Action, 10* (2), 37–46.

Vaughn, B. E. (1994b). Teaching cultural diversity courses from a balanced perspective. *Exchanges: Newsletter of the California State University System Institute for Teaching and Learning, 2*(5), 17–18.

5

Working from Within

Contextual Mental Health and Organizational Competence

Patricia Arredondo, Ed.D.
Arizona State University

Tiffany M. Rice
Arizona State University

> We cannot seek achievement for ourselves and forget about progress and prosperity for our community.... Our ambitions must be broad enough to include the aspirations and needs of others, for their sakes and for our own.
>
> —César Chavez

The "fourth force" of multiculturalism in counseling and psychology has created new avenues for understanding and meaning with respect to context and contextual mental health. Whereas traditional models of counseling and psychology have focused almost exclusively on the individual, the new models emphasize the social structures that impact the individual, including organizations and communities. "We know there is a necessary distinction between the processes of multicultural contact including the behaviors, attitudes, perceptions, and feelings of participants, and the institutional structures that characterize, support, or hinder intercultural contact" (Pederson, 2000, p. 185). Multiculturalism attends to both the individual and institutional structures.

The new models of mental health indicate that social action is a mandate for counselors and therapists (Lee & Walz, 1998; Lewis & Bradley, 2000; Lewis et al., 1998) and that educators and practitioners have a responsibility to advance a community based agenda. This change in professional roles for the twenty-first century has been given more attention due to external forces that continue to affect the delivery of services, including technological advances, changing demographics, and major reorganizations in the health/mental health care fields. In particular, the downward spiral in the quality of services associated with reorganization of the general health care delivery system has led to a diffusion of practices and innovations at the same time. This spiral influences mental health care, catalyzing new opportunities for institutional change from seeming chaos and upheaval (Schlesinger & Bradford, 1999). The ultimate outcome of these opportunities, however, depends on a paradigm shift that emphasizes interventions at the organizational level based on principles of empowerment, client self-efficacy, and a contextual understanding of mental health.

Fortunately, it seems as though the counseling and psychology professions have acknowledged this point. Multiculturalism is not confined to the helping relationship but rather is embedded in the fabric of all institutions (APA Guidelines, 2002; D'Andrea et al., 2001; Neville et al., 2001). Multicultural organizational development models have been introduced to promote systems of change so that context does not remain a backdrop but becomes integral to understanding the behavior of organizational practitioners and clients alike (Arredondo, 1996; Sue, 2001).

Springboards for Contextual Practice

Instruments catalyzing new visions and paradigms for change within the counseling and psychology fields are Multicultural Counseling Competencies and Guidelines, evolving through different forms since 1982. Multicultural Counseling Competencies (see Figure 5.1) have been promulgated by the Association of Multicultural Counseling and Development (AMCD) and Guidelines on Multicultural Education, Training, Research, Practice, and Organizational Change for Psychologists (2002) have been prepared by a taskforce of Division 17 (Counseling Psychology) and Division 45 (Society for the Psychological Study of Ethnic Minority Issues) of the American Psychological Association (APA). These documents provide a rationale for culture-centered approaches to mental health, with attention to the importance of multiple contexts that influence clients, practitioners, and organizations (APA Guidelines, 2002; Arredondo et al., 1996; Sue et al., 1992; Sue et al., 1982).

A further validation for contextual mental health emanates from the report issued by the U.S. Surgeon General David Thatcher (2000, 2001). "Culture counts" is the mantra stated throughout this comprehensive study on the gaps in mental health care for the four predominant racial ethnic minority groups in the United States. There is compelling evidence in the report for culture-centered mental health care practices in order to ameliorate the differential needs of ethnic-specific groups. For example, studies indicate that there are different rates of metabolism for individuals of Asian and American Indian heritage in comparison to that of European Americans. However, consideration of such differences in the prescription of psychotropic medications has not always occurred, leading to what can be termed *cultural malpractice.*

Because "culture counts" and because health centers become the source for treatment of both physical and mental health needs, administrators and practitioners must be more mindful of cultural differences and how context directly affects individuals from specific groups. Factoring in context and culture will allow for more appropriate and relevant interventions.

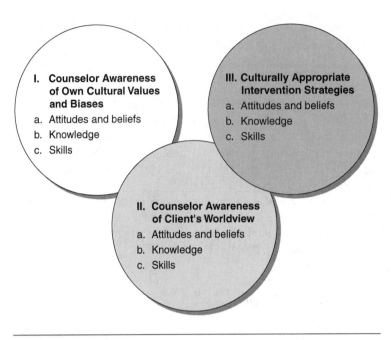

FIGURE 5.1 *Multicultural Counseling Competencies: Domains of Education and Practice (Arredondo et al., 1996)*

Multicultural counseling and psychology advocates remember that this was not always the mindset in the profession. A lack of recognition of culture persisted for many years. Although resistance to change introduced by attention to multiculturalism, changing demographics, and demands of accrediting bodies has not vanished, there is more reason to be hopeful. At the onset of the twenty-first century, multicultural competencies and attention to other dimensions of human diversity seem to be eliciting the attention of professional associations, accrediting bodies, behavioral health care payers, legislators, and the business world. The call to action from these various entities is beckoning new culture-centered paradigms and practices for mental health.

Overview

The purpose of this chapter is to articulate a rationale for the development of organizational cultural competency based on the principles of community counseling and psychology. Topics addressed include the underpinnings of contextual mental health, prototypical cultural issues in organizations including institutional racism, specific Multicultural Competencies to guide contextual mental health practices, and a blueprint for institutional change. Three case examples will be used to illustrate the ethical dilemmas inherent in organizations when "old" models of service are used, ones that are not culturally informed or responsive. Ultimately, promoting contextual mental health means that counselors and

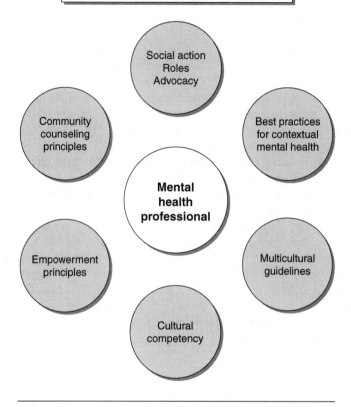

FIGURE 5.2 *Contextualism and the Mental Health Professional's Spheres of Influence*

psychologists must perceive themselves as agents of change, the hub for interpersonal and organizational empowerment (Figure 5.2).

Underpinnings of Contextual Mental Health

Discourse on multicultural-centered counseling and psychology has continued to evolve since the early 1970s. Initial discussions advocated an acknowledgement of cultural differences and the dynamics of difference in education and training and the delivery of mental health services. The focus was the individual client. Through landmark special issues of the

Personnel and Guidance Journal in the late 1970s, professionals began to receive validation about the importance of cultural issues.

Many of the early publications addressed the culturally different or ethnic/racial minority individual and the shortcomings of counseling and therapy processes on their behalf. Social categorization and descriptions by cultural group identity were prevalent as counselors, psychologists, and other helping professionals attempted to know how to counsel African Americans and other ethnic minority clients successfully. The "other" focus, however, allowed for the perpetuation of culture-bound, Eurocentric education and training (Arredondo, 1985; Atkinson et al., 1993).

Research findings in the late 1970s and early 1980s indicated that context counted. Outcome studies revealed that ethnic minorities dropped out of treatment after the first or second visit for very specific "controllable" reasons (Acosta & Evans, 1982; Sue, 1978). Reasons often cited were the lack of bilingual therapists, distance of the mental health facility, a sense of cultural disconnection in the counseling environment, and the inexperience and discomfort of clinicians working within cross-cultural counseling contexts. It was not that clients did not need help, but their needs were compromised by the cultural naivete or benign neglect of clinicians and institutions alike. A common statement in those days was that clients were difficult or resistant, a form of "blaming the victim." These statements also failed to consider the possible shortcomings of monocultural, culture-bound treatment strategies and ethnocentric institutions.

As the multicultural emphasis continued to evolve, the focus expanded to competencies and standards for the educator and practitioner. Introduction of Multicultural Competency Standards and Guidelines presented an argument for expanding the paradigm about multicultural counseling beyond the counseling relationship (APA Guidelines, 2002; Arredondo et al., 1996; Sue et al., 1992; Sue et al., 1982). These documents indicate that multiple forces and contexts play a role in the life experiences and worldviews of clinicians and clients alike, and that organizational culture and practices are also contributing factors to the outcome of mental health services. Particular behavioral statements have been suggested to insure that context is considered (Arredondo et al., 1996). For example, culturally skilled counselors

- Are aware of institutional barriers that prevent minorities from using mental health services (p. 69)
- Can give examples of how they may modify a technique or intervention or what alternative intervention they may use to more effectively meet the needs of a client (p. 71)
- Can recognize and discuss examples in which racism or bias may actually be imbedded in an institutional system or in society (p. 71)
- Work at an organizational level to address, change, and eliminate policies that discriminate, create barriers, and so forth (p. 73)

These statements are underpinnings for promoting the relationship between systems and contexts, and for helping to better reflect the worldview and life experiences of clients and communities where well-intentioned services are provided. In short, multicultural counseling competencies have brought momentum and meaning to contextual mental health, challenging the status quo and simultaneously shifting the focus to models of practice that are culture-centered and promote social justice through advocacy. The nondirective individual session lasting 50 minutes is no longer sufficient. Rather, counselors and administrators must now adapt their mindset to new ways of "giving help" and to new roles of intervening.

Specific Contextual Rationale from the Multicultural Competencies

It has already been stated that Multicultural Competencies have become the bedrock for transforming the counseling and psychology professions. Rather than assuming that all counselors and psychologists are familiar with the Competencies, the salient themes of these documents will be summarized.

Premises articulated in multicultural competency guidelines are that (1) all relationships are cross-cultural and culture-bound; (2) individuals must be understood in their totality by noting the intersection of different dimensions of an individual's identity; (3) the concept of worldview invites an understanding of similarities and differences of beliefs, values, and practices, from individual/intrapersonal, interpersonal, group, and organizational perspectives; (4) clinician cultural competency is essential to ethical practice; (5) cultural competency development for individuals and institutions is a developmental process; (6) organizational change in psychology education and training, research, assessment, and clinical practices, and through accreditation processes must drive the contextual mental health paradigm; (7) collaboration among community agencies, advocacy groups, practitioners, and educators is necessary in order to create strategies for considering the individual within context; and (8) historical, sociopolitical, and economic forces are continuous influences on trust and power-sharing for individuals, cultural groups, and organizations (D'Andrea & Daniels, 2001; Lee & Walz, 1998; Lewis et al., 1998; Robinson & Howard-Hamilton, 2000).

The eighth point advances the importance of understanding individuals and organizations in context. Community counseling and psychology specialists refer to this as "contextualism," a perspective that "views human development as a process in which individuals undergo continuous changes stimulated by their unique biological, environmental, social, and cultural contexts" (Lewis et al., 1998, p. 145). Contextualism also invites ecological considerations in counseling practice, including micro-, meso-, exo-, and macro-systems (Lewis et al., 1998; Neville & Mobley, 2001). From the contextual perspective, the APA multicultural guidelines suggest that mental health professionals aspire to expand their purview of interventions to organizations and communities. "Psychologists' knowledge about the roles of organizations, including employers and professional psychological associations are potential sources of behavioral practices that encourage discourse, educational and training, institutional change, and research and policy development that reflect rather than neglect cultural differences" (APA Guidelines, 2002, p. 19).

The exploration of cultural and multicultural issues in organizations is receiving increased attention through the focus on workforce diversity initiatives in corporations. However, this attention is also finding its way into universities, behavioral health care organizations, accrediting bodies, legislative bodies, and domestic political agendas— powerful contexts for shaping the legitimacy of cultural competency. The consequence of this attention does trickle down or directly impact community mental health organizations and other agencies designed to provide human services.

Organizational Dilemmas

Organizations often seek consultation because of some misalignment in their systems and practices in relation to particular constituencies (e.g., clients). Since 1985, the first author of this chapter has been engaged as a consultant by many different types of organizations confronted with culture-centered dilemmas. In all instances, there were no simple solutions. Rather, each situation had to be examined from multiple yet interdependent perspectives—those of the client, the practitioner, and the institution in context. Inherent in the counselor-consultant approach has always been an immediate scan of the environment with respect to cultural practices in the given setting. Working from a strength versus deficit perspective, the chapter author has wanted to understand the purpose or mission of the organization and how its worldview, or values and beliefs, is successfully applied or not through existing practices. Moreover, she has wanted to diagnose the organizational culture, its operating norms and its motivators for change. The examples that follow will serve to demonstrate that although a problem may seem quite singular and specific in nature, attending to the entire organization and its interdependent contexts is required.

Case 1: Santa Teresa's Battered Women's Shelter

Santa Teresa's had the reputation of being the only shelter in the city that served a multicultural clientele. "Hidden" in a culturally diverse, residential neighborhood, the shelter administration endeavored to provide a range of services for the women, including childcare for those who continued to be employed. Among the clinicians was one Spanish-English-speaking therapist named Clara. Her language skills allowed her to see all clients, a practice that became the issue for the administration. Clara sought bilingual supervision, exemptions from weekend assignments, and extra time to prepare her notes for case review. She indicated that the bilingual, culturally different caseload required more time than a monolingual caseload. Clara, an immigrant from Colombia, knew that she had been hired at a lower salary than her counterparts, but she was told that this was based on differences in experience. With respect to weekend assignments, Clara was told that since she was single and her peers had children, it would be easier to give her the assignment. Following a weekend assignment, Clara was told by the shelter administrator that she was going to be placed on probation for not being a team player and for her resistance to comply with job responsibilities, namely working weekends. Dismayed, Clara submitted her resignation, stating that she was being victimized just like the women she was trying to serve.

Case 2: Hilltop Healthcare Services

The Barry Hospital human resource director was asked to investigate a complaint of racism brought by a group of clinicians and interns at the Hilltop

Healthcare Services (HHS). The complaint stated that the senior administrative team, consisting of the medical and nursing director and the vice-president of operations, were operating in a cultural vacuum. The majority of the patients seen at HHS were of lower socioeconomic and ethnic minority background from the Caribbean and Central America. Many spoke English minimally. The staff members were concerned about the restriction on the involvement of indigenous health care workers. Apparently, the staff had requested a consultation from experts in non-Western medical practices, but they were told that because these services were ultimately not reimbursable, there was no point in bringing in cultural outsiders. The interns, prepared in the latest cultural-competency based research, argued that to use only Western approaches was unethical. They indicated that the patients should be treated by people who know their beliefs and have experiences with interventions that will help to improve their conditions. After failing three times to receive a positive response from administration, the interns decided to file a complaint through the human resources department.

Case 3: Blue State Counseling Center

The Blue State Counseling Center decided to initiate a cultural diversity initiative. Its rationale was based on the attrition of first-time college students from African American, Latino, and American Indian heritage who sought services but failed to return after a first visit. The advisor for the ethnic minority student groups began to make referrals of students who were manifesting academic issues. She knew, however, that there were sociocultural and developmental stressors affecting the students' performance and sense of belonging. Counseling center personnel were primarily Caucasian men and women. There was only one African American psychologist. Staff indicated that they wanted to help but felt there were cultural barriers in communication. In most cases language was not the issue, but rather cultural values and personal practices that were unfamiliar to the clinicians.

These are but three of multiple examples that could be given of how organizational structures, systems, and practices impact mental health service delivery and, ultimately, individual clients. More and more frequently, counselors and psychologists recognize the need to intervene at the organizational level, taking on the role of consultant and using principles derived from models of community-based approaches to mental health.

Community Mental Health Practices

In the early 1970s, there was discourse about the future of the mental health hospital and mental health delivery systems. In the last three decades, we witnessed and experienced numerous benchmark events that have led to a more commerce-driven approach to the mental health industry. Deinstitutionalization of the chronically mentally ill in many states, the proliferation of HMOs and managed care practices, and more recent policies by insurance companies have marginalized mental health services except in the most dire situations. All of these events have constituted setbacks for clients and practitioners alike. Recommendations for reorganization suggest creating networks and interdependent systems of hospitals and community mental health clinics that would better serve the needs of the client in context—in his or her community (Schlesinger & Gray, 1999). While the latter is the purpose of community mental health, fiscal objectives continue to serve as barriers to the implementation of systems. It is in these instances that revisiting the roots and rationale for community counseling can serve to revalidate the rationale for contextualism.

The Promise of Community Mental Health and Contextualism

Through the lenses of community counseling, contextual approaches would include four service components: "direct client, indirect client, direct community and indirect community services" (Lewis et al., 1998, p. 5) with the effectiveness of these services influenced by the socialization experiences of clients and practitioners alike (APA Guidelines, 2002). In other words, the service components must be adapted to particular contexts in order to be relevant and useful for different client constituencies.

Second, one of the premises underlying proposed multicultural-centered guidelines for psychologists is that "culturally appropriate psychological applications assume awareness and knowledge about one's worldview as a cultural being and as a professional psychologist, and the worldview of others, particularly as influenced by ethnic/racial heritage" (p. 46). To enhance sensitivity and understanding further, psychologists are encouraged to become knowledgeable about federal legislation including the Civil Rights Act, Affirmative Action, and Equal Employment Opportunity (EEO) that were enacted to protect groups marginalized due to ethnicity, race, national origin, religion, age, gender, and so forth (APA Guidelines, 2002).

A third perspective for defining culture-centered contextual mental health is based on the application of culture-specific practices in traditional clinical work. Rituals, the use of indigenous providers such as *curanderos* and *espiritistas,* invoking *dichos/*proverbs, and encouraging clients to express emotions in their language are examples that have been discussed and demonstrated by practitioners (Society for the Psychological Study of Ethnic Minority Issues, 2001). More culture-specific practices or alternative approaches to treatment may better demonstrate respect for a client's worldview and culture. Rituals allow for spiritual and religious expression and also acknowledge individuals' history and reminders of that history in contemporary life. Brought into a counseling session or as part of a community-based experience, rituals and other practices serve to validate salient dimensions of an individual's identity contributing to cultural self-efficacy (Arredondo & Glauner, 1992).

Empowerment

In the midst of these examples and statements lies the concept of empowerment. To practice contextual mental health requires a worldview that values power-sharing and personal development through interdependent and culturally authentic processes of change. The constructs of power and empowerment have been conceptualized as relational and motivational in workplace settings (Conger & Kanungo, 1988). As such, it is hypothesized that the empowerment of subordinates can lead to individual and organizational effectiveness. There is a parallel application of this construct to mental health practice because empowerment is a developmental process, and the role of counselors and therapists is to facilitate and promote individual and group self-efficacy. "Empowerment refers to a sense of personal power, confidence, and positive self-esteem. Empowerment involves a process of change that can be achieved in relation to specific goals" (Arredondo, 1996, p. 17).

In the context of community mental health, a definition offered by McWhirter (1994) also seems to apply:

> Empowerment is the process by which people, organizations, and groups who are powerless or marginalized (a) become aware of the power dynamics at work in their life context, (b) develop the skills and capacity for gaining some reasonable control over their lives, (c) which they exercise, (d) without infringing on the rights of others, and (e) which coincides with actively supporting the empowerment of others in the community. (p. 12)

The definitions and examples for contextual mental health have become more prevalent through the influence of the Multicultural Counseling Competencies (Arredondo et al., 1996; Sue et al., 1992). Essentially, the Competencies have enriched counseling and psychology by bringing deliberate attention to issues that were not being addressed for both individuals and institutions of training and service delivery.

Demographic Shifts

Census 2000 data point to major shifts in the current makeup of the U.S. population, and projections indicate increases for cultural groups historically defined as ethnic/racial minorities. The multicultural literature and competencies have advocated the importance of understanding and working from the client's worldview. In all situations, this means appreciating the heterogeneity of all cultural groups, the diversity within the diversity. Models that assist in appreciating within-group differences and contexts of socialization and influence include the Dimensions of Personal Identity Model (Arredondo & Glauner, 1992), the Minority Identity Development Model (Sue & Sue, 1999), an Ecological Model for Social Identities in Context (Neville & Mobley, 2001), and the Tripartite Framework of Personal Identity (Sue, 2001).

The community mental health movement of the 1960s and early 1970s was established to respond to low-income families in urban centers, mainly ethnic/racial minority and immigrant families. However, immigrants are now residing in rural areas and states not historically home to recent immigrants. Western Nebraska, southern Alabama, central Tennessee, and Arkansas are a few examples of areas faced with new challenges by the arrival of new immigrants. Not only may language be different, but cultural differences will also likely be found in lifestyle patterns, religious and spiritual affiliations, and health care practices. Failure by mainstream organizations to understand the stressors experienced by immigrants often leads to marginalization and devaluing of the contributions they make to a community's economy (Arredondo, 2002).

The key to understanding both differences and similarities is often the concept of worldview—beliefs, values, and attitudes. Cultural differences can catalyze positive change but not before there is an understanding of factors that interfere with respecting and valuing culture-specific perspectives and practices.

Barriers to Cultural-Centered Practice

Over the years, multicultural-centered mental health professionals have reported on proto-typical issues of resistance in academic training programs and service provision agencies. These data are now augmented and perhaps further legitimized by the work of organizational diversity consultants, some of whom are counselors and psychologists by training. Through their work as practitioners and researchers with a multicultural and diversity focus, there is now more information about barriers and enablers to contextual mental health. Identification and removal of these barriers can facilitate institutional change.

Racism

Fundamental to a discussion of barriers to contextual mental health is the concept of racism and the similar concepts of sexism, ageism, ableism, classism, homophobia, and so on. Racism and other forms of pervasive bias are both ideological and structural (Neville et al., 2001; Ridley, 1995). That is, the biases are not only beliefs but also social systems. For example, race is frequently falsely understood in biological terms (a belief). Viewing race in this way gives the impression that race is an unchangeable, fixed human condition (rather than an arbitrary social division based on some physical features but not others). When viewed as static, race takes on ascribed meanings, with social differences, rewards, opportunities, and privileges (systems) being reinforced across the perceived racial categories. These differences in treatment produce differences in behaviors, which further reinforce beliefs about race and racial hierarchies (since there are apparent behavioral differences, then the racial hierarchies must be justified). The obvious outcomes are discriminatory practices and other unfair treatment of racial minorities. The same principle holds for other historically marginalized groups including women, the other-abled, and gays and lesbians. Although some beliefs and social systems have been changing toward greater inclusion and tolerance over the past several decades, it is important to acknowledge that these biases are pervasive and continue to harm members of society. To protect the rights of citizens in education, employment, and housing, federal legislation through the Civil Rights Act of 1964 and the Americans with Disabilities Act of 1990 has been necessary. In certain states, legislation has been passed to protect gays and lesbians in these various contexts. Further action is needed to combat social hierarchies and the resulting oppression whenever it occurs, particularly at the organizational/institutional level.

Failure to Take Personal Responsibility for Institutional Racism

Institutional racism is the structural form of racism (described above) that is reflected through policies and practices that adversely affect the access to opportunities and services for certain groups of individuals. Though the attribution for racism is made to the institution, it is important to note that organizations exist because of the presence of people. Thus, to separate clinicians from responsibility for institutional racism is erroneous. Helping professionals too often externalizes responsibility by invoking institutional racism as the culprit for the lack of cultural competency, rather than admit to their own passivity when faced with social injustices and opportunities to change inequities in the system.

Individuals tend to take personal responsibility for institutional racism when they are harmed by the result of those policies. It is therefore important to emphasize that institutional racism ultimately hurts all parties. Unfair organizational systems and malpractices adversely affect not only the employees but the future stability of the organization. In the context of mental health organizations, in which the vast majority of practitioners and administrators are currently European Americans, the largest positive influence toward the eradication of institutional racism would be for European American practitioners to advocate for equitable policies and practices.

Even though many practitioners acknowledge the importance of multicultural aims, with virtually all mental health organizations making aspirational statements about respect for cultural differences and valuing diversity, *Anglo conformity* continues to dominate public policies in education, language, law, and religion (Homan, 1999, p. 16). The status quo is characterized by an ethnocentrism that is difficult to overcome. Anglo conformity is a path of least resistance that organizations typically follow. Eradicating institutional racism and facilitating cultural pluralism in organizations require true effort in the face of both overt resistance and apathetic inertia, and efforts needed to reverse the pervasive influences of white privilege (McIntosh, 1989), color-blind racial attitudes, cultural mistrust, and defensiveness.

White Privilege

From a cost-benefit analysis framework, it is easier to be European American than to be a person of color in North American society and in organizations administered by predominantly European American leadership. The advantages that accrue as a consequence of light skin color and European facial features have been called White privilege (McIntosh, 1989). White privilege is based on premises of White superiority and on deficit thinking about ethnic/racial minorities that leads to separate and unequal treatment. From such a perspective, power typically resides in the hands of a few, usually white, middle and upper class men, with the resulting abuse of power and access benefiting Whites over all other constituencies. In her well-known article, Peggy McIntosh (1989), a White woman, lists benefits she and her family accrue in society because of their White privilege, ranging from small and subtle benefits such as being able to find personal hygiene products that match her features (e.g., "flesh colored" Band-Aids) to serious and consequential benefits such as being treated for who she is as opposed to who she represents.

With respect to mental health services, White privilege manifests itself in clinical practices that are not culturally informed or that do not adapt to other groups' needs. For example, consider the unavailability of bilingual therapists and non-clinical staff, the insufficient insurance coverage available for low income clients, the adherence to traditional 9 to 5 hours that impose hardship on low income persons, and the location of the mental health facilities, often in predominantly White areas and far from diverse residential areas. Each of these factors restricts the ease with which people of color can access mental health services. A multicultural contextual mental health agenda aims to overcome these structural disadvantages that perpetuate cultural mistrust.

Cultural Mistrust

Cultural mistrust and *healthy cultural paranoia,* broadly speaking, affect individuals based on different dimensions of personal and social identity (Arredondo & Glauner, 1992; Dorland & Fischer, 2001; Neville & Mobley, 2001; Whaley, 2001). For ethnic minority groups, gays and lesbians, and the other-abled, inequitable systems of care are often perceived as real barriers to participation. These barriers include heterosexist language, non-adaptive facilities, and cumulative experiences of discrimination within mainstream institutions that are insensitive to issues of diverse cultural groups.

Clients who pick up cues of organizational inflexibility to diversity will respond with mistrust. Such cues need not be blatant. The very language, words, and inflections of an administrator or practitioner are powerful and can serve to communicate respect and inclusion or the opposite. For example, the automatic use of "he" to discuss a female client's partner without knowledge of the partner's gender or the use of the terms "husband" and "wife" but not "partner" on client intake and insurance forms can send the message that gays and lesbians are not welcomed. Organizations that use such heterosexist terminology can become a means of institutional oppression (Dorland & Fischer, 2001). Organizations should therefore be on guard to present messages of inclusion to all clients so as to decrease the levels of cultural mistrust that already exist concerning mental health organizations and practices.

Color-Blind Racial Attitudes

Related to both cultural mistrust and white privilege are Color-Blind Racial Attitudes (CoBRAs) (Neville et al., 2001). CoBRAs are those that fail to account for group heterogeneity in perceptions and experience, including historical oppression, rates of acculturation, ethnic identity status, communication patterns, manifestation of psychological symptoms, coping mechanisms, etc. CoBRAs are imbedded in society, perpetuating beliefs that what is good for one group must be good for all, that all people receive equal treatment under the law, that racism is not a serious issue, etc. These types of beliefs can become embedded into mental health institutions and practices, rendering invisible historical and contemporary injustices in the delivery of mental health services. These beliefs can influence administrators and clinicians, both European Americans and people of color, to advocate for "sameness" or uniformity of policies and procedures without taking into account the cultural, linguistic, and socioeconomic differences that may give rise to unique consequences of those policies across groups of people. Effective mental health practice therefore does not assume that all people think and act alike, but rather assumes that both similarities and differences need to be considered. Optimal organizational policies do not emphasize rigid equality of treatment so much as flexible treatment that leads to equality of outcomes.

Defense Mechanisms

It is not unusual for some individuals to deny that the several barriers heretofore described exist. While denial is one of the most basic defense mechanisms, others that typically occur are displacement, projection, rationalization, splitting, idealization, fixation, and re-action formation. Of course, defense mechanisms operate at both interpersonal and institutional levels. In fact, organizations may be even more sensitive to threat than individuals. As a consequence, they are more likely to rigidly persist in their ways of doing things or resist input from other sources. Morgan (1997) uses the metaphor of *psychic prisons* to describe defensive organizations.

To use a specific example, it is common for culturally resistant organizations to have characteristics of a patriarchal family. With predominantly male leadership, a mental health organization may implicitly espouse traditionally male values of authority and task-oriented performance as opposed to traditionally female values of nurturance and networking. An organization with a male-centered ethos may therefore react defensively when authority and use of power are questioned or when alternative forms of administration are suggested. Institutional change is most likely to occur when the dynamics of defensiveness and resistance are acknowledged and addressed effectively.

Openly Addressing Resistance among Counselors and Psychologists

This chapter has posited that multiculturalism is central to the practice of contextual mental health. However, not all educators and practitioners would agree with this assertion. After more than twenty years of advocating multicultural competence in education and training practice, the first author of this chapter is no longer surprised, but rather disappointed, when she continues to hear that "counseling is counseling" regardless of client background. This denial underscores both an unwillingness to recognize the centrality of multiculturalism to counseling and a lack of leadership of the profession in this domain.

"Despite their role as change agents, many counselors and psychologists continue to be ill-prepared to address the revolutionary challenges that underlie the multicultural movement in this country" (D'Andrea et al., 2001, p. 224). D'Andrea and Daniels (2001) conjecture that most mental health professionals, educators, and students who are in positions of power and privilege respond to the barriers of racism, cultural mistrust, etc., through (1) overt expressions of anger, (2) generalized apathy, or (3) intellectual detachment. Each of these emotional responses can be understood in terms of racial identity development models (Helms, 1990), which serve as useful mirrors for practitioners in reflecting one's racial identity status, with subsequent implications for how one has internalized beliefs that maintain the privileges of one's own racial group at the expense of others (see Chapter 3).

Of the three responses reported by D'Andrea et al. (2001), it is "intellectual detachment" that is perhaps most often invoked by mental health professionals. For example, many White persons are aware of racism and other forms of oppression in society but often do not take direct action. "The knowledge they had about this subject was usually not connected to any pragmatic action to ameliorate white racism in the places where they lived and worked" (D'Andrea & Daniels, 2001, p. 308). Similar dynamics occur with men relative to sexism, middle- to upper-class people relative to classism, and heterosexual people relative to homophobia.

"Walking the talk" is an expression often used in multicultural centered discussions. The point of this expression is that although counselors may espouse principles about valuing differences, it is quite possible that this valuing occurs only at the cognitive level. The Multicultural Competencies remind professionals of the importance of being aware of our attitudes, beliefs, and emotions, and how these influence assumptions and judgments we make about others. "Culturally skilled counselors recognize their sources of discomfort with differences that exist between themselves and clients in terms of race, ethnicity, and culture" (Arredondo et al., 1996, p. 58) and how these affect our assessments, judgments, and decisions about others.

Multidimensional Activism for Change

Promoting contextual mental health requires a deliberate process to promote institutional change at multiple levels—education and training, clinical services, organizational policies and practices, and community relations development. By following the framework and guidelines provided in the Multicultural Competencies (Arredondo et al., 1996; Sue et al., 1992), the *Blueprint* (see Figure 5.3) for successful diversity initiatives (Arredondo, 1996), and other cultural competency models (Cross et al., 1989; Cox, 1993; Sue, 2001), it is possible to begin to develop and implement structural and service level adaptations.

To become involved in processes of change and adaptation requires consultation with individuals experienced and knowledgeable in change management processes through a focus on diversity and cultural competency. However, as with any change-oriented process, promoting contextual mental health must begin with visionary and transformational thinking. "Fundamental to arriving at a state of multicultural actualization is a shared vision" (Arredondo, 1996, p. 65).

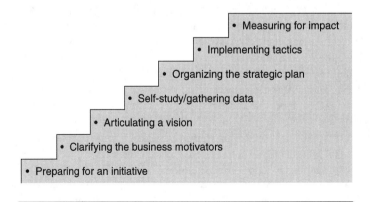

FIGURE 5.3 *Organizational Diversity Blueprint © Empowerment Workshops, Inc., 1997. Used by permission of the author.*

According to D'Andrea et al. (2001), fostering multicultural organizational change, based on tried and proven strategies, involves the following: "(a) belief in the revolutionary potential of the multicultural movement; (b) commitment to work to help transform the fields of counseling and psychology; and (c) dedication to positively impact our society at large" (pp. 249–50).

The Contextual Mindset for Change

Interventions must occur in education and training programs, at agency levels, led by the senior administrators and the board of directors, and by community activists who understand the reality of quality care connected to contextual multicultural values and practices. The recommended approach is through a systemic diversity or cultural competency initiative. Both reflect contextualism. By following a *Blueprint* (Figure 5.3) for multicultural-centered organizational change, administrators and boards of directors have the opportunity to establish measurable objectives that will lead to enhanced contextual mental health practices.

Imbedded in the *Blueprint* approach are self-studies that will inform an organization about its diversity status quo from a costs-benefits analysis framework. Studies provide data about different constituencies within a shared context and how experiences vary or are similar based on position, ethnicity, gender, age, disability, sexual orientation, and other dimensions of human diversity. The interaction of systems, policies, and practices among individuals cannot be understood without hearing the voices of those who are affected (Arredondo, 1996). "Contextual intervention models consider interventions within multiple systems, including macro- (e.g., racial ideology, values, political economic structure), exo- (e.g., profession and organization level), meso- (e.g., interaction among specific departments or institutions), and microsystems (e.g., specific program area, department, or individual)" (Neville et al., 2001, pp. 282–83).

At the education and training level, it is recommended that color-conscious policies and practices in counseling and psychology be applied. "Policies with the explicit goal of promoting social justice and racial inclusion (e.g., color-conscious policies) are an essential ingredient in the eradication of white privilege within our profession, and ultimately, our society" (Neville et al., 2001, p. 282).

Applying Contextual/Multicultural Frameworks and Strategies

The case examples introduced earlier invite an examination of possible approaches to enhance contextual practices through the multicultural counseling competencies, the model "Contextualism and the Mental Health Professional's Spheres of Influence" (Figure 5.2), and community counseling strategies. In all three examples, the Multicultural Competencies can help to explain the seemingly culturally competent behavioral shortcomings of administrators, and at the same time point out how counselors could assume the roles of an internal consultant, activist, cultural broker, and advocate. Additionally, the contextual model (Figure 5.2) offers to organizations and clinicians alike a framework to assess barriers to multicultural-centered contextual practices and enablers to address difficult culture-specific situations. With the mental health professional at the hub of this model, there are several premises: (1) the professional has the opportunity and responsibility to become knowledgeable about the designated principles, roles, and practices (e.g., social action roles for advocacy); (2) the professional is directly and indirectly impacted by the four external and internal forces—institutional racism, economics, sociopolitical climate, and demographic changes—and therefore must be aware of the effects on clients and organizations as well; (3) contextualism is always part of the mental health professional and an organization's existence; and (4) the purview of the mental health professional is more expansive than interpersonal clinical practices.

The case examples presented earlier of Santa Teresa's Battered Women's Shelter, Hilltop Healthcare Services, and the Blue State Counseling Service all provide rich opportunities for contextual consultation interventions. All organizations seem to be unaware that racism and other forms of bias, such as linguisism, are imbedded in the institutional culture. In each setting, there are opportunities to become more contextual based on the client population, the setting for the services, the issues at stake, and the roles and skills that clinicians may leverage for the organizations.

Two Multicultural Competencies (Arredondo et al., 1996) that apply in these three examples are: "Culturally skilled counselors can recognize and discuss examples in which racism or bias may actually be imbedded in an institutional system or in society" (p. 71) and "Culturally skilled counselors should attend to, as well as work to eliminate biases, prejudices, and discriminatory contexts…and should develop sensitivity to issues of oppression, sexism, heterosexism, elitism, and racism" (p. 73). A brief analysis for each case follows.

Santa Teresa's Battered Women's Shelter.   It appears that the supervisors and administrators at Santa Teresa's do not value Clara's bilingualism, biculturalism, or her status as a single woman. Additionally, because she is assertive and is trying to set limits on expectations, she is accused of being a maverick, not a "team player." Ironically, in American culture, assertiveness and direct communication are encouraged. Stereotypically, immigrants are often perceived as quiet, passive, and uneducated. This case points out the risks for under-represented individuals when being the only provider of a particular cultural group in mental health facilities. On the one hand, their skills are essential to the delivery of services, but quite often disrespect is communicated by others. Administrators seem to be unaware of "their stereotypes and preconceived notions that they may hold toward other racial and ethnic minority groups" (Arredondo et al., 1996, p. 63).

What do the administrators need to do to ensure that their clients receive the services that are culturally relevant, ethical, and in their best interest? It is recommended that responses need to occur at two levels: organizational mission and practices. Perhaps administrators can examine the *Blueprint* and how it can assist them in actualizing their mission in a culturally diverse context. They must also identify the benefits of keeping Clara, because she represents a cultural broker for the women as well as for the shelter in the larger community. Second, administration must also examine the organizational inefficiencies and client-centered turbulence that will result by removing Clara. Third, dismissing Clara will likely raise questions about the inability for the shelter to retain employees of color. Finally, administrators must revisit their agency mission for empowerment. They must recognize how color-blind racial attitudes (Neville et al., 2001), White privilege, and Anglo conformity (Homan, 1999) are consciously or unconsciously influencing their decisions. Continuing to work with Clara would suggest that they value her and her work, and would signal that they are living according to their mission and principles.

Hilltop Healthcare Services.   Empowered employees can be an agency's worst nightmare. It is not unusual, however, for politically conscious interns or students to begin to challenge the status quo. The Hilltop case is one of activism on several levels: individual/interpersonal, institutional, and community. The opportunity for HHS administrators to model activist leadership became apparent. The *Blueprint* was recommended to guide a diversity initiative, the approach the administrators decided would allow for a developmental change process to unfold. For example, this meant engaging a consultant to first de-escalate the tension that was permeating the organization. Crisis management was required as well as facilitated discussion to creating meaningful communication about varying perspectives. APA multicultural guideline 5 reminds us that "psychologists strive to apply culturally appropriate skills in clinical and other applied psychological practices" (APA Guidelines, 2002, p. 46). In this situation and others of a similar nature, mental health professionals must employ many of the same practices we learn to apply with clients. Once tensions subsided, the consultant was able to guide administrators and staff to clarify the motivators for a diversity initiative, the necessary data to plan for measurable change, and the best strategies to have an inclusive process that promotes the principles of empowerment, community counseling and multicultural competency.

In the change management process, consultants often introduce learning organization models (Morgan, 1997; Senge, 1990). These advocate for organizations to anticipate and recognize contextual forces, "developing an ability to question, challenge, and change operating norms and assumptions" (Morgan, 1997, p. 90).

Included in the HHS initiative task force were some of the very same interns who had lobbied for change. It was also through the interns' advocacy that clients became part of the task force. The premise was that they had great culture-specific contacts and legitimacy within their communities to seek them out. Through focus groups, the administration learned about institutional strengths and barriers to care. What began as a crisis led to a positive change process for HHS and is exemplified in the Multicultural Competencies. Counselors become engaged in processes to reduce organizational biases and become proactive, working "at an organizational level to address, change, and eliminate policies that discriminate, create barriers, and so forth…[and] if an organization's policy creates barriers for advocacy, the counselor works toward changing institutional policies to promote advocacy against racism, sexism, and so forth" (Arredondo et al., 1996, p. 73).

Blue State Counseling Center.   The counseling center staff immediately recognized its cultural-competency shortcomings. Fortunately, a critical core group decided to become proactive. They recognized their social action and advocacy roles as outlined in the contextualism model and also identified areas to enhance cultural competency. They sought out cultural brokers on the campus, individuals of the specific cultural backgrounds, and individuals already involved in mentoring and supporting of ethnic minority students. "Culturally skilled counselors are not averse to seeking consultation with traditional healers or religious and spiritual leaders and practitioners in the treatment of culturally different clients when appropriate" (Arredondo et al., 1996, p. 71).

Rather than embark on a self-study, the center decided to engage in multicultural counseling training. Workers expressed a need for content knowledge and discussions with culturally informed psychologists and counselors to process the new learning material. Through this approach, they wanted to increase their self-efficacy and usefulness as clinicians working with students culturally different from themselves. Again, two Multicultural Competencies (Arredondo et al., 1996) are invoked: "Culturally skilled counselors are able to recognize the limits of their multicultural competency and expertise" (p. 58) and "Culturally skilled counselors seek out educational, consultative, and training experiences to improve their understanding and effectiveness in working with culturally different clients" (p. 61).

Conclusion

Multiple forces affect the well-being of clients. Counselors and psychologists schooled in theories developed by European and European Americans must be mindful of the culture-bound nature of many interventions (e.g., rational-emotive and behavioral therapies) as well as assumptions that only one modality, such as Reality Therapy, should be applied with all ethnic/racial minority individuals. Counselors are thus encouraged to "participate or gather adequate information regarding indigenous or community helping resources to make appropriate referrals (e.g., be familiar with the American Indian community enough to recognize when, how, and to whom it may be appropriate to refer a client to indigenous healers)" (Arredondo et al., 1996, p. 72).

Community counseling advocates also provide strategies to promote contextual mental health. These include visionary, revolutionary thinking, color-conscious policies and practices, and strategic diversity-centered processes for organizational change. As an internal and external consultant, working with all three strategies is essential because the spheres of contextual influences are ever present. There are no shortcuts to promoting contextual mental health—it is a life-long process. With unpredictable change introduced by technology, terrorism, economic disparities, globalism, and a decreasing European American population, counselors and psychologists have many opportunities to spearhead humanistic societal progress. We have multiple skill sets and resources that can engage us in facilitating change at individual, interpersonal, group, and institutional levels, but we cannot be shy about this. The opportunity to work from within is now. The legacies we leave to the profession and to society must be ones of cultural competency, empowerment, and social action.

References

Acosta, F. X., & Evans, L. A. (1982). Effective psychotherapy for low income minority patients. In F. X. Acosta, J. Yamamoto, & L. A. Evans (Eds.), *Effective psychotherapy with low income and minority patients* (pp. 51–82). New York: Plenum Press.

American Psychological Association. (2002). *Guidelines on multicultural education, training, research, practice, and organizational change for psychologists.* Washington, DC: Author.

Arredondo, P. (1996). *Successful diversity management initiatives.* Thousand Oaks, CA: Sage.

Arredondo, P. (2002). Counseling individuals from specialized, marginalized and underserved groups. In P. Pedersen, J. G. Draguns, W. J. Lonner, & J. E. Trimble (Eds.), *Counseling Across Cultures* (5th ed). (pp. 233–250). Thousand Oaks, CA: Sage.

Arredondo, P. (1985). Cross cultural counselor education and training. In P. Pedersen (Ed.), *Handbook of Cross Cultural Counseling and Therapy* (pp. 281–289). Westport, CT: Greenwood Press.

Arredondo, P., & Lewis, J. (2001). Counselor roles in the 21st century. In D. C. Locke, J. E. Myers, and E. L. Herr (Eds.), *The Handbook of Counseling* (pp. 257–268). Thousand Oaks, CA: Sage.

Arredondo, P., & Glauner, T. (1992). *Personal dimensions of identity model.* Boston: Empowered Workshops, Inc.

Arredondo, P., Toporek, R., Brown, S. P., Jones, J., Locke, D. C., Sanchez, J., & Stadler, H. (1996). Operationalization of the multicultural counseling competencies. *Journal of Multicultural Counseling and Development, 24,* 42–78.

Atkinson, D., Morten, G., & Sue, D. W. (1993). *Counseling American minorities* (3rd ed.). Dubuque, IA: Wm. C. Brown.

Conger, J. A., & Kanungo, R. N. (1988). The empowerment process: Integrating theory and practice. *Academy of Management Review, 13,* 471–482.

Cox, T. (1993). *Cultural diversity in organizations: Theory, research and practice.* San Francisco: Berret-Koehler Publications.

Cross, T., Bazron, B., Dennis, K., & Issacs, M. (1989). Toward a culturally competent system of care. Vol. 1: *Monograph on effective services for minority children who are severely emotionally disturbed.* Washington, DC: CASSP Technical Assistance Center. Georgetown University Child Develoment Center.

D'Andrea, M., Daniels, J., Arredondo, P., Ivey, M. B., Ivey, A. E., Locke, D. C., O'Bryant, B., Parham, T. A., & Sue, D. W. (2001). Fostering organizational changes to realize the revolutionary potential of the multicultural movement. In J. G. Ponterotto, J. M. Casas, L. A. Suzuki, & C. M. Alexander (Eds.) (pp. 222–253). *Handbook of Multicultural Counseling* (2nd ed.). Thousand Oaks, CA: Sage Publications.

D'Andrea, M., & Daniels, J. (2001). RESPECTFUL counseling: An integrative model for counselors. In D. Pope-Davis & H. Coleman (Eds.), *The Interface of Class, Culture, and Gender in Counseling,* pp. 417–466. Thousand Oaks, CA: Sage.

Dorland, J. M., & Fischer, A. R. (2001). Gay, lesbian, and bisexual individuals' perceptions: An analogue study. *The Counseling Psychologist, 29,* 432–547.

Helms, J. E. (Ed.) (1990). *Black and white racial identity: Theory, research and practice.* Westport, CT: Greenwood Press.

Homan, M. S. (1999). *Promoting community change* (2nd ed.). Pacific Grove, CA: Brooks/Cole Publishing Company.

Lee, C. C., & Walz, G. R. (1998). *Social action: A mandate for counselors.* American Counseling Association.

Lewis, J., & Bradley, L. (Eds.) (2000). *Advocacy in counseling: Counselor, clients & community.* Greensboro, NC: ERIC/CAPS, pp. 45–54.

Lewis, J. A., Lewis, M. D., Daniels, J. A., & D'Andrea, M. J. (1998). *Community counseling* (2nd ed.). Pacific Grove, CA: Brooks/Cole Publishing Company.

McIntosh, P. (1989, July/August). White privilege: Unpacking the invisible knapsack. *Peace and Freedom,* pp. 8–10.

McWhirter, E. H. (1994). *Counseling for empowerment.* Alexandria, VA: American Counseling Association.

Morgan, G. (1997). *Images of organization* (2nd ed.). Thousand Oaks, CA: Sage Publications.

Neville, H. A., & Mobley, M. (2001). Social identities in contexts: An ecological model of multicultural counseling psychology processes. *The Counseling Psychologist, 29,* 471–486.

Neville, H. A., Worthington R. L., & Spanierman, L. B. (2001). Race, power, and multicultural counseling psychology: Understanding white privilege and color-blind racial attitudes. In J. G. Ponterotto, J. M. Casas, L. A. Suzuki, & C. M. Alexanders (Eds.). *Handbook of Multicultural Counseling* (2nd ed.) (pp. 257–288). Thousand Oaks, CA: Sage.

Pederson, P. (2000). *A handbook for developing multicultural awareness* (3rd ed.). Alexandria, VA: ACA Press.

Ridley, C. R. (1995). *Overcoming unintentional racism in counseling and therapy.* Thousand Oaks, CA: Sage.

Robinson, T. L., & Howard-Hamilton, M. (2000). *The convergence of race, ethnicity, and gender.* Upper Saddle River, NJ: Prentice-Hall, Inc.

Schlesinger, M., & Gray, B. (1999). Institutional change and its consequences for the delivery of mental health services. In A. V. Horowitz & T. L. Scheid (Eds.), *A Handbook for the Study of Mental Health: Social contexts, theories, and systems.* New York: Cambridge University Press (pp. 427–448).

Senge, P. (1990). *The fifth discipline.* New York: Doubleday.

Sue, D. W. (2001). Multicultural facets of cultural competence. *The Counseling Psychologist, 29,* 787–821.

Sue, D. W., Arredondo, P., & McDavis, R. J. (1992). Multicultural counseling competencies and standards: A call to the profession. *Journal of Counseling and Development, 70,* 477–483.

Sue, D. W., Bernier, J., Durran, M., Feinberg, L., Pedersen, P., Smith, E., & Vasquez-Nuttall, E. (1982). Position paper: Multicultural counseling competencies. *The Counseling Psychologist, 10,* 45–52.

Sue, D. W., & Sue, D. (1999). *Counseling the culturally different: Theory and practice* (3rd ed.). New York: Wiley & Sons.

U.S. Department of Health and Human Services (2000; 2001). *Mental health: culture, race, and ethnicity—A supplement to Mental Health: A report of the Surgeon General.* Rockville, MD: U.S. Department of Health and Human Services, Public Health Office, Office of the Surgeon General.

Whaley, A. L. (2001). Cultural mistrust and mental health services for African Americans. *The Counseling Psychologist, 29,* 513–531.

The Society for the Psychological Study of Ethnic Minority Issues, Division 45 of the American Psychological Association & Microtraining Associates, Inc. (Sponsors and producers) (2000). *Culturally-competent counseling and therapy: live demonstrations of innovative approaches.* [Films.] (Available from Microtraining Associates, Inc., PO Box 9641, North Amherst, MA 01059-9641.)

6

A Contextual Approach to Assessment

Timothy B. Smith
Brigham Young University

After treating a 23-year-old college sophomore for symptoms of depression for several weeks, a therapist was puzzled that the client did not show signs of improvement. The student dressed in expensive clothing, was popular among her friends, and attended many social functions each week. The therapist had tried to be sensitive to issues related to race, gender, upper class values, etc. Upon further questioning, the therapist finally learned that for the past two months the client had been homeless, sleeping in her car or with a different friend each night. She was having difficulty maintaining a drug habit because increased national and local security made it difficult for her to obtain and sell as much as she had in previous years. The client had previously alluded to these issues and thought that the therapist had understood her street jargon. Up until that point, the therapist had focused treatment on the client's self-critical cognitions and low self-esteem because the client had not marked a box on an intake form that indicated alcohol use and because she dressed as if she were from an upper class background.

A 6-year-old Latino boy was referred to a school psychologist for an evaluation during the second week of kindergarten. The teacher indicated that the boy was constantly squirming in his seat and would not pay attention in class. The previous week the teacher had started a behavioral management program that was meant to keep the child in his seat because he had frequently disrupted the class by asking for a hall pass or by suddenly running out of the room. Although Spanish was his primary language, the child was able to communicate effectively in English, so the teacher was certain that he understood her instructions to remain seated quietly until "break times." The school psychologist conducted an in-class observation and confirmed the teacher's report of the boy's behavior. She administered a computerized test for symptoms of Attention-Deficit Hyperactivity Disorder and found a Spanish translation of a behavioral checklist for the parents to complete. Upon finishing the written report, the school psychologist found a note written in Spanish in the child's folder. When the note was translated, after the referral to a pediatrician had already been mailed to the parents, the psychologist learned that the child was on a medication that required him to drink large amounts of liquids and that he had a small bladder, necessitating frequent urination. The teacher later admitted that the boy had repeatedly indicated that he needed to go to the bathroom, but she had assumed that the constant requests were an excuse to leave the classroom.

Mental health professionals often fail to account for the multiple contexts that impact clients' behavior and well-being. Assessment (and consequently treatment) focuses almost exclusively on the individual and on psychological causes for symptoms. Consultation with family members or other people who are close to the client is rare, and assessment is often limited to a brief interview about the presenting problem and to the administration of a pencil-and-paper survey on the severity of symptoms. External contexts, including resources and supports that could facilitate treatment, are hardly considered.

All this merely says that counseling and psychotherapy are Western modes of healing, embedded in a sociohistorical context that favors symptom reduction, individualism, time-efficiency, etc. Counseling and psychotherapy are indeed effective within this context (e.g., Seligman, 1995). However, the efficacy of contemporary mental health treatment may be restricted in other situations (Fancher, 1995; Pedersen, 1999; Pope-Davis & Coleman, 2001; Sue & Sue, 1999). As emphasized in previous chapters of this book, monocultural approaches do not work well in multicultural settings. A multicultural perspective requires that multiple contexts be considered and addressed in the process of assessment.

This chapter will present an overview of the major issues involved with contextual assessment. First, the need to address multiple sources of client diversity will be highlighted. Second, specific guidelines regarding assessment procedures will be presented. Third, factors and biases that restrict the abilities of counselors and therapists to conduct accurate assessments are enumerated, and suggestions for reducing therapist biases are provided. Thus this chapter is organized around three essential components of assessment: the client, the assessment procedure, and the counselor or therapist conducting the assessment.

Assessing Client Contexts

Although clients are not always aware of the causes of their problems, they are usually aware of more background information than the counselor or therapist could ever hope to assess in a few 50-minute sessions. Because time is limited, counselors and therapists tend to focus on collecting information that *they* believe to be pertinent to the presenting problem, rather than making time to gather information on contexts that may be relevant from the client's perspective. Ironically, had the professionals treating the previously described

23-year-old college sophomore and 6-year-old kindergartener taken more time to gather background information, they might have found effective treatment solutions more rapidly than they did.

Moreover, because counselors and therapists are almost exclusively trained to identify psychological causes for problems, they often fail to assess other possible sources of influence, such as economic conditions, neurochemistry, family dynamics, etc. Assessment of the individual in isolation from his or her contexts reinforces the belief that only psychological factors are responsible for the client's condition. Consequently, the interventions of most counselors and psychologists are meant to change the individual, yet research has shown that interventions targeting the individual are less effective than interventions designed to change the environment (e.g., Kazdin, 2001). Counselors and therapists who do not address environmental influences undermine the efficacy of the services they provide.

Recognizing the individualistic biases inherent in counseling and psychotherapy, professionals in the field have developed two very similar conceptual frameworks that affirm the need for a complex understanding of the many factors that influence a client's identity and well-being. Although somewhat different, both frameworks offer a useful template to facilitate effective recognition and assessment of clients' multiple contexts.

The framework developed by Pamela Hays (1996, 2001) uses the acronym ADDRESSING to capture several aspects of diversity that should be considered when conducting an assessment. This acronym represents the following content areas:

A	**A**ge and generational influences
DD	**D**evelopmental and acquired **d**isabilities
R	**R**eligion and spiritual orientation
E	**E**thnicity and race
S	**S**ocioeconomic status
S	**S**exual orientation
I	**I**ndigenous heritage
N	**N**ational origin
G	**G**ender

Michael D'Andrea and Judy Daniels (2001) developed a similar framework with the acronym RESPECTFUL to indicate an approach to assessment and treatment that considers each of the following contextual issues:

R	**R**eligious and spiritual identity
E	**E**thnic, cultural, and racial background
S	**S**exual identity
P	**P**sychological maturity
E	**E**conomic class standing and background
C	**C**hronological-developmental challenges
T	**T**hreats to well-being and trauma
F	**F**amily history, values, and dynamics
U	**U**nique physical characteristics
L	**L**ocation of residence and language differences

A major purpose of the ADDRESSING and RESPECTFUL frameworks is to make explicit a contextual approach to assessment and treatment. Both Hays (2001) and D'Andrea and Daniels (2001) recognize that their framework represents only some of the areas that mental health practitioners must keep in mind as they work with clients. However, both frameworks are highly useful in that they provide an easy-to-recall acronym that emphasizes the salience of a comprehensive contextual assessment. Counselors and therapists who remember to assess these multiple aspects of diversity will be more likely to understand clients' worldview, along with their perceptions about well-being, coping strategies, and available external resources. Because the remaining chapters in this book deal specifically with these several aspects of client diversity, the rest of this chapter will focus on the assessment procedure and on factors that influence counselors' and therapists' ability to conduct accurate assessments.

Evaluating Procedural Contexts

Accurate assessment should consider not only the contextual issues highlighted in the ADDRESSING and RESPECTFUL frameworks, involving characteristics of the client, but also the objectives, characteristics, relevance, and impact of the assessment procedures. This section will review each of these issues.

Assessment Objectives

The overall objectives of any assessment procedure are to establish a working alliance with the client (including working through client mistrust), to clearly define the clinically relevant issues, to gather useful contextual information, and to develop hypotheses and/or tentative diagnoses based on the data obtained (Takushi & Uomoto, 2001). *However, the primary objective of assessment is to inform treatment decisions.* The information collected and the hypotheses generated are useful only inasmuch as they facilitate effective interventions and improved outcomes. In line with these considerations, the following are among several questions that if addressed adequately could improve the quality of assessment:

- Why is this particular evaluation being conducted, and how might the results impact the client?
- What effects might the assessment routine have on the client and on the client-therapist relationship?
- What are the risks and benefits of conducting a thorough evaluation vs. proceeding with a preliminary intervention?
- What procedures could be included to minimize the failure to acquire pertinent information or to prevent an inaccurate conceptualization/diagnosis?
- What standardized measures would be most useful to administer, and what are the psychometric properties and potential biases associated with those measures with this particular client population?
- How can the evaluation results be best communicated to the client?

These and similar questions can inform the overall assessment process, including the particular assessment structure that would most likely benefit the client.

Assessment Structure

Assessment can be formal, informal, or a blend of the two approaches. Counselors and therapists should consider the potential impact of formality and structure upon their relationship with the client, recognizing that although formal procedures can aid objectivity, the impersonal nature of formal assessments can create distance between the client and therapist (Dana, 2000a). This concern is particularly salient for clients whose cultural or personal values emphasize relationships over time efficiency (e.g., Sue & Sue, 1999). Clients who are in emotional distress and/or nervous about sharing their concerns with a stranger should not be immediately requested to start divulging personal information or to complete tests that enumerate a host of problems, only some of which are relevant to their reason for seeking help. Such approaches cause many clients to attend only one session and drop out before adequate interventions can be provided (Hansen, Lambert, & Forman, 2002).

As indicated above, the first objective of assessment is to facilitate a working alliance with the client and to work through client mistrust. Counselors or therapists who use such processes effectively will not only prepare the client for subsequent formal evaluations but also conduct informal observation and assessments during the initial relationship-building period. Observations about how clients express themselves, which material comes up repeatedly, which symptoms are emphasized verbally, and which symptoms are apparent in the client's demeanor, etc., can help the therapist decide on the nature and extent of subsequent formal testing that will be used in confirming/disconfirming initial hypotheses and in generating new information.

This does not mean that informal assessment should always precede formal evaluations. Professionals are encouraged to consider the immediate needs and likely preferences of the client, making decisions on sequencing, timing, and selection of specific procedures that will likely facilitate the retention of the client. Only when clients are retained can the information gathered in assessment eventually be put to use in intervention.

Assessment Duration

As the primary objective of assessment is to inform treatment, assessment should not be considered an end in itself. Rather it could be considered an ongoing process. Too often counselors and therapists see assessment as an isolated activity that occurs prior to or at the beginning of treatment. A more effective approach is to integrate assessment throughout treatment. New information uncovered over time can alter treatment, sometimes drastically (as with the 23-year-old woman and the 6-year-old boy described at the beginning of the chapter). Furthermore, client responses to interventions should be tracked, providing a beneficial feedback loop regarding treatment efficacy. For example, recent research has shown that client outcomes improve when therapists respond to indicators that clients who complete brief ratings of symptoms at every session are not showing expected improvement (Lambert, Hansen, & Finch, 2001). Counselors and therapists can also benefit from evaluating client satisfaction following the completion of services, making modifications in their subsequent work with other clients as needed. Assessment can therefore inform intervention from the first visit to beyond termination.

Assessment Consequences

Problems with assessment frequently occur when it is conducted once, in isolation from other data, and when it is used to inform decisions that have clear consequences for the client's future. These conditions are sometimes reinforced by the current trend to conduct *high-stakes testing* (e.g., Sackett, Schmitt, Ellisgson, & Kabin, 2001), wherein important and potentially far-reaching consequences are based on a single assessment. Examples of high-stakes testing include academic placement decisions, university admissions decisions, employment eligibility decisions, child custody evaluations, etc. In some cases, these decisions are based on data that explain only a very small amount of variance in the desired outcome (Padilla, 2001). Counselors and therapists should therefore consider the consequences of any assessment and advocate for more valid and comprehensive assessment practices whenever the stakes are high (Sackett et al., 2001).

Measurement Bias and Equivalence

Reliance on high-stakes testing in making decisions has increased along with increased professional and public reliance on standardized instruments. Certainly standardized testing has multiple benefits (e.g., Kaplan & Saccuzzo, 2001). However, professionals should not make unquestioning use of these instruments. Rather they should select tests and procedures only after considering the issues of bias and equivalence.

Tests are considered biased whenever the content of the items, mode of administration, conditions for testing, or interpretation of results give advantage to one group over another (Padilla, 2001). It is virtually impossible to create an instrument free of bias (Reynolds, 1995). Nevertheless, test developers are becoming more and more aware of the problems associated with bias, and the field continues to refine instruments and make them more equivalent across groups (e.g., Samuda, Feurstein, Kaufman, Lewis, & Sternberg, 1998; Suzuki, Ponterotto, & Meller, 2001). Clinicians are therefore encouraged to seek out instruments that have the following four characteristics:

1. *Functional equivalence.* That the construct assessed performs the same role and is associated with comparable behavioral responses in both mainstream and non-mainstream cultures.
2. *Conceptual equivalence.* That the stimuli that comprise the test have similar meanings across cultures.
3. *Linguistic/translation equivalence.* That the language, symbols, affective impact, and format (e.g., formats for illiterate or deaf persons) used are indeed comparable for members of mainstream and non-mainstream cultures.
4. *Metric/scalar equivalence.* That the data show similar psychometric properties and internal structures across cultures (Rollock & Terrell, 1996, p. 125).

Evidence of equivalence includes similar distributions of data (mean, variance, kurtosis, and skewness), similar reliability and internal consistency coefficients, and similar factor structures and validity coefficients across different populations (men vs. women, adolescents vs. adults, etc.) (Poortinga, 1995).

Description of the psychometric properties and cultural equivalence of commonly used tests of personality, intellectual ability, academic and vocational aptitude, neuropsychological functioning, and social and emotional functioning is beyond the scope of this chapter. However, several excellent resources are available to guide the use and interpretation of commonly used standardized instruments (Dana, 2000a, 2000b; Samuda et al., 1998; Suzuki et al., 2001). Clinicians are encouraged to familiarize themselves with up-to-date information on the measures they frequently use and to locate research evidence that can support an instrument's equivalence prior to using that instrument with a specific population.

Diagnostic Considerations

The same principles of reliability, validity, and equivalence that apply to tests of cognitive or emotional functioning also apply to diagnostic classification systems, such as the *Diagnostic and Statistical Manual of Mental Disorders* (DSM-IV-TR) (American Psychiatric Association, 2000). Just as it is virtually impossible to develop an instrument that is free of bias, it is impossible to find a diagnostic system that is completely free of bias, particularly because such systems rely heavily on clinical judgment. It is to be expected that the DSM-IV-TR and other diagnostic systems developed in Europe and North America contain Eurocentric assumptions about health and about diagnostic categories and symptom clusters (Mezzich, Kirmayer, & Kleinman, 1999). For example, the DSM-IV-TR and similar systems take a universalistic approach, implying that all conditions exist across all cultures. Several problems can arise when mental health professionals exclusively adhere to a universal (etic) approach to diagnosis: biological causality is inferred, the context of the client's symptoms is minimized, and in many cases, the diagnostic system becomes more real/important to the mental health professional than the client's presentations and interpretations. Although the DSM-IV-TR includes more information on contextual issues and cultural influences than previous editions, ongoing refinement is needed based on cultural differences in symptom expression and interpretation (Dana, 2000a).

Individuals from distinct cultures can manifest symptoms of distress and mental illness in a wide variety of ways. How symptoms are expressed depends largely on emotional display rules and other social mores specific to a given society. For example, some groups may tend to mask depression with substance abuse, which is more socially acceptable than open emotional disturbance, while other groups may weep or mourn in public based on norms of social extroversion, collective awareness, and support.

Moreover, symptoms can have different meanings across groups. Contemplating suicide has unique ramifications for individuals from cultures where it is considered honorable compared to individuals from cultures where it is unacceptable, potentially bringing punishment upon surviving family members. Similarly, cultures can attribute symptoms and illnesses to different causal mechanisms. Whereas some groups may believe in demonic possession, imbalanced energy fields, or shameful personal behavior as being responsible for a condition, others consider only genetic, biochemical, or psychological explanations. Problems can occur when a diagnosis made from one of these perspectives is imposed upon a client who takes another perspective. Therefore, in conjunction with the guidelines for multicultural assessment that follow, clinicians are encouraged to use the client's perspective on the illness in forming a treatment plan that accurately reflects the client's contexts.

Practical Guidelines for Contextual Multicultural Assessment

The development and implementation of effective treatment plans depend largely on the accuracy of the assessment conducted. To improve the accuracy and utility of clinical assessment, Charles Ridley and colleagues (Ridley, Hill, Thompson, & Ormerod, 2001) have provided the field with 10 useful guidelines for multicultural assessment. These guidelines are based on an idiographic perspective, meaning that the individual client should be perceived as a unique individual, not merely as a set of characteristics (race, gender, age, sexual orientation, abilities, etc.). From an idiographic perspective, understanding clients' characteristics is indeed important, but generalizations about characteristics can obscure clients' unique experiences and the interactions between multiple attributes. Hence, the guidelines emphasize both the complexity of the individual and the importance of context.

Guideline 1.   Psychological functioning reflects the interactions of several aspects of identity, particularly those listed in the ADDRESSING and RESPECTFUL frameworks. Accurate assessment accounts for how these different sources of identity impact one another. For example, using the ADDRESSING framework, different age cohorts (A) have different values and expectations about gender roles (G), which also differ across ethnic groups (E) and socioeconomic status (S). Similarly, national origin (N) is often highly related to religious background (R), which may influence beliefs and expectations for a person with different abilities (D). In sum, every aspect of a person's identity overlaps to some degree with every other aspect, and professionals who recognize and understand these interactions are more likely to conduct an accurate assessment.

Guideline 2.   Macro-level factors (sociopolitical forces, economic conditions, etc.) greatly influence an individual's behavior and well-being. Situations and external pressures are powerful determinants of behavior. For example, assessment should account for the effects of discrimination, historical oppression, and other social biases upon the client and their network of relationships.

Guideline 3.   Assessment should include strengths and opportunities as well as difficulties and limitations. Problematic behaviors often represent attempts to cope with challenging situations. A holistic perspective that considers assets and talents along with desires and motivations will more accurately represent individuals' attempts to cope with their situation.

Guideline 4.   Therapists need to recognize when trauma has occurred. Trauma undermines coping strategies, leading to a wide range of deleterious effects, from relationship difficulties to substance abuse and from hopelessness to psychosis. Nearly every mental disorder can be triggered by some form of trauma. The indistinct effects of trauma make it difficult for therapists to understand the resulting pattern of symptoms unless they first recognize how clients perceive traumatic events and circumstances.

Guideline 5.   Physiology, physical illness, and related genetic predispositions impact mental functioning. Medical conditions, particularly those that involve the nervous system, often produce psychological symptoms. Moreover, psychological symptoms can linger even after a medical condition has been treated. As illustrated in the case of the 6-year-old boy presented earlier, assessment of mind-body interactions is essential to effective practice.

Guideline 6.   Given that a multiplicity of factors influences identity and wellness (including those listed in the ADDRESSING and RESPECTFUL frameworks), assessment should determine which of these have the most salience for a particular individual. Each person's identity is a unique blend emphasizing certain characteristics over others. For some individuals, political activity or nationality may be more salient than race or ethnicity; for others, sexual orientation or gender may be more salient than age or religious background. Moreover, the relative hierarchy of importance of each aspect may change over time and across situations, such as when individuals begin to pay more attention to their age and abilities once they reach late adulthood and begin to notice evidence of ageism and ableism in their interactions with others. Effective assessment therefore seeks to identify the type and degree of influence each aspect of diversity has upon the individual client, along with the particular experiences that have been most influential in shaping the client's identity and worldview.

Guideline 7.   Assessment should be informed by prevalence and incidence data. Information on the base rates of conditions can balance the essential idiographic nature of mental health assessment by keeping diagnoses and conditions in perspective. For example, if therapists know that a particular condition is either relatively rare or incorrectly over-diagnosed among people of a certain background, they may be more likely to conduct additional assessment prior to making a diagnosis.

Guideline 8.   Psychological symptoms frequently overlap with other psychological symptoms. For example, symptoms of anxiety often overlap with symptoms of depression, substance abuse often appears simultaneously with depression, and low caloric intake among individuals with eating disorders frequently produces symptoms characteristic of depression (e.g., low energy, altered sleep patterns). As illustrated in the case of the 23-year-old drug addict presented at the start of the chapter, differential diagnosis and assessment for comorbid conditions are essential to effective treatment.

Guideline 9.   Psychological testing is most valuable when used to test hypotheses based on other information collected first. Too often therapists use a set battery of standardized instruments as the first approach or, unfortunately, the only approach to assessment. Optimally, clinicians should select the instruments that are the most appropriate to hypotheses generated about the case, interpret the results in light of other evidence, and then make decisions about severity of symptoms and diagnosis.

Guideline 10.   Clinical judgments are susceptible to bias. Bias comes in many forms, both positive and negative. Biases due to race, gender, sexual orientation, age, abilities, and socioeconomic status are common, and they adversely impact the quality of the assessment. Biases of the therapist can prevent accurate understanding of the context and experiences of the client. A complex contextual approach to assessment and treatment therefore requires that personal biases be recognized and corrected to the extent possible.

Facilitating Accurate Counselor and Therapist Perceptions of Context: Recognizing and Correcting Personal Biases

Common Sources of Bias in Assessment

As illustrated by the examples of the 23-year-old college student and the 6-year-old kindergartener given at the beginning of this chapter, individualistic biases prevalent in society restrict the ability of mental health professionals to consider multiple contexts that impact clients' behavior. However, it takes a great deal of vigilance to recognize and correct for personal biases, *particularly the tendency to focus exclusively on evidence from our own interpersonal interactions with a client,* thereby minimizing the importance of external contexts.

Biases that obscure context are also prevalent because social values of individualism and related psychological factors combine to maintain and reinforce them. These factors include attribution errors, similarity-seeking and transference/countertransference, defensiveness, reductionism, failure to recognize conflicting and non-stereotypic contexts, and tendencies to abuse power through motives of self-interest, each of which is briefly reviewed below.

Attribution Errors.   Research has shown that it is a natural tendency among people from individualistic cultures to see other peoples' behavior in isolation from their context (Fay, 1996; Morris & Peng, 1994). We overestimate the role of psychological/dispositional factors and underestimate the role of situations and environmental causes (i.e., the fundamental attribution error; Baron & Byrne, 2000). We attribute others' success to circumstances (luck, favoritism, etc.) and our own success to hard work. We attribute others' negative behavior to their dispositions/characters ("what a jerk") and our own negative behavior to circumstances (bad mood, lack of support, etc.). In sum, it is our natural inclination to be patently unjust in our judgments of ourselves and others. Counselors and psychotherapists should be trained to recognize attribution errors and follow assessment procedures such as those described in the previous section that can help to counteract these natural tendencies.

Selective Attention, Transference, and Similarity Seeking.   If you take a moment to think of the attributes of some of the people you enjoy being around, chances are you would notice that they share many of your own attributes and interests. Alternatively, if you think of a time when you have been mildly disappointed in another person, you might find that the disappointment came when you realized that they did not demonstrate an attribute or interest that you had assumed they had in common with you. This tendency to seek out and selectively attend to similarities between oneself and others has been widely documented (Baron & Byrne, 2000). We feel comfortable with people who are like us (which similarity implicitly supports our own way of doing things), and we feel uncomfortable around people who are different (which difference implicitly challenges our own way of doing things).

This tendency to seek out similarities and minimize differences is problematic from a multicultural perspective (Comas-Diaz & Jacobsen, 1991). For example, in the case of the 23-year-old college student presented previously, the therapist selectively attended to certain information and missed other information that the client presented. The therapist was attuned to upper class values as a projection of personal values and experiences, but the drug subculture of the client was foreign to the therapist's personal experience such that the client's experiences were misinterpreted. To the extent that we selectively attend to others through the filter of our own experiences, needs, and assumptions, we fail to see them for who they are and thus fail to establish mutually enriching relationships. Consider the following personal example. The author of this chapter was chatting with a new acquaintance that he found pleasant and friendly. The person shared the author's values on multiculturalism, and they talked about how great life would be if everyone supported egalitarian ideals. They bashed proponents of an "English only" law that was recently enacted, and they passed the time pleasantly criticizing people not committed to diversity initiatives. Only afterward did the author recognize the irony of the situation and his own contribution to social intolerance! Although obvious in hindsight (or to an external observer), even blatant, it is hard to see in the moment. Psychological defenses further obscure bias to make constant personal vigilance a requirement of effective multicultural assessment and practice.

Defensiveness.   All people use psychological defenses, which are natural reactions to perceived threat or actual pain (Cramer, 2000; Rychlak, 1981). Of course, defenses provide no ultimate solution. They limit the ability of an individual to accurately perceive reality, to experience a wide range of emotions, and to maintain positive relationships. More often than not, defensiveness creates additional problems worse than the original threat. In therapy, defensiveness undermines the foundations of multiculturalism, open dialogue, and a contextual understanding of others.

Because multiculturalism poses real and perceived threats to monocultural values and privileges, defensive reactions to multiculturalism are common. No other subject in the mental health professions seems to consistently evoke as much emotionality, rigidity, and distress among practitioners (except perhaps financial threats associated with managed care). Reactions differ greatly from individual to individual, but the following are examples of several types of common defenses preventing a multicultural approach to practice.

Avoidance. A heterosexual individual realizes that she or he has never conversed meaningfully with an openly gay man or lesbian woman.

Blaming the victim. "If mental health treatment and everything that it entails is so wrong for those from other backgrounds, why do they even care to have counseling?"

Denial. "I can honestly say that in my heart, I know I do not have racist feelings against any minority. That is why it is so frustrating that minorities keep complaining about Whites being racist."

Identification. A psychologist with no prior experience working with Native Americans secures a job on a reservation and soon begins wearing silver bracelets, feathered earrings, and woven hair ornaments.

Projection. An instructor publicly accuses members of his class of being insensitive to interpersonal differences. (By making the accusation publicly, the instructor demonstrates the insensitivity supposedly characteristic of the students.)

Rationalization. An administrator shown statistics demonstrating inequities in the quality of care among certain groups of clients at her clinic feels a sense of relief when she learns that the same results were found at another clinic across town, and she puts the report away.

Reaction-formation (negative feelings disguised by acting out the opposite feeling). Following a heated class discussion on affirmative action, a member of the class slaps on the back a student who had been very vocal during class and acts very friendly with him as they walk out of the room together but then does not interact with him again in the future.

Suppression. During the first session of therapy with a client in a wheelchair, a therapist makes a concerted effort to keep from gazing at the client's thin legs.

Withdrawal. A student in a multicultural course remains silent during class discussions.

Many more examples could be listed. But it is so much easier to present examples of other people's behavior than to consider those that characterize our own. We do not like to see ourselves as reacting defensively, and so most often we do not (even though others do!). Professionals who learn to recognize their own blend of avoidance, denial, projection, etc., admit it openly, and seek feedback from others on how to improve are on their way to practicing multiculturalism. The following is an example of a therapist who has begun that very process:

> I don't consider myself a racist. I fervently believe that all people should be equal and that there is much in the world that prevents people of color from achieving their full potential. So it shouldn't bother me when I hear others accuse me of being racist. But why does it?
>
> As I consider this difficult question, I think that I revel in the thought that somehow I am not capable of racism. I am not like others. I am different and above the fray. I am...BETTER.
>
> Facing my own arrogance and hypocrisy has been a shock. My particular brand of racism is not that I have actively sought power over others but that I

have implicitly put myself in a position of moral superiority over others. I have believed that "all people should be equal" to the extent that it favors my own agenda, which is to keep myself above the fray and smugly condemn others for perpetuating inequality publicly, while I perpetuate it privately. I am a racist who has hid from the scrutiny of others but who can no longer hide from my own conscience.

Psychological Reductionism, Stereotyping, and Labeling. Diversity is everywhere. But diversity is complex and multifaceted, and that complexity competes with a human tendency to keep things simple (e.g., van der Helm, 2000). Simplicity is nearly always preferred to complexity in interpersonal interactions. Therefore, the complexities that do exist are often simplified through generalizations and labels (gay, Italian American, blind, etc.) that become more real than the person they are meant to represent. Such reductionism masks diversity. Not only is there a great deal of diversity across groups, but there is also a great deal of diversity within groups (Comas-Diaz & Jacobsen, 1995). For example, gay men are far more diverse than the word "gay" implies, and people over age 80 are far more diverse than the term "elderly" depicts. Moreover, we have a tendency to form impressions of others quickly, based on the limited data of the label and its associated stereotypes (Abreu, 2001), *but then those early impressions shape all of our subsequent perceptions and interactions* (e.g., Baron & Byrne, 2000). When we label a person, we end up engaging with them as if they were primarily or exclusively that label. For example, we treat an Arab American as if she or he represented all Arabs and a lesbian as if she matched our internalized image of lesbians in general. Categories and labels can be useful, even affirming at times, but they mask the complexity of an individual's background and experience, and they can restrict the ability of mental health professionals to conduct accurate evaluations (Abreu, 1999).

Failure to Address Conflicting and Nonstereotypic Contexts. Related to the tendency to simplify complex issues is the tendency to overlook conflicting and nonstereotypic contexts. Although overlaps between one context and another frequently complement each other (e.g., Native American identity is strengthened and deepened by participation in traditional religious ceremonies), there are many times when contexts may conflict with one another. For example, a given culture may proscribe gender role distinctions that conflict with certain educational and political tenets or proscribe normative behaviors that contradict certain religious tenets. Although the sources of conflicts are many, individuals who find themselves in conflicting contexts face particular challenges that impact their well-being and mental health. Therapists who take an individualistic approach and minimize such conflicts are likely to look for psychological causes for clients' distress, rather than to contextual factors that underlie the predicament.

Moreover, certain groups of people are more likely to be caught "at the intersections" of diversity than others. For example, people of Japanese ancestry from South America are incorrectly stereotyped as Asian Americans when they immigrate to North America because of their physical appearance. Similarly, Blacks immigrating from the Dominican Republic or Haiti are labeled as African Americans, despite their linguistic and cultural differences. Sikhs are often incorrectly labeled as Muslims and treated as extremists because the men wear a turban and carry a *kirpan* (dagger).

A particularly salient example of this point is represented in the experiences of many biracial and multiracial individuals (e.g., Root, 2001). In a social world where in-group/out-group boundaries are common and highly scripted, individuals whose ancestry reflects multiple racial groups must negotiate a place in between perceived extremes. Many multiracial individuals therefore develop a multiracial identity, which has complex and unique processes only partially addressed in the race-specific theoretical models of racial identity development (Chapter 3). Factors that influence multiracial identity development include family of origin dynamics, language fluency, surname, relative social status of each group in the person's heritage, racial composition of the community and school, degree of acceptance by members of each group in the person's heritage, and physical appearance (Johnson, 1992). The process of multiracial identity development clearly exemplifies the complex interaction of the individual within multiple contexts that sometimes conflict with one another.

To conduct an effective contextual assessment, therapists should consider both the potential benefits and challenges associated with particular intersections of diversity. For example, a multiracial identity may lead to a heightened awareness of one's own racial and cultural heritage and an accompanying appreciation for those of others, an increased ability to communicate across divergent cultures, and a more complex understanding of cultural and power dynamics. However, a multiracial identity is not always valued in society, where multiracial individuals are sometimes marginalized. Feelings of inferiority or isolation may occur, although multiracial individuals may experience relatively few severe adverse effects despite some of the additional challenges they face (e.g., White Stephan, 1992). Challenges include facing stereotypes about the myth of "racial purity," experiencing pressure to "choose" a racial identity aligned with one group over another, having to exert special efforts to "prove" that they are really who they say they are, or being labeled a "sellout" when they align with one group instead of another or when they engage in "passing" between both groups (Root, 1992). In sum, therapists should be attuned to non-stereotypic contexts and the resulting benefits and challenges found at the intersections of diversity.

Self-Interest and the Abuse of Power.   Social, cultural, political, and economic power are similar to all other forms of power, such as nuclear energy; they can be used to build or destroy, to enrich or oppress. The positive use of power is often taken for granted (e.g., public works that ease congestion and improve sanitation, children expressing gratitude to parents), so it is less well documented or noticed in society than the abuse of power. Moreover, it is a common tendency that whenever an individual or group has an advantage over others, that advantage is used to further self-interest (Fay, 1996; Miller, 1999). The privilege of the advantage is abused, in that power becomes compulsion, the ability to limit the agency or opportunities of others. Those inherently disadvantaged are required to play by rules that favor the advantaged. There are enough extreme examples of this principle at the macro level (domination by military force, breaking treaties, and slavery) and examples from every culture (the new wave of immigrants to any region of the world being resented and oppressed by the previous wave who was resented and oppressed by the previous wave) to effectively demonstrate that *bias and self-interest lack only unchallenged power to be expressed openly.*

At the interpersonal level, the same principle holds true: self-interest and bias nearly always appear when an imbalance of power heavily favors one person over the other. Even normally congenial and "unbiased" individuals tend to show bias, become overly prideful, or otherwise seek self-interest as soon as they obtain an imbalance of power over someone else. Biases will appear whenever the opportunity to do so without penalty presents itself. Therefore, unless counselors and therapists recognize their own privileges and power, they will tend to abuse them through the common tendency to seek self-interest.

Self-interest and the resulting abuse of power are the fundamental causes of many failed or harmful interactions. Therapists infrequently recognize how their self-interests in the therapy setting may adversely impact a client. Self-interest comes in many forms, from overt efforts to increase the amount of compensation for services to subtle feelings of criticism or boredom that arise in a particular session. Regardless of the form, self-interest creates blinders that minimize a therapist's ability to accurately perceive and treat clients in their contexts.

By way of summary, personal bias can greatly limit the ability of therapists to accurately assess other people. Attribution errors, similarity-seeking and transference/countertransference, defensiveness, reductionism, failure to recognize conflicting and nonstereotypic contexts, and tendencies to abuse power through motives of self-interest all combine to limit the accuracy of multicultural assessment. The following section describes ways in which therapists can facilitate accurate assessment by evaluating and modifying personal biases where appropriate.

Self-Evaluation and Correction of Personal Bias

Skilled therapists learn to listen carefully to a client, but gifted therapists learn to observe all client expression, body language, and behavior. Although it is enlightening to hear clients speak, it is more enlightening to understand *how* they communicate and interact (e.g., Prochaska & Norcross, 1999; Tryon, 2002).

This principle is parallel to the process of developing contextual assessment skills. Although therapists may find it enlightening to consider sources of personal bias that may restrict their assessment and intervention skills, more significant is the way in which they act on that understanding.

The personal change needed for therapists to evaluate their own biases and subsequently to monitor the impact of these biases on their work with clients is exactly what multicultural competence requires (e.g., Abreu, 2001; American Psychological Association, 2002; Roysircar Sodowsky, 1997). Although difficult in the short term, overcoming initial inertia and taking meaningful steps to raise personal awareness and monitor personal biases can set a pattern for practice that will benefit potentially thousands of clients over the long term. This section provides some preliminary suggests as to how that can be accomplished.

Openness to Learning. Unless a therapist has successfully treated over 100 persons from a particular background, that individual cannot really be considered "expert" in working with that population. Although this statement may seem extreme, it is no more unreasonable than the common assumption that therapists are skilled with a given population just because they share the background, or have friends from the background, or particularly enjoyed a client from that background in 50-minute increments. Even if therapists have seen over 1,000 clients with a particular problem, they may be no more effective in treating the problem than when they saw the very first client. Their efficacy depends on what they have learned from the 999 clients seen subsequently. Therapists who open themselves to personal change based on their clients' cues have taken a first step toward accurate self-evaluation and eventual multicultural proficiency.

External and Internal Motivations.   A second useful process in self-evaluation is to consider the sources of motivation that produce long-term commitments to personal growth and to effective service to clients. The social pressures to be politically correct and avoid offending others or to appear knowledgeable and competent so as to gain others' favor are among the *external* sources of motivation that can produce reluctant compliance but fail to produce mutual enrichment, the aim of multiculturalism (e.g., Ridley et al., 1994).

The influence of external pressures can be appropriately recognized (Roysircar & Sodowsky, 1997), but the goal is to integrate them with internal motivations, such as a desire to communicate effectively with others, a desire to stand beside those who suffer, a respect for the resilience of the human spirit, a desire to defend principles of justice, fairness, etc. Such motivations can produce long-term change, and they do not depend on the presence/pressure of others to enforce compliance. Moreover, in contrast to external motivations, these internal factors are pro-social, not sustained exclusively by self-interest ("What's in it for me?"), such that they support the aim of *mutual* enrichment. Scrutiny of one's motivations and subsequent realignment of those motivations toward pro-social outcomes can help to secure the desired mutual enrichment, which itself can become a source of continued motivation.

Awareness of Past Experiences and Themes.   A third process is for therapists to consider their own personal history and background to see how multiple aspects of diversity have influenced their personal and professional development (perhaps using the ADDRESSING or RESPECTFUL frameworks as a guide) (Abreu, 2001). A systematic evaluation of past experiences may be particularly enlightening, since people often repeat behaviors and maintain perceptions from the past unless they have sufficient motivation to do otherwise (e.g., Prochaska & Norcross, 1999). Questions similar to the following may be useful in this process:

- What have I explicitly and implicitly been taught by society in general and by family and peers in particular regarding diversity and classification of people? How have I acted as if these classifications were real?
- What have been my most memorable/emotional experiences interacting with those who see the world differently? What emotions/lessons do I still carry with me from those interactions?
- How have I maintained negative feelings and how have I successfully changed negative feelings to positive ones?

- Where have I shown flexibility in adapting to others and under what conditions have I maintained my position without compromise?
- Which of the defenses listed in the previous section (e.g., avoidance, projection) have characterized my own behavior, particularly when I am under stress?

If answered candidly, these kinds of questions should produce specific awareness of patterns and themes, discrepancies and contradictions, including self-deceptions and distortions that are embedded in society but consequently internalized by the individual. Once consistent themes and patterns have been recognized, the real work of unlearning harmful distortions and mastering empathic, non-defensive ways of relating to others can begin.

Trying New Ways of Being.   Self-awareness entails more than introspection. Because humans have distorted perceptions of themselves, mentally rehearsing previous experiences provides only a partial picture of who they are. Just as a culture is invisible without contrast (Chapter 1), individuals may have difficulty seeing themselves accurately unless they put themselves into situations they have not previously encountered. New experiences provide the necessary contrast for re-examining previous assumptions and beliefs.

This suggestion parallels the recommendation for mental health professionals to immerse themselves in another culture as a necessary aspect of acquiring multicultural competence (Pope-Davis, Breux, & Lui, 1997; Ridley et al., 1994). The rationale is that personal experience is the best way of learning new material and unlearning inaccurate assumptions. For example, if an individual believes stereotypes about a certain group of people, those stereotypes will likely remain until proven inaccurate when the individual interacts positively and meaningfully with members of that group (Abreu, 2001). Such interactions not only facilitate a more accurate understanding of the worldviews and experiences of the other group, they provide an opportunity for a person to see his or her own worldview in contrast to that of others. Such interactions can also demonstrate the heterogeneity of the other group, challenging previously held assumptions and generalizations. Moreover, when individuals truly immerse themselves in another group, they can better recognize the difficulties that come from doing so, optimally increasing their empathy in the process (Roysircar Sodowsky, 1997). Empathy, emotional understanding, and genuine respect for others can then become the filter through which generalizations can be viewed: "How would the client feel about that label? Would I want someone to characterize me that way?"

Feedback and Support.   A fifth process, seeking external resources and support, is an essential component of self-evaluation and self-improvement. Asking others for feedback is invaluable. Supervision and consultation specific to multicultural issues can facilitate the learning and support needed to confront difficult problems. Many find it helpful to join a professional organization, informal discussion group, or listserv, thereby developing a network of consultants concerning multicultural issues. Other useful resources are professional guidelines for multicultural competence (e.g., American Psychological Association, 2002), available from professional organizations such as the Society for the Psychological Study of Ethnic Minority Issues (www.apa.org/divisions/div45) or the Association for Multicultural Counseling and Development (www.amcd-aca.org). Using the points from these guidelines as a checklist and/or as ongoing reminders can provide a structure for continuing development.

Attending to Emotions.   Sixth, perhaps the most important process in working toward self-awareness is acknowledging the emotional component of interpersonal interactions. It is well known that the same stimulus can elicit highly disparate emotional reactions across people (e.g., Baron & Byrne, 2000). What is pleasant to one person may be threatening to another, etc. Therefore, emotional reactions can say more about the person than about the stimulus. For example, a person who responds to a given event with fear may have been hurt by a similar event in the past, whereas a person who responds with joy may have had positive experiences earlier that same day that created "rose-colored glasses" through which the subsequent event was seen. Our own emotional reactions can say more about ourselves than we are willing to admit.

Applying this principle to multiculturalism, it should be clear that the differences, real and perceived, that exist among and between people should elicit a variety of emotions across individuals. A person could react to difference with anger, apathy, appreciation, or awe—any of which would reflect the internal state of the person more than any other influence. Counselors and therapists can therefore learn about themselves by taking note of their own emotional reactions, considering why they selected one reaction as opposed to others ("What was that about?") and then watching for themes that arise over time. For example, a therapist who is consistently overly anxious to help the perceived underdog may realize ways in which unresolved personal issues make the role of nurturer particularly comforting. A therapist who passively waits to see what the majority of others will do or think before acting or forming an opinion may become aware of ways in which their reliance on others has shaped nearly all of their perceptions. And a mental health professional who resents having to adapt her practice to meet the needs of some unique client may discover ways in which other people have inflexibly misused power *over her* in the past, modeling inflexible behaviors and attitudes that are subsequently perpetuated, often unwittingly. The assumption here is that emotional reactions to multiculturalism reflect previous experience (patterns of reinforcement and punishment, cognitive schemas, developmental dynamics, etc.) that need to be recognized and, where appropriate, replaced with new experiences, thoughts, desires, etc., that are more conducive to therapeutic outcomes (Roysircar Sodowsky, 1997).

There are several ways in which this monitoring of emotional reactions can be facilitated. Therapists can set up a routine to remind themselves of the need to engage in this process prior to each session and subsequently remain self-aware (but not self-focused!) throughout the session. Therapists may wish to keep a journal for observing and processing their own emotional reactions, making regular entries between sessions or at the end of each workday. Some may find supervision or consultation useful in exploring these issues. Others will purposefully work to establish relationships with those who are very different from themselves and then learn from the experience, monitoring their own insecurities and tendencies to retreat to familiar ground. Regardless of the process used, therapists who commit to monitor their own emotional reactions and learn from them will find that they become more effective in their work, modeling adaptive skills for others to emulate. Consider the following narrative from a developing professional:

Last week I was walking by a school playground when I noticed a little boy sitting alone by the fence, with his head between his hands. I walked past him thinking "What a loner!" but then I remembered what I had read about being judgmental and about making a difference "one moment at a time." This child was not my responsibility, but when I knelt beside him and heard his muffled whimpers, I knew I was responsible to help. He did not speak much, but he looked up and nodded his head when I asked if he felt hurt being left out of the games. He had a noticeable facial deformity. As it turned out, my neighbor's son was playing across the sandpit, and I invited him to include one more new friend. I stayed until I saw consistent smiles.

I similarly fought with my feelings and prejudices when I was in a packed lecture hall and a woman with purple hair, sunglasses (still on), and a huge nose ring entered the room but could not find an open seat. My first reaction was to guess at her sexual orientation and to privately ridicule her wardrobe. My second reaction was to recognize what I had just done and simultaneously take responsibility to do better. I sat down on the floor and motioned for her to take my chair, and to my surprise she did, thanking me profusely. We chatted at the conclusion of the seminar. I cannot tell you how good it felt to have my initial feelings disconfirmed and replaced with respect. I also realize that in both cases my actions were maternalistic and that I may offend someone in the future if I try to "solve" every dilemma I encounter, but I have a new resolve to respond to others as I feel appropriate, trusting instinct and the signals I receive from others' cues, in spite of (or because of?) my initial emotional reactions.

Although neither of these experiences occurred in session with a client, the young professional in the vignette was able to challenge beliefs that would otherwise eventually impact her work with clients who shared similar attributes to the child and the woman. In fact, if counselors or therapists limit themselves to self-monitoring during sessions, they will likely only be partially successful in the endeavor. As with most therapeutic skills, learning from one's emotional reactions is an ongoing process, developed and refined across settings and circumstances.

Before concluding this section, it is important to emphasize that the process of self-evaluation should not result merely in a simple admission of inadequacy or in an extensive list of things to change about oneself or others, such that one quickly feels overwhelmed with the impossibility of it all. Although guilt can be an appropriate internal/pro-social motivation at times, feelings of inadequacy and self-blame can paralyze action and smother the desires for improvement that prompted the self-evaluation in the first place. Rather than paralyze our progress, emotional reactions such as feeling guilty or overwhelmed should further teach us about how we react to difficult circumstances. Multiculturalism is difficult. Many people feel guilty or overwhelmed when confronted with the realities of multicultural competence (e.g., Gillespie, Ashbaugh, & DeFiore, 2002). Individuals who have been oppressed often struggle to find ways to make a difference, changing the seemingly unchangeable. Individuals who have unwittingly benefited from racism, sexism, etc., find it awkward to take personal responsibility for something so diffuse and so pervasive. Yet personal resolve to make a difference, despite the overwhelming nature of the problem, and willingness to take personal responsibility, despite the inevitable consequences, are both potential outcomes of a thoughtful, reflective, and sincere self-evaluation against professional standards of multicultural practice (e.g., American Psychological Association, 2002). Personal resolve to do what is possible to improve oneself and one's environment relative to those standards brings a quiet confidence, whereas motivations that are external ("What will others think of me?") and motivations that stem from unfinished emotional business (e.g., previous hurt) tend to produce stress that amplifies discouragement.

Therapists can increase the accuracy of their assessments by considering the multiple contexts that impact the assessment process, including their own ability to perceive the client accurately. Accurate perception of others is facilitated by openness to learning, a requisite for any self-evaluation. Scrutiny of the motivations for routine practice and for personal change, along with an exploration of previous experiences and personal history, can clarify the lenses through which we see others. External resources such as supervision, consultation, and professional guidelines can facilitate the process, which optimally includes monitoring our own emotional reactions and working through initial discomfort until we accept and desire to learn from the client (thus continuing the circular process). The following is a brief vignette of a professional working on these very issues:

> Although my primary reason for choosing a career was to help others, I have found myself increasingly preoccupied with the daily hassles and burnout that accompany full-time practice. My caseload has been fairly homogeneous, but I became revitalized by an opportunity to work part-time with a group of physicians treating low-income expectant mothers (a welcomed contrast to the upper-middle class malaise that I knew only too well myself!). At the same time, I began taking a serious look at my own values and past experiences relevant to multicultural issues. I recognized that I was nervous working with the women who did not speak English well, and I could see that I had a lot to learn about family dynamics across several cultures. I admitted to being very timid with clients whose backgrounds were unfamiliar to me, and I constantly worried what they were thinking about me (my insecurities again!). So, to make a long story short, I started a supplemental reading program and sought out an old friend who could provide phone consultation—and a needed source of humor! After about three months of this, the obstetrician reviewing my charts commented that she was surprised that the degree and types of mental health difficulties among the women had been increasing. My previous diagnoses had mostly reflected symptoms of depression and anxiety, but my recent assessments were uncovering a range of issues that were much more complex. I took this as validation that what I was doing was working!

Conclusion

This chapter has emphasized the counselor's professional responsibility to conduct contextual assessments. Contextual assessments carefully consider the multiple influences on a client's worldview and well-being, the assessment procedures optimal for informing interventions, and the ability of the person conducting the assessment to accurately interpret the resulting information. The suggestions provided in these three areas are far from comprehensive, but they are foundational.

Contextual understanding of a client can be facilitated through recognition and evaluation of multiple aspects of diversity, such as those listed in the RESPECTFUL and ADDRESSING frameworks (D'Andrea & Daniels, 2001; Hays, 2001). The subsequent chapters in this book provide additional information regarding these aspects of diversity.

Contextual understanding of assessment procedures includes recognition of the purpose, structure, duration, and consequences of the assessment. Optimally, assessment shapes interventions in an interactive process consisting of both informal and formal methods. In selecting formal methods, the therapist should consider the instruments' functional, conceptual, linguistic/translation, and metric/scalar equivalence for the particular group being evaluated. Limitations of universal diagnostic systems such as the DSM-IV-TR should be acknowledged, and diagnoses should be informed by culture-specific consideration of manifestations and interpretations of symptoms. Idiographic guidelines for multicultural assessment indicate that although therapists or counselors should seek to understand the client's *cluster* of symptoms, *type* of personality, *status* of racial/ethnic identity development, *degree* and *type* of acculturation, *scores* from testing, diagnostic *category,* etc., they never feel comfortable categorizing the person.

Finally, accurate assessment is facilitated when mental health professionals recognize common tendencies that obscure context, including attribution errors, defensiveness, reductionism, and self-interest. Combating these tendencies requires introspection, motivation, external support and resources, and analysis of personal reactions to multicultural content. Although most counselors and psychologists acknowledge the need to conduct effective multicultural assessments, the interesting part is how they work to increase the accuracy of those assessments.

References

Abreu, J. M. (1999). Conscious and nonconscious African American stereotypes: Impact on first impression and diagnostic ratings by therapists. *Journal of Consulting and Clinical Psychology, 67,* 387–393.

Abreu, J. M. (2001). Theory and research on stereotypes and perceptual bias: A didactic resource for multicultural counseling trainers. *Counseling Psychologist, 29,* 487–512.

American Psychiatric Association (2000). *Diagnostic and statistical manual of mental disorders* (4th edition, text revision). Washington, DC: Author.

American Psychological Association (2002). *Guidelines on multicultural education, training, research, practice, and organizational change in psychology.* Washington, DC: American Psychological Association.

Baron, R., & Byrne, D. (2000). *Social psychology* (9th ed.) Boston: Allyn & Bacon.

Bellah, R. N., Madsen, R., Sullivan, W. M., Swidler, A., & Tipton, S. M. (1985). *Habits of the heart: Individualism and commitment in American life.* Los Angeles, CA: University of California Press.

Comas-Diaz L., & Jacobsen, F. M. (1991). Ethnocultural transference and counter transference in the therapeutic dyad. *American Journal of Orthopsychiatry, 61,* 392–402.

Comas-Diaz, L., & Jacobsen, F. M. (1995). The therapist of color and the White patient dyad: Contradictions and recognitions. *Cultural Diversity & Ethnic Minority Psychology, 2,* 93–106.

Cramer, P. (2000). Defense mechanisms in psychology today: Further processes for adaptation. *American Psychologist, 55,* 637–646.

Dana, R. (2000a). Psychological assessment in the diagnosis and treatment of ethnic group members. In

J. F. Aponte & J. Wohl (Eds.), *Psychological inter-vention and cultural diversity* (2nd ed.). Boston: Allyn & Bacon.

Dana, R. (Ed.) (2000b). *Handbook of cross-cultural and multicultural personality assessment.* Mahwah, NJ: Lawrence Erlbaum Associates.

D'Andrea, M., & Daniels, J. (2001). Respectful counseling: An integrative multidimensional model for counselors. In D. Pope-Davis & H. Coleman (Eds.), *The intersection of race, class, and gender in multicultural counseling* (pp. 417–466). Thousand Oaks, CA: Sage.

Fancher, R. T. (1995). *Cultures of healing: Correcting the image of American mental health care.* W. H. Freeman & Co.

Fay, B. (1996). *Contemporary philosophy of social science: A multicultural approach.* Malden, MA: Blackwell Publishers.

Gillespie, D., Ashbaugh, L., & DeFiore, J. (2002). White women teaching White women about White privilege, race cognizance, and social action: Toward a pedagogical pragmatics. *Race, Ethnicity, and Education, 5,* 237–253.

Hansen, N., Lambert, M. J., & Forman, E. M. (2002). The psychotherapy dose response effect and its implications for treatment delivery services. *Clinical Psychology: Science & Practice, 9,* 329–343.

Hays, P. (1996). Addressing the complexities of culture and gender in counseling. *Journal of Counseling and Development, 74,* 332–338.

Hays, P. (2001). *Addressing cultural complexities in practice: A framework for clinicians and counselors.* Washington, DC: American Psychological Association.

Ivey, A. E., D'Andrea, M., Ivey, M. B., & Simek-Morgan, L. (2002). *Theories of Counseling and Psychology: A Multicultural Perspective* (5th ed.). Boston: Allyn and Bacon.

Johnson, D. (1992). Developmental pathways: Toward an ecological theoretical formulation of race identity in black-white bi-racial children. In M. P. P. Root (Ed.) *Racially mixed people in America* (pp. 37–49). Thousand Oaks, CA: Sage.

Kaplan, R. M., & Saccuzzo, D. (2001). *Psychological testing: Principles, applications, and issues* (5th ed.). Belmont, CA: Wadsworth/Thomson Learning.

Kazdin, A. E. (2001). *Behavior modification in applied settings* (6th ed.). Belmont, CA: Wadsworth/Thomson Learning.

Lambert, M. J., Hansen, N., & Finch, A. (2001). Patient-focused research: Using patient outcome data to enhance treatment effects. *Journal of Consulting & Clinical Psychology, 69,* 159–172.

Mezzich, J. E., Kirmayer, L. J., & Kleinman, A. (1999). The place of culture in DSM-IV. *Journal of Nervous & Mental Disease, 187,* 457–464.

Miller, D. T. (1999). The norm of self-interest. *American Psychologist, 54,* 1053–1060.

Morris, M. W., & Peng, K. (1994). Culture and cause: American and Chinese attributions for social and physical events. *Journal of Personality and Social Psychology, 67,* 949–971.

Padilla, A. (2001). Issues in culturally appropriate assessment. In L. A. Suzuki, J. G. Ponterotto, and P. J. Meller (Eds.), *Handbook of multicultural assessment: Clinical, psychological, and educational applications* (2nd ed.) (pp. 5–27). San Francisco: Jossey-Bass.

Pedersen, P. (Ed.) (1999). *Multiculturalism as a fourth force.* Philadelphia, PA: Brunner/Mazel.

Poortinga, Y. (1995). Cultural bias in assessment: Historical and thematic issues. *European Journal of Psychological Assessment, 11,* 140–146.

Pope-Davis, D., Breaux, C., & Lui, W. (1997). A multicultural immersion experience: Filling a void in multicultural training. In D. Pope-Davis & H. Coleman (Eds.), *Multicultural counseling competencies: Assessment, education and training, and supervision.* (pp. 227–241). Thousand Oaks, CA: Sage.

Pope-Davis, D. B., & Coleman, H. L. K. (Eds.). (2001). *The intersection of race, class, and gender in multicultural counseling.* Thousand Oaks, CA: Sage.

Prochaska, J., & Norcross, J. (1999). *Systems of Psychotherapy: A transtheoretical analysis.* New York: Brooks/Cole.

Reynolds, C. R. (1995). Test bias and the assessment of intelligence and personality. In D. Saklofske & M. Zeidner (Eds.), *International handbook of personality and intelligence* (pp. 545–573). New York: Plenum Press.

Ridley, C. R., Hill, C. L., Thompson, C., E., & Ormerod, A. L. (2001). Clinical practice guidelines in assessment: Toward an idiographic perspective. In D. Pope-Davis & H. Coleman (Eds.), *The intersection of race, class, and gender in multicultural counseling* (pp. 191–211). Thousand Oaks, CA: Sage.

Ridley, C. R., Mendoza, D., & Kanitz, B. (1994). Multicultural training: Reexamination, operationalization, and integration. *The Counseling Psychologist, 22,* 227–289.

Rollock, D. & Terrell, M. D. (1996). Multicultural issues in assessment: Toward an inclusive model. In J. DeLucia-Waack (Ed.), *Multicultural counseling competencies: Implications for training and practice* (pp. 113–153). Alexandria, VA: Association for Counselor Education and Supervision.

Root, M. P. P. (Ed.) (1992). *Racially mixed people in America.* Thousand Oaks, CA: Sage.

Root, M. P. P. (2001). Negotiating the margins. In J. G. Ponterotto, J. M. Casas, L. A. Suzuki, & C. M. Alexander (Eds.), *Handbook of multicultural counseling* (2nd ed.) (pp. 113–121). Thousand Oaks, CA: Sage.

Roysircar Sodowsky, G., Kuo-Jackson, P., & Loya, G. (1997). Outcome of training in the philosophy of assessment: Multicultural counseling competencies. In D. Pope-Davis & H. Coleman (Eds.), *Multicultural counseling competencies: Assessment education, training, and supervision* (pp. 3–40). Thousand Oaks, CA: Sage.

Rychlak, J. F. (1981). *Introduction to Personality and Psychotherapy*. Massachusetts: Houghton Mifflin Company.

Sackett, P., Schmitt, N., Ellisgson, J., & Kabin, M. (2001). High-stakes testing in employment, credentialing, and higher education: Prospects in a post-affirmative-action world. *American Psychologist, 56,* 302–318.

Samuda, R. J., Feurstein, R., Kaufman, A. S., Lewis, J. E., & Sternberg, R. J. (1998). *Advances in cross-cultural assessment.* Thousand Oaks, CA: Sage.

Seligman, M. E. P. (1995). The effectiveness of psychotherapy: The Consumer Reports study. *American Psychologist, 50,* 965–974.

Sue, D. W., & Sue, D. (1999). *Counseling the culturally different: Theory and practice* (3rd ed.). New York: Wiley.

Suzuki, L. A., Ponterotto, J. G., & Meller, P. J. (Eds.) (2001). *Handbook of multicultural assessment: Clinical, psychological, and educational applications* (2nd ed.). San Francisco, CA: Jossey-Bass/Pfeiffer.

Takushi, R., & Uomoto, J. M. (2001). *The clinical interview from a multicultural perspective.* San Francisco: Jossey-Bass.

Tryon, G. S. (2002). *Counseling based on process research: Applying what we know.* Boston: Allyn & Bacon.

van der Helm, P. A. (2000). Simplicity versus likelihood in visual perception: From surprisals to precisals. *Psychological Bulletin, 126,* 770–800.

White Stephan, C. (1992). Mixed-heritage individuals: Ethnic identity and trait characteristics. In M. P. P. Root (Ed) *Racially mixed people in America* (pp. 50–63). Thousand Oaks, CA: Sage.

Part III

Considerations for Multicultural Practice with Specific Populations

7

Effective Interventions with Children of Color and Their Families

A Contextual Developmental Approach

Daisuke Akiba

Queens College of the City University of New York

Cynthia Garcia Coll

Brown University

The proportion of people of color in the United States is projected to increase from 26.4 percent in 1995 to 47.2 percent in 2050, and the rate of increase in the number of children of color under the age of 18 exceeds that of European Americans under that age (Census Bureau of the United States, 1996).[1] These trends clearly suggest that the future of this country cannot be discussed meaningfully without including children and families of color. Nevertheless, the projected increase in numbers of individuals of color has not necessarily translated into an increase in research involving this population, much less an increase in access to the power and resources that should be available to people of color, who are disproportionately likely to suffer from poverty, mental health issues, and other challenges

---

[1]Scholars and professionals have traditionally used the term *minorities* to refer to people of color. The notion of *minority* implies quantitative dimensions—that they are oppressed because they are outnumbered by the majority. However, it is important to note that racial/ethnic minority status in the current context is more concerned about qualitative differentials, and it has more to do with lack of resources and power than lack of numbers. Accordingly, we use such terms as *children of color* and *families of color,* instead of *minority children* or *minority families.*

(Garcia Coll & Garrido, 2000). Therefore, there is an urgent need for a systematic under-standing of the lives of children and families of color. The primary aim of this chapter is to review major psychosocial characteristics of the development of children and families of color; in the process, we will also consider models for conceptualizing child development, methodological issues, and clinical applications.

Interaction of Factors Influencing Child Development: The Ecological Systems Approach

In the past, mental health professionals have invested much time and effort in debating whether heredity or environment—or if a combination, what proportion of each—was re-sponsible for a wide variety of developmental outcomes. More recently, however, there has been a movement toward conceptualizing child development in terms of the interactive processes between a child and various layers of factors surrounding the child. Bronfenbren-ner's (1979) framework, often characterized as following the *ecological systems* approach, is useful in visualizing this paradigm. His ideas focus on the reciprocal relationship be-tween "an active, growing human being and the changing properties of the immediate set-tings in which the developing person lives, as this process is affected by relations between these settings, and by the larger contexts in which the settings are embedded" (p. 21). Chil-dren, therefore, are viewed neither as passive recipients of the environment nor as agents whose existence is independent of environmental influences. This perspective does not fol-low the idea that the characteristics of the child and the nature of the environment contrib-ute autonomously to these children's development. Instead, it is theorized that a child's own characteristics and contextual factors are interactive as they affect the child's develop-mental pathways. These ideas are of critical importance in explaining within-group varia-tions in development, which are in some instances considerably more dramatic than between-group variations. As seen in Figure 7.1, Bronfenbrenner's theory further recog-nizes the interactions within as well as among various layers of factors, ranging in imme-diacy to a child from most immediate, such as family, peers, and neighborhoods (i.e., microsystems), to most distant, such as cultural ideologies (i.e., macrosystem). There is more to what a child experiences than is readily apparent; a multitude of attitudes, beliefs and practices present in larger institutions—current or past—interact with his/her own in-dividual characteristics, directly and indirectly affecting the phenomenological experience of this child.

Garcia Coll et al.'s (1996) integrative model of development expands on this ecolog-ical and interactionist approach, and it deals explicitly with children of color. It illustrates how the social stratification system and its correlates within a society play critical roles in human development by interacting with an individual's own characteristics (Figure 7.2). This model, like Bronfenbrenner's framework (1979), posits that a person's psychosocial characteristics can only be fully understood when s/he is viewed as an agent within the context of a historically established social stratification system, with its surrounding micro and macro elements, throughout her/his life. Individuals, in other words, are not viewed as existing independent of such elements at any given moment. In the U.S. society, social po-

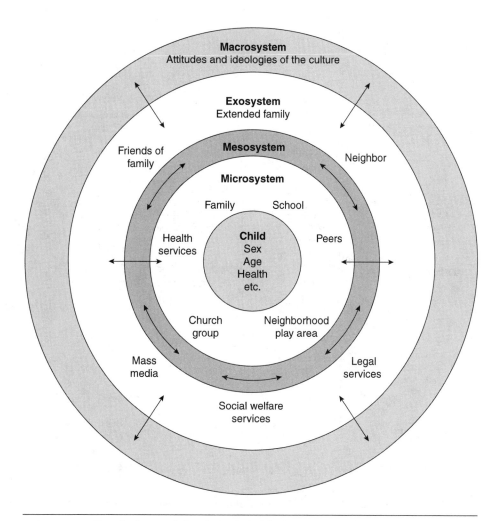

FIGURE 7.1 *Bronfenbrenner's Ecological Model of Human Development*

Source: The Child (p. 648) by C. B. Kopp and J. B. Kaslow, 1982. Reading, MA: Addison-Wesley. Copyright 1982 by Addison-Wesley Publishing Co., Inc. Reproduced by permission of Pearson Education, Inc.

sition is often marked along such dimensions as socioeconomic status, gender, and race/ethnicity. These dimensions often correlate, and each can also be further divided into sub-categories. The racial/ethnic dimensions, for example, share related sub-characteristics, such as skin color and other physical features that are perceived to signal racial and ethnic backgrounds.

These markers of social position often predict the quality of life and the range of options a person has available in this society; they also tend to elicit varying reactions

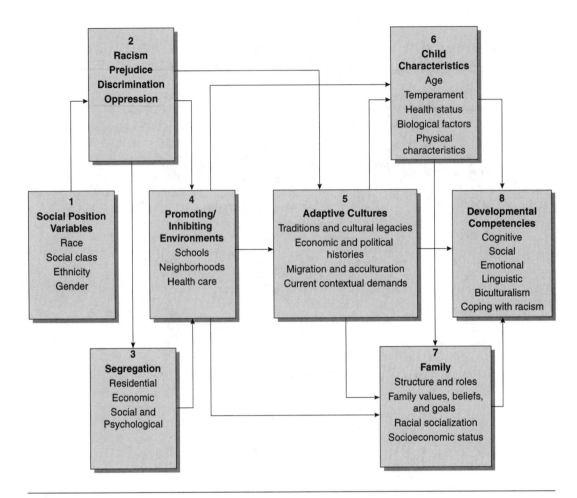

FIGURE 7.2 *An Integrative Model for the Study of Developmental Competencies in Children of Color*

Source: Adapted from Garcia Coll et al., 1996. Copyright 1996 by the Society for Research in Child Development. Reproduced by permission.

from the individuals and institutions in children's lives, even in mundane social interactions. For instance, African Americans on average may find themselves in social positions where some educational and career opportunities are not readily available to them, and there may be other compelling factors (e.g., socioeconomic status and neighborhood factors) discouraging them from pursuing goals that are valued in the mainstream U.S. culture. These discouraging influences would interact with such factors as the individuals' own characteristics or their teachers' and counselors' expectations, to affect developmental pathways. The interactive relationships among a range of macro and micro factors are mediated and moderated by other systems such as local governments, schools, families, and peers. Specifically, therefore, the social position factors are theorized to directly and indirectly affect the developmental processes of children and families of color, through a series of social mechanisms pertaining to exclusion associated with such factors. In short, no single factor is theorized to exert enough influence by itself to determine an outcome. Hence, it is crucial that psychology professionals consider both individual characteristics and larger contexts, focusing on interactive relationships among them. Thus to ensure adequate cultural sensitivity in psychological and educational practices entails much more than simply translating the European American models of therapy into various languages or dialects. Cultural sensitivity may also require practitioners and researchers to reexamine such models by considering larger contexts within which their clients have lived.

Human development cannot be fully understood without reflecting on a client's individual characteristics, his/her family, relevant neighborhoods, and the larger society, as well as a wide range of other elements within which an individual exists. Consideration of these complex interactions is particularly meaningful in discussing people of color, since they tend to have actual or perceived characteristics that are non-normative and may be stigmatized in this society; yet they are expected to fully participate as members of the mainstream society. In the following sections, basic concepts and issues will be reviewed, in order to facilitate a more detailed discussion on how these models are useful in understanding the developmental characteristics of children and families of color.

Biases in Research and Practice That Trivialize the Importance of Context

Following D'Andrea and Daniels's (2001) model, we propose that the "universal" goal of counseling and other forms of mental health intervention is to promote children's development within the range of contexts in which they have lived, currently live, and will live in the future. Children across cultures often share phenomenologically similar sets of affective, behavioral, and cognitive challenges associated with growing up, such as entry into formal education and formation of peer networks. Nevertheless, as discussed in detail in the following sections, various contextual factors (e.g., cultural value priorities, the characteristics of the larger communities) create a unique and complex multidimensionality that is a monumental influence in the development of each child, whose own unique characteristics interact with such contextual factors. Although clinicians and researchers have long addressed the psychological characteristics of children of color and their families, such attempts have frequently failed to adequately consider contextual factors. This trend can be attributed to biases prevalent in the research and practice with these populations. In the current section, we will discuss two biases that have too often adversely impacted professionals' work with children of color: overemphasizing race and minimizing race.

Overemphasis on Race and Ethnicity

Some researchers and practitioners tend to inappropriately attribute almost all psychosocial characteristics of people of color to their race/ethnicity (Gibbs & Huang, 1989). In their seminal work in 1968, *Black Rage,* Grier and Cobbs discussed the case of a young African American mother who demonstrated no interest in maintaining proper hygiene or in acting responsibly as a parent. A European American clinician concluded that this woman simply needed training in parenting and family management, reportedly because of a widespread belief that African American women in general lacked proper family management skills. Grier and Cobbs stated that the woman was actually severely psychotic, a fact that was undetected because the clinician had made a diagnosis without looking beyond a racial stereotype and surface symptoms. In this case, the "color obsession" led to nondiagnosis of a serious mental disorder, because psychosis was considered a "non-Black" disorder, while lack of parenting skills was thought to be common among this population.

The opposite outcome, overdiagnosis, occurs as a result of overemphasis on disorders that are thought to be prevalent among a particular demographic group. For example, attention deficit hyperactivity disorder (or ADHD) is widely believed to be common among African American children, particularly boys (Barbain & Soler, 1993). Given the prevalence of this diagnosis among this population, teachers and clinicians have been accused of being excessively eager to diagnose African American children with ADHD, despite the fact that their behavioral tendencies may stem from causes unrelated to ADHD, such as poor vision, learning differences, and unconventional communication styles (Hsu, 1996).[2] This overemphasis may cause the real problems to remain unaddressed, since the focus of clinicians and teachers is diverted to factors that are not necessarily related to the actual etiology of the characteristics.

Overemphasis of some group traits can also minimize contextual understanding of relevant sub-group traits. For example, Lopez & Espiritu (1990) suggest that terms such as *Asian* and *Latino* represent *pan-ethnicity,* grouping individuals who have little in common yet are perceived to belong together in the mainstream of American society. Their within-group diversity reflects the absence of meaningfully cohesive units, as the groups include peoples with varying races and ethnicities. Therefore, any cultural generalizations or assumptions in psychological practice must be made with extreme caution when dealing with the members of these groups. For example, it is often argued that the Japanese culture attaches a wide variety of meanings to the act of suicide, and under certain circumstances suicide is glorified and even expected (Leenaars et al., 1993). Since such cultural notions may be transmitted within Japanese American families, suicidal thoughts expressed by a Japanese American child in a school setting might not necessarily reflect the same psychological conditions or motives as similar ideation expressed by children from other backgrounds, and strategies for addressing such thoughts should thus allow for such differences. However, practitioners must avoid generalizing this trend of "suicide glorification" in treating non-Japanese Asian American clients who probably do not share this

---

[2]Hsu suggests that a statistical model by Bayes is useful in explaining the tendency to base clinical diagnoses on the clients' membership in particular "high-risk" groups.

tendency. In addition, it is crucial for clinicians to recognize the within-group variability—that not all Japanese Americans have been exposed to and/or internalized this trend. Overemphasis on race/ethnicity can obscure other contextual factors.

What factors are responsible for the "color obsession" among professionals who overemphasize race? One contributing factor is that researchers and practitioners have the inclination to consider race and ethnicity as etiological factors without controlling for crucial confounding variables such as socioeconomic status (McLoyd, 1998).[3] In the anecdote cited earlier from Grier and Cobbs (1968) about an African American mother with "lack of parenting skills," for instance, it can be argued that researchers and clinicians misattributed lack of parenting skills to her racial background. However, clinicians should have considered the possibility that her non-standard parenting practices might instead have been attributable to a wide variety of factors, such as lower socioeconomic status, chronic exposure to stress, inadequate resources, or a psychological disorder. Since such factors often correlate with race/ethnicity, past research and practice on race/ethnicity may be grossly confounded with these variables.

Also there has been a notable tendency for professionals to selectively focus on the problem characteristics of children and families of color; these groups have historically been studied and treated in the context of highlighting their deficiencies (Ogbu, 1999). Consequently, subsets within these populations (e.g., delinquent "urban" African American youths, excluding successful African American youths) have been heavily investigated. Yet, as Ogbu suggests, the characteristics of these selective samples are erroneously generalized to the entire ethnic/racial group. As a consequence, for example, the psychosocial properties of delinquent urban African American youths would be generalized to all African American youths, despite the fact that a large majority of them may not have the problem in question—delinquency—and thus may not share such properties. This trend of focusing solely on problem characteristics is not found in the research literature on European Americans. For example, such heinous criminal acts as serial murders and indiscriminant school shootings are almost exclusively committed by European Americans. However, no researchers or practitioners would suggest that these crimes show something inherently wrong with European American children or their families, let alone generalize such tendencies to the entire European American population.

In addition to the risk of this selective overgeneralization, this trend poses a more serious concern: With the process of selective sampling, "healthy" and normative children and families of color, who do not have these problems, are systematically excluded from consideration. As a result, we have yet to isolate the factors that *facilitate* success among children and families of color, as our focus has been on isolating the factors that inhibit success. Adequately addressing the range of within-group variances, rather than between-group variations, may hence be the key to understanding the lives of a specific population. Such information would facilitate practitioners' efforts to maximize the quality of life for these populations.

---

[3]However, it should be noted that, in the authors' view, socioeconomic status need not be controlled if the aim of a given study were to describe and understand "typical" families or children in each racial group, rather than to simply highlight group differences.

The "Color-Blind" Approach

We have so far discussed how color obsession may lead to inadequate understanding of the psychosocial properties of children and families of color. Would the opposite stance, color blindness, be the solution? Consider the following examples:

> When a clinical social worker from Massachusetts was asked about her philosophy on dealing with clients of color, she responded: "When dealing with minority consumers, I try to see beyond their nationality. I think I treat them as individuals who have the same concerns and issues as any other consumer would, regardless of their skin color."

> A teacher commented on her experience in an inner-city public school with predominantly Dominican and Cambodian students in Rhode Island: "I don't focus on skin color when I look at my students; I see human beings and I don't treat them based on the color of their skin or the shape of their eyes."

These examples illustrate the "color-blind" approach, which appeals to many perhaps because it is consistent with the philosophy that all people are equal and should therefore be treated accordingly. Unfortunately, this seemingly innocent and well-intended view can lead to adverse consequences when educators and practitioners fail to recognize that people and families of color often have specific needs that are not necessarily compatible with the theories and practices generated largely from European American middle-class standards, as will be discussed in later sections.

The need to openly address cultural contexts rather than minimize them is apparent in all phases of practice—from measurement and diagnosis to treatment and outcome evaluations. Even professionals who advocate cultural relativity have underestimated the importance of cultural sensitivity; for instance they administer surveys or diagnostic measures designed for use with middle-class European American individuals without addressing limitations to validity for diverse populations, (e.g., Akiba & Klug, 1999). This is a typical mistake: researchers and clinicians often forget that such instruments may not be valid across cultures, even with perfect semantic translations, because the questions and issues addressed may (1) not carry the same definitions in the minds of non-European Americans and (2) inadequately encompass the issues relevant to a specific population on a given dimension. One must thus first identify what questions and issues are prevalent in a particular population, instead of assuming their universality. Exploratory studies, focus group sessions, ethnographic research, and the inclusion of researchers, clinicians, and informants of color may afford the advantage of an "insiders' view" of the group such that contextual material is better understood—and biases that either overemphasize or minimize race and ethnicity are reduced.

Effective Practice with Children of Color through Understanding Unique Cultural Contexts

Children and families from all backgrounds in North America experience similar challenges and stresses associated with growing up and living in this country. For example, around the age of five years children must adjust to attending school daily, spending an extended amount of time away from their primary caretakers in a structured environment where social and academic learning takes place. Regardless of their backgrounds, children go through puberty, many proceed to gain employment, and they may form a marriage-type arrangement and raise children, as Duvall's (1988) theory of family development would suggest—though not necessarily in that order. However, in addition to these sequences of events shared by children and families of all backgrounds, children and families of color face the added tasks of reconciling and navigating their ways through the mainstream culture, despite their non-normative backgrounds.

For example, children of color may have limited academic success if the context of their learning conflicts with their opportunities for success (see Figures 7.1 and 7.2). Factors that mediate child well-being include: cultural mismatch, cultural devaluation, exclusion experiences, self-defensive reactions, identity development, and support structures such as family, religion, and community. The most effective practitioners account for these factors, which are addressed in the sections that follow.

Cultural Mismatch

It is apparent that cultural differences in values, attitudes, and practices must be considered in understanding and working with children of color and their families, as such differences can profoundly impact children's opportunities for success—regardless of how success is defined. However, we challenge the notion commonly held by educators and psychological care providers that problems (e.g., low levels of academic aspiration, higher instances of psychological and behavioral disorders) among people of color stem largely from *cultural value deficits,* which reflects an assumption that children and families of color do not share the mainstream American values placed on vocational success, individualism, and independence (e.g., Kiselica, Changizi, Cureton, & Gridley, 1995). Quite the contrary—it has been widely acknowledged that, when controlled for various factors such as parental education levels and socioeconomic status, children of color who are recent immigrants to the United States appear to value vocational success and independence more than do their more "Americanized" counterparts (e.g., Garcia Coll et al., in press; Suarez-Orozco & Suarez-Orozco, 1999).

Instead, following Thomas and Chess's (1977) model, we propose to focus on the *match* between characteristics of children and families and characteristics that are demanded in their environment. For example, some religions strongly emphasize the notion of fatalism. A parent, based on her firm adherence to this belief, may therefore desire *not* to "interfere" with the developmental pathways taken by her child. For example, despite her wish for her child to grow up "successful," she may actively avoid intervening when the child engages in unproductive activities, such as joining a gang (Smith-Hefner, 1999). This belief and subsequent action (or her "parenting ethnotheory") may perfectly match the demands in cultural systems where the belief in fatalism is expected and hence accommodated. Unfortunately, however, this ethnotheory may not match the demands of the culture in which the family lives—the United States—where parents are expected to assert proactive control over their children's conduct. This mismatch can result in detrimental developmental outcomes in the child. In short, we propose that this *mismatch,* rather than *cultural value deficits,* may account for the challenges associated with the developmental processes among children and families of color.

Cultural Devaluation and Discontinuity.   When the characteristics prevalent in communities of color do not match those in the mainstream culture, children and families of color may perceive their own cultural backgrounds (e.g., people, customs, religion, languages, etc.) to be less desirable than those of the European American mainstream. They may feel that they are destined to maintain their less-than-optimal social position, simply because the characteristics common in their communities are considered inadequate—or unacknowledged altogether—in the larger society. Although such perceptions may or may not be phenomenologically warranted, they nevertheless contribute to disillusionment among children as well as their caretakers (see also Hardy & Laszloffy, 1999). It is therefore plausible that children and families who are unaware of this devaluation, such as recent immigrants, may perform relatively well, since they are less discouraged by the prospect of not being able to gain social, academic, and economic power. Professionals need to keep in mind that this disillusionment, rather than inadequate values, may be responsible for less-than-optimal outcomes among some children of color.

These situations may also cause children of color to experience "discontinuity"— the awareness of discrepancy in standards and demands (e.g., value priorities, expectations, communication styles, etc.) among various ecological systems within their lives, such as home, schools, neighborhoods, and beyond. Children of color may also find it demanding, both affectively and cognitively, to have to navigate their ways through greatly incompatible contexts and act appropriately across these situations (Cooper, 1999; Nieto, 2000). Counselors and psychologists should perhaps consider the benefits of bridging among a multitude of contexts within which a child of color lives (e.g., demonstrating how pursuing a particular academic goal can actually help a child of color contribute to her own family and community in the long run without compromising her strong sense of cultural membership), rather than on forcing her into prioritizing them as adults often do (e.g., isolating a child from neighborhood peers from the housing projects and placing her in an unfamiliar after-school program in another neighborhood). In short, following Bronfenbrenner's (1979) and Garcia Coll's (1996) schemes, an individual child's psychosocial needs may be most effectively addressed when educators and counselors view them within a larger framework of contexts in which this child exists rather than isolating such factors.

The Experience of Exclusion

Kayoko, an Asian American female adolescent, and her family enjoy dining out with their friends. Recently, Kayoko has noticed a disturbing trend: whenever her family is with her friend, Ramien—who is African American—and his family, they are seated in the back of a restaurant, near the bathroom, even if there appear to be plenty of empty tables. This never happens to Kayoko's family when they are with their non-African American friends or even when they are by themselves. When Kayoko mentions this to Ramien, he replies, "Hello, welcome to America. We've been dealing with this kind of treatment all our lives." This anecdote illustrates how activities as mundane as eating out can have racial implications and cause stress to the members of some groups. It also shows that people of color from various backgrounds may experience exclusion to different degrees.

Children and families of color routinely face negative stereotypes (unfavorable beliefs based solely on group membership), prejudice (typically negative attitudes toward a group and its members), and discrimination (behavior, typically negative, toward individuals due to their perceived membership in particular groups). Some scholars refer to these adverse experiences inclusively as "exclusion" (Garcia Coll & Garrido, 2000). Although this exclusion may be actual, perceived, or anticipated, it does impact people's lives. Despite legislative and other efforts to outlaw discrimination based on race, ethnicity, or national origin, as manifest in differential access to educational, health, and economic resources, children and families of color are still subject to various forms of exclusion. Social mechanisms of exclusion may be differentiated in terms of both (1) their blatancy, ranging from most blatant to subtle and perhaps unintended, and (2) their agents, varying from individuals to larger institutions. Physical or verbal attacks against people of color are blatant forms of individual exclusion, and the example of restaurant seating practices involving African Americans would also be blatant. By contrast, Word, Zanna, and Cooper (1974) describe a subtler form of exclusion. They studied the difference in European Americans' behavior when they are dealing with other European Americans and with African Americans. They experimentally demonstrated that European American individuals tend to keep greater physical distance, make more speech errors, and keep the interactions short when dealing with African American individuals than when they were interacting with other European American individuals. This consistently occurred no matter how courteous they were acting otherwise toward African Americans.

In the experiment just described, no matter what their intentions may have been, European American individuals treated African Americans quite differently than they did European Americans, leaving the African Americans perhaps feeling excluded. These subtler forms of exclusion may also include, for instance, teachers knowingly or unknowingly setting lower standards and expectations for students of color than those set for their European American counterparts (Ferguson, 1998) or practitioners not expecting children of color to have conditions that are typically seen among middle-class European American children, such as eating disorders (Petersons, Rojhani, Steinhaus, & Larkin, 2000).

Examples of institutional exclusion include people of color being systematically denied employment, housing, or financial benefits primarily based on their actual or presumed cultural backgrounds, or the police systematically and selectively targeting people of color as suspects (i.e., racial profiling). Subtler forms of institutional exclusion may include such phenomena as the media systematically compromising the visibility of people of color or portraying them in stereotypic and demeaning fashion. It has been shown that even these subtle forms of exclusion have dramatic adverse consequences on people of color, such as lower-than-justifiable academic performance, or feelings of detachment and institutional disengagement (Word, Zanna, & Cooper, 1974). All in all, these subtle forms of exclusion perpetuate the second-class citizen status that people and families of color are perceived to hold. Given the extent of the adversities they face, it is useful to analyze how people, families, and communities of color react to these experiences of exclusion.

Self-Defensive Reactions to Mismatch, Devaluation, and Exclusion

In this section, we will review some recent findings on the reactions to exclusion that serve ego-protective functions and promote psychosocial well-being among people of color.[4] It is widely acknowledged in the psychological community that people of color, despite the exclusion and social stigmas they may face, appear to have reasonable or even higher-than-expected self- and group-esteem (Crocker et al., 1991). Recent research on interethnic social attribution shows that this counterintuitive phenomenon results from various strategies people and families of color have developed in reaction to their stigmatized status in this society. One of the possible ego-protective measures occurs when people of color eagerly attribute all negative experiences to bias, hence wholly avoiding personal accountability for adverse events in their lives—even though they may have been personally responsible for at least some of these adverse results (Crocker & Major, 1994).

Consider an African American male being rejected for a part in a school performance or a Latino elementary student receiving unfavorable feedback from her teacher. Since most people in power outside of their communities (i.e., teachers and administrators) tend to be European Americans, the following two types of attribution are plausible. First, it is possible that these negative results actually reflect these individuals' limited qualifications and achievements, as defined according to the standards of the drama coach or the teacher. However, a second explanation is that considering the long history of exclusion collectively faced by people of color in the United States, these unfavorable outcomes could be interpreted to reflect racial bias, which motivates European Americans to act negatively toward People of Color and perhaps inaccurately perceives People of Color to be less intellectually capable than their European American counterparts. These two potential explanations generate a situation of attributional ambiguity, whereby people of color decide for themselves which of the two potential causes represents the true reason for the undesirable outcomes.[5]

Crocker and her colleagues (1989, 1991, 1994) suggest that People of Color are indeed more likely to experience exclusion than their non-stigmatized European American counterparts, and attribution of negative results to bias is "not only plausible, it is often accurate" (1994, p. 291). Since this attribution guards People of Color from having to face the possibility that they themselves may have contributed to the negative outcomes, it serves a powerful ego-protective function, which may explain the healthy self-esteem among People of Color (also see Weiner, 1986). In the same vein, Akiba (2000) found that anticipation of negative outcomes in interethnic social transactions can function as a psychological *buffer,* preparing people of color for potentially unpleasant social transactions

---

[4]Aside from these recent works on ego-protective factors, interested readers are encouraged to explore Allport's (1954) book, which lists a wide variety of characteristics people of color are theorized to develop as a result of exclusion.

[5]It is important to stress that people of color are chronically exposed to such ambiguities, while this type of ambiguity does not normally exist for most European-American individuals. Nevertheless, it is possible for European-Americans to have similar experiences based on such dimensions as gender, sexual-orientation, physical conditions, and socioeconomic status.

with European Americans. He also demonstrated experimentally that positive outcomes, just like negative ones, may be distrusted. Specifically, in dealing with European Americans, African American female students attributed both negative and positive interethnic outcomes to bias, which implies that the skeptical attribution in question may be *self-protective* (i.e., discounting both negative and positive outcomes) but not self-enhancing (i.e., discounting negative but taking credit for positive outcomes) in this population, as these students did not take credit for what may have been a deserved success.

Similarly, Johnson (2001) suggests that African American parents and other elders transmit what she calls *racial coping skills* to help African American children survive the experiences of exclusion. She demonstrates that both intended and unintended expression of mistrust toward European Americans is abundantly present in mundane intergenerational dialogues between adults and children, parenting practices, child-rearing behaviors, and other interactions (also Hughes & Chen, 1997). Not surprisingly, the underlying skepticism toward the mainstream culture is reflected in statements made by children as young as in first grade (Akiba, Garcia Coll, & Magnuson, 2001). Johnson believes that these dialogues serve as proactive ego-defensive measures for children of color, preparing them for the adversities they are likely to face because of their race/ethnicity. This anticipation of possible negative treatment by European Americans has been called *healthy cultural paranoia* or *cultural mistrust* (Grier & Cobbs, 1968, p. 161; Thompson, Neville, Weathers, Poston, & Atkinson, 1990).[6] This shared knowledge of racial coping skills can be utilized by children in dealing with actual or perceived exclusion, which, in turn, further reinforces the importance of sharing these skills among African Americans, for example. In general, then, it can be reasonably concluded that adjectives such as "distrustful" and "skeptical" describe the reactions of People of Color when dealing with European Americans. However, equally important with defenses against exclusion are social supports and systems that serve to facilitate a child's success in the face of exclusion, such as family involvement, community supports, and religion.

Sources of Support and Coping

Family Involvement.   One of the main predictors of child academic success and well-being is positive family involvement, but school counselors and school psychologists frequently fail to involve families of children of color in their intervention efforts (Kiselica et al., 1995). Optimal interventions facilitate parental involvement in the schools by explaining how the school environment works in the United States, detailing the expectations of teachers, informing school personnel of cultural conflicts, and working to reduce bias in educational policies and systems. A school counselor or school psychologist best serves children of color by acting as a liaison between the school and the family.

Ways of increasing parental involvement that have been found effective include outreach parent training programs, community meetings, and, best of all, personalized telephone calls and discussions (Kiselica et al., 1995). Of course, every cultural group has

---

[6]It is important to reiterate that, as suggested earlier, such skepticism is often accurate; therefore, the use of the term "paranoia" in the current context does not imply psychopathology.

unique familial characteristics that need to be considered when working with children of color in the schools. For example, our own research (Garcia Coll et al., 2002) shows that average Cambodian American parents do not get actively involved with their children's education, based on the notion of "parental involvement" as it is usually defined in North America. Despite what some may speculate, this trend is not because these parents do not value academic and vocational "success" among their children.[7] Instead, their hesitation appears to be related to the belief common in the Cambodian and Khmer Buddhist communities that teachers are the absolute authority figures as far as children's academic pursuits are concerned, and Cambodian American parents, on average, do not believe that they have a role in facilitating such pursuits (Smith-Hefner, 1999). For parents to be involved in a child's education may even be considered to signal disrespect toward the child's teachers. This particular belief, which appears to be deeply ingrained in the Cambodian American culture, may be perfectly adaptive in a society in which all educational systems operate under such assumptions. Nevertheless, in the United States, the educational systems consider active parental involvement (e.g., supervision of homework, keeping close contact with teachers) to be essential to a child's academic and vocational pursuits, and lack of parental involvement is often linked to less-than-optimal academic and behavioral outcomes (Kiselica et al., 1995). Cambodian American parents, as we have found in our research, might be better able to help their children if they were informed that teachers in this country do not consider themselves solely responsible for the children's education, and that teachers in fact expect and value active participation by parents in facilitating children's academic efforts. Adapting interventions with the family based on the family's needs and structures is key to successful work with children of color. Interventions should align with the way that the family perceives the challenges or opportunities that the intervention is meant to address. Learning the nuances of each racial-cultural group requires additional effort, but without such understanding, interventions may be unproductive.

When working with families, it is also important to consider the other contextual factors that influence their attitudes and values concerning education and child development (Figure 7.2). For example, when working with families that have recently immigrated, it is important to assess their previous experience with education, the circumstances surrounding the immigration, and the impact of immigration on the family and on each individual family member (see Chapter 13). Moreover, it is important to remember that different members of the family will have different and unique reactions to the immigration experience—particularly across generations. In most cases, loss of community resources and support networks cause some emotional distress within the family, particularly if the family immigrated alone or if their relative socioeconomic power and/or social position changed notably with their immigration.

The efforts of working with families may be facilitated by—or sometimes require—the use of interpreters and translators as school personnel encounter situations where the

---

[7]It should be noted that the definition of "success" may vary across cultures, although our research appears to indicate that, on average, economic independence, academic achievement, and good citizenship seem to be valued across various communities within the U.S. For example, in our study (Garcia Coll et al., 2002), it was found that 88 percent of Cambodian American, 98 percent of Dominican American, and 85 percent of Portuguese American parents expressed their desire to have their children complete college.

primary or the preferred language of the family is other than English. In fact, providing written materials already translated into a language and/or cultural contexts with which a family is comfortable accomplishes more than merely improving the linguistic communications between the school and parents. Doing so serves the critically important function of demonstrating to the parents that the school professional values and acknowledges the presence of the student and is willing to meet the educational needs of this student. As with all mental health interventions, there is no substitute for the genuine commitment and interest of the professional, and families can quickly discern whether that commitment and interest are present. Even when solutions to dilemmas are not immediately found, families will be more willing to work with professionals who have demonstrated interest in them and in the well-being of the student.

Community Resources.   Mental health practitioners working with children too often ignore community resources that may be available to facilitate treatment or enhance academic success. Service organizations, universities, social groups, public libraries, professional associations, youth clubs, and city/county offices can often provide sources of aid to individual children or to large groups of children if they are aware of need. Public and private schools also provide some resources that can greatly benefit practitioners working with children.

However, practitioners working in the schools tend to rely solely on school resources (often meager) and to neglect community resources that might be available. School counselors and psychologists too often consider that they have to "do it all on their own," with minimal resources to support their work. They may feel that the community does not support the school, and it is true that many communities will not support a school if that school provides no visible benefits back to the community or if the school is perceived as perpetuating institutionalized oppression. Practitioners in the schools should therefore work to make the school a truly integral part of a community, hosting community functions and providing a positive place for community members to receive benefits, organize, socialize, etc.

For example, to combat community apathy towards the school, a school counselor in an inner city area facilitated a community clean-up project organized by two local agencies. Children from all grades helped in the project, and teachers donated time to lead small group initiatives to maintain conditions following the clean-up. The school's efforts were mentioned in the local press, and a local businesswoman who read the article provided a small donation for new books at the school library.

In another instance, a rural school began a series of community presentations on Native American culture, in conjunction with several aspects of the curriculum, and they saw a dramatic increase in the number of parents volunteering to work with the children during school hours, which allowed teachers the time to add music and art classes. A tribal college several hours away invited the children on an expenses-paid field trip to put on one of their productions on the campus and to learn about opportunities for higher education.

Inclusion of these community groups brings about another important benefit. Collaborations between schools and communities may create greater continuity in various contexts within which children and families of color live, and this sense of continuity has been shown to contribute to healthy development in these individuals (Cooper, 1999), as discussed earlier in this chapter. In sum, apathy toward education can be reduced, volunteers can be recruited, and efforts to solicit additional funding from local businesses may be more successful when relevance of the school to the community is highly visible.

Religion and Spirituality.   In addition to family socialization and community resources that can buffer children of color against anticipated and inevitable experiences of exclusion, social scientists have found that participation in religious and spiritual organizations often provides opportunities for people of color to bond, to organize political and civic activities within their communities, and to promote cultural coping skills (Gibbs, 1989). African American churches have served as significant social institutions in their communities since the days of slavery (Williams, 1996). A wide variety of communities of color in the United States have historically developed around churches and temples (Smith-Hefner, 1999; Suarez-Orozco & Suarez-Orozco, 1999), and religious organizations have been vital, if not primary, sources of support for non-African American people of color as well (Min, 1996). Aside from opportunities for mutual support, several notable benefits have been associated with religious involvement in promoting mental health among people of color. First, religion may influence a person's affect, cognition, and behavior, and such influence can be positive for the individuals as well as for larger communities (Gilkes, 1990). From a psychological view, the significance of spirituality may rest on the hope it provides for people to momentarily escape the hardships experienced in their lives by focusing on an "authority figure" beyond those they encounter daily. Finally, Gilkes also suggests that religious settings allow attendees to freely express their emotions, which may give people of color the opportunity for catharsis, to "let the guard down" and release their frustration and stress.[8] Hence spirituality may compensate for the chronic sense of uncertainty and helplessness generated by the skepticism and distrust experienced by people of color, discussed earlier in this chapter (also see Smith-Hefner). Together with family and community support, religion and spirituality can protect children of color against negative experiences and enhance their developmental experiences.

Identity and Cultural Inversion

Tajfel's (1978) seminal work on affective consequences of identity focused on individuals drawing self-esteem from the status of the group to which they belong. Ogbu (1994) introduced the concept of *cultural inversion* to refer to the tendency among members of subordinate groups to resist characteristics that are valued by their oppressors. In particular, this resistance appears to be most pervasive in areas traditionally considered "European American privileges," such as high academic and career performance and status. The psychological advantage of this process is intuitively clear: By devaluing and "disidentifying" with what is valued by the mainstream, people of color are able to define their own values and priorities so as to justify their positions in the society—positions which may appear less than optimal from the mainstream standards (Steele, 1990). Cross (1995) discusses a similar notion, which he calls the "oppositional identity," among Af-

---

[8]We do not claim that these functions of religion are unique to people of color. Rather, our hope here is to illustrate how feelings of exclusion may be comforted in these settings.

rican American youths. Although negative academic and career outcomes from cultural inversion have been documented (Cook & Ludwig, 1997), Cross states that a subtype of oppositional identity called *defensive oppositional identity* is useful in fostering healthy psychosocial development among African American individuals by providing such advantages as heightened sense of ingroup cohesion and unity (also Cooper, 1999).[9] The issues of identity, therefore, seem to be of great relevance to understanding the lives of children of color.

Identity formation has been theorized to be one of the most consequential processes in a person's development, as it has been known to affect various dimensions of psychosocial characteristics, including how one acts, feels, and thinks (e.g., Rosenthal, 1987). During middle childhood, children begin to construct their own sense of personal (e.g., personality) characteristics and social (e.g., race/ethnicity) identities; the process involving the latter is typically much more complex for people of color because of what they perceive as a stigmatized status from which they cannot escape (Waters, 1996). Children of color must reconcile discrepancies in value priorities across "multiple worlds" (Cooper, 1999). Specifically, Waters (1996) proposes that the ethnic identity of a European American merely serves symbolic functions: It is typically inconsequential to identify oneself as a British American, Irish American, or Mediterranean American because, despite any subidentification, the individual is still European American, unlikely to face systematic exclusion. According to Waters, optional identification normally represents a pleasant opportunity for European Americans to celebrate their heritage without fearing negative consequences. By contrast, identification as a person of color (e.g., African American or Chinese American) is not optional since these identity labels have been historically and sociopolitically imposed by the mainstream society, often for the purpose of justifying exclusion (e.g., African Americans being forced into slavery; Chinese laborers being denied immigration to the United States; Japanese Americans being placed in internment areas during the second World War).

Although children of color around five years of age or younger have been shown to be aware of their own race and ethnicity (Aboud, 1987), most of the previous research on this topic is on populations older than adolescents, partly because an abstract notion like identity is difficult to study among young populations, who are not as articulate or capable of abstract thinking as their older counterparts. Thus research on young children has involved mostly concrete tasks such as racial preference (e.g., having children choose dolls that they like or dolls that do or do not look like them), which may or may not reflect their identities. Also most research on identity addresses ethnic identity in the absence of other dimensions, following the dilemma model (e.g., "Are you Black or are you White?"). In addition, the Eriksonian (1968) theories of identity imply that achieving objectively *appropriate* ethnic identity prompts race/ethnicity to become a fixed presence, dictating a child's construction of self. Nevertheless, practitioners should consider that even if an African American child "correctly" and rather strongly identifies with his or her own race, being

---

[9]To test these theories, we are currently undertaking a study linking the quality and the strength of identity, attitudes and values concerning education and occupational attainment, and actual scholastic outcomes among children of color.

African American may still represents one segment of the child's identity: he may instead define himself primarily as a boy, a figure skater, and a Christian. Also the weight of certain identity dimensions may be heightened in specific circumstances. For example, among a group of boy figure skaters, his identity as *African American* may temporarily become salient to the child if his race sets him apart from the other boy skaters, who are mostly European Americans.

It is thus vital to note that the relative salience (or fluidity) of identity dimensions may vary across *situations* and across *time,* being dependent on a child's situation at a given moment (e.g., Rumbaut, 2001). Gender has been identified as the dominant dimension of identity in various studies involving Europeans and White North Americans (Martin & Halverson, 1987); the relative importance of gender and race/ethnicity in children of color has not received similar attention. But it is important to recognize that "ethnic identity" should be considered within a complement of characteristics children possess. To address these issues, we have devised a method of exploring the identity of children in middle childhood, ranging in age from 6 to 12 as described below.[10,11]

This method consists of a scenario involving a peer interaction. An interviewer conducted the following role play with the child:[12]

> "Let's play a pretend game. Pretend that we are making a phone call. When I say 'ring, ring,' pick up the phone, okay? Pretend that we can't see each other, we've never met before, and we don't know each other. Let's begin." [interviewer turns around]
>
> *Interviewer:*   "Ring, ring." [Child answers the phone]
>   "Hi, my name is [experimenter's name]. What's yours?"
> *Child:*   [Child says his/her name].
> *Interviewer:*   "Hi, [child's name]. I just moved here and I don't know anybody, and I want you to be my friend. Can you tell me a little about yourself, so I can get to know you?"
> *Child:*   [proceeds to telling the interviewer about him- or herself]

Most elementary school children should be able to participate in this dialogue, as it puts the abstract notion of *self* into a concrete context: describing oneself to another person in the everyday situation of a telephone call. Over 800 children were interviewed. The response of a European American girl in the second grade was typical of those of European American children: "I am a girl, and I have long hair. I am a little short. I like playing." European Americans tended to focus on gender, activities, and physical descriptions that are not specific to a particular racial/ethnic group. In fact, European American children virtually

---

[10]We collaborated with Diane Ruble (NYU) and her associates in developing this measure.

[11]Specific statistical analyses on these results are beyond the scope of this chapter and will therefore not be discussed here. However, interested readers should contact the first author for further information.

[12]The interviewers and the children were matched for race and ethnicity.

never cited characteristics associated with their race, ethnicity, or language, suggesting that these children perhaps take such dimensions for granted. Children of color, by contrast, gave somewhat different answers. An African American second grade boy of Nigerian descent said, "I'm Black, I am a boy, and I am good." Similarly, a Hmong girl in the third grade stated, "I'm a girl, and I have a big sister. I'm Hmong and I like Teletubbies" [name of a TV show/characters].

This pattern is consistent with various professionals' supposition that ethnic identity is more salient to children of color than to their European American counterparts in early or middle childhood, although it should be noted that ethnic identity does not appear to be salient enough to replace universal sources of identity such as gender or activity preferences altogether. Younger children were as likely to mention race/ethnicity-related words as were older children, further demonstrating the relevance of these dimensions in the lives of even the youngest children of color (Akiba, Garcia Coll, & Magnuson, 2001). To summarize, these children's responses suggest the multifaceted nature of their construction of self, and race and ethnicity seem to be quite relevant at early ages.

How these identity issues relate to the psychosocial characteristics of these children remains to be fully understood, particularly for non-African American children of color. However, the preliminary analyses of our ongoing study (Akiba, DiMartino, & Rodriguez, 2001) reveal some notable tendencies. Among the 301 Dominican American and Cambodian American elementary school children we interviewed, those with strong "minority" identity (e.g., Dominican, Latino, Spanish, Cambodian, Asian, etc.) tended to have lower overall school engagement scores: attitudinal and behavioral tendencies toward various aspects of schooling, such as academics, peer and teacher relations, and tardiness. Particularly intriguing is the tendency of Dominican American children with strong "minority" identity, older ones in particular, to score low on the academic engagement dimension (e.g., "How important is it to you that you get good grades?") and the attitudes concerning teachers dimension (e.g., "How important is it to you that your teacher likes you?"). Although these results seem to confirm Cross's (1995) and others' suppositions based on African Americans (i.e., the oppositional identity), further explorations are necessary to make sense of these findings. For example, there was an unexpected yet statistically reliable tendency for Cambodian American children with strong "minority" identity to score *high* on the conduct dimension (e.g., "How important is it to you that you don't miss school?"), despite their earlier-mentioned trend for *lower* overall school engagement scores. This unexpected result reminds us of the complex role of culture in understanding children's development, as well as the culturally relative nature of its effects on the developmental outcomes among children. Still it is evident that identity as persons of color predicts various aspects of school engagement, though such predictions may differ per cultural background.

Conclusion

This chapter has illustrated that understanding the development of children and families of color requires that scholars and practitioners consider various layers of elements as these elements interact with each other and with the characteristics of the children themselves. In addition to the developmental tasks commonly faced by all children and families in the United States, children and families of color face the added challenge of dealing with cultural devaluation and exclusion. The integrative model by Garcia Coll and her associates (1996) helps one conceptualize the interactive relationship among a wide variety of forces that influence an individual's life and the potential impact of these forces on his or her development. Being culturally sensitive in educational and psychological practice does not mean merely communicating in Spanish with Spanish-speaking consumers; rather it entails understanding the dynamics of the forces within the consumers' lives. Also, as illustrated, families and communities often assume central roles in preparing children of color for the adversities they may inevitably face because of their oppressed status. Families and other institutions function—directly and indirectly—to help children effectively navigate their ways through the multiple worlds. Reflecting such multiplicity, children appear to incorporate a wide variety of dimensions in establishing the sense of self. In addition, the prevalence of "minority" identity in children appears to predict some aspects of their psychosocial characteristics, such as school engagement.

Acknowledging and further investigating these forces designed to promote healthy development of people of color, rather than focusing on the development of negative characteristics among them, will help professionals establish theories of normative development for this population. These theories will be crucial if people of color are to identify proactive measures for attaining desired developmental outcomes. Such normative theories may also allow them to have greater control over the destiny of their own families and communities.

References

Aboud, F. E. (1987). The development of ethnic self-identification and attitudes. In J. S. Phinney & M. J. Rotheram (Eds.), *Children's ethnic socialization* (pp. 32–55). Newbury Park, CA: Sage.

Akiba, D., & Miller, F. (2001). *The expression of racial insensitivity in the presence of African Americans: When racist humor isn't funny.* Manuscript submitted for publication.

Akiba, D. (2000). *Mistrust toward teachers: Implications for ethnic difference in affect, cognition and behavior in the classroom.* Unpublished doctoral dissertation, Brown University.

Akiba, D., Garcia Coll, C. T., & Magnuson, K. (2001). *Children of color and children from immigrant families: The development of social identities, school engagement, and interethnic social attribution.* Manuscript submitted for publication.

Akiba, D., & Klug, W. (1999). The different and the same: Reexamining East and West in a cross-cultural analysis of values. *Social Behavior and Personality, 27,* 467–473.

Alarcon, O. (April, 1999). The construction of race among urban Puerto Rican youths. A poster presented at the biennial meeting of Society for Research in Child Development, April 15–18, Albuquerque, NM.

Allport, G. W. (1954). *The nature of prejudice.* Reading, MA: Addison Wesley.

Bain, S. K., & Pelletier, K. A. (1999). Social and behavioral differences among African American preschool sample. *Psychology in the Schools, 36,* 249–259.

Barbain, O. A., & Soler, R. E. (1993). Behavioral, emotional, and academic adjustment in a national probability sample of African American children: Effects of age, gender and family structure. *Journal of Black Psychology, 19,* 423–446.

Bernstein, B. (1960). Language and social class. *British Journal of Sociology, 11,* 271–276.

Bronfenbrenner, U. (1979). *The ecology of human development: Experiments by nature and design.* Cambridge, MA: Harvard University Press.

Cook, P. J., & Ludwig, J. (1997). Weighing the burden of "acting white": Are there race differences in attitudes toward education? *Journal of Policy Analysis and Management, 16,* 656–678.

Cooper, C. (1999). Multiple selves, multiple worlds: Cultural perspectives on individuality and connectedness in adolescent development. In A. S. Masten (Ed.), *Cultural processes in child development. The Minnesota Symposia on Child Psychology, 29,* 25–57. Mahwah, NJ: Lawrence Erlbaum Assoc.

Crocker, J., & Major, B. (1989). Social stigma and self-esteem: The self-protective properties of stigma. *Psychological Review, 96,* 608–630.

Crocker, J., & Major, B. (1994). Reactions to stigma: The moderating role of justifications. *The Psychology of Prejudice: The Ontario Symposium, 7,* 289–314.

Crocker, J., Voelkl, K., Testa, M., & Major, B. (1991). Social stigma: The affective consequences of attributional ambiguity. *Journal of Personality and Social Psychology, 60,* 218–228.

Cross, W. E. (1995). Oppositional identity and African American youth: Issues and prospects. In W. D. Hawley & A. W. Jackson (Eds.), *Toward a common destiny: Improving race and ethnicity in America* (pp. 185–204). San Francisco, CA: Jossey-Bass.

D'Andrea, M., & Daniels, J. (2001). Respectful counseling: An integrative multidimensional model for counselors. In D. B. Pope & H. L. K. Coleman (Eds.), *The intersection of race, class, and gender in multicultural counseling* (pp. 417–466). Thousand Oaks, CA: Sage.

Denenberg, V. H. (1970). *Education of the infant and young children.* NY: Academic.

Duvall, E. M. (1988). Family development's first forty years. *Family Relations, 37,* 127–134.

Erikson, E. H. (1968). *Identity: Youth and crisis.* New York: Norton.

Ferguson, R. F. (1998). Teachers' perceptions and expectations and the Black-White test score gap. In C. Jenks and M. Phillips (Eds.), *The Black-White test score gap.* (pp. 273–317). Washington, DC: Brookings Insitute Press.

Fuligni, A. J., Burton, L., Marshall, S., Perez-Febles, A., Yarrington, J., Kirsh, L., & DeVries, C. (1999). Attitudes toward family obligations among American adolescents with Asian, Latin American, and European backgrounds. *Child Development, 70,* 1030–1044.

Garcia Coll, C. T., Akiba, D., Palacios, N., Bailey, B., Chin, C., & DiMartino, L. D. (in press). Parental involvement in children's education: Lessons from three immigrant groups. *Parenting: Science and Practice.*

Garcia Coll, C. T., & Garrido, M. (2000). Minorities in the United States: Sociocultural context for mental health and developmental psychopathology. In A. J. Sameroff, M. Lewis, & S. M. Miller (Eds.), *Handbook of Developmental Psychopathology* (pp. 177–195). New York: Kluwer-Plenum.

Garcia Coll, C. T., Lamberty, G., Jenkins, R., McAdoo, H. P., Crnic, K., Wasik, B. H., & Vazquez, H.

(1996). An integrative model for the study of developmental competencies in minority children. *Child Development, 67,* 1891–1914.

Garcia Coll, C. T., & Thorne, B. (in press). Beyond categories. In C. Cooper (Ed.), *America's new diversity and successful pathways through childhood: How do families, schools and communities matter?*

Gibbs, J. T. (1989). Black American adolescents. In J. T. Gibbs & L. N. Huang (Eds.), *Children of color: Psychological interventions with minority youth* (pp. 179–223). San Francisco, CA: Jossey-Bass.

Gibbs, J. T., & Huang, L. N. (1989). A conceptual framework for assessing and treating minority youth. In J. T. Gibbs & L. N. Huang (Eds.), *Children of color: Psychological interventions with minority youth* (pp. 1–29). San Francisco, CA: Jossey-Bass.

Gilkes, C. T. (1990). "Liberated to work like dogs!": Labeling Black women and their work. In H. Y. Grossman & N. L. Chester (Eds.), *The experience and meaning of work in women's lives* (pp. 165–188). Hillsdale, NJ: Lawrence Erlbaum Assoc.

Graham, S. (1992). "Most of the subjects were white and middle-class." Trends in published research on African Americans in selected APA journals, 1979–1989. *American Psychologist, 47,* 629–639.

Grier, W. H., & Cobbs, P. M. (1968). *Black rage.* New York: Basic Books.

Hardy, K. V., & Laszloffy, T. A. (1999). The development of children and families of color: A supplemental framework. In W. C. Nichols & M. A. Pace-Nichols (Eds.), *Handbook of family development and intervention* (pp. 109–128). New York: John Wiley & Sons.

Hsu, L. M. (1996). On the identification of clinically significant client changes: Reinterpretation of Jacobson's cut scores. *Journal of Psychopathology and Behavioral Assessment, 18,* 371–385.

Hughes, D., & Chen, L. (1997). When and what parents tell children about race: An examination of race-related socialization among African American families. *Applied Developmental Science, 1,* 200–214.

Hunt, J. (1969). *The challenges of incompetence and poverty.* Urbana, IL: University of Illinois Press.

Jensen, A. R. (1969). How much can we boost IQ and scholastic achievement? *Harvard Educational Review, 39,* 1–123.

Johnson, D. (2001). *The ecology of children's racial coping: Family, school, and community influences.* Paper presented at the Conference on Successful Pathways in Children's Development: Mixed methods in the study of childhood and family life meetings, January 25–27, 2001, Santa Monica, CA.

Kiselica, M., Changizi, J., Cureton, V., & Gridley, B. (1995). Counseling children and adolescents in schools. In J. Ponterotto, J. Casas, L. Suzuki, & C.

Alexander (Eds.). *Handbook of multicultural counseling* (pp. 516–532). Thousand Oaks, CA: Sage.

Leenaars, A. A., Berman, A. L., & Cantor, P. (1993). *Suicidology: Essays in honor of Edwin S. Schneidman.* New Jersey: Jason Aronson.

Lopez, D., & Espitiru, Y. (1990). Panethnicity in the United States: A theoretical framework. *Ethnic and Racial Studies, 13,* 198–224.

Macionis, J. J. (1991). *Sociology.* Englewood Cliffs, NJ: Prentice-Hall.

McLoyd, V. (1998). Conceptual and methodological issues in the study of ethnic minority children and adolescents. In H. E. Fitzgerald, B. M. Lester, & B. S. Zuckerman (Eds.), *Children of color: Research, health and policy issues* (pp. 3–24). New York: Garland.

Martin, C. L., & Halverson, C. F. (1987). The roles of cognition in sex role acquisition. In D. B. Carter (Ed.), *Current conceptions of sex roles and sex typing: Theory and research* (pp. 123–137). New York: Praeger.

Min, P. G. (1996). The entrepreneurial adaptation of Korean immigrants. In S. Pedraza & R. G. Rumbaut (Eds.), *Origins and destinies: Immigration, race and ethnicity in America* (pp. 302–314). Belmont, MA: Wadsworth.

Nieto, S. (2000). *Affirming diversity: The sociopolitical context of multicultural education.* NY: Longman.

Ogbu, J. (1999). Cultural context of children's development. In H. E. Fitzgerald, B. M. Lester, & B. S. Zuckerman (Eds.), *Children of color: Research, health and policy issues* (pp. 73–92). New York: Garland.

Ogbu, J. (1994). Racial stratification in the United States: Why inequality persists. *Teachers College Record, 96,* 264–298.

Petersons, M., Rojhani, A., Steinhaus, N., & Larkin, B. (2000). Effect of ethnic identity on attitudes, feelings, and behaviors toward food. *Eating disorders: The Journal of Treatment and Prevention, 8,* 207–219.

Ponterotto, J., Rivera, L., & Adachi Sueyoshi, L. (2000). The Career-in-Cultural Interview: A semi-structured protocol for the cross-cultural intake interview. *Career Development Quarterly, 49,* 85–96.

Portes, A., & Rumbaut, R. G. (1996). *Immigrant America: A portrait.* Berkeley, CA: UC Press.

Rosenthal, D. A. (1987). Ethnic identity development in adolescents. In J. S. Phinney & M. J. Rotheram (Eds.), *Children's ethnic socialization* (pp. 156–179). Newbury Park, CA: Sage.

Rumbaut, R. (2001). *Sites of belonging: Shifts in ethnic self-identities among adolescent children of immigrants.* Paper presented at the Conference on Successful Pathways in Children's Development: Mixed Methods in the Study of Childhood and Family Life Meetings, January 25–27, 2001, Santa Monica, California.

Smith-Hefner, N. J. (1999). *Khmer American: Identity and moral education in a diasporic community.* Berkeley: University of California Press.

Steele, S. (1990). *The content of our character: A new vision of race in America.* New York: Harper Perennial.

Tajfel, H. (1978). *The social psychology of minorities.* New York: Minority Rights Group.

Thomas, A., & Chess, S. (1977). *Human developmental theories: Windows of culture.* Thousand Oaks, CA: Sage.

Thompson, C. E., Neville, H., Weathers, P. L., Poston, W. C., & Atkinson, D. R. (1990). Cultural mistrust and racism reaction among African American students. *Journal of College Student Development, 31,* 162–168.

U.S. Census Bureau (1996). *Population projection of the United States by age, race, and Hispanic origin: 1995 to 2050.* Washington, DC: U.S. Bureau of the Census.

Vernon, P. E. (1969). *Intelligence and cultural environment.* London: Methuen Press.

Waters, M. (1996) Optional ethnicities: For Whites only? In S. Pedraza & R. G. Rumbaut (Eds.), *Origins and destinies: Immigration, race and ethnicity in America* (pp. 444–454). Belmont, MA: Wadsworth.

Weiner, B. (1986). Attribution, emotion and action. In R. M. Sorrentino & E. T. Higgins (Eds.), *Handbook of motivation and cognition* (pp. 281–312). New York: Guilford.

Williams, D. R. (1996). The health of the African American population. In S. Pedraza & R. G. Rumbaut (Eds.), *Origins and destinies: Immigration, race and ethnicity in America* (pp. 404–416). Belmont, MA: Wadsworth.

Word, C. O., Zanna, M. P., & Cooper, J. (1974). The nonverbal mediation of self-fulfilling prophecies in interracial interaction. *Journal of Experimental Social Psychology, 10,* 109–120.

8

Counseling and Psychotherapy with African American Clients

Leonie J. Brooks
Towson University

Deborah G. Haskins
Loyola College in Maryland

Judith V. Kehe
Community College of Baltimore County–Essex Campus and Loyola College in Maryland

Descriptive Information

A clear understanding of the term *African American* is a necessary prerequisite for culturally competent counseling and psychotherapy with this population. Historically, the term has been used to describe those persons of African descent who were born in the United States, and who may have experienced or inherited a history of slavery and oppression. The authors would like to include in this category of *African Americans* those persons who have immigrated to the United States and who choose the term "African American" because it best fits their group identity. Such persons of color include those from the African Diaspora such as African countries, the West Indies, the Caribbean, and South America who do not classify themselves as Caucasian, Asian, Hispanic, or Native American. Such an inclusion of persons from diverse ethnic and cultural backgrounds (whose forced or voluntary displacement from their homeland brought them to the New World) fosters a more comprehensive understanding of the term *African American*. And while this inclusion creates the tendency towards generalization, the authors offer useful strategies and insights for innovative practices that value and appreciate multiculturalism. Additionally, the authors bring their unique perspectives: an African American who was born in the USA and two immigrants of African descent from the Caribbean—one having entered the high school system on arrival and the other having entered the workforce.

Demographic information on "African Americans" has traditionally classified them as "Blacks," and these two terms are often used interchangeably in the literature. White and Parham (1990) suggest that the use of "Black" and "African American" refer, respectively, to the experience of blackness in a white supremacy environment and the endorsement of cultural roots that can be traced back to Africa. The experience of being "Black" or "African American," therefore, must be understood within the context of an individual's experiences. For a therapist, it is important to keep in mind that either term can create conflicts for clients based on their personal stories, their racial identity development, and the sociopolitical context of their experiences, especially in the context of racism, classism, discrimination, and prejudice. Some clients may prefer the term *African American* over *Black* or *Negro* since more negative stereotypes have been attributed to the latter two, while others may indicate a preference for either of the latter two based on their racial identity development and their personal experiences. There are also age and generational differences in the preference for these terms. The younger often choose *African American,* while the older prefer the term *Black,* and a preference for *Black* is strongest among college-educated, affluent, and executive households, as well as in rural areas and in the South (Edmonson, 1993). In addition, Blacks who are immigrants may not readily identify with being "African American" or with having a minority status, making salient the need to differentiate among the African American population. As Watkins-Duncan (1992, p. 453) noted, it is important for psychotherapists to know if their clients consider themselves American Black, European Black, Caribbean Black, Southern Black, and so on. As will be emphasized in this chapter, African Americans are a very diverse group with respect to skin color, nationality, education, language, socioeconomic status, spirituality, faith denomination, sexual orientation, heritage, and geographic location of birth.

According to the U.S. Census Bureau information, there are 35.1 million Blacks in the United States, comprising 13 percent of the total population; most Blacks reside in the South (55 percent), with 19 percent living in the Northeast, 18 percent in the Midwest and 8 percent in the West; Blacks are more likely than non-Hispanic Whites to live in metropolitan areas (McKinnon & Humes, 2000). Cities with the largest African American population are New York City, Houston, Los Angeles, Philadelphia, Washington D.C., Detroit, New Orleans, Baltimore, and Memphis, with over 50 percent of the African American population found in the latter five cities (U.S. Census Bureau, 1990).

Based on the 1999 Current Population Survey (CPS), McKinnon and Humes (2000) have indicated that even though the life expectancy of Blacks (African Americans) has increased, their median age continues to be about 6 years younger than the non-Hispanic White population, with 33 percent of the Black population falling under age 18 as compared to 24 percent of the non-Hispanic White population. Black families are also larger than their non-Hispanic White counterparts in that married couples are more likely to have three or more children (20 percent and 12 percent, respectively). The numbers of Blacks employed in professional jobs such as lawyers, doctors, and engineers have also increased over the past several decades. However, Blacks participate in the labor force at lower rates than non-Hispanic Whites, and Black men are less likely than non-Hispanic White men to be employed in managerial and professional jobs. Similar proportions of Black men and women (25 years and over) are at least high school graduates, but Black women are more likely to have completed a bachelor's degree (McKinnon & Humes, 2000).

McKinnon and Humes (2000) compared Blacks and non-Hispanic Whites on poverty and unemployment rates. In 1998, the poverty rate, which was 13 percent for the overall population, was 26 percent for Blacks and 8 percent for non-Hispanic Whites. Among all children under age 18, the poverty rate was 19 percent, but for Blacks, this rate was three times as high (37 percent) when compared to non-Hispanic White children (11 percent). In March 1999, the employment rate for Blacks was more than twice that of non-Hispanic Whites, and while the median income of African American married couples is increasing, African American married couples are less likely than their non-Hispanic White counterparts to have an annual income of $50,000 or more (28 percent as compared to 52 percent). In sum, even though improvements in the socioeconomic situations of some African Americans have been made in recent years, vast inequities still exist. These inequities and the history of injustices that shaped them provide a context from which to understand cultural conflicts that can arise in counseling and psychotherapy.

Key Cultural Conflicts Encountered When Working with African Americans

There are several important cultural conflicts that therapists can consider when conducting psychotherapy with African Americans. These cultural conflicts are likely to influence the willingness of African Americans to seek help, the interpersonal relationship between the therapist and the client, and also the process of psychotherapy. African Americans as a group have a long history of traumatic events including slavery, racism, poverty, and a host of other individual and social problems. The most blatant indicators of the cumulative effects of trauma are evidenced in health, income, education, and occupational success (Dana, 1993). Thus, African Americans' experiences with slavery and racism in America continue to impact their daily survival, their intrapersonal and interpersonal behavior, and their willingness to seek help from others.

Acknowledgment of Oppression

Therapists will be most effective if they develop a personal awareness of how oppressive experiences, like racism and discrimination, influence help-seeking behaviors and overall psychological functioning. As Cook and Wiley (2000) and Helms and Cook (1999) have stated, many African Americans will share their experiences of oppression in psychotherapy. Therapists who have limited knowledge of the history of racism and oppression among African Americans or those who have not developed increased cultural empathy to validate an African American's experience could, unknowingly, perpetuate conflicts during the therapeutic process.

Impact of External Coping Resources

Second, although oppressive events have been significant and often insidious, African Americans possess the resiliency to cope, and they have learned to rely on their own resources instead of seeking outside help. Several researchers (Baldwin & Hopkins, 1990; Boyd-Franklin, 1989; Cook & Wiley, 2000; Nobles, 1991) have discussed the value African Americans place on religion and spirituality and the influence of these factors on clients' ability to solve seemingly insurmountable problems. Therefore, another cultural conflict may involve "selling" psychotherapy as an optimal or useful coping strategy, since African Americans have traditionally used religious, spiritual, and personal resources for healing internal and external problems. Excluding spirituality and religion from the assessment process can, therefore, be a source of conflict for clients.

Differences in Worldview

Third, Baldwin and Hopkins (1990) have stated that African Americans develop a particular worldview that emphasizes beliefs often derived from their racial and cultural experiences. This worldview includes their assumptions and guiding beliefs about life existence (Cook & Wiley, 2000; Helms & Cook, 1999; Jackson & Meadows, 1991). For example, one African American worldview places a dominant value on harmony with nature, emphasizing the search for balance or harmony. Harmony and balance are achieved through survival of the corporate whole, such as the family, community, and nation, versus an emphasis on survival of the individual (Baldwin & Hopkins, 1990). Since this African American worldview stresses communal harmony and emphasizes interdependence, another key cultural conflict may arise if psychotherapy focuses primarily on the client's individual needs instead of the client's connectedness with community (i.e., family and support networks such as friends, church, and other organizations). Since many of the traditional psychotherapy models stress individualism versus collectivism (Helms & Cook, 1999; McGoldrick, Giordano, & Pearce, 1996; Sue & Sue, 1999), therapists working with African Americans can be more effective if they validate an African American's interdependence with others when conceptualizing the client's presenting problem and its resolution.

Racial Identity Development

Racial identity is a fourth factor that has an impact on the African American's willingness to seek help the development of a therapeutic relationship, and participation in the psychotherapy process. Mental health professionals who do not become aware of their own racial identity and recognize the African American's racial identity may encounter conflicts when attempting to provide therapeutic services (Cook & Wiley, 2000; Helms & Cook, 1999; Pierce & Pierce, 1984; Sue & Sue, 1999).

One of the first racial identity models was the Cross (1971) Nigresence Model. *Nigresence* is defined as the psychology of becoming Black (Cross, Parham, & Helms, 1998). The 1971 Cross model included five stages: the Preencounter stage, which describes the old identity or the identity to be changed; the Encounter stage, which defines the events and experiences causing an individual to feel the need for change; the Immersion-Emersion stage, which illustrates the transition between the old and the developing identities; and two final stages, Internalization and Internalization-Commitment, which identify behaviors, attitudes, and psychological development that accompany habituation to the new identity (p. 96). To illustrate these stages the following examples are provided:

Preencounter Stage. An African American woman is in her first week at a new office job. Her boss says, "You know I am so impressed with your work. The only African American woman working for me has been my housekeeper, and she is so efficient! I never have to worry about my house being clean." The African American employee replies, "Thank you so much for the compliment. It is really important for me to do my work accurately." The employee does not appear conscious of her employer's stereotyped images of African Americans as working solely in manual labor jobs.

Encounter Stage. An African American child moves to a suburban neighborhood from the city. His old neighborhood was primarily African American, but the new neighborhood is primarily European American. He forms many friends in the new neighborhood, but one day one of the children tells him, "My father said I cannot play with you because you are Black." The African American child never had anyone in his old neighborhood say this to him before. Previously, the boy down the street did not play with him because he did not have the toy he wanted. The African American child is hurt and confused, and he asks his parents what is wrong with being Black. This little boy has just had an Encounter stage experience, facing opposition and racism for the first time. His parents' ability to help him understand the incident and their ability to affirm his Blackness will potentially influence his progression to the next Nigresence stage.

Immersion-Emersion Stage. An African American employee notices that most of her fellow employees question her attachment to African culture. They question her placement of African artifacts in her office. She is aware that when she was younger she was not particularly familiar with her African heritage, but as she matured her ancestral heritage became more important. At a recent Diversity Awareness Training day, employees were encouraged to integrate their rich multicultural experiences in the workplace. She decided that it was important to share her African heritage even at work.

During the Immersion stage, the person immerses him- or herself in the world of Blackness. The person attends political or cultural meetings that focus on Black issues, joins new organizations, and incorporates more Afrocentric values (Ponterotto et al., 1995). The second part of the Immersion-Emersion stage is that the person emerges from the emotionality of the Nigresence identity and begins to "level off" and feel in control of his or her emotions and intellect about the developing Blackness.

Internalization Stage. The person at this stage has naturally incorporated Blackness in everyday life, which also serves as a psychological buffer against racism and other challenges. A range of racial and ethnic diversity in the world is recognized, and the person internalizes an identity wherein Blackness becomes one of several possible bicultural or multicultural identities. This internalized identity also makes transactions with people, cultures, and human experiences beyond solely a Black experience (Ponterotto et al., 1995).

Internalization-Commitment Stage.   The African American is committed to a lifetime of developing a Black identity and personal action. The individual may devote time and energy to helping African American children in the community learn about African culture. This person may mentor other African American children or become an advocate for civil rights with the National Association for the Advancement of Colored People (NAACP).

Acculturation

Finally, the process of acculturation can also be a source of conflict in the therapy process. Berry and Annis (1974) and Brislin, Lonner, and Thorndike (1973) proposed that acculturation is a multidimensional psychosocial phenomenon reflected in psychological changes that occur in individuals encountering a new culture. Examples of psychological changes could include culture shock, isolation from familiar cultural experiences, communication difficulties, and lack of support systems (Winkelman, 1994). Berry and Annis (1974) have provided a model for understanding the stress associated with acculturation. In this model, clients can experience stress as a result of their efforts to negotiate their cultural identity in a new culture. Racial identity issues sometimes compound issues of acculturation. For example, a Black immigrant from the Caribbean, whose primary identity might have been based on national or geographic origin, will be confronted with being defined solely by his or her race upon arrival in the United States. In addition to the stress of acculturation, this immigrant will have to deal with the issue of classifying self as an African American, a foreign concept to one who previously considered self as West Indian or Caribbean. Therapists should be cognizant of the psychological consequences of acculturation, as well as its interface with racial identity issues.

Contextual Issues

As emphasized throughout this book, effective multicultural counseling and psychotherapy considers the multiple contexts of an individual client. Although the following sections do not cover every aspect of a client's experience (see Hays, 1996 for a comprehensive framework), they serve as an overview of several important contextual issues that should be considered when working with African American clients.

Family Dynamics

There is a range of family constellations among African American families, including multigenerational and single parent families. Estimates from the Census Bureau indicate that in 2001 approximately 48 percent of the 8.7 million African American families were married-couple families (U.S. Census Bureau, 2001). The number of Black households, especially female-headed Black households, has increased since 1980, with approximately 45 percent of Black families maintained by women with no spouse present in 1999 (McKinnon & Humes, 2000). While this increase may be partly due to the increased rates of divorce and separation in the population at large, it could also be due to the national trend of women and men choosing to live alone. In addition, African Americans have a higher rate of choosing not to marry than do European Americans (Boyd-Franklin, 1989).

According to Boyd-Franklin (1989), African American families are extremely diverse in their values, characteristics, and lifestyles, due to a number of factors including acculturation, geographic origin, socioeconomic status (SES), education, and religious background. Sexual orientation and history of colonization could be added to this list. Historically, families have included extended kinship networks that extend beyond the traditional bloodlines to include non-blood relations described as uncles, aunts, big mamas, older brothers and sisters, deacons, preachers, etc. (McGoldrick et al., 1996). This practice of having strong extended kinship bonds within African American families can be traced back to the time when their ancestors were brought from Africa to the United States and the Caribbean as slaves. While many families were broken up during the practice of slavery, many slaves established new family units including non-blood relatives. Immediate and extended family members form interdependent relationships, pool resources, and share in many tasks, which include rearing children and caring for the elderly. It is not unusual for extended family members to step in and raise other family members' children if parents are unable to or if extended family members can provide a better life (Hines & Boyd-Franklin, 1996). Many African American families have also included the church as part of their extended family network, with church members assisting in rearing the children and in preparing and supporting them for adulthood (Cook & Wiley, 2000). In the past, many young adults were assisted in pursuing higher education by their home church through scholarships and other fundraisers.

Another common dynamic within African American families is the parental–child system (Hines & Boyd-Franklin, 1996). In this system, an older child is selected or volunteers to assist with parental responsibilities for younger siblings because parents work or because there are many children in the family (p. 72). When working with African American families, it is important for the therapist to be flexible in his or her definition of family. Asking clients whom they include in their designation of family should be a part of the assessment process.

Gender Issues

Gender influences therapy with the African American population. Both African American men and African women were subjected to the trauma and devastation of slavery. Both were exploited, families were torn apart, and women were often, out of necessity, left primarily responsible for taking care of and providing for their children when the children themselves were not sold away. While many men and women have created and sustained healthy families, this legacy of broken families and egalitarian gender roles (where both men and women are heads of households and providers) has continued, due in part to ongoing discrimination against African American men and women in the larger society.

As with many other ethnic groups, the identity of African American men continues to be linked to their ability to provide for their families (Abreu, Goodyear, Campos, & Newcomb, 2000). "Success in being a provider, however, is often limited by discrimination" (McGoldrick et al., 1996, p. 69). According to Franklin (1996), this limitation may cause many African American men to feel marginalized and invisible because of the seemingly insurmountable obstacles they face when trying to provide for their families. While African American men are diverse in their SES, educational achievement, principles, and lifestyles (Lee & Bailey, 1997), they have had to deal with the issue of racism, which can have a deleterious impact on their overall mental health and function. Although the reaction to racism varies greatly among African American men, the difficulty in fulfilling their traditional masculine role has led to a number of problems including difficulties with anger, frustration, low self-esteem, and depression (Gary, 1985; Washington, 1987). Despite these challenges, African American men, like most other men, have traditionally been reluctant to enter therapy (Lee & Bailey, 1997). It is very important for therapists working with this group to take time to develop rapport by being respectful, genuine, and open to being questioned, remaining sensitive to issues of racism and discrimination and to the unique challenges faced by African American men in America.

Historically, African American women have generally been perceived as the strength or backbone of their families and of their communities. Relationships between African American men and women have been described as more egalitarian than those of other ethnic groups due in part to the expectation that women will be participating in the workforce. However, these egalitarian relationships still function within the context of a patriarchal society (Hines & Boyd-Franklin, 1989, p. 70). Many male-female relationships for Caribbean- and African-born Blacks, in particular, tend to reflect more traditional and stereotypical gender roles, with males seen as authority figures and providers and women viewed as responsible for the emotional well-being and nurturing of their families (Gopaul-McNicol, 1993; Nwadiroa, 1995). Therefore, it is important for a therapist to be sensitive to gender role and power dynamics issues when working with African American families.

Spirituality and Religious Issues

Within the United States, African Americans belong to a variety of religious denominations (see Cook & Wiley, 2000). However, the literature often uses the term "the Black Church" to refer to the many denominations whose membership is predominantly African American. Historically, religion and the Black Church have provided authentic validation of the African American's cultural and racial identity and have contributed to their identity formation. Cook and Wiley (2000) stated that it was in the Black Church that African Americans could escape the rejection often imposed by society and find solace and acceptance in their religious experience. Through their church many African Americans learned to read, hold leadership positions, access housing and financial resources, and find increased social supports.

Religion and spiritual experiences have traditionally been ignored in the field of psychology. However, during the last decade many codes of ethics within psychology, counseling, and social work have mandated that members of the professions integrate religion and spirituality to address cultural diversity needs within mental health service delivery (American Counseling Association, 1995; American Psychological Association, 1992, 1993; National Association of Social Workers, 1993). Social and human service fields are learning to be sensitive to religious and spiritual diversity. Many persons of African descent validate the importance of religion and spirituality in their lives. Cook and Wiley

(2000) recommend that therapists need to assess whether these clients are using religion or spirituality in positive or negative ways.

Helms and Cook (1999) provided a clear understanding of religious spirituality. The authors stated that while many religious practices focus on the supernatural, for purposes of their discussion they focused on the relationship that members of a culture have with their "God figure." The authors explained that various religions propose that persons should rely on a "higher (or universal) spiritual power" to direct them in their lives and that through prayer and other worship techniques, persons can "call upon" this higher power for guidance and for emotional strength when problems arise. Psychological distress is considered to be related to an individual's failure to follow the edicts or life process of his or her religion; therefore, the healing process involves calling on the higher power to heal believers of their distress, and religious helpers assist in this process through prayer and instructions for devout living (p. 259). It is important, therefore, for therapists to understand how clients may call on their "higher power."

Smith (1981) discussed the positive contribution of religion in the mental health of African Americans. This author maintained that religion is one of the most vital aspects of culture that African Americans have retained over the years and that African Americans use religion and spirituality for mental health and survival. Smith discussed Grier and Cobb's (1968) appraisal of the religion–mental health link in African American communities, describing how mental health and religious entities can develop partnerships for African Americans in healing psychological disturbances. Smith also emphasized that African Americans will be further alienated in American society if they are not allowed to use the creative and spiritual tools which often define their existence. Finally, Smith also pointed out that psychotherapy is often not available or helpful to the poor, uneducated, and African American populations. As a result, many African Americans have found that identifying with and participating in the churches is more affirming of mental health than psychotherapy. He advocated the need for mental health professionals to recognize the Black Church as a mental health resource and noted that in traditional African societies a person's mental health issues were not separated from the individual's spiritual well-being. In African culture, spirit is recognized to be "in everything and everywhere" (Mbiti, 1991). On the other hand, Grier and Cobbs' (1968) model of religion considered Black religions to be pathological and detrimental to the mental health of African Americans. These authors believed that African Americans cover up rage and anger during the process of seeking solace through religion, and this cover-up causes additional psychological damage. Grier and Cobbs stated that African Americans must accept certain psychological truths, including harsh realities of racism, poverty, and other social ills.

It is true that some African Americans, like some members of other racial and ethnic groups, may use religion to the extent that they decrease personal control and responsibility, for example, using the Bible to substantiate extreme physical abuse with the scripture "spare the rod and spoil the child." However, it is important to remember that religious and spiritual practices may be healthy alternatives in resolving difficult crises or problems. Smith (1981) proposed that a therapist should look for a balance of religious maturity, psychic stability, and cultural integration to examine whether an African American exhibits a healthy or unhealthy religious orientation. A therapist can use traditional psychological assessments and incorporate additional religious and spiritual assessment questions before reaching a psychological diagnosis and before conceptualizing the case. Examples of religious and spiritual assessment questions will be provided in a subsequent section.

Social Groups and Significant Support Networks

Many African American families embrace the concept of reciprocity, incorporating a collectivist or group identity that encourages families to help and support each other and to share resources that help to ensure the survival of their communities (Boyd-Franklin, 1989). Social support for many African American families is found primarily in extended kinship networks, in the church and surrounding community, and through civic and other organizations including sororities and fraternities. African Americans form significant social support networks through participating in church-related activities and through membership in civic and political organizations including the NAACP, Urban League, National Council of Negro Women, Concerned Black Men, as well as cultural organizations that reflect their geographic origin including Caribbean and African organizations. Involvement in these organizations serves multiple purposes such as reinforcing shared values, attitudes, and beliefs; fostering pride in the group's cultural identity; providing a venue for effectively organizing members for a particular cause such as voter registration or fundraising; and mobilizing critical resources in times of crises.

Families and extended kin are the primary socializing agents for African American children, and many communities incorporate both formal and informal cultural activities such as rites of passage, mentoring, and cultural celebrations like Kwanzaa that help to connect individuals to their cultural heritage and values. In assessing the social support of African Americans, the therapist should be cognizant of the communal identity among African Americans which leads them to first seek help from members of their own communities, particularly within their extended family/kinship network. As noted earlier, the role flexibility that exists within extended kin networks tends to be mobilized during times of crisis (McGoldrick et al., 1996, p. 71). The "church family" has often been utilized as an important social service resource for many African Americans, both when they face crises such as homelessness and illness and when individuals are geographically isolated from their families (Boyd-Franklin, 1989). The relationship that is established with the African American client can, therefore, be the crux of therapy.

View of Mental Health

Several research studies have documented the disparity in the mental health utilization rates of various ethnic minorities (Sue & Sue, 1999). African Americans seldom use private therapists but may more often access community mental health centers. In 1976, the American Psychological Association Task Force on Health Research found that large numbers of disadvantaged and minority citizens lacked access to adequate health care. This was also true of mental health care. In addition, the Task Force found that racism affected service delivery in both direct and subtle ways. Sue (1977) analyzed detailed information on approximately 14,000 clients seen in 17 community mental health centers over a 3-year period. Sue found that African Americans and Native Americans were overrepresented in the community mental health centers and that African Americans were significantly more likely to terminate prematurely.

Sue, Fujino, Hu, Takeuchi, & Zane (1991) later investigated community mental health services to determine whether changes had occurred in mental health services that had adopted culturally responsive interventions in service delivery and outcomes for minority group clients, as compared to the 1977 study. The authors examined premature termination rates, number of sessions, and treatment outcomes and found that African Americans had a significantly higher dropout rate than other groups. Ethnic match between therapist and client proved to have a greater impact on the number of sessions attended than did treatment outcomes. While there appears to be progress in culturally responsive treatment, services for African Americans did not seem to improve, a finding which emphasizes the need to address ethnic match in therapy. The following is an experience of one of the authors at a counseling center that focused on this issue of ethnic match. This center was attempting to expand outreach to ethnic members on campus:

> At a counseling center in a private college located in a metropolitan city, African American students were asked whom they would consult if they experienced personal problems. Consistently, the students' verbal reports were that when experiencing problems they would first consult with a parent, family member, or extended family member. In some cases, the students indicated that they would also seek solace through their religion. When asked if they would seek help if the counseling center had an African American psychologist, many of the students indicated that they might if they were uncomfortable talking with someone in their personal network.

While these students' responses may be similar to those of students from other ethnic groups, the literature confirms that ethnic match may influence a client's willingness to request help and remain in treatment rather than affecting the actual therapy outcome. Often an ethnic match is helpful because the African American client perceives that an African American therapist shares a similar worldview or may be familiar with his or her culture (Helms & Cook, 1999). However, research also documents that clients cannot assume that similar ethnicity will guarantee culturally sensitive psychotherapy. Being an African American therapist does not guarantee sensitivity to or knowledge about African American cultures. There is also great diversity in African American culture (Cook & Wiley, 2000; Helms & Cook, 1999; McGoldrick et al., 1996), and it is quite possible that many African American therapists identify more with European American culture (since most training emphasizes theories based in European schools of thought) than African American culture. It is important, therefore, for therapists to be culturally competent regarding service delivery to African American clients because ethnic match is not always possible, due to the low percentage of African Americans in the mental health field (Dana, 1993; Sue & Sue, 1999), and, as stated previously, ethnic match does not guarantee culturally competent therapeutic interventions.

Recommended Approaches to Counseling and Therapy

There are many texts that include useful information on approaches to therapy with African Americans (Dana, 1993; Helms & Cook, 1999; Lee, 1997; McFadden, 1993; Parham, White, & Ajumu, 2000; Ponterotto et al., 1995; Sue & Sue, 1999). In addition, Boyd-Franklin's (1989) work on *Black Families in Therapy* is a useful resource. Given the available information on treatment issues with African American or Black families, the authors will highlight those elements that have been found to be most effective with this population: racial identity, trust building, family therapy, group work, gender-sensitivity, and the assessment of spiritual and religious content in therapy.

Racial Identity Issues

The exploration of racial identity issues is crucial when working with African Americans. Internalized oppression and the coping methods for dealing with racism influence identity development (Helms & Cook, 1999). Jones (1985) has provided a model of racism as internalized trauma, comprising a four-pronged approach that explores the following factors: reactions to racial oppression, influence of the majority culture, influence of Afro-American culture, and personal experiences and endowments. It is also helpful to keep in mind that personal experiences may vary within groups. For example, African Americans who immigrate to the United States may struggle with the status of being considered "minority" and may not share the same experience or history of oppression as African Americans who were born in the United States. Yet both groups may have experienced oppression since, for example, it is not uncommon for class distinctions to occur within groups based on skin color, where those with lighter skin are more prized (Boyd-Franklin, 1989).

The United States has struggled for some time with race relations. It will be important for psychotherapists to understand the sociopolitical issues of slavery and oppression. The following exercise can foster this understanding:

> Imagine that you are taken to another country against your will and that you are separated from family and loved ones.
>
> Imagine that when you go to a new country, even though you were a doctor, lawyer, or business owner in your own place of origin, you are told you do not speak "standard English" or because of your "accent" you cannot communicate clearly enough to have access to certain jobs.
>
> Imagine that in this new country you cannot seem to transfer your talents and skills because there is a perception that your education or skills are not equivalent to those of persons in the new domicile.
>
> Imagine that when you interact with others, persons refer to you by the color of your skin.
>
> Imagine that you are treated by others not on the basis of your unique talents, intelligence, or self-worth but on the basis of the color of your skin.

Imagine that you notice that others, because they have a different skin color, have access to education, economics, certain neighborhoods, and certain jobs.

Imagine that when you turn on the television you see people of your skin color portrayed in destructive and negative ways and that television portrays your families as those without a father, but you know that there are many families in your culture with mothers and fathers.

What are some of your thoughts, feelings, and reactions to these "imagined" experiences? These *imagined* experiences are the reality for many African Americans.

Building Trust

Historically, African Americans have exhibited mistrust of formal mental health and medical institutions due to their experiences with prejudice, discrimination, or culturally insensitive treatment. Their reluctance to utilize formal mental health systems, along with their preference to seek help from family, extended kin, or religious or spiritual sources, may make building trust initially challenging. Therapists are encouraged to adopt a multisystemic approach with African American families, considering the impact of social, political, socioeconomic, cultural, and other broader environmental conditions on the client and the process of therapy (Boyd-Franklin, 1989).

Therapists need to explore their African American clients' fears about mental health interventions, to respectfully challenge their misperceptions about the treatment process, and to educate them about the process, including issues related to confidentiality and to client and counselor roles and responsibilities. Therapists should be open to questions about the process and be patient while actively working to gain trust by being genuine, empathic, and respectful when interacting with African American clients. Knowledge about African American culture and sensitivity to cultural differences and their possible impact on the therapy process are crucial. Therapists should also take the time to carefully examine and clarify clients' expectations and culturally influenced values. They must be willing to explore differences that may exist between themselves and their clients in these areas.

Self-disclosure by the therapist may also help reluctant African American clients who may initially feel uncomfortable talking about their "business" with a stranger. Therapists should be willing to disclose relevant information about themselves, as clients are more likely to open up if they feel they know something about the therapist as a person. Therapists should also be willing to be more directive in the beginning of therapy, as many clients will want concrete solutions and may view the therapist as an expert.

Family Therapy

In utilizing family therapy approaches, the therapist must seek to understand the client's definition of the family, its structure, and its function. As mentioned earlier, Hines and Boyd-Franklin (1996) have recommended that a genogram, a schematic diagram that visually depicts the structure of a family, can be a very effective method of obtaining information about family relationships and roles. Genograms typically include all significant family members, indicating their relationships to one another, ages, dates of marriage, births, deaths, and geographic locations (readers are encouraged to utilize McGoldrick and Gerson's (1985) text as a useful guide to constructing a genogram). It is crucial for therapists to recognize the diversity among families and to consider that the "typical" nuclear family is not the only kind of family that exists for African Americans. It is especially important to differentiate between *matrilineal* and *patrilineal* family relationships and to avoid confusing these terms with *patriarchal* and *matriarchal,* respectively. The former terms are kinship designations that do not imply rule by women or rule by men (Ingoldsby & Smith, 1995) but refer to the affiliation and inheritance that are passed on by the father and mother, respectively. Therapists who are willing to recognize diversity among families, and who are willing to challenge their assumptions, are in a position to be therapeutically effective with the African American client. Therapists must also be aware of their own definition of "family," as well as the definition and goal of their particular theoretical orientation.

Ingoldsby and Smith (1995) have provided an overview of the various definitions that family therapy approaches endorse, along with the contribution of these approaches to multicultural studies. For example, from a family system perspective the family is defined as "an organic system striving to maintain a balance as it confronts external pressures," whereas from a structural-functionalism viewpoint the family is "a structure that satisfies members' needs and operates for the survival and maintenance of society" (p. 30). Each theoretical framework offers its unique definition. Therefore, therapists may want to clarify their own definition of the family and ask themselves whether this definition is congruent with their theoretical framework. The following self-internalization questions may be useful to consider when working with African American clients:

What is my definition of family?

Does my definition of family fit with my theoretical orientation?

How can I integrate my definition of family and my theoretical framework with the client's definition of his or her family structure and function?

The role of extended kinship among African Americans must be a part of the clinical assessment. It is useful to consider that it is not uncommon for families to adopt blood relatives and non-blood relatives as part of their family without a legal process. Failure to consider these "adopted" members would be a disservice to clients. It is also not uncommon for family members to talk about the deceased as ongoing forces in the therapeutic process. The importance of spirituality and religion for the family and the roles of godparents are also underscored in the assessment process.

A particularly useful approach when working with Black families is the structural family therapy approach. The structural approach, which is primarily a problem solving approach, is well suited to therapy with Black families because it is clear, focused, specific, and directive (Boyd-Franklin, 1989). According to this approach, problems occur in families when the family structure, or the way in which the family is organized (including who is in charge of the family), is inflexible and/or poorly organized. Typically, family structures need to be well organized and flexible enough to adapt to changing circumstances. Families with poorly organized or inflexible structures fail to adjust adequately to changing circumstances, such as encountering stressful situations. The goal of structural family therapy is to alter and strengthen the family structure so the family can solve its own problems. Many African American families tend to have diverse structures, with extended and nontraditional family configurations. Therefore, it is important that therapists recognize all of the members considered as family by the African American client and work with all relevant family members. For a more detailed description and conceptual framework of this approach, see Aponte and Van Deusen (1981) and Minuchin, Lee, and Simon (1996).

Group Work

Group work can be extremely effective for African Americans. The traditional African view of nature is characterized by cooperative interdependence and group centeredness in human relationships (Lee, 1997). These allocentric tendencies can provide the context for change within a group setting since there is a tendency toward purpose (*nia*) and unity (*umoja*)—two of the seven principles of Kwanzaa. Matsumoto (1996) defines allocentrism as "the collectivistic tendencies on the individual level" (p. 32).

Research indicates that addressing issues of racial identity can be beneficial in a racially homogenous environment (Fukayama & Coleman, cited in Ponterotto et al., 1995; Shipp, 1983). Because most African Americans tend to present practical rather than personal problems (Ponterotto et al., 1995), groups that focus on issues and resolutions and that have clear boundaries and expectations can be most effective. Groups must also be structured in a way that fosters respect for individual differences and experiences.

Gender-Sensitive Practices

Many of the underlying principles of feminist theory, a form of gender-sensitive practice, are especially useful for the African American population. The increase of female elderly African Americans, the increased percentage of female-headed households, and the attention that has been given to African American males argue favorably for gender-sensitive theories. Ballou and Gabalac (1984) summarized the major tenets of feminist therapy, and two of these tenets, psycho-educational liberation and personal validation, will be highlighted as particularly useful in working with African Americans.

A strong psycho-educational component exists in feminist approaches to therapy. The therapist often is cast in the role of educator, not merely educating clients about therapy, but also providing instruction in social and historical facts concerning sexism, racism, and discrimination, as well as the impact of these facts on cultural conditioning and racial identity development. Issues of discrimination and prejudice can arise during therapy with the African American client. Therapy can be enhanced, therefore, by providing an external emphasis, where appropriate, to assist clients in placing their experiences in a social context. It is important to explore the sociopolitical context of clients' experiences. To simply dismiss the importance of the sociopolitical context will invalidate clients' stories. It is not enough that therapists focus primarily on helping clients to feel better about themselves.

Therapists also need to consider key issues such as social context, oppression, racism, discrimination, and power as part of the assessment process and to become knowledgeable regarding the effects of these social constructs in influencing clients' worldviews and their perceptions. Ignoring context is one of the major downfalls of traditional therapies.

Another aspect of feminist therapy is an emphasis on personal validation, including respect for individual differences. In working with African Americans, the therapist must value differences and treat clients in a respectful manner. This is a core ethical principle for professionals in clinical practice (Principle D: Respect for People's Rights and Dignity) expressed in the Ethical Principles of Psychologists and Code of Conduct (APA, 1992). Valuing clients' rights includes valuing pluralism and taking into account the interface between gender and other forms of diversity such as religion and spirituality. For example, African American Islamic women, because of their faith and beliefs, may present with issues that are different than those of African American Christian women. The etiology, symptomatology, and participation in treatment may vary. Other diversity issues such as physical ability, gay or lesbian identity, and ageism are useful constructs for the psychotherapist to take into consideration when working with the African American client. Therapists who assume that the needs of all African Americans are the same, without recognizing the interplay of diversity and the uniqueness of the individual's cultural heritage as valuable to the therapeutic relationship, do a disservice to clients. This is especially important for African American clients whose values have been attacked over the years. Incidents such as the Moynihan (1965) report and the Tuskegee incidents have contributed to a lack of validation of the African community.

Spiritual and Religious Assessment and Intervention

Because many African Americans tend to use their spirituality and religion as sources of support, particularly during difficult times, therapists working with African American clients need to be comfortable incorporating these variables in therapy. Therefore, therapists must first assess their own beliefs and their level of comfort with religion and spirituality before conducting a religious or spiritual assessment. This personal assessment may reduce the effects of negative counter-transference or indicate areas where knowledge deficits related to religion and spirituality may need to be corrected. Such deficits may include understanding the difference between religion and spirituality; being aware of one's own religious and spiritual beliefs, including how they are similar to and different from those of the client; working to understand the client's religious and spiritual beliefs; recognizing the limits of one's tolerance of spiritual and religious phenomena; and, when necessary, being able to make appropriate referrals; having the ability to assess the relevance of religious and spiritual issues associated with the client's concerns; being able to utilize the client's spiritual and religious beliefs and expressions within sessions to meet the client's therapeutic goals and understanding how these beliefs affect treatment (Fukuyama & Sevig, 1999). The knowledge and comfort that a therapist exhibits regarding these issues will facilitate the development of a trusting relationship with many African American clients. Personal reflection on the following questions, typically directed to clients when conducting an assessment of their religious/spiritual beliefs, may provide an opportunity to develop or increase awareness of one's own spiritual/religious beliefs:

Describe your early experiences with religion or spirituality: What were the religious or spiritual backgrounds and experiences of your family members, and how did they introduce you to religion or spirituality? Were these experiences positive and/or negative? Were any particular religious practices or spiritual beliefs emphasized or de-emphasized in your family? In a crisis, did your family rely on God or a higher power, and if so, how?

How have your beliefs changed over time, and what has influenced that change? Were there any particular life events that impacted you in a positive and/or negative way, which may have influenced your religious or spiritual development? Did any experience cause a religious or spiritual crisis in your life?

What is the role of God or the higher power in your life right now? Would it be beneficial for you to use religion or spirituality during counseling or psychotherapy? If so, how?

Asking these or similar questions of clients can facilitate accurate understanding of their spiritual and religious contexts—and how these contexts may impact clients' current difficulties and coping. Once therapists are aware of these issues and clients have affirmed their desire to include spiritual or religious perspectives in therapy, relevant spiritual interventions can be incorporated. Common interventions include helping the client to clarify his or her spiritual values, using spiritual language or metaphors, acknowledging the client's prayer life, exploring religious concepts such as forgiveness, exploring spiritual elements in dreams, and using spiritual practices to cope with grief/loss. In doing so, therapists should remember that clients may have had negative experiences with religion or spirituality, and therapists should never impose their own beliefs on the client. Readers may benefit from obtaining Richards and Bergin's *A Spiritual Strategy for Counseling and Psychotherapy* (2003) and *Handbook of Psychotherapy and Religious Diversity* (2000) to gain additional information about religious and spiritual diversity issues.

Working from within an African American Worldview: Final Recommendations

Culturally sensitive attitudes, knowledge, and skills have already been identified. The following considerations are beneficial for therapists when integrating African American worldviews into the therapy process.

First, it is important that therapists adopt a strength-focused model when working with African Americans. Ford (1997) has pointed out that much of the literature on ethnic minorities has focused on those who are lower class, unemployed, or on welfare. This has been especially true of African Americans. While past research depicted African American families from a deficit or disadvantaged viewpoint (Frazier, 1966; Moynihan, 1965), more recent works have adopted a more balanced view of these families, including an emphasis on such strengths as family role flexibility, strong kinship bonds, education and work achievement, and religiosity (Billingsley, 1992; Boyd-Franklin, 1989; Hill, 1999).

Second, therapists must be willing to have clients share those experiences which involve the client's perception of reality, which often includes living in a world in which treatment is based on race (Helms & Cook, 1999). If the therapist is uncomfortable listening to and discussing these experiences, then it is likely that the client will not feel validated and will terminate therapy (Sue & Sue, 1999).

Third, therapists must recognize that although there may be universal characteristics that are found across ethnic groups, these characteristics may not be based on a similar worldview. For example, many European Americans, Asian Americans, Latino/as, African Americans, and West Indians value education and family, but each cultural group may approach the experiences with its own set of beliefs, expectations, roles, and rules.

Fourth, therapists must recognize that clients may experience varying levels of locus of control and locus of responsibility. Sue (1978) stated that mental health professionals further oppress minority clients when they approach problems expecting the client to adopt a worldview of internal control and internal responsibility. Sue noted that most psychology training programs emphasize internal control and internal responsibility, yet clients may approach life from a different locus.

Fifth, many therapists have been trained in individual therapy models and are not skillful in working with multisystems (Boyd-Franklin, 1989). Many clients may need practical assistance (e.g., citizenship concerns, housing); thus therapists must become familiar with integrating multiple systems into the treatment plan. Additionally, therapists can integrate spirituality and religious resources (e.g., prayer and meditation, reading spiritual and religious literature) into the therapy process. Finally, therapists most commit to developing and integrating multicultural competency as an ongoing professional goal.

Case Study of an African American Client

Allen was an 18-year-old African American male referred by his pediatrician for therapy. Allen intended to begin college, and his grandmother, Mrs. P., took him for a physical examination. The pediatrician called the therapist and stated that the grandmother was concerned about Allen because he appeared to be very stressed. The grandmother stated that she believed Allen's stress was related to the marital conflict between his stepmother and his father. The pediatrician referred Allen and his grandmother to this particular therapist because they had wanted someone who was sensitive to religious and spiritual issues. Upon receiving the referral and hearing the pediatrician's observations about Allen's high anxiety level and symptoms, the therapist concluded that it would be desirable to include a psychiatric evaluation by a consulting psychiatrist. The pediatrician responded, "Oh, no—he is a very bright young man and that is not necessary."

The grandmother accompanied Allen to the first session. She reported that Allen's father was retiring from the military and relocating his family from abroad. She also indicated that she and her husband had raised Allen and his brother Jeffrey from ages 5 and 7 until ages 9 and 11. She further indicated that the relationship of her son and the boys' mother had not lasted, and her son had felt it was in the boys' best interest for the grandparents to raise them while he was out of the country. The grandmother never explained why the mother could not raise the sons. The grandmother also reported that the father had retrieved his sons at ages 9 and 11 and had married a woman who had a daughter, age 5. He and his wife had then had two additional children. At age 17, Allen had decided that he wanted to have a relationship with his mother, so he had planned to attend a college near his mother's home. After only a few months of living with his mother, Allen realized the relationship was not as he had desired. He made the decision to leave quite suddenly, and he now sought to enroll in a college near his grandparents' home.

At the initial session, the therapist noted that Allen met most of the criteria for Generalized Anxiety Disorder. It was evident that he was experiencing a great deal of anxiety over his relationships with his parents and over numerous environmental transitions. The therapist obtained Allen's permission to contact his father and to solicit the father's input and involvement in treatment, even at a distance.

The next six sessions of therapy focused on building rapport, incorporating Allen's value for religion and for spiritual practices, exploring his emotions and thoughts related to the many conflicts and transitions in the family, and applying cognitive-behavioral strategies to help Allen learn relaxation skills. Therapy appeared to progress well until the seventh week when Allen skipped a session. He called and said that schoolwork was intense due to upcoming midterm examinations. Allen then missed the eighth week as well. The therapist was concerned because Allen was active in therapy. The next morning Allen's grandmother called and reported that Allen had had a nervous breakdown the day before and was in a local psychiatric clinic. When the therapist visited Allen in the clinic, his grandparents, father, and stepmother (who had flown home) were also present, and they reported that Allen had always demonstrated some unusual behaviors. The grandmother then reported that Allen had begun "cleansing his food in the oven" and talking "strangely during the past 3 weeks." The father reported that Allen's mother had seemed to have psychiatric problems and that she had been addicted to drugs. He wondered if Allen's behavior might be related to a genetic disorder. Allen was diagnosed with bipolar disorder with psychotic ideation, and he received medication and both individual and family treatment upon his release from the clinic. His symptoms notably decreased over time. He remained on medication, but he was able to discontinue therapy and succeed in his academic work.

This case provides examples of several issues that may arise in therapy with African American clients. The therapist validated the importance of the grandmother and of religious beliefs in Allen's life. The therapist was willing to have the client share experiences, such as family and religion, that were important in the client's worldview. The therapist also included the father and stepmother, even though doing so meant taking an additional step. Boyd-Franklin (1989) discussed the importance of including the extended family and working hard to include fathers, even if they are absent. The therapist recognized that while family is important to many ethnic groups, the definition and roles of family are not confined to the typical nuclear family. Upon first hearing Allen's symptoms, the therapist had wanted a psychiatric evaluation but trusted the evaluation of the pediatrician, who apparently had known the boy longer. The pediatrician's concern about a psychiatric evaluation (and she was an African American) was possibly related to mistrust of the establishment (Pierce & Pierce, 1984) and to concern that Allen would become part of the mental health system as an African American. The therapist later realized that the pediatrician was protective of Allen due to her concern of how this African American male may become part of a system that often treats people based on racial biases within the profession. The therapist realized that in the future she could trust her own intuition and clinical judgment, while at the same time acknowledging concerns related to the sociopolitical and cultural fears of African Americans. Knowledge of the sociopolitical context is important, but clinical acumen is paramount when dealing with all clients. The therapist also realized that many African American families might not initially report their observations (such as Allen's odd behavior) if they believe the child may be identified as abnormal. Research documents the history of pathologizing many African American clients (Helms & Cook, 1999), and Allen's family's realistic fear resulting from this unfortunate history almost prevented him from getting comprehensive mental health care. Multicultural competencies were demonstrated in this case by the awareness of the sociopolitical context, an understanding of the client's worldview, the ability to include various members of the mental health care team, and the continuation of treatment even after a major setback. The importance of therapists increasing multicultural awareness, knowledge, and skills is underscored.

References

Abreu, J. M., Goodyear, R. K., Campos, A., & Newcomb, M. D. (2000). Ethnic belonging and traditional masculinity ideology among African Americans, European Americans and Latinos. *Psychology of Men and Masculinity, 1*(2), 75–86.

American Counseling Association (ACA) (1995). *Code of ethics and standards of practice.*

American Psychological Association (APA) (1992). Ethical principles of psychologists and code of conduct. *American Psychologist, 47,* 1597–1611.

American Psychological Association (1993). Guidelines for providers of psychological services to ethnic, linguistic and culturally diverse populations. *American Psychologist, 48,* 45–48.

Aponte, H., & Van Deusen, J. (1981). Structural family therapy. In A. Gurman & D. Knickern (Eds.), *Handbook of Family Therapy* (pp. 310–360). New York: Brunner/Mazel.

Baldwin, J. A., & Hopkins, R. (1990). African American and European American cultural differences as assessed by the worldviews paradigm: An empirical analysis. *The Western Journal of Black Studies, 14,* 38–52.

Ballou, M., & Gabalac, N. (1984). *A feminist position on mental health.* Springfield, IL: Charles C Thomas.

Berry, J. W., & Annis, R. C. (1974). Acculturative stress: The role of ecology, culture and differentiation. *Journal of Cross-Cultural Psychology, 5,* 382–405.

Billingsley, A. (1992). *Climbing Jacob's ladder: The enduring legacy of African-American families.* New York: Simon & Schuster.

Boyd-Franklin, N. (1989). *Black families in therapy.* New York: Guilford Press.

Brislin, R. W., Lonner, W. J., & Thorndike, R. M. (1973). *Cross-cultural research methods.* New York: Wiley.

Cook, D. A., & Wiley, C. Y. (2000). Psychotherapy with members of African American churches and spiritual traditions. In P. S. Richards & A. E. Bergin (Eds.), *Handbook of psychotherapy and religious diversity* (pp. 369–396). Washington, DC: American Psychological Association.

Cross, W. E. (1971). The Negro-to-Black conversion experience. *Black World, 20,* 13–27.

Cross, W. E., Parham, T. A., & Helms, J. A. (1998). Nigrescence revisited: Theory and research. In R. L. Jones (Ed.), *African American identity development.* Hampton, VA: Cobb and Henry Publishers.

Dana, R. H. (1993). *Multicultural assessment perspectives for professional psychology.* Boston: Allyn & Bacon.

Edmonson, B. (1993). What do you call a dark-skinned person? *American Demographics, 15*(10), 35.

Ford, R. (1997). *Counseling strategies for ethnic minority students.* Tacoma, WA: University of Pugent Sound. (ERIC Document Reproduction Service No. ED 247 504).

Franklin, A. J. (1996). The invisibility syndrome. *Family Therapy Networker,* pp. 33–39.

Frazier, E. F. (1966). *The Negro family in the United States.* Chicago: University of Chicago Press.

Fukuyama, M. A., & Sevig, T. (1999). *Integrating spirituality into multicultural counseling.* Thousand Oaks, CA: Sage.

Gary, L. (1985). Correlates of depressive symptoms among a selected population of Black males. *American Journal of Public Health, 75,* 1220–1222.

Grier, W. H., & Cobbs, P. M. (1968). *Black rage.* New York: Basic Books.

Gopaul-McNicol, S. (1993). *Working with West Indian families.* New York: Guilford Press.

Hays, P. (1996). ADDRESSING the complexities of culture and gender in counseling. *Journal of Counseling and Development, 74,* 332–338.

Helms, J. E., & Cook, D. A. (1999). *Using race and culture in counseling and psychotherapy: Theory and process.* Boston: Allyn & Bacon.

Hill, R. (1999). *The Strengths of African American Families: Twenty-five years later.* Lanham, MD: University Press of America.

Hines, P., & Boyd-Franklin, N. (1989). *Black families.* New York: Guilford.

Hines, P. M., & Boyd-Franklin, N. (1996). African American families. In M. McGoldrick, J. Giordano, & J. Pearce (Eds.), *Ethnicity and family therapy* (pp. 66–84). New York: Guilford Press.

Ingoldsby, B., & Smith, S. (Eds.) (1995). *Families in multicultural perspective.* New York: Guilford Press.

Jackson, A. P., & Meadows, F. B. (1991). Getting to the bottom to understand the top. *Journal of Counseling and Development, 70,* 72–76.

Jones, A. C. (1985). Psychological functioning in Black Americans: A conceptual guide for use in psychotherapy. *Psychotherapy, 22,* 363–369.

Lee, C. (1997). *Multicultural issues in counseling* (2nd ed.). Alexandria, VA: American Counseling Association.

Lee, C., & Bailey, D. F. (1997). Counseling African American male youth and men. In C. Lee (Ed.), *Multicultural issues in counseling* (2nd ed.) (pp. 123–154). Alexandria, VA: American Counseling Association.

Matsumoto, D. (1996). *Culture and psychology.* Pacific Grove, CA: Brooks Cole.

Mbiti, J. S. (1991). *Introduction to African religion* (2nd ed.). Oxford, England: Heinemann Educational Publishers.

McFadden, J. (1993). *Transcultural counseling: Bilateral and international perspective.* Alexandria, VA: American Counseling Association.

McGoldrick, M., & Gerson, R. (1985). *Genograms in family assessment.* New York: W. Norton and Company.

McGoldrick, M., Giordano, J., & Pearce, J. K. (Eds.) (1996). *Ethnicity and family therapy* (2nd ed.). New York: The Guilford Press.

McKinnon, J., & Humes, K. (2000). The black population in the United States: March, 1999. U.S. Census Bureau. Current Populations Report, Series P20-730. Washington, DC: U.S. Government Printing Office.

Minuchin, S., Lee, W. Y., & Simon, G. M. (1996). *Mastering family therapy: Journeys of growth and transformation.* New York: Wiley.

Moynihan, D. P. (1965). *The Negro family: The case for national action.* Washington, DC: U.S. Department of Labor.

National Association of Social Workers. (1993). *Code of ethics.* Washington, DC: Author.

Nobles, W. W. (1991). African philosophy: Foundations for black psychology. In R. L. Jones (Ed.), *Black Psychology* (pp. 47–63). Berkeley, CA: Cobb & Henry.

Nwadiora, E. (1995). Alienation and stress among Black immigrants: An exploratory study. *Western Journal of Black Studies, 19,* 59–71.

Parham, T. A., White, J., & Ajumu, A. (2000). *The psychology of Blacks: An African centered perspective.* Upper Saddle River, NJ: Prentice Hall.

Pierce, L. H., & Pierce, R. L. (1984). Race as a factor in the sexual abuse of children. *Social Work Research and Abstracts,* 9–14.

Ponterotto, J. G., Casas. J., Suzuki, L. A., & Alexander, C. M. (1995). *Handbook of multicultural counseling.* Thousand Oaks, CA: Sage.

Richards, P. S., & Bergin, A. E. (Eds.) (2003). *A spiritual strategy for counseling and psychotherapy.* Washington, DC: American Psychological Association.

Richards, P. S., & Bergin, A. E. (Eds.) (2000). *Handbook of psychotherapy and religious diversity.* Washington, DC: American Psychological Association.

Shipp, P. L. (1983). Counseling Blacks: A group approach. *Personnel and Guidance Journal, 62,* 108–111.

Smith, A. (1981). Religion and mental health among blacks. *Journal of Religion and Health, 20,* 264–287.

Sue, D. W. (1977). Barriers to effective cross-cultural counseling. *Journal of Counseling Psychology, 24,* 420–429.

Sue, D. W. (1978). Eliminating cultural oppression in counseling: Toward a general theory. *Journal of Counseling Psychology, 25,* 419–428.

Sue, D. S., Fujino, D. C., Hu, L., Takeuchi, D. T., & Zane, N. W. S. (1991). Community mental health services for ethnic minority groups: A test of the cultural responsiveness hypothesis. *Journal of Consulting and Clinical Psychology, 59,* 533–540.

Sue, D. W., & Sue, D. S. (1999). *Counseling the culturally different: Theory and practice* (3rd ed.). New York: John Wiley and Sons, Inc.

United States Census Bureau. (1990). We, the American Blacks. Report issued on September, 1993. U.S. Government Printing Office.

United States Census Bureau. (February 22, 2001). *Census bureau facts for features.* Retrieved October 19, 2001 from http://www.census.gov/Press-Release/www/2000/cb00-158.html

Washington, C. S. (1987). Counseling Black men. In M. Scher, M. Stevens, G. Good, & G. A. Eichenfield. (Eds.), *Handbook of counseling and psychotherapy with men* (pp. 192–202). Newbury Park, CA: Sage.

Watkins-Duncan, B. (1992). Principles for formulating treatment with Black patients. *Psychotherapy, 29,* 452–456.

White, J. (1972). Toward a Black psychology. In R. Jones (Ed.), *Black psychology* (pp. 43–50). New York: Harper & Row.

White, J. L., & Parham, T. A. (1990). *The psychology of Blacks: An African American perspective.* New York: Prentice Hall.

Winkleman, M. (1994). Cultural shock and adaptation. *Journal of Counseling and Development, 73,* 121–126.

9

Counseling and Psychotherapy with Latino and Latina Clients

Alberta M. Gloria
University of Wisconsin–Madison

Ester L. Ruiz
Arizona State University

Elisa M. Castillo
Northeastern University

Because many Latinos and Latinas do not differentiate between physical and emotional health, they often come to mental health services via the medical system. Many Latinos and Latinas believe that strong emotions may cause physical illness and thus perceive the psyche as affecting one's physical condition (Cuellar & Roberts, 1984). Similarly, illness and misfortune are often believed to be external to the individual, and their cause is thought to be spiritual (Koss-Chioino, 1995). Consequently, it is not uncommon for Latinos and Latinas to seek or to expect some form of medical treatment (e.g., medication) for their psychological issues. In addition to standardized treatments, clinicians need to be aware of and open to the use of indigenous or traditional cultural methods (e.g., referral to a traditional folk healer) as part of their treatment modalities when necessary and appropriate.

Although the field of professional psychology has called for culturally appropriate and sensitive therapy (Sue, Arredondo, & McDavis, 1992), Latinos and Latinas are slow to seek mental health services, and more than half of those who do seek services terminate therapy after one session (Thurman, Swaim, & Plested, 1995). A high tolerance for psychopathology among Latino and Latina families (Molina & Aguirre-Molina, 1994) delays the consideration of psychological services. Barriers such as economics, language, environment, and sociocultural factors account for early termination and underutilization rates (Sue & Sue, 1999). In particular, lack of bilingual and bicultural therapists and lack of cultural sensitivity account for therapy attrition of Latino and Latina clients (González, 1997).

The purpose of this chapter is to provide an overview of issues for counselors and therapists to consider when working with Latino and Latina clients. With recommendation for a psychosociocultural approach (Gloria & Rodriguez, 2000), practical information relevant to case conceptualization and treatment interventions for Latinos and Latinas is presented. Treatment implications will be integrated throughout this chapter, and vignettes taken from our professional practice will be used to illustrate concepts and explicate cultural nuances. Issues such as acculturation, ethnic identity, traditionalism-modernism, core beliefs/values, and gender roles will be discussed. Specific core values pertinent to the vignettes will include *familismo, personalismo,* and *simpatía.* Issues for specific subpopulations (i.e., youth, older adults, college students, and migrant workers) and treatment applications are integrated throughout the chapter to provide a working framework.

Descriptive Information about Latinos/Latinas

Reference Terms

As with most racial, ethnic, or cultural groups, any one term that is used to describe millions of racially, ethnically, or culturally diverse individuals is inadequate and subsequently the target of academic and community critique. Specifically, debates continue regarding the most inclusive and least culturally offensive term to describe *Latinos* and *Latinas,* particularly as preferred self-descriptors vary by generation, geography, nationality, or personal preference. Some individuals are incensed by the use of the term *Hispanic* (e.g., a census descriptor that has colonial implications), whereas others choose it to self-identify (García & Marotta, 1997). Comas-Díaz (2001) recently presented a "taxonomic panorama" addressing the various terms that range from generic to specific in describing *La Raza Cósmica,* or the Cosmic Race.

Despite relevant and meaningful self-reference debates, Padilla (1995) insisted that the social and cultural "politics" must be secondary to the psychological implications. Because a terminology debate is beyond the scope of this paper, the terms *Latino, Latina,* and *Latino/as* will be used. It is important to note, however, that the self-identifying term *Latino* was used for the first time during Census 2000 (Guzmán, 2001). Although there are limitations to these terms, their use is not intended to negate or minimize the varied realities experienced by Mexican-, Cuban-, Puerto Rican-, Dominican-, and South and Central American-descended individuals who currently reside in the United States.

As the term *Latino* is nongendered, additional attention to the use of this descriptor is warranted. When referring to both males and females, scholars have been cautious to use both *Latino* and *Latina* or to include postscripts (i.e., a/o or o/a) to ensure clarity (Gloria, 2001). Even use of postscripts has incurred political or ideological conflict (Dernersesian, 1993), as the use of the *o/a* postscript identifies race/ethnicity first, whereas the *a/o* postscript identifies gender first. Although it may appear a superficial aspect of spelling, the postscripting allows for a sociopolitical shift for Latina identities, as reference to Latinas has been traditionally omitted from group characterizations and cultural systems that are typically male-privileged (Dernersesian, 1993). Specifically, Latinas are challenging their male-oriented characterization by subverting gender and racial/ethnic identities and proclaiming their self-defined and subjective realities (Gloria, 2001). Thus, the terms *Latino* or *Latinos* will refer only to males within the context of this chapter.

Population Estimates

Of the 281.4 million persons counted in the 2000 U.S. Census (excluding the Commonwealth of Puerto Rico and U.S. island areas), 12.5 percent were Latinos and Latinas (Guzmán, 2001). Since 1990, the Latino/a population has increased from 22.4 million in 1990 to 35.3 million in 2000. The 57.9 percent increase is more than four times the percentage of the total U.S. population. Current population projections suggest that Latinos and Latinas will number 63 million persons by 2030 and 88 million persons by 2050.

Heterogeneity of Subpopulations

Latinos and Latinas comprise many distinct subgroups from North, Central, and South America, who have different geographic distributions, language, cultural nuances, and economic and political reasons for migration (García & Marotta, 1997). A defining aspect of Latino/as is the heterogeneity of different subpopulations. Specifically, the Mexican-origin population constitutes the largest group of Latinos and Latinas (66.1 percent), followed by South and Central American- (14.5 percent), Puerto Rican- (9 percent), and Cuban-origin individuals (4 percent) (Therrien & Ramirez, 2001). Persons identified as "Other Hispanic" by the 2000 Current Population Reports of the U.S. Bureau of the Census comprise 6.4 percent of the Latino/a population.

Geographic Distribution

Although Latinos and Latinas live in every state of the U.S., there are particular geographic regions that are more heavily populated by different subpopulations. According to 2000 Census information, Latino/as are more likely to live in the West than the Northeast or the Midwest. Specifically, 44.7 percent of Latino/as live in the West, followed by 32.2 percent who live in the South, 14.1 percent in the Northeast, and 7.9 percent in the Midwest. Those of Mexican heritage are more likely to reside in the West (56.8 percent) and South (32.6 percent), whereas those of Puerto Rican heritage are more likely to live in the Northeast (63.9 percent). Persons of Cuban heritage are highly concentrated in the South (80.1 percent), particularly Florida. South and Central American Latinos and Latinas are distributed throughout the South (34.6 percent), Northeast (32.3 percent), and West (28.2 percent) (Therrien & Ramirez, 2001).

Age

The U.S. Latino/a population is considered young, with over one-third (35.7 percent) being less than 18 years of age and only 5.3 percent being over 65 (Therrien & Ramirez, 2001).

Latino/as have a younger median age (25.9 years) than that of the total U.S. population (35.3 years) (Guzmán, 2001), with the non-U.S.-born Latino/as being typically younger than those who are U.S.-born (Lollock, 2001). Among subgroups, individuals of Mexican origin had the highest percentage of persons less than 18 years old (38 percent, median age = 24.2), and persons of Cuban origin had the highest percentage (21 percent) of individuals who were 65 years of age or older. Currently, Latino/a children represent 16 percent of all children in the United States (Therrien & Ramirez, 2001).

Family Composition

Data indicate that for 30.6 percent of family households in which either a Latino or Latina was the primary "householder" (as compared to 11.8 percent of non-Latino/a Whites), there were five or more persons in the home (Therrien & Ramirez, 2001), with non-U.S.-born Latino/as typically having larger families than U.S.-born Latino/as (Lollock, 2001). Households with five or more persons were generally of Mexican descent (35.5 percent), whereas Cuban-descended individuals were most likely to have only two persons in the household (41.3 percent) (Therrien & Ramirez, 2001). Of Latino/a families, 1 in 4 are headed by Latinas, whereas only 17 percent of non-Latino/a families are headed by females (U.S. Bureau of the Census, 1995).

Language

Many Latino/as do not speak English well or do not speak English at all (U.S. Bureau of the Census, 1990), with more than three-fourths of Latino/as speaking Spanish in the home (Koss-Chioino & Vargas, 1999). Latino/as often have adequate knowledge of English to function in their daily lives (e.g., at work), particularly as approximately 17 million small businesses were able to conduct transactions in Spanish as of 1992 (U.S. Bureau of the Census, 1997). The command of English, however, may not be sufficient for Latino/as to discuss intimate and personal matters that are emotion laden with subtle cultural nuances (Echeverry, 1997), which are more readily expressed in one's first language (Koss-Chioino & Vargas, 1999).

Educational Attainment

As a whole, Latinos and Latinas tend to have high rates of undereducation, with educational attainment varying by subgroup. Over one-fourth of Latino/as have less than a ninth grade education, and approximately two in five persons have not graduated from high school (Therrien & Ramirez, 2001). Although they comprise the largest percentage of elementary- and secondary-level children (National Center for Education Statistics [NCES], 2000a), Latino/a presence in high school and college does not proportionally reflect their entry into the educational system (NCES, 2000b). Many Latino and Latina school children and adolescents are misplaced into special education classrooms and directed into non-college-bound tracks, with monolingual teachers, culturally insensitive teachers, and low achievement expectations (Gay, 2001).

Employment and Income

As of March 2000, almost 7 percent of Latinos and Latinas age 16 and older were unemployed, as compared to 3.4 percent of non-Latino/a Whites (Therrien & Ramirez, 2000), with non-U.S.-born Latino/as more likely than U.S.-born Latino/as to be unemployed, earn less, and live in poverty (Lollock, 2001). Puerto Ricans have the highest unemployment rates (8.1 percent), whereas Central and South Americans have the lowest (5.1 percent). For those employed full time throughout the year, less than one-fourth of Latino/as earned $35,000 or more, as compared to almost half of non-Latino/a Whites. By subgroup, Mexican-origin persons had the lowest percentage of persons earning $35,000 or more (20.6 percent), and Cuban-origin persons (34.4 percent) had the highest percentage of persons earning $35,000 or more (Therrien & Ramirez, 2001).

Religion and Spirituality

No single religious or spiritual tradition typifies Latino/a culture, as Latinos and Latinas range in their religious and spiritual practices (Zea, Mason, & Murguía, 2000). The predominant religion of many Latino/as, however, is Catholicism (Falicov, 1998). Indigenous traditions are central to the spiritual beliefs and practices of many Latino/as, as reflected in the three most prominent U.S. Latino/a ethnomedical healing systems: Curanderismo with individuals of Mexican descent, Espiritismo with individuals of Puerto Rican descent, and Santería with individuals of Cuban descent (Koss-Chioino, 1995). Although there are primary subpopulations that are more likely to engage in certain indigenous activities, the practices are not bound by ethnicity (Zea et al., 2000).

Implications of Diversity for Services for Latino and Latina Subpopulations

Because of the diversity among Latinos and Latinas, identifying particular characteristics, experiences, support systems, and living environments is critical in providing culturally appropriate, sensitive, and individualized therapy. Considering the rapid increase in the U.S. Latino/a population, Zea et al. (2000) have aptly stated that "Anglo therapists may have no choice but to work with Latino[a] clients" (p. 407). All mental health providers and counselors will need to provide services that recognize and integrate psychological, social, and cultural values and nuances. More specifically, counseling and therapy must attend to the dynamic and interdependent relationships of psychological, social, and cultural constructs in order to provide comprehensive and context-specific interventions for Latino/as (Gloria & Rodriguez, 2000).

Gloria and Rodriguez (2000) originally presented a *psychosociocultural* (PSC) approach to provide holistic, context-specific, and culturally relevant services to Latino/a university students; however, the framework assumes that various contextual aspects and issues (e.g., socioeconomic status, age, sexual orientation, immigration status) could and should be incorporated into counseling or therapy. The context of the university environment was of particular importance, as Latino/a college students encounter barriers and experiences different from those faced by other students. Similarly, Latino/a experiences within the context of societal values and assumptions about Latino/as often result in difficult interactions such as lower socioeconomic status, underemployment, and experience of oppression and racism (Rivers & Morrow, 1995).

Despite the interdependent and dynamic relationships of these psychosociocultural constructs, specific issues should be considered; these are presented in several case examples. The cases are presented not as stereotypical dilemmas faced by Latinos and Latinas, but rather as individual experiences that highlight salient Latino and Latina issues.

Psychosociocultural and Diversity Considerations

The following brief discussions of acculturation, ethnic identity, traditionalism-modernism, specific core values, and gender roles are intended to provide a basis from which culturally relevant and sensitive therapy can begin to address the needs of selected Latino/a subpopulations. Mental health professionals must attend to the individual needs of Latino/a clients and simultaneously recognize the unique cultural and value systems that must be incorporated into counseling and therapy in order to provide relevant and sensitive treatment.

Acculturation

Despite controversy in the psychological research concerning the measurement of acculturation, failing to consider the acculturation level of any racial and ethnic minority client is a violation of ethical standards (Board of Ethnic Minority Affairs, 1990). Acculturation has been defined as cognitive and behavioral changes that occur in an individual as a result of first-hand contact with a new or alternate cultural environment (Mendoza & Martinez, 1981). Some consider acculturation as a bidirectional process that focuses on the degree of assimilation into a new (majority) culture and the retention of the old (minority) culture (Berry, 1980). Others believe acculturation is a multifaceted process consisting of composite profiles in which individuals may reject, assimilate, or integrate various aspects of a culture (Sodowsky, Lai, & Plake, 1991). Kim and Abreu (2001) provide an extensive discussion of acculturation, reviewing definitions, measurement models, and instrumentation. Importantly, Kim and Abreu (2001) have identified the need to differentiate acculturation to the dominant culture from enculturation to the indigenous culture.

Numerous measures are available for Latino/as and specific subgroups of Latino/as (Kim & Abreu, 2001). For example, the Acculturation Rating Scale for Mexican Americans (ARSMA; Cuellar, Harris, & Jasso, 1980), the Bidimensional Short Acculturation Scale for Hispanics (BSASH; Marín & Gamba, 1996) and the Acculturation Rating Scale for Mexican Americans II (ARSMA-II; Cuellar, Arnold, & Maldonado, 1995) are a few of the standardized scales that can be used to make assessments. In particular, the ARSMA-II measures acculturation by assessing an orientation to Mexican culture and an orientation to Anglo culture. Knowing the Latino/a client's acculturation level is critical if therapists are to form appropriate and sound treatment plans (Ponterotto, 1987). For example, expectations of therapy may differ by level of acculturation (Aponte, Rivers, & Wohl, 1995).

It is inappropriate to rely solely on an instrument for the assessment of acculturation, however, as many factors influence how acculturation is manifested in an individual. Age and gender consistently attenuate acculturation. For instance, being male and young seems to accelerate the acculturative process (Rogler, 1994). Other factors positively correlated with acculturation include higher education (Negy & Woods, 1992), English language preference and proficiency, socioeconomic and generational status, and migrational history (Rogler, 1994). The process of acculturation is stressful as Latino/as contend with the demands of adapting and adopting a different culture (Smart & Smart, 1994).

Given the many factors that influence acculturation, counselors and therapists must assess factors for *each* individual client rather than work from general assumptions about Latino/a culture. The clinical interview allows therapists to assess for aspects (e.g., relational interactions) of acculturation that a paper-pencil test may not capture.

Ethnic Identity

Ethnic identity is another relevant concept to consider when providing mental health services to Latinos and Latinas. Ethnic identity refers to an individual's self-classification into an ethnic group based on characteristics representative of that group (Fernandez & Sanchez, 1992). Ethnic identity encompasses the extent to which an individual values his/her origin, engages in ethnic behavior, possesses information about that behavior, and understands the importance infused in that behavior and knowledge (Bernal & Martinelli, 1993). As part of one's social identity, ethnic identity is a developmental process that includes past cultural traditions and psychological dimensions from early socialization along with present sociological factors (Rosenthal & Feldman, 1992). Ethnic identity also is positively related to adjustment. Those who have a clear sense of their ethnic identity tend to have higher social and personal-emotional adjustment (Rodriguez, 1994).

The Multiethnic Identity Measure (MEIM) (Phinney, 1992) assesses three aspects of ethnic identity: positive ethnic attitudes and sense of belonging, ethnic identity achievement, and ethnic behaviors. It is important to note that although *acculturation* and *ethnic identity* are interrelated, they are not the same concept. *Acculturation* refers to how much the dominant culture has been incorporated and native culture maintained, whereas *ethnic identity* is part of one's self-identity—how one perceives oneself. Variations of these two concepts provide some understanding for the heterogeneity and worldviews within Latino/a cultures. The following vignette illustrates the complexity of acculturation and ethnic identity:

> Marco and Roberto are both second generation Latinos who grew up in low middle-class homes where Spanish was regularly spoken. Both are eldest children who attended college and completed a bachelor's degree. Both achieved a similar score on an acculturation measure. Marco, however, refuses to speak Spanish and identifies as an "American," whereas Roberto prefers to speak Spanish and describes himself as "muy Puertoriqueño." When troubled with an issue, Marco rationalizes and redirects his dissonance toward "doing" or working (e.g., yard work) and Roberto seeks the solace of good friends and family to discuss his concerns. When referred for psychological counseling for

different issues, Roberto adamantly refused to participate. He could not tell a stranger his "business" nor could he risk shaming his family. In contrast, Marco agreed to talk with someone for two sessions. He did not believe in "internal work" but thought that the therapist might offer some advice that might prove helpful.

Both Marco and Roberto were able to function well in the U.S. culture; however, their self-identification as ethnic individuals differed. Marco viewed himself as "American," whereas Roberto saw himself as "muy Puertoriqueño." Integrating both ethnic identity and level of acculturation of Latino/a clients appropriately attends to the social distance and trust levels experienced in the counseling relationship (Parham, 1989). Given Parham's (1989) implications for therapy in counselor-client dyads, Latino/a clients with ethnic identities congruent with the dominant culture (e.g., Marco) may more readily trust and be open with White counselors than would Latino/a clients with more traditional identities (e.g., Roberto). Because different ethnic identities and acculturation levels influence decisions to pursue counseling, interventions must parallel Latino/a clients' worldviews and values. A solution-oriented or brief treatment model would be more appropriate for Marco, whereas community-based outreach programming might reach clients like Roberto. Acculturation and ethnic identity are also valuable indicators to help clinicians assess clients' adherence to cultural concepts of *familismo, personalismo,* and *simpatía.*

Traditionalism-Modernism

The literature on Latino/as frequently refers to values that distinguish them from the dominant society, such as *familismo, personalismo,* and *simpatía* (Comas-Díaz, 1997). As a whole, these values underscore what Ramírez and Castaneda (1974) referred to as the traditionalism-modernism dimension. Modernistic belief systems embrace change and encourage an individual's separation from family and community early in life, whereas traditional belief systems resist change and emphasize family and community. Traditional Latino/a beliefs encompass several domains (Castro & Guiterres, 1997; Ramírez, 1991), including (1) strict and separate role definitions for men and women, (2) strong family and community (group) identity and loyalty as contrasted with individualism, (3) time orientation to the past and present versus the future, (4) valuing of age (elderly) versus youth, (5) valuing of traditions and rituals, (6) subservience to conventions and authority versus a questioning of authority, and (7) valuing of spirituality versus secularism. Understanding values within the traditionalism-modernism dimension helps mental health professionals conceptualize and respond to presenting concerns from Latino and Latina worldviews. As a result, interventions are strengthened, client participation and compliance improves, and treatment efficacy increases.

Familismo.   Familism or *familismo* refers to Latino/as' profound sense of family. Central and basic to the Latino/a culture (Marín & Marín, 1991), *familismo* is typified by strong feelings of loyalty, unity, solidarity, commitment, and reciprocity (Gloria & Peregoy, 1996). Interdependence, cooperation, and affiliation are also central to *familismo* (Falicov, 1996). Family needs supercede individual needs, and family honor must be upheld.

Latino/a families are characterized by extended kinship systems, including nuclear family, extended family, and non-related family members (Comas-Díaz & Griffith, 1988). Nonrelated members include *compadres* or *comadres* (godparents, literally coparents), *padrinos* or *madrinas* (godparents, literally best man and best woman), or *hijos de crianza* (legal and informally adopted children). *La familia* serves as a natural support system, providing physical, emotional, and social support to its members and acting as a buffer against stress (Briones et al., 1990). Latino/a families are also noted for the flexibility to reconfigure (Nichols & Schwartz, 1995). The ability of Latino/a nuclear families to expand to include extended family members, nonblood-related members, new generations, and adult members who have left the household and subsequently returned is a perceived strength. The adaptability of family structure also enables Latino/a families to handle change (Rodriguez, 1996a).

The following vignette illustrates several aspects of *familismo*. The vignette also demonstrates how traditionalism in a Mexican family may impact treatment.

A 64-year-old Mexican woman, Señora H, was brought to an outpatient mental health center by her husband and 32-year-old son who lived with his parents. The family spoke only Spanish, although the son could speak some English. The husband and son were farm laborers, and the family resided in a segregated Mexican community. Señora H had been psychotic for six months. Her symptoms included not caring for her personal hygiene, not performing her household duties, responding with intense emotions, and, more recently, throwing pebbles at passing cars and neighbors. Her husband and son responded by bathing and dressing her, performing her household tasks, and brewing sedative teas for her "nerves." Acting against her wishes to not seek help outside the family, her husband and son sought professional assistance when the neighbors complained about her behavior. Because of the considerable shame and guilt for having brought her to the clinic, they were unwilling to proceed with any additional interventions without the woman's consent. When asked to describe her presenting concerns, Señora H replied that she had been hexed by the local curandero. Both husband and son also believed she was cursed; however, they had been unable to locate another curandero to undo the hex. The therapist recognized the need to consider all treatment methods, and supplied them with the name and address of another curandero. Señora H agreed that following treatment from the curandero she would proceed to the local inpatient psychiatric facility.

As this vignette indicates, family support can also be both a strength and a liability. In this case, the family's help with the functional day-to-day activities delayed their pursuing treatment. Taken to an extreme, the risk of feeling obligated to an unhealthy family system or situation may unintentionally enable a family member's pathology by delaying service utilization (Molina & Aguirre-Molina, 1994). Similarly, the belief that emotional or personal concerns are a result of weakness, bad luck, a supernatural event, or God's will (Echeverry, 1997) was addressed with Señora H and her family to increase her comfort and compliance with treatment. This vignette also demonstrates how therapists can sensitively enter into a Latino/a client's world to promote compliance and facilitate appropriate treatment. In this instance, the counselor respected and utilized the strength of *familismo* and nontraditional methods of treatment in providing a holistic and relevant intervention. It is important that the counselor did not ignore or pathologize Señora H's or her family's spiritual beliefs and was willing and able (i.e., by a referral) to integrate alternative forms of treatment.

Personalismo.   *Personalismo* is a communication style emphasizing personal interactions (Comas-Díaz, 1989) that complements and is essential to the value of *familismo* (Gloria & Peregoy, 1996). Most Latino/as value the qualities that encompass worth of self, dignity of self and others, and reciprocity of respect for other people (Ho, 1987). As interpersonal behaviors are considered more important than task achievements (Triandis, Marín, Lisansky, & Betancourt, 1984), external characteristics of an individual are of secondary importance. For instance, a Latino/a who provides emotional support, personal connection, and encouragement for his/her family is more highly valued than a Latino/a who provides material goods and has high societal standing (Comas-Díaz, 1997; Gloria & Peregoy, 1996).

Because of the value placed on interpersonal interactions, Latino and Latina clients may desire a personal connection with their therapist prior to establishing a working relationship (Gloria & Peregoy, 1996). Thus the client may invite the therapist to family functions, bring small gifts (e.g., food), or ask about the therapist's family. If a therapist rejects such attempts to personalize the relationship, some Latino/a clients may feel offended, ultimately limiting client trust in the therapeutic relationship. Therefore, therapists should carefully consider invitations from their Latino/a clients; should they choose not to accept an invitation, they should decline respectfully, continuing to affirm and acknowledge the importance of the relationship. Although a therapist may find a personal connection uncomfortable, he/she needs to recognize that *personalismo* is necessary and central to relational interactions, important in ensuring future interactions with Latino/a clients (Gloria & Peregoy, 1996).

Simpatía.   Closely related to the value of *personalismo* is *simpatía. Simpatía* is a permanent personal quality "where an individual is perceived as likeable, attractive, fun to be with, and easygoing" (Triandis et al., 1984, p. 1363). Identified as a cultural script, *simpatía* emphasizes promotion and maintenance of harmonious and pleasant interpersonal relationships (Yep, 1995). Accordingly, individuals maintain certain levels of conformity, behave with dignity and respect toward others, and attempt to maintain interpersonal harmony. In maintaining harmony, individuals avoid conflicts by emphasizing positive behaviors and de-emphasizing negative behaviors (Triandis et al., 1984).

Triandis et al. (1984) identified five instances in which Latino/as are more likely to adhere to the *simpatía* script than are non-Latino/as:

> (a) greater emphasis on talking with friends, even if that makes one late for an appointment, (b) greater importance given to the values of loyalty, respect, duty, and graciousness, (c) more emphasis on cooperation and interpersonal helping, (d) greater willingness to sacrifice oneself for the sake of attending family functions, (e) preference for service (physician, lawyer) received from friends, even if the friends are not too competent. (p. 1374)

Thus great value is placed on manners, courtesy, and harmonious relationships. As conflict, direct argument, and contradiction are considered rude, interactions will likely be detailed and indirect. Such a cultural script for Latino/as and non-Latino/as suggests that non-Latino/as who deviate from the *simpatía* are likely to be rejected by more traditional Latino/as.

Counselors and therapists need to be cognizant of and sensitive to *simpatía* and to resist pathologizing Latino/as who appear to "socialize" during client sessions. Therapists need not automatically conceptualize socializing as resistance or denial of the issues, but rather as an effort to maintain cultural propriety (Gloria & Peregoy, 1996). By responding appropriately, therapists can become *una persona de confianza* (a person of trust). Ultimately, gaining the confidence of Latino/a clients will help to establish therapeutic working alliances.

Gender Roles

Gender roles are an aspect of Latino/a cultures that are frequently represented as negative stereotypes. Specifically, *machismo, hembrismo,* and *marianismo* are often misunderstood concepts. Although many Latino/as continue to adhere to traditional gender roles, many have modified their adherence to these more traditional roles (Vasquez-Nuttal, Romero-Garcia, & De Leon, 1987). Thus therapists must assess the degree to which each individual maintains or adheres to *machismo, hembrismo,* and *marianismo* in order to understand cultural roles and their influence on Latino/a clients' issues (Gloria & Peregoy, 1996).

Machismo refers to Latino/as who promote traditional sex roles by categorizing activities as "manly" or "womanly." Siantz de Leon (1994) indicated that the historical Mexican concepts of machismo evolved during tumultuous political and social periods in Mexico's history. Without support from military or police, local citizens patrolled roads and highways to protect their homes and families from the lawless. Just and fair authority, courage, honor, and respect were necessary for men to participate in these patrols.

Although *machismo* has both positive and negative connotations, the construct is most often negatively defined (Félix-Ortiz, Abreu, Briano, & Bowen, 2001). At one extreme, *machismo* refers to Latinos who perceive their roles as breadwinners and protectors of their families, hold benign and flexible attitudes, and provide structure to family relationships. At another extreme, *machismo* refers to Latinos who rigidly adhere to gender roles that cause distress to their families, such as consuming great quantities of alcohol, being sexually available to women, taking risks, exerting extreme authoritarianism, or psychologically and physically dominating women (Abreu, Goodyear, Campos, & Newcomb, 2000; Comas-Díaz & Griffith, 1988; Félix-Ortiz et al., 2001; Ho, 1987). Any of these attributes are problematic to family relationships, yet labeling these behaviors as *machista* without first understanding the underlying or cultural context of the behavior limits the therapist's ability to have significant impact.

The negative stereotypes and perceptions of Latinos and Latinas are many (Niemann, 2001). Some of the less than favorable views often emanate from the interconnected concepts of *marianismo* and *hembrismo,* commonly held ideals within patriarchal Latino/a value systems. *Marianismo* is the value that women are expected to revere and emulate the Virgin Mary (Rivers, 1995) and to endure suffering (Mirandé, 1985). *Hembrismo* embodies "femaleness," where Latinas are expected to work in and out of the home and competently fulfill multiple roles (Comas-Díaz, 1989). Subsequently, Latinas may be expected to live "cultural paradoxes" in which they are expected to be "morally and spiritually superior to men, while they are expected to accept male authority" (Boyd-Franklin & Garcia-Preto, 1994, p. 253).

Unfortunately, the essence of *marianismo* and *hembrismo* (i.e., strength, perseverance, flexibility, ability to survive, and willingness to serve) has been overlooked and undervalued (Comas-Díaz, 1989). Some Latinas successfully modify their roles and values, some completely reject traditional Latino/a cultures, and others never fully resolve the conflict and thus experience difficulties (Rivers, 1995). Counselors and therapists need to assess adherence to traditional values, assist in values clarification, and ultimately support their clients' decisions to adhere to particular values (Gloria & Peregoy, 1996). Counselors and therapists must also examine their own biases and assumptions to avoid negative and inappropriate stereotypes and to prevent discrimination and oppression within the therapeutic relationship (Vasquez, 1994).

The following vignette illustrates how *marianismo* and *hembrismo* may manifest themselves differently as a function of cultural environment.

> A highly-educated professional, Alicia presented at a counseling training center for help to "sort out marital issues." She revealed that she held a high-level managerial position and was successful. At home, she behaved traditionally: her husband made major purchase and vacation decisions and was the perceived head of the family. Although Alicia considered herself to be better able to handle the family's monies and make family decisions, she nevertheless believed and presented him as "head of the family." Alicia was assertive at her workplace; however, at home she felt her assertiveness would be disrespectful and disloyal to her husband and family. This paradox was contributing to her depressive symptoms. She had recently been offered a position that would increase her salary beyond her husband's and thus was uncertain about accepting the offer.

Examination and clarification of gender roles would be necessary with Alicia to support her in making decisions congruent with her professional and personal values. The counselor helped Alicia clarify that she valued her own *hembrismo* and consequently sought her husband's help in making the career decision. Thus Alicia honored her cultural values (i.e., *hembrismo, familismo*), resolved her dilemma, and her depressive symptoms abated. Given the knowledge of differing traditional gender roles, culturally effective counselors honor and support the gender role choices (and other culturally based decisions) of their clients rather than pathologize their clients' choices.

Considerations with Latino/a Subpopulations

Within Latino cultures, subgroups of clients have unique circumstances and particular needs. Among these subgroups are youth, older adults, college students, and migrant farmworkers. Information about these subpopulations becomes important as both youth and older adults are increasing in number within the Latino/a population, thus increasing the likelihood that counselors will interact with either. Focusing on college students and migrant farmworkers is also relevant, as these subpopulations have unique experiences and needs.

Youth

The experiences and needs of Latino/a youth warrant attention, as a large proportion of Latino/as are under 17 years of age. The fastest growing group of young people in the nation, Latino/a youth are projected to triple from six million in 1982 to almost 19 million in 2020 (Chapa & Valencia, 1993). Children are a source of pride in Latino/a cultures, and many young adults marry and/or have children at an early age, in part accounting for the high Latino fertility rates (Sue & Sue, 1999). Along with the issues associated with being a young spouse or parent, Latino/a youth also grapple with unique mental health issues (e.g., acculturation gap with parents), given their cultural membership, lower socioeconomic status, undereducation, negative stereotypes, and experiences of oppression and racism (Rivers & Morrow, 1995).

It is important to note that two-thirds of Latino/a youth are first or second generation immigrants (Chapa & Valencia, 1993), with most Latino/a youth having been exposed to another language and culture before entering the U.S. school system. The contradiction between home culture and U.S. culture is often more salient for girls than for boys, due to cultural differences in what constitutes gender-appropriate behavior (Espín, 1997). In addition, children and adolescents tend to acculturate faster than their parents, resulting in intergenerational tension for many Latino/a families (Ramirez, 1991). Tension is created when youth serve as language and social mediators for their parents, resulting in an imbalance in the parent-child relationship (Falicov, 1996). Latino/a youth also contend with migrational stress as a result of having left family members behind in the process of relocating to the United States (Espín, 1997).

Within Latino/a families, parents are expected to provide for their children through adulthood and marriage, as the parent-child relationship is a lifelong commitment and expectation. Children are expected to be obedient, contribute monetarily to the family whenever possible, and care for household functioning (Ho, 1987). Older children are also expected to care for and protect their younger siblings, with the oldest sister often acting as a surrogate mother, and with brothers protecting sisters. Although these cultural values allow for multigenerational families to support each other, many Latino/a youth lack the resources to cope with the multiple stresses they experience. For example, Kobus and Reyes (2000) found that Mexican American youth are more likely to use active coping (e.g., information seeking and problem solving), family social support, self-reliance, and behavioral avoidance in stressful situations than are non-Latino/a White youth. Latino/a youth are also more likely to use religion as a means of coping (Copeland & Hess, 1995).

Latino/a youth also struggle with gender and sexual norms. Boys are generally allowed greater freedom to come and go as they please, whereas girls are more closely restricted (Ho, 1987). Despite heavy emphasis on family interactions, sexuality and sexual issues are rarely discussed with Latino/a youth by their families (Centers for Disease Control, 1991; Sue & Sue, 1999). However, Latinos often have more accurate knowledge of contraceptives than Latinas (Scott, Shifman, Orr, Owen, & Fawcett, 1988). Complicating the lack of information is the traditional Latino/a belief that "'good' Latinas are not supposed to know about sex" (Marín & Gómez, 1997, p. 79). Levels of homophobia within the Latino/a culture also minimize discussions about sexuality, as gay or lesbian youth often fear rejection and stigmatization from their families and communities (Morales, 1992). Important to note are the inconsistent findings regarding the degree to which religion or religiosity influences Latino/a sexuality (Marín & Gómez, 1997, p. 79).

Unlike non-Latino/a White adolescents, who are encouraged to be independent and assertive, Latino/a youth are encouraged to be interdependent and cooperative (Siantz de Leon, 1994). By overlooking or minimizing the cultural norm of interdependence and collaboration, mental health professionals often pathologize Latino/a clients as "codependent" or "enmeshed." Counselors working with Latino/a youth must recognize and constructively use the strength, support, and interdependency that often characterize Latino/a families. The following vignette illustrates family interdependence and the difficulty of addressing sexuality.

> Monica, who prefers to be called Monique, is a 16-year-old high school sophomore who was brought into a mental health clinic by her mother. Monique's mother reports that she has been talking back, missing school, and climbing out her window at night. Mrs. Jimenez has not yet told her husband about Monique's activities because she fears that he will become angry with Monique. When seen alone, Monique reveals that she suspects that she is pregnant and is afraid to tell her parents, particularly her father. Although Monique is aware of contraceptives and that intercourse can lead to pregnancy, she acquiesced to her boyfriend's wish not to use a condom. She fears that her father will make her leave home because she has "shamed" their family. Upon further exploration of possible options and resources, Monique reveals that she could live with her paternal grandmother if her father kicked her out and that her father would most likely help support her once the baby was born.

A family member who refers Latino/a youth to counseling may be concerned about the stigma that is often associated with receiving psychological services. It is therefore important to explain and demystify the counseling process as part of developing a trusting, safe therapeutic relationship (Falicov, 1996). In working with Latina clients such as Monique, counselors and therapists need to recognize and call upon the strengths of the family (González, 1997). In this example, a counselor could easily assess the family as overly enmeshed; however, a more culturally appropriate, relevant, and helpful conceptualization would be to embrace and mobilize the intergenerational supports of Latino/a family systems. Recognizing cultural lines of communication would also facilitate strategies for Monique to communicate her concerns to her father. For example, Monique could communicate her concerns to her grandmother and mother, who could then discuss Monique's issue with the father. As a result, verbally acknowledging the realities of sexual behavior would break the "sexual silence" often supported by Latino/a cultures (Marín & Gómez, 1997). Additional issues for consideration include helping Mrs. Jimenez (a) anticipate potential blame from her husband for her role in Monique's dilemma, (b) address her guilt for not telling her husband of the situation earlier, and (c) deal with the loss of her dreams for Monique. This is particularly salient because Latinas are often held responsible for the spiritual, physical, social, and emotional well-being of the children.

Older Adults

For older Latino/as, physical and emotional difficulties of aging are compounded by transcultural alienation, racial discrimination, language barriers, lack of health insurance, limited financial resources, different cultural customs and beliefs, and poverty (Parra & Espino, 1992). As almost half of older Latino/as live at or below the poverty level, many do not have access to health care (Wray, 1992). Influenced by acculturation level and beliefs about health and illnesses, older Latino/as are more likely to access the medical profession than to seek mental health services. As with physical illness, they may treat psychological problems with brewed teas, special massages, church attendance, and prayer (McKenna, 1995) or seek the services of a traditional healer (Koss-Chioino, 1995). For example, Applewhite (1995) found that elderly Mexican Americans' cultural knowledge, belief, and faith systems played distinct roles in their health practices and preferences, with 76 percent of the sample choosing to treat themselves with common folk treatment, herbs, or self-medication. Seeking spiritual services or practicing some form of spiritism is common, particularly as many Latino/as believe that illness and misfortune are external to the individual and primarily spiritual in nature (Koss-Chioino, 1995). For example, altars that pay homage to God or to one's higher spirits are commonplace in many Latino/a homes.

Although older Latino/as may not regularly or traditionally choose to access mental health services for themselves, they can facilitate the services for other family members, particularly as many Latino/as live in intergenerational households or with extended relatives residing nearby (Hurtado, 1995). Older Latino/as perform many roles in the family, such as socializing younger family members, providing emotional support, and transmitting culture and language (Sotomayor, 1989). Zuniga (1997) called for the use of reminiscence work to maintain and strengthen traditional roles of Mexican elderly, thereby promoting continued intergenerational transmission of cultural values and ethics, as well as helping to alleviate alienation and deal with discrimination. Further, Mayers and Souflee (1991) suggested that counselors and therapists access and strengthen social support systems of aging Latino/as through the use of mutual aid/self-help programming and informal network strategies. Accessing potential resources within the Latino/a communities can also augment and supplement services for older Latino/as.

As depicted in the vignette with Señora H, adult children may seek assistance regarding the mental health of their elderly parents. Frequently these adult children coordinate and mediate services, transport their parents, and interpret for the counselor and their parents. Thus counselors need to acquire a working understanding of the roles of family members in contact with their older Latino/a clients.

College Students

As the most undereducated segment of the U.S. population (Pérez & de la Rosa Salazar, 1993), Latino/as face multiple barriers in their academic careers, ranging from educational tracking and alienation on campuses to a lack of Latino/a faculty members and mentors (Aguirre & Martinez, 1993). Two factors particularly relevant to the nonpersistence of Latino/as in higher education are perceptions of the college environment (Ponterotto, 1990) and cultural congruity (Gloria & Robinson Kurpius, 1996). Latino/as are likely to report feelings of isolation in an inhospitable climate on predominantly White campuses (Ponterotto, 1990). Although Latino/as are recruited and tolerated on campus, their cultural values are often unaccepted or unappreciated in academia (Ponterotto, Martinez, & Hayden, 1986).

Where academia is based upon a middle class White male orientation, Latino/a students often encounter "cultural incongruence" (Gloria & Robinson Kurpius, 1996). Isolation and alienation may occur from being one of only a few Latino/as on campus and from their attempt to balance their cultural values with the institutional values in order to succeed academically (Gloria & Rodriguez, 2000). As a result, both students and faculty are forced to examine their own identities as Latino/as (Cervantes, 1988). All college students have adjustment issues, but Latino/a students have few Latino/a faculty to seek out as mentors or guides (Gloria & Rodriguez, 2000).

As a result, university counselors, faculty, and staff (e.g., academic advisors) must serve as resources to Latino/a students (and/or campus and community organizations) by providing a systematic structure for social support, psychoeducational information, and advocacy for their academic and social well-being (Gloria & Rodriguez, 2000). An example of how the college experience may trigger value conflicts is reflected in the following vignette:

> Carmen is a first year, first generation college student at a predominately White four-year institution. Because Carmen had been crying frequently and having trouble concentrating on class assignments, her residence hall advisor referred her to the university counseling center. Her parents, who live in a different state, were pressuring her to return home for a week to take part in an important family event, her grandfather's 80th birthday. From Carmen's perspective, not attending her grandfather's party would mean that she is a "bad daughter" or *mal educada* (poorly educated), and she is also concerned that her family will think that she is "better" than they are. Carmen reports feeling "torn." She wants to return home for the family party, yet at the same time feels she cannot afford to miss a week of school and still maintain her grades. This is Carmen's first time away from home, and she reports feeling lonely and isolated.

Counselors and therapists can help Latino/a college students like Carmen balance family and school commitments through values clarification. When working with a student like Carmen, the meaning of attending or not attending family events needs to be clarified. For example, Carmen's counselor could help her identify something that she could do for her grandfather and family in lieu of attending, thereby letting her family know that she values them. In addition, Carmen may need to address issues of guilt, betrayal, selfishness, and confusion that may have resulted when she left her family to attend school (Arredondo, 1991). Counselors and therapists can also help Latino/a students identify social and emotional supports on campus (e.g., "older" Latino/a students) and/or in the local community (e.g., attending local church services) to help decrease feelings of isolation. Similarly, seeking out other Latinas with similar struggles could validate her need and provide guidance in balancing the demands of home and school (Gloria, 1999).

Migrant Farmworkers

The estimated number of migrant farmworkers has not changed; however, two major shifts have occurred in the composition of the migrant farmworker population in the United States (COSSMHO, 1990). First, the number of migrants with dependents and family members (i.e., children and older adults) who travel as part of a work crew has increased, as has the number of migrant family units traveling in private vehicles. Second, the number of Latino/a farmworkers has increased relative to the numbers for other racial and ethnic groups (Siantz de Leon, 1994). Although there are migrational streams in the United States (west, midwest, east), Latino/as account for 90% of migrant farmworkers in the Midwest and more than 50% in California, Nevada, and Arizona (COSSMHO, 1990).

The migrant lifestyle is uncertain and transient. Long hours, six- to seven-day work weeks, poor working conditions, low wages, and lack of job security contribute to stressful living (Siantz de Leon, 1994). Inadequate housing, transportation, nutrition, and medical care limit migrant farmworkers from seeking services. Similarly, many have insufficient time or are otherwise unwilling to seek medical or psychological attention (Hibbeln, 1996). If Latino/as do seek services, Echeverry (1997) has estimated, many miss at least two hours of work for one hour of counseling—one hour for therapy and one hour for round-trip transportation. Time constraints result because many Latino/as have more than one job, family responsibilities, no personal transportation, and jobs that do not allow for sick leave (Echeverry, 1997). Thus counselors must be willing to provide weekend services or late evening sessions or to travel to a location that can be easily reached (e.g., community center or church) so that services are accessible.

Although economic necessity forces a transient lifestyle, there is great variability in the degree of socialization in the life of a migrant farmworker. For many immigrants, migrant farmworking is a temporary way of making money until they return to their homeland. For second, third, and later generation Latino/as, however, the migrant farmwork experience often defines who they are and how they perceive themselves: that is, they often resign themselves to the migrant way of life and do not foresee a different socioeconomic future.

Latino/a migrant farmworkers are at high risk for psychological concerns (Vega, Warheit, & Palacio, 1985). For example, farmworkers are at risk for depression if isolated from their support systems (Siantz de Leon, 1994). For Latino/as, depression is buffered by localized social support (Briones et al., 1990), including family members who live with the individual, people from his/her region, or fellow workers. Once social networks are identified, counselors and therapists can assess the feasibility of incorporating family and nonfamily members into the treatment plan. Organista and Organista (1997) have suggested group psychoeducational interventions and workshops as a psychotherapeutically effective means of intervention for migrant farmworkers that is more likely to be accepted than individual sessions. Despite a psychoeducational focus on a specific topic, counselors and therapists should anticipate questions and discussion about unrelated topics. For example, Latino/as may convene for a parenting skills class and introduce the topic of domestic violence or physical concerns (Rodriguez, 1998). Also a brief therapy model that respects the client's mobile lifestyle and is accessible (e.g., late hour appointment times that accommodate workers' schedules and do not require them to forgo pay from their jobs) may be more effective and appropriate. Counselors are referred to Miramontes' (1995) *Under the Feet of Jesus* for a fictional but accurate description of the migrant lifestyle.

Psychosociocultural Implications for Counseling and Psychotherapy

In providing holistic counseling that integrates the multiple dimensions of Latino/a culture, counselors must address and work within belief systems that they may not value or fully appreciate. As a result, Latino/as may not be willing to discuss sensitive issues such as sexuality or religion and spirituality due to persecution, prejudice, or belief of pathology (Zea et al., 2000). Further, because the relationship one has with God or one's spirits is highly personal, even if they are brought up these issues may not be open for challenge or discussion. It is necessary to establish a trusting and personable relationship, in which belief systems can be addressed in a nonjudgmental and caring manner.

Central to all of the traditional belief systems espoused by many Latinos and Latinas are the values of harmony and balance, in which "imbalance is a moral issue" (Koss-Chioino, 1995, p. 148). The underlying aspect of homeostasis can be an important aspect of the therapeutic conversation in "striving for mental balance and personal harmony by counteracting or neutralizing excesses and imbalances" (Falicov, 1998, p. 137). The belief of some Latino/a clients that their concerns are caused by external influences may be challenging to counselors, particularly as many Latino/as believe that only God (or deities, energies, or spirits likened to God) can solve a problem or illness (Echeverry, 1997) or that a higher power is punishing an individual or a family (Zea, Belgrave, García, & Quezada, 1997). For example, gay Latinos (Arguelles & Rivero, 1997), Latino/as with physical disabilities (Zea et al., 1997), or Latino/as with substance use/abuse issues (Gloria & Peregoy, 1996) often attribute their "affliction" to punishment from God. As a result, Latino/as may engage in spiritual work for their families and communities (Zea et al., 2000), activities that can supplement and complement culturally relevant and competent therapeutic work.

Conclusion

It is imperative that *each* Latino or Latina client be considered individually in order for treatment to be effective. Providing culturally sensitive, contextually appropriate, and individualized service for each Latino/a client entails that the mental health professional accurately assess and understand the client's worldview and sociocultural context (Rodriguez, 1996b). In particular, an understanding of ethnic identity and acculturation must be applied in providing culturally relevant counseling for Latino/a clients (Padilla, 1995). After the significance of ethnic identity and acculturation is determined, the cultural, historical, linguistic, and sociological uniqueness of each client must be further integrated and considered in providing an approach that is holistic and context-specific (Gloria & Rodriguez, 2000). For example, addressing gender roles (e.g., *machismo, hembrismo, marianismo*) and other cultural values (e.g., traditionalism, *personalismo, simpatía*) is critical when working with different Latino/a subpopulations (e.g., youth, elderly, college students, migrant farmworkers). Finally, counselors and therapists must not only understand the significance of family, social networks, and belief systems of their Latino/a clients, but they must also examine their own stereotypes and biases, including those biases imposed as a result of their clinical training. Doing so will enhance the quality and effectiveness of mental health services provided to *all* clients and allow them to move toward culturally competent services for Latino/a clients in particular.

References

Abreu, J., Goodyear, R. K., Campos, A., & Newcomb, M. (2000). Ethnic belonging and traditional masculinity ideology among African Americans, European Americans, and Latinos. *Psychology of Men and Masculinity, 1*(2), 75–86.

Aguirre, A., Jr., & Martinez, R. O. (1993). *Chicanos in higher education: Issues and dilemmas for the 21st century.* ASHE-ERIC Higher Education Report No. 3. Washington, DC: The George Washington University, School of Education and Human Development.

Aponte, J. F., & Crouch, R. T. (1995). The changing ethnic profile of the United States. In J. F. Aponte, R. Y. Rivers, & J. Wohl (Eds.), *Psychological interventions and cultural diversity* (pp. 1–18). Boston: Allyn & Bacon.

Aponte, J. F., Rivers, R. Y., & Wohl, J. (Eds.) (1995). *Psychological interventions and cultural diversity.* Boston: Allyn & Bacon.

Applewhite, S. L. (1995). Curanderismo: Demystifying the health beliefs and practices of elderly Mexican Americans. *Health and Social Work, 20,* 247–253.

Arguelles, L., & Rivero, A. (1997). Spiritual emergencies and psycho-spiritual treatment strategies among gay/homosexual Latinos with HIV disease. In M. P. Levine, P. M. Nardi, & J. H. Gagnon (Eds.), *In changing times: Gay men and lesbians encounter HIV/AIDS* (pp. 83–98). Chicago: The University of Chicago Press.

Arredondo, P. (1991). Counseling Latinas. In C. C. Lee & B. L. Richardson (Eds.), *Multicultural issues in counseling: New approaches to diversity* (pp. 143–156). Alexandria, VA: American Association for Counseling and Development.

Bernal, M. E., & Martinelli, P. C. (1993). *Mexican American identity.* Encino, CA: Floricanto Press.

Berry, J. W. (1980). Acculturation as varieties of adaptation. In A. M. Padilla (Ed.), *Acculturation: Theory, model, and some new findings* (pp. 9–25). Boulder, CO: Westview.

Board of Ethnic Minority Affairs (1990). *Guidelines for providers of psychological services to ethnic, linguistic, and culturally diverse populations.* Washington, DC: American Psychological Association.

Boyd-Franklin, N., & Garcia-Preto, N. (1994). Family therapy: The cases of African American and Hispanic women. In L. Comas-Diaz & B. Greene (Eds.), *Women of color: Integrating ethnic and gender identities in psychotherapy* (pp. 239–264). New York: Guilford Press.

Briones, D. F., Heller, P. L., Chalfant, H. P., Roberts, A. E., Aguirre-Hauchbaum, S. F., & Farr, W. F. (1990). Socioeconomic status, ethnicity, psychological distress and readiness to utilize a mental health facility. *American Journal of Psychiatry, 147,* 1333–1340.

Castro, F. G., & Guiterres, S. (1997). Drug and alcohol use among rural Mexican Americans. *NIDA research monograph.* Rockville, MD: National Institute on Drug Abuse.

Centers for Disease Control (1991). Characteristics of parents who discuss AIDS with their children—United States 1989. *Morbidity and Mortality Weekly Report, 40,* 789–791.

Cervantes, O. F. (1988). The realities that Latinos, Chicanos, and other ethnic minority students encounter in graduate school. *Journal of La Raza Studies, 2,* 33–41.

Chapa, J., & Valencia, R. R. (1993). Latino population growth, demographic characteristics, and educational stagnation: An examination of recent trends. *Hispanic Journal of Behavioral Sciences, 15,* 165–187.

Coalition of Spanish Speaking Health and Human Service Organizations: COSSMHO (1990). *Delivering preventive health care to Hispanics.* Washington, DC: Author.

Comas-Diaz, L. (2001). Hispanics, Latinos, or Americanos: The evolution of identity. *Cultural Diversity and Ethnic Minority Psychology, 7,* 115–120.

Comas-Diaz, L. (1997). Mental health needs of Latinos with professional status. In J. G. García & M. C. Zea (Eds.), *Psychological intervention and research with Latino populations* (pp. 142–165). Boston: Allyn and Bacon.

Comas-Diaz, L. (1989). Culturally relevant issues and treatment implication for Hispanics. In D. R. Koslow & E. Salett (Eds.), *Crossing cultures in mental health* (pp. 31–48). Washington, DC: Society for International Education Training and Research (SIETAR).

Comas-Diaz, L., & Griffith, E. E. H. (1988). *Clinical guidelines in cross-cultural mental health.* New York: Wiley & Sons.

Copeland, E. P., & Hess, R. S. (1995). Differences in young adolescents' coping strategies based on gender and ethnicity. *Journal of Early Adolescence, 15,* 203–219.

Cuellar, I., Harris, L. C., & Jasso, R. (1980). An acculturation scale for Mexican American normal and clinical populations. *Hispanic Journal of Behavioral Sciences, 2,* 199–217.

Cuellar, I., Arnold, B., & Maldonado, R. (1995). Acculturation Rating Scale for Mexican Americans-II: A revision of the original ARSMA Scale. *Hispanic Journal of Behavioral Sciences, 17*(3), 275–304.

Cuellar, I., & Roberts, R. E. (1984). Psychological disorders among Chicanos. In J. L. Martinez, Jr., & R. H. Mendoza (Eds.), *Chicano Psychology* (2nd ed., pp. 133–161). New York: Academic Press.

Dernersesian, A. C. (1993). And, yes…the earth did part: On the splitting of Chicana/o subjectivity. In A. de la Torre & B. M. Pesquera (Eds.), *Building with our hands: New directions in Chicana studies* (pp. 34–56). Los Angeles: University of California Press.

Echeverry, J. J. (1997). Treatment barriers: Accessing and accepting professional help. In J. G. García & M. C. Zea (Eds.), *Psychological intervention and research with Latino populations* (pp. 94–107). Boston: Allyn and Bacon.

Espín, O. M. (1997). *Latina realities: Essays on healing, migration, and sexuality.* Boulder, CO: Westview Press.

Falicov, C. J. (1998). *Latino families in therapy: A guide to multicultural practice.* New York: Guilford Press.

Falicov, C. J. (1996). Mexican families. In M. McGoldrick, J. Giordano, & J. Pearce (Eds.), *Ethnicity and family therapy* (pp. 169–182). New York: Guilford Press.

Fernandez, D. M., & Sanchez, J. I. (1992, August). Multidimensional measurement of ethnic identification: Hispanic versus American of Hispanic-American? Paper presented at the annual meeting of the American Psychological Association, Washington, DC.

Félix-Ortiz, M., Abreu, J. M., Briano, M., & Bowen, D. (2001). A critique of machismo measures in psychological research. In F. Columbus (Ed.), *Advances in psychology research, Volume III* (pp. 63–90). Huntington, NY: Nova Science.

Firestone, J. M., & Harris, R. J. (1994). Hispanic women in Texas: An increasing portion of the underclass. *Hispanic Journal of Behavioral Sciences, 16,* 176–185.

Gay, G. (2001). Educational equality for students of color. In J. A. Banks & C. A. McGee Banks (Eds.), *Multicultural education: Issues and perspectives* (4th ed., pp. 197–224). New York: John Wiley.

García, J. G., & Marotta, S. (1997). In J. G. García & M. C. Zea (Eds.), *Psychological interventions and research with Latino populations* (pp. 1–14). Boston: Allyn & Bacon.

Gloria, A. M. (2001). The cultural construction of Latinas: Practice implications of multiple realities and identities. In D. B. Pope-Davis & H. L. K. Coleman (Eds.), *The intersection between race, gender, and class: Implications for multicultural counseling* (pp. 3–24). Thousand Oaks, CA: Sage.

Gloria, A. M. (1999). Apoyando estudiantes Chicanas: Therapeutic factors in Chicana college student support groups. *Journal for Specialists in Group Work, 24*(3), 246–259.

Gloria, A. M., & Peregoy, J. J. (1996). Counseling Latino alcohol and other drug abusers: Cultural issues for consideration. *Journal of Substance Abuse Treatment, 13,* 1–8.

Gloria, A. M., & Robinson Kurpius, S. E. (1996). The validation of the Cultural Congruity Scale and the University Cultural Environment Scale with Chicano students. *Hispanic Journal of Behavioral Sciences, 18,* 533–549.

Gloria, A. M., & Rodriguez, E. R. (2000). Counseling Latino university students: Psychosociocultural issues for consideration. *Journal of Counseling and Development, 78,* 145–154.

González, G. M. (1997). The emergence of Chicanos in the twenty-first century: Implications for counseling, research, and policy. *Journal of Multicultural Counseling and Development, 25,* 94–106.

Guzmán, B. (2001). *The Hispanic population.* Current Population Reports, C2KBR/01-3. U.S. Census Bureau, Washington, DC.

Hibbeln, J. A. (1996). Special populations: Hispanic migrant workers. In S. Torres (Ed.), *Hispanic voices: Hispanic health educators speak out* (pp. 162–192). New York: NLN Press.

Ho, M. K. (1987). *Family therapy with ethnic minorities.* Beverly Hills, CA: Sage.

Hurtado, A. (1995). Variations, combinations, and evolutions: Latino families in the United States. In R. E. Zambrana (Ed.), *Understanding Latino families: Scholarship, policy, and practice* (pp. 40–61). Thousand Oaks, CA: Sage.

Kim, B. S. K., & Abreu, J. M. (2001). Acculturation measurement: Theory, current instruments, and future directions. In J. G. Ponterotto, J. M. Casas, L. A. Suzuki, & C. M. Alexander (Eds.), *Handbook of multicultural counseling* (2nd ed., pp. 394–424). Thousand Oaks, CA: Sage.

Kobus, K., & Reyes, O. (2000). A descriptive study of urban Mexican American adolescents' perceived stress and coping. *Hispanic Journal of Behavioral Sciences, 22,* 163–178.

Koss-Chioino, J. D. (1995). Traditional and folk approaches among ethnic minorities. In. J. F. Aponte, R. Y. Rivers, & J. Wohl (Eds.), *Psychological interventions and cultural diversity* (pp. 145–163). Boston: Allyn & Bacon.

Koss-Chioino, J. D., & Vargas, L. A. (1999). *Working with Latino youth.* San Francisco: Jossey-Bass.

Lollock, L. (2001). *The foreign-born population in the United States: March 2000.* Current Population Reports, P20-534. U.S. Census Bureau, Washington, DC.

Marín, G., & Gamba, R. J. (1996). A new measurement of acculturation for Hispanics: The Bidimensional Acculturation Scale for Hispanics (BAS). *Hispanic Journal of Behavioral Sciences, 18,* 297–316.

Marín, B. V., & Gómez, C. A. (1997). Latino culture and sex: Implications for HIV prevention. In J. G. García & M. C. Zea (Eds.), *Psychological intervention and research with Latino populations* (pp. 73–93). Boston: Allyn and Bacon.

Marín, G., & Marín, B. V. (1991). *Research with Hispanic populations.* Newbury Park, CA: Sage.

Mayers, R. S., & Souflee, F. (1991). Utilizing social support systems in the delivery of social services to the Mexican-American elderly. *Journal of Applied Social Sciences, 15,* 31–50

McKenna, M. A. (1995). Transcultural perspectives in the nursing care of the elderly. In M. M. Andrews & J. S. Boyle (Eds.), *Transcultural concepts in nursing care* (pp. 203–234). Philadelphia, PA: Lippincott.

Mendoza, R. H., & Martinez, J. L. (1981). The measurement of acculturation. In A. Baron, Jr. (Ed.), *Explorations in Chicano psychology* (pp. 71–82). New York: Praeger.

Miramontes, H. M. (1995). *Under the feet of Jesus.* New York: Dutton.

Mirandé, A. (1985). *The Chicano experience: An alternative perspective.* Notre Dame, IN: University of Notre Dame Press.

Molina, C. W., & Aguirre-Molina, M. (1994). *Latino health in the US: A growing challenge.* Washington, DC: American Public Health Association.

Morales, E. (1992). Latino gays and Latina lesbians. In S. Dworkin & F. Gutiérrez (Eds.), *Counseling gay men and lesbians: Journey to the end of the rainbow* (pp. 125–139). Alexandria, VA: American Association for Counseling and Development.

Negy, C., & Woods, D. J. (1992). A note on the relationship between acculturation and socioeconomic status. *Hispanic Journal of Behavioral Sciences, 14,* 248–251.

Niemann, Y. F. (2001). Stereotypes about Chicanas and Chicanos: Implications for counseling. *The Counseling Psychologist, 29,* 55–90.

Nichols, M. P., & Schwartz, R. C. (1995). *Family therapy: Concepts and methods* (3rd ed.). Boston, MA: Allyn and Bacon.

Organista, P. B., & Organista, K. C. (1997). Cultural and gender sensitive AIDS prevention with Mexican migrant laborers: A primer for counselors. *Journal of Multicultural Counseling and Development, 25,* 121–129.

Padilla, A. M. (1995). *Hispanic psychology: Critical issues in theory and research.* Thousand Oaks, CA: Sage.

Parham, T. A. (1989). Cycles of nigrescence. *The counseling psychologist, 17,* 187–226.

Parra, E. O., & Espino, D. V. (1992). Barriers to health care access faced by elderly Mexican Americans. *Clinical Gerontologist, 11,* 171–177.

Pérez, S. M., & de la Rosa Salazar, D. (1993). Economic, labor force, and social implications of Latino educational and population trends. *Hispanic Journal of Behavioral Sciences, 15,* 188–229.

Phinney, J. S. (1992). The Multigroup Ethnic Identity Measure: A new scale for use with diverse groups. *Journal of Adolescent Research, 7,* 156–176.

Ponterotto, J. G. (1990). Racial/ethnic minority and women students in higher education: A status report. *New Directions for Student Services, 52,* 45–59.

Ponterotto, J. G. (1987). Counseling Mexican Americans: A multimodal approach. *Journal of Counseling and Development, 65,* 308–312.

Ponterotto, J. G., Martinez, F. M., & Hayden, D. C. (1986). Student affirmative action programs: A help or hindrance to development of minority graduate students? *Journal of College Student Personnel, 27,* 318–325.

Preciado, J., & Henry, M. (1997). Linguistic barriers in health education and services. In J. G. García & M. C. Zea (Eds.), *Psychological intervention and research with Latino populations* (pp. 235–254). Boston: Allyn and Bacon.

Ramírez, M. (1991). *Psychotherapy and counseling with minorities: A cognitive approach to individual and cultural differences.* New York: Pergamon Press.

Ramírez, M., & Castaneda, A. (1974). *Cultural democracy, bicognitive development and education.* New York: Pergamon Press.

Rivers, R. Y. (1995). Clinical issues and intervention with ethnic minority women. In J. F. Aponte, R. Y. Rivers, & J. Wohl (Eds.), *Psychological interventions and cultural diversity* (pp. 181–198). Boston: Allyn & Bacon.

Rivers, R. Y., & Morrow, C. A. (1995). Understanding and treating ethnic minority youth. In J. F. Aponte, R. Y. Rivers, & J. Wohl (Eds.), *Psychological interventions and cultural diversity* (pp. 164–180). Boston: Allyn & Bacon.

Rodriguez, E. R. (1998). Addressing the needs of diverse populations. In S. E. Robinson Kurpius, S. L. Roth-Roemer, & S. Carmin (Eds.), *The emerging role of counseling psychology in health.* Evanston, IL: Norton.

Rodriguez, E. R. (1996a). Mexican families: Strengths and limitations. Unpublished manuscript.

Rodriguez, E. R. (1996b). The sociocultural context of stress and depression in Hispanics. In S. Torres (Ed.), *Hispanic voices: Hispanic health educators speak out* (pp. 143–158). New York: NLN Press.

Rodriguez, E. R. (1994). *The role of psychological separation, ethnic identity, and worldview in college adjustment.* Unpublished dissertation. Arizona State University, Tempe, AZ.

Rogler, L. H. (1994). International migrations. *American Psychologist, 49,* 701–708.

Rosenthal, D. A., & Feldman, S. S. (1992). The nature and stability of ethnic identity in Chinese youth. *Journal of Cross-Cultural Psychology, 23,* 214–227.

Scott, C. S., Shifman, L., Orr, L., Owen, R. G., & Fawcett, N. (1988). Hispanic and Black American adolescents' belief relating to sexuality and contraception. *Adolescence, 23,* 667–688.

Siantz de Leon, M. L. (1994). The Mexican-American migrant farmworker family. *Mental Health Nursing, 29,* 65–72.

Smart, J. S., & Smart, D. W. (1994). The rehabilitation of Hispanics experiencing acculturative stress: Implications for practice. *Journal of Rehabilitation, 60,* 8–12.

Sodowsky, G. R., Lai, E. W. M., & Plake, B. S. (1991). Moderating effects of sociocultural variables on acculturation attitudes of Hispanics and Asian Americans. *Journal of Counseling and Development, 70,* 194–204.

Sotomayor, M. (1989). The Hispanic elderly and the intergenerational family. *Journal of Children in Contemporary Society, 20,* 55–65.

Sue, D. W., Arredondo, P., & McDavis, R. J. (1992). Multicultural counseling competencies and standards: A call to the profession. *Journal of Counseling and Development, 70,* 477–486.

Sue, D. W., & Sue, D. (1999). *Counseling the culturally different: Theory and practice* (3rd ed.). New York: John Wiley & Sons.

Therrien, M., & Ramirez, R. R. (2001). *The Hispanic population in the United States: March 2000.* Current Population Reports, P20-535. U.S. Census Bureau, Washington, DC.

Thurman, P. J., Swaim, R., & Plested, B. (1995). Intervention and treatment of ethnic minority substance abusers. In J. F. Aponte, R. Y. Rivers, & J. Wohl (Eds.), *Psychological interventions and cultural diversity* (pp. 215–233). Boston: Allyn & Bacon.

Triandis, H. C., Marín, G., Lisansky, J., & Betancourt, H. (1984). Simpatía as a cultural script of Hispanics. *Journal of Personality and Social Psychology, 47,* 1363–1375.

U.S. Department of Commerce, Bureau of the Census (1998). *Hispanic population nears 30 million* (Census Bureau Reports, CB/98-137). Washington, DC: Government Printing Office.

U.S. Department of Commerce, Bureau of the Census (1997). *Almost half of all U.S. small businesses home-based* (Census Bureau Reports, CB/97-182). Washington, DC: Government Printing Office.

U.S. Department of Commerce, Bureau of the Census (1995). *The nation's Hispanic population—1994* (Statistical Brief, SB/95-25). Washington, DC: Government Printing Office.

U.S. Department of Commerce, Bureau of the Census (1990). *We the American...Hispanics* (WE-2R). Washington, DC: Government Printing Office.

U.S. Department of Education, National Center for Education Statistics. (2000a). *Racial and ethnic distribution of elementary and secondary students.* NCES 2000-005. Washington, DC: U.S. Government Printing Office.

U.S. Department of Education, National Center for Education Statistics. (2000b). *The condition of education 2000.* NCES 2000-062. Washington, DC: U.S. Government Printing Office.

Vasquez-Nuttal, E., Romero-Garcia, I., & De Leon, B. (1987). Sex roles and perceptions of femininity and masculinity of Hispanic women. *Psychology of Women Quarterly, 11,* 409–425.

Vasquez, M. J. T. (1994). Latinas. In L. Comas-Díaz & B. Greene (Eds.), *Women of color: Integrating ethnic and gender identities in psychotherapy* (pp. 114–138). New York: Guildford Press.

Vega, W., Warheit, G., & Palacio, R. (1985). Psychiatric symptomatology among Mexican-American farmworkers. *Social Science and Medicine, 20,* 39–45.

Wray, L. A. (1992). Health policy and ethnic diversity in older Americans: Dissonance or harmony? *Western Journal of Medicine, 157,* 357–361.

Yep, G. A. (1995). Communicating the HIV/AIDS risk to Hispanic populations. In A. Padilla (Ed.), *Hispanic psychology: Critical issues in theory and research* (pp. 196–212). Thousand Oaks, CA: Sage.

Zea, M. C., Mason, M. A., & Murguía, A. (2000). Psychotherapy with members of Latino/Latina religions and spiritual traditions. In P. S. Richards & A. E. Bergin (Eds.), *Handbook of psychotherapy and religious diversity* (pp. 397–419). Washington, DC: American Psychological Association.

Zea, M. C., Belgrave, F. Z., García, J. G., & Quezada, T. (1997). Socioeconomic and cultural factors in rehabilitation of Latinos with disabilities. In J. G. García & M. C. Zea (Eds.), *Psychological intervention and research with Latino populations* (pp. 217–234). Boston: Allyn and Bacon.

Zuniga, M. E. (1997). Counseling Mexican American seniors: An overview. *Journal of Multicultural Counseling and Development, 25,* 142–155.

10

Counseling and Psychotherapy with Asian American Clients

Nolan Zane
University of California, Davis

Teru Morton
Alliant International University, San Diego

June Chu and Nancy Lin
University of California, Davis

This chapter addresses the mental health issues involved in the clinical treatment of Asian American clients. The guidelines and resulting recommendations are based on the most current research in the field and on well-documented clinical and professional experiences in working with this clientele.

In working with Asian American populations, it is important to appreciate and account for the social and psychological diversity that exists among members of this ethnic minority group. Generalizing about any group is perilous, particularly when considering peoples with roots in Asia, which comprises 30 percent of the Earth's total land mass and is home to over three-fifths of this planet's population, with the inhabitants ranging from preliterate hunter-gatherers to cosmopolitan multilingual urbanites (Columbia Encyclopedia, 2001). It is therefore best to consider the specific background of an Asian American client and to be cautious in the tendency to generalize information across distinct ethnic groups.

Moreover, to make counseling or treatment recommendations for such a diverse group becomes even more challenging in view of the limited amount of empirically based information available on cultural influences in treatment. The bulk of the research reviewed in this chapter involves primarily group or population-focused studies in which research has examined ethnic or cultural group influences on therapy process and outcomes. Although this parameter-based research has provided important information about the mental health treatment experiences of ethnic minorities, the focus on group differences often has obscured important variations among members of a particular minority group. More significantly, the descriptive nature of this research has precluded exact determination of how culture affects the treatment experience and eventual outcomes. Recently, greater emphasis has been placed on variable-focused studies that examine how specific psychological elements associated with ethnic or cultural group differences affect treatment or moderate treatment effectiveness. This shift to study culturally based variables such as cultural value orientation, cultural identity, control orientation, shame and stigma, etc., allows us to better explain and understand the specific effects of cultural influences.

Given these limitations, we proceed as judiciously as we can, outlining the demographics and sociopolitical history of Asian American subgroups, reviewing key cultural tendencies, issues, and conflicts likely to be encountered in counseling and psychotherapy, drawing out some implications for working with this population and offering several illustrative case studies. We recognize that culture is only one relevant factor in establishing an explanatory model for mental illness, and that, depending on the circumstances, other aspects may be more influential. The literature reviewed represents trends that have been observed and should be considered as general guidelines for working with Asian American clients. However, when possible (as addressed by the research), we will also discuss individual differences in psychological dimensions, as well as inter-ethnic and intra-ethnic group differences.

Demographics and Sociopolitical History

Asians began immigrating to North America in the 1840s, up to six generations ago. More recently, new waves of immigrants have once again substantially augmented the Asian population. The 2000 United States Census showed Asian Americans increasing from 7.27 million in 1990 to 10.24 million in 2000, a 46 percent growth rate (U.S. Census Bureau, 1990; U.S. Census Bureau, 2000). They are presently the fastest growing ethnic group in North America. The percent of foreign-born people in this country is higher than it has been in more than half a century, and more of these foreign-born individuals (28 percent) come from Asia than any other continent. The largest subgroups among the overall Asian American community are Chinese Americans (2.4 million), Filipino Americans (1.9 million), Asian Indians (1.7 million), Vietnamese Americans (1.1 million), Korean Americans (1.1 million), and Japanese Americans (0.8 million). Smaller subgroups together represent 1.3 million additional Asian Americans.

Asian Americans are a very heterogeneous group, not only because of clearly distinct countries of origin but also because of unique sociopolitical histories concerning their arrival in North America. The first Asian immigrants were men from southern China, who began arriving in 1848 for the Gold Rush in California and western states. Soon after, Americans' fears of losing jobs to Chinese workers led to the 1882 Chinese Exclusion Act, banning further immigration. This ban was repealed in 1943 when the United States recognized China as an ally in World War II and relaxed its immigration laws somewhat. With the 1882 ban on Chinese immigration, Japanese immigrants began to arrive to work Hawaii's sugar plantations, but anti-Japanese sentiments grew there as well. A 1907 Executive

Order prohibited Japanese migration to the U.S. mainland from Hawaii and Mexico, the 1908 Gentlemen's Agreement restricted immigration from Japan to wives of Japanese already in the United States, and the 1924 Immigration Bill ended further immigration from Japan altogether. Relations with Japan deteriorated just prior to World War II, a conflict characterized by markedly anti-Japanese sentiments. In 1942, Executive Order 9066 permitted forcible removal of Japanese Americans from the west coast to internment camps. This political history is unique to Japanese Americans, but other aspects of anti-Asian discrimination and racism have targeted all of the Asian American groups.

Laborers from Korea began arriving in Hawaii to work the sugar plantations in 1903. The 1907 Executive Order banned them, along with the Japanese, from migrating to the mainland United States, and the 1924 Oriental Exclusion act prevented almost all Korean migration to this country. Korean migration resumed after World War II ended, with the arrival of the Korean wives and children of United States military servicemen. U.S. support during and after the Korean War was influential in later waves of immigration.

When Spain ceded the Philippines to the United States in 1892, Filipinos became United States nationals, and unrestricted immigration was permitted so that they could work the cane fields and pineapple plantations of Hawaii, orchards of California, and fisheries and canneries of Washington, Oregon, and Alaska. More Filipino immigrants arrived in response to the 1946–1965 recruitment drives of the U.S. Armed Forces during the Cold War of the 1950s. Immigration was severely reduced when the Philippines later achieved commonwealth status. However, the Immigration Act of 1965 resulted in substantial increases in Asian immigration when the national origins system was replaced with the fixed quota system of 20,000 people from each foreign country.

Large numbers of Vietnamese war refugees came to the United States in the 1970s after the fall of Saigon. The United States resettlement policy often distributed refugees across diverse areas of the United States to sponsoring individuals and groups responsible for helping them find employment, education, and other services (Tran, 1991). Recently, diplomatic ties between the United States and Vietnam have been reestablished, prompting a second wave of Vietnamese immigrants (Banerjee, 2001).

Profiles of other recent immigrants differ widely. Many Southeast Asians, Laotians, Hmong, Cambodians, and Vietnamese were refugees who fled retaliatory persecution for supporting United States. Many of these refugees have often experienced economic and psychosocial adjustment challenges upon their arrival in the United States. By contrast, the Asian Indian population tends to have a higher mean income and level of education than all other Asian American groups, and it has grown the fastest in the last decade (106 percent), growth which is attributed in part to the creation of H-1B visas that encourage high-tech industry immigrants from Asia (KTVU/Fox 2, 2001).

As a whole, Asian Americans reside predominantly in urban settings (96 percent live in metropolitan areas). About half of all Asian Americans live in the western United States, with 20 percent in the Northeast, 19 percent in the South, and 12 percent in the Midwest. Their rate of growth from 1990 to 2000 was significant across many states: e.g., 10 percent in Arkansas, 110 percent in South Dakota, 94 percent in New Jersey, 83 percent in Pennsylvania (Armas, 2001), 78 percent in Florida (Word, 2001), 71 percent in Michigan (Warikoo, 2001), 61 percent in California (KTVU/Fox 2, 2001).

Family Dynamics and Issues

Although substantial inter-group heterogeneity exists among Asian Americans, these groups share certain commonalities of family structure and functioning. A number of factors mitigate these tendencies, the most notable being the effects of acculturation on Asian American families and their members (cf. Lee, 1989). However, certain family tendencies in child rearing practices, communication patterns, role relations and expectations, as well as potential sources of interpersonal conflict persist among Asian Americans despite societal pressures to acculturate in social, political, financial, and educational domains (Ching, McDermott, Fukunaga, Yanagida, Mann, & Waldron, 1995).

Child Rearing Practices

Confucius laid the general template for Asian families centuries ago—a vertical structure with father at its head, mother deferential and supportive of him, and children obedient to and respectful toward both authority figures. To reinforce core family values such as work ethic and academic achievement, parents may use shame, guilt, or an appeal to duty and responsibility to help children understand that they must not embarrass, shame, or dishonor their families (Isomura, Fine, & Lin, 1987). Even across many generations residing in North America, Asian Americans continue to see families as responsible for their individual members' behavior (Lin, Miller, Poland, Nuccio, & Yamaguchi, 1991). Asian Americans value family lineage, considering that the behavior of any individual reflects upon and impacts both preceding and future generations of the family. Thus, it is vital that counselors and therapists understand an individual's identity and place within the family context whenever conducting therapy with Asian Americans (Sodowsky, 1991). Traditional Asian emphases on paternal hierarchy, authoritative parenting, filial piety, interdependence, conformity, and saving face can contrast with the Western preference for more child independence and egalitarian parenting, an approach in which children are taught about individuality, the need for autonomous functioning, self-reliance, and the uniqueness of their personal qualities.

There are, of course, variations in how Asian groups socialize these traditional Asian values (Uba, 1994). For example, Chinese Americans tend to closely supervise children, emphasize achievement, and view childrearing as a mother's responsibility. Filipino Americans tend to lull, carry, and play with their infants, but Korean Americans may view playing with children as undermining the children's respect for adults. Southeast Asian parents tend to become more restrictive as children grow older, gradually increasing their emphasis on such things as disobedience, failure to fulfill responsibilities, and aggression toward siblings. Taken as a whole, however, many Asian American parents still differ appreciably from mainstream American parents. For example, in contrast to Asian parents, White American parents tend to see play with children as an integral part of the learning process, and they often treat their children as equals or at least as participants in the decision making process. Asian American mothers often anticipate the needs of their children, while White American mothers are inclined to want their children to verbalize their needs. Attachment and interaction patterns between mother and child reflect cultural values, and differences in these practices across cultures often result in unique socioemotional, identity development, and individuation processes (cf. Takahashi, 1986).

Communication Patterns and Norms

Traditional Asian families emphasize collectivist values of interdependence, conformity, and harmony; communication is indirect, implicit, nonverbal, and intuitive. Direct confrontations are avoided (Hsu, 1983). Japanese consider emotional expression to be "bad form," and Japanese language has restrictive words for affect expression (McDermott, Char, Robillard, Hsu, Tseng, & Ashton, 1983; Takeuchi, Imahori, & Matsumoto, 2001). Filipino women demonstrate the use of *delicadeza* for nonconfrontational communication (Araneta, 1993), and Koreans use *noonchi*, a "measuring with eyes," or intuitive perception of others (Kim, 1993). Love and affection are not expressed verbally as much as shown through the mutual fulfillment of obligations and consideration of tending to physical needs. A language of emotions is characteristic of Western cultures, and traditional Asian cultures tend to view emotions as a sign of weakness and disgrace. For example, as Chinese Americans report becoming more "American," their reports of affective behavior show increased variation (Tsai & Levenson, 1997), reflecting the Westernized tendency for more open and verbal affective expression.

Because so much of communication in Asian cultures is through indirect means, intra-familial conflict and misunderstandings often occur. Older generation parents who have grown accustomed to certain styles of interacting may not be able to fully express themselves directly, but their more Americanized children may not be fully able to "read" these meaningful cues. The more acculturated children may also be more vocal, and this further upsets the family hierarchy, as the younger generation family members may unwittingly overstep certain cultural norms and expectations such as the appropriate display of deference and respect to elders.

Attitudes toward Marriage and Relationships

With the more traditional, less acculturated families, marriage is not seen as an individual decision based upon love but as a union between families, emphasizing the appropriate match in economic and social status of the families rather than the romantic inclinations of the spousal relationship. Whereas Westerners raise children to become autonomous individuals who are able to lead their own lives separate from their parents, Asians raise their children with a respect for the familial role in their present and future lives. Asian Americans who are raised by parents holding one worldview of family and marriage, yet grow up in a society where love and affective emotion are bases for relationships, may find themselves in conflict when they choose to marry an individual for love. The difficulties that individuals may encounter when marrying someone from another culture must also be kept in mind. Some Asians look down on Asian women who marry non-Asians; they see these women as "business girls" whose only goal is economic advancement (Ratliff, Moon, & Bonacci, 1978). And the strong in-group and out-group inclinations of Asian American groups (Tanaka, Ebrero, Linn, & Morera, 1998) may cause interracial marriage to be considered a betrayal of the family heritage. Factors that increase the rates of out-group marriage include acculturation and assimilation to North American society (Kitano, Fujino, & Sato, 1998) and dissatisfaction among Asian women with the gender hierarchy of traditional Asian cultures (Kitano et al., 1998).

Worldviews Relative to the Family and Extended Relationships

The collectivistic values characteristic of many Asian Americans also have a large impact on identity and sense of the self, which differ markedly from typical Western self-perceptions (Landrine, 1992; Markus & Kitayama, 1991). The Western view of "self" assumes that people are completely independent and separate from others, whereas the Asian view of "self" emphasizes social influences, with each person defined in relation to others. Sense of self, particularly in first generation immigrants, is strongly tied to family and ethnic groups (Sodowsky, Kwan, & Pannu, 1995). With so much of psychotherapy predicated on the Western perspective of self, it is not surprising that therapy dropout rates are so high for Asian American clients. Enmeshment, codependence, lack of individuation, social anxiety, and other psychopathological labels are frequently given erroneously to this group by practitioners who impose the Western conceptualization of self onto the behavior of Asian Americans.

Holistic cognitive orientations, which emphasize interrelationships and interconnectedness, also clearly influence the perceptions of many Asian Americans. Compared to other groups, Asians are highly context-sensitive, attending to the whole environment rather than to its focal features (Ji, Peng, & Nisbett, 2000; Tsai, 1999). Additionally, they are more inclined towards dialectical thinking, the "cognitive tendency towards acceptance of contradiction" (Peng & Nisbett, 2000, p. 742). They are able to deal with contradictions by compromising and finding truth in two contradictory ideas, rather than insisting upon only one correct premise. For example, Morris and Peng (1994) found that Chinese individuals process behavior using situational factors, preserving contextual information in their mental representations and simulating counterfactual situations in addressing problem situations, which results emphasize to the salience of context, audience, and dialectic thinking. The Asian worldview, whereby attention is directed towards the environment rather than inward to the self, has important implications for cognitively oriented practitioners, in that highly context-specific problem formulations and dialectic thinking that encourage compromises in conflict resolution can be used by the therapist in treatment.

Similarly, the holistic thinking of Asian philosophies is counter to the mind-body dualism of Western thinking. Asian languages typically blend descriptors of psychological experiences with physical body sensations. Moreover, excessive emotions are believed to endanger both relationships with others and one's own physical well-being (Hsu, 1983). Asians may therefore voice mental illness in somatic terms, and their children may monitor physical symptoms and communicate with somatic representations, which poses problems for Western practitioners, who are unaccustomed to working with somatic complaints as indicators of mental distress. This tendency also creates difficulty in Asian American families, where older generations call for help indirectly or somatically, but their more Westernized children require more verbal and explicit descriptions of mental health problems than elders are able to provide.

In sum, East-West cultural differences involve collectivism/interdependence versus individualism/autonomy, hierarchical versus egalitarian structures, indirectness versus emotional expressiveness, holistic integration versus separation of mind, body, and spirit, an interconnected versus separated sense of self, and a sense of belonging to a small nuclear family versus an extended clan, including a web of past ancestors and yet-to-be-born progeny. For Asian Americans, these cultural conflicts and tensions take place as much in the family as they do within the individual, and they continue to present in various forms across generations as acculturative forces that vary in their effects on different family members.

Age and Cohort Issues

Adolescents and Young Adults

Asian American adolescents and young adults face cultural challenges in the developmental issues of establishing their identity, establishing a career of some kind, and choosing a partner. In identity development, they must navigate the powerful cross pressures to adhere to more traditional family and cultural traditions and to become "more American." The question "Who am I?" is often quite a different issue to Asian American youth than it was for their parents. Table 10.1 shows the dominant frameworks for conceptualizing the development of Asian American ethnic identity. All three frameworks listed assume that an identity acknowledging and integrating both ethnic and majority cultures results in optimal psychological well-being and functioning (Phinney, Cantu, & Kurtz, 1997). In some ways, the ambivalence and, at times, hostility often observed among Asian American youth toward their ethnicity and culture may be considered "rational" and normal in view of the bicultural pressures and demands usually experienced by these youth. It is important that mental health professionals help them work through filial piety/individuation and other differential acculturation-accelerated conflicts (e.g., overt expression of emotions and caring vs. emotional self-restraint, asserting one's opinion and needs vs. deference and respect for elders, promoting oneself vs. modesty and self-effacement), enabling them to leave treatment with a better integrated answer to their "Who am I?" question, irrespective of the presenting problem.

Another stressor commonly experienced by Asian American youth is the enormous pressure they feel to excel academically. The Chinese, like many other Asian groups, have a long tradition of academic aspirations for their children, dating back to the centuries-old Mandarin system (Lam, Chan, & Leff, 1995). This parental emphasis on work ethic and academic achievement is reinforced by the reality that many Asian American youth are excluded or discouraged from pursuing other avenues of achievement (Sue & Okazaki, 1990). In addition, the "American Model Minority" myth can often marginalize this group as docile, hard working, and upwardly mobile—respected but disliked (Lin & Fiske, unpublished manuscript). Given these circumstances, many Asian American youth feel that they have little choice but to excel in academics, and they see scholastic failure as unacceptable personally and as a major disappointment to the family.

TABLE 10.1   *Models of Ethnic Identity and/or Ethnic Identity Development*

Racial/Cultural Identity Development Model (R/CID) (Sue & Sue, 1990)

Stage 1	Conformity—individual rejects ethnic identity in favor of host culture
Stage 2	Dissonance—individual begins to question their initial rejection of their ethnic group
Stage 3	Resistance & Immersion—individual completely identifies with Asian American culture, actively rejecting the host culture
Stage 4	Introspection—individual questions their complete immersion in their ethnic culture, and begins search for self-identity
Stage 5	Integrative Awareness—individual is secure in ethnic identity and appreciates other racial/ethnic groups

Tse's (1999) Stage Model of Ethnic Identity Development

Stage 1	Ethnic unawareness—individual is unaware of minority status
Stage 2	Ethnic ambivalence/evasion—individual actively distances self from ethnic group; adopts the host group culture
Stage 3	Ethnic emergence—individual realizes that joining the ethnic group is not possible, and begins to seek other affiliations
Stage 4	Ethnic identity incorporation—individual joins their ethnic minority group

Phinney's (1989) Model of Ethnic Identity Development

Stage 1	Diffusion/Foreclosure—individual does little exploration of ethnic identity
Stage 2	Moratorium—individual engages in active ethnic identity search, increased awareness about the importance of ethnicity
Stage 3	Identity achieved—individual has come to terms with their ethnic identity and emerges identified with their ethnic group

Elderly

Elderly Asian Americans face very different problems from the youth. They experience developmentally related losses of their parental, work, marital, and other roles (Merton, 1957). Moreover, aging in a culturally incongruent society exacerbates these losses. Traditionally the elderly are revered and respected in Asian countries; traditions of filial piety dictate that elderly parents' children fulfill their needs, care for them, treat them with reverence, and obey their wishes and plans (Hines, Garcia-Preto, McGoldrick, Almeida, & Weltman, 1992). If Americanized adult children do not fulfill these obligations and expectations, the personal and cultural incongruencies that elderly Asian Americans feel can lead to increasing tension, conflict and dysphoria (Kim, Hurh, & Kim, 1993). Among people age 75 and older in San Francisco during 1987–1996, 20% of suicides were committed by Asian Americans, a rate disproportionately higher than that of other ethnic groups (Shiang, 1998).

Refugees and Recent Immigrants

There is a clear contrast in the circumstances of refugees vs. immigrants (Matsuoka, 1990). While immigrants voluntarily left their native lands to pursue better opportunities or reunite with loved ones in North America, refugees were forced to abandon their homes and seek safety elsewhere. Asian refugees, particularly those from Southeast Asia, have typically experienced significant and protracted trauma involving persecution or genocidal campaigns, torture or containment as prisoners of war, abrupt severance from ancestral homelands, rupture of extended kinship networks, loss of family members often through traumatic events, and protracted family separation or long stays in crowded refugee camps en route to this country (Matsuoka, 1990; Nicholson & Kay, 1999). As a group, refugees are typically burdened with more mental health problems and have fewer resources than other Asian immigrants for coping with the continuing stresses of adjusting to their new environment.

Recent or new immigrants from Asia vary widely in education, income, and country of origin, but all experience some degree of acculturative stress as they struggle to adjust to their new environment, find employment, enter schools, and learn English. Western education, employment, urbanization, and settlement patterns, along with changes in socialization practices and pressures to conform to the Western culture are just a few of the many new stressors that may be encountered when adapting to American culture (Sodowsky, Lai, & Plake, 1991). Settling in a densely Asian community can provide supports for traditional structures and values but can correspondingly diminish the speed of adaptive acculturation. In any case, new immigrant families often must work long hours, isolating themselves from local culture and practices (Lam et al., 1995). The immigrant wife who works outside the home may help relieve financial stress on the family but augment other difficulties by inadvertently undermining the patriarchal family structure. Commonly, immigrant children become English-fluent faster than their parents, thereby becoming the primary interpreters and culture brokers, further destabilizing the traditional family system.

Experience as an Ethnic Minority

Asian Americans are oftentimes the targets of racism in its various forms. This country's long history of anti-Asian legislation (exclusionary acts, the internment of the Japanese Americans during World War II, anti-miscegenation laws, etc.) reflects the fact that Asian Americans have not been seen as Americans, but as foreigners. Ying, Lee, and Tsai (2000) found that racial discrimination decreases subjective competence ratings for both foreign-born and U.S.-born Chinese Americans, with this effect being stronger for the latter. These researchers hypothesize that immigrants, retaining psychological attachment to their native culture, may be more able to distance or buffer themselves from discrimination than are persons of Asian descent who are born in the United States. American-born Asian Americans, though in their home country, must repeatedly confront the question *"Where are you from?"*

which implies foreign status. For Asian Americans, being accepted as American is considered "achieved and provisional, rather than a taken-for-granted and stable" (Kibria, 2000). Research indicates that racial discrimination produces the same psychological and physical stress effects that other psychosocial stressors do (Williams, Spencer, & Jackson, 1999), and mental health practitioners should anticipate the additional issues that Asian clients may bring to therapy concerning their place in this society that often involve their experiences of marginalization, alienation, and discrimination.

Gender Issues

Traditionally, Asian societies have well-defined social roles, especially in the context of family (Marsella, 1993; Uba, 1994; Sue, 1999). Social roles across genders are no exception. Although there is a trend towards increasing gender equality, Asian cultures tend to encourage men and women to hold different responsibilities and to abide by rules of conduct that emphasize social stability over individual rights. For East Asian societies such as those found in China, Korea and Japan, Confucian teachings have strictly differentiated proper behavior for each sex (Hong et al., 1993).

"The most beautiful and gifted girl is not so desirable as a deformed boy" (Hong, Yamamoto, Chang, & Lee, 1993) reflects the traditional pre-eminence and perceived desirability of boys, who are needed to carry on the family name and perform necessary family rituals. With a legacy of male favoritism, it is not surprising that even today implicit expectations for boys and girls can be very unequal. Among Asian Americans, eldest sons (as well as individuals with no siblings) may feel special pressure to carry on the family line (L. Nguyen & Peterson, 1992; N. A. Nguyen & Williams, 1989), succeed economically (Espiritu, 1999), and become caretakers of aging parents (Sue, 2001). This dutiful familial role is at odds with the freewheeling, independent, "own-man" image of American masculinity and career success (Sue, 1999). Therefore, Asian American men may present with conflicts over family responsibility and obligations versus the emphasis on autonomy, overt masculinity, and self-reliance that characterizes male behavior in American society. Historically, Asian daughters have been devalued, expected to be obedient and modest, and perceived as belonging to their future husband's household (Morrow, 1989; Lee & Cynn, 1991). Strict adherence to these values is now rare among modern Asian American households, but the tendency to be more liberal with sons than with daughters often persists. Less acculturated parents typically grant less social freedom to daughters than they would to sons. If women marry, they are usually expected to subordinate their personal agendas and careers to those of their spouses and to share the husband's family responsibilities, including taking care of the parents-in-law in their old age. If husbands spend most of their time away from home, care of elderly in-laws can become solely the daughter-in-law's responsibility. Many Asian American women feel caught in competing cross-pressures to defer to their husbands and take care of in-laws, while being assertive and independent achievers in the context of American society.

Homosexual and transgender Asians and Asian Americans may experience emotional distress compounded by a cultural heritage emphasizing family (Baytan, 2000). Research aimed at describing the experiences of these individuals is needed. Because many Asian cultures are family-based and do not have acceptable models for different lifestyles, lesbian and gay individuals may understandably feel the need to hide their sexuality from their families in order to avoid both personal rejection and family shame. In addition, most Asian cultures do not openly discuss issues of sexuality. Therefore, the idea of "coming out" is not likely to be a familiar concept. Consequently, there may be few social supports for individuals experiencing the double jeopardy of being both an ethnic and sexual minority.

Spiritual Beliefs, Values, and Practices

Hundreds, if not thousands, of religions are practiced in Asia (Central Intelligence Agency, 2001). For more than 2000 years, the elements of Confucianism, Buddhism, Taoism, Hinduism, animism, and shamanism have blended to yield some main principles as well as a host of alternative belief systems and attendant alternative therapies. Even though some Asian immigrants bring a tradition of Christianity with them from their country of origin or convert to Christianity after arriving in North America, the underlying beliefs, values, and philosophies of their earlier religious traditions continue to exert powerful and inchoate influences on them (Tan & Dong, 2000).

Unlike the Confucian doctrine of righteous action and moral codes of conduct, Buddhism prescribes a program of passive acceptance, detachment from desire, and meditation. A Buddhist believes that only by extinguishing one's personal desires and attachments can suffering be overcome and the spiritual self liberated and fully awakened. The Buddhist practice of meditation to elicit "evenly hovering attention" is compatible with the here-and-now "mindfulness" of some humanistic treatments, such as gestalt approaches, and with certain cognitive-behavioral approaches (Finn & Rubin, 2000).

Taoism emphasizes the inseparability of the body, psyche, and spirit, as well as a connection with nature through quiet reflection, balanced diet, breathing techniques, and disciplined living to promote health and longevity. It is the basis of traditional Chinese medicine, which provides a variety of cures to ailments attributed to an imbalance of the social or physical world (Unschuld, 1985). *Feng shui,* a form of geomancy addressing physical environmental factors, and *tai chi chuan,* a martial art form combining physical exercise and mental discipline, are two of the derivatives. The worldviews of many Asian Americans incorporate the complementary forces of *yin* and *yang,* and of *chi,* one's life energy. Many Taoist concepts are making their way into a variety of new Asian-influenced alternative approaches to restoring and maintaining well-being which are beginning to coalesce in North America.

Hinduism, originating in the Indian subcontinent, posits numerous gods and goddesses, is reflected in numerous rituals, prescribes yoga as a spiritual path, and explains the development of a soul through karma and reincarnation. Karma is inherently a belief in one's personal responsibility—"as a man sows, so shall he reap," if not in this lifetime then in the next—and in the essential fairness of life (Sharma, 2000).

Animism, the oldest spiritual tradition worldwide, deifies Nature in spirit forms that can then be worshipped and interacted with symbolically. Illnesses can result from malevolent or displeased spirits, sometimes sent by other people casting a curse or spell (Unschuld, 1985). Rituals to appease or distract the spirits are prescribed, often involving the actual or symbolic sacrifice of an animal or object in exchange for the nature spirit's release of the sick person's spirit. Shamanism is closely related to animism. The human and spirit worlds are held to be linked, such that disturbance in one creates disturbance in the other, and problem solving in one brings peace in the other (Vitebsky, 1995). Shamans, chosen by the spirits (Howard, 1998), may manifest their spiritual calling through hearing voices, speaking in tongues, having a physical or mental anomaly or possessing an unusual ability to communicate with animals or read the signs of nature. They are both celebrated and marginalized in their own society. Shamanism is widespread in Asia, particularly among people marginalized from the official power structure: individuals from rural areas, women, and ethnic minorities (K. Howard, personal communication, March 18, 1999).

Together, the strains of Confucianism, Buddhism, Taoism, Hinduism, animism, and shamanism have woven an almost countless number of specific cults across the vast continent of Asia, most of which identify afflictions along with their etiologies and remedies. Asian spiritual beliefs emphasize the centrality of family and clan, the place of individuals in a larger cosmos, the spiritual connection with deceased ancestors as a link to the spirit world, and a holistic view of body, mind, and spirit. Beyond this, the therapist must tactfully probe for spiritual and culture-specific explanations of the manifest symptoms and attendant culture-prescribed remedies.

Culture-bound syndromes, symptom clusters that are identified and mediated in particular cultural contexts, may sometimes be observed in Asian clients, particularly if they are immigrants from rural areas. Table 10.2 shows some of the better-documented Asian culture-bound syndromes, although there are many others not yet commonly seen in the West. These syndromes can only be understood by viewing their etiologies and symptom manifestations from a spiritual and culturally relativistic perspective.

View of Mental Health Professions

By tradition, Asian Americans see mental health problems as shameful—reflecting moral weakness in the individual and family, disgracing ancestors and future generations, and resulting from the past sins by family members. Families often shield mentally ill members from the public to save face and to avoid shame and stigma. Many only seek outside help as a last resort in acute stages (Zane & Sue, 1996). Moreover, many Asian Americans conceptualize mental illness very differently from views of mental health professionals. Many Western forms of psychotherapy require (a) a separation of mental from physical problems in symptoms, causes, and cures, which can be at odds with Asian holistic approaches; (b) a level of self-disclosure that offends notions of privacy and propriety in a face-conscious culture; (c) a focus on interpersonal conflict and direct confrontation, which is difficult for harmony-oriented individuals; (d) a language of emotion not always consonant with cultural cognitive and communication forms; and (e) an emphasis on individuation and pursuit of personal wants and needs in contrast to collectivistic norms and obligations emphasized by the Asian cultures. In view of these cultural incongruities between psychological treatment and Asian values and worldviews, it is not surprising that Asian Americans are relatively skeptical about the Western mental health profession, relatively unlikely to present for treatment, and relatively likely to drop out prematurely (from the therapist's

TABLE 10.2 *Asian Culture-Bound Syndromes*

Name in English	Asian Names	Endemic Area	Cultural Explanation	Symptoms
Divine Illness	*Shin-byung*	Korea	Invasion by angry ancestral spirits onto a descendant with weak constitutions, caused by improper observance of ritual.	Sense of double-facedness (*ijung inkyukja*), persistent and sometimes acute physical pain, sleeplessness, fatigue, anxiety, sudden outbursts of anger and distress.
Penis Retraction Syndrome	*Koro* *Suo yang, Siok iong,* or *Shuk yang Rok-joo* *Jinjinia bemar*	Malaysia China, Hong Kong & Taiwan Thailand Assam	Spirit invasion, excessive masturbation.	Sudden intense fear and sensation of the penis retracting into the abdomen resulting in death; a female correlate, in which the vulva and nipples recede into the body, also exists.
Qi-gong Psychotic Reaction or Cultivation Insanity	*Zho hwo ru mwo*	China	Practicing *qi gong* with an unrighteous mind, resulting in spirit or animal possession and has various mentalities such as pursuing a *qi gong* state to show off.	Time-limited psychotic episode of dissociative, paranoid, or other psychotic and non-psychotic symptoms after participating in qi-gong (a folk health-enhancing body movement/meditative exercise).
Neurasthenia	*Shenjing shuairuo* *Shinkei shitsu*	China Japan	Imbalance of the body, environmental stress, weak bodily constitution.	Physical and mental fatigue, dizziness, headaches and other pains, difficulty concentrating, memory loss, sleep disturbance.
Spirit Possession	*Hsieh-ping* *Shin-byung*	Taiwan Korea	Possession by an ancestral spirit who is trying to communicate with family members.	Tremor, delirium, visual or auditory hallucinations, disorientation; trancelike state.
Fear of Wind/Fear of Cold	*Pa-feng/Pa-leng*	China	Fear of excessive *yin* energy from wind and cold.	Phobic fear of wind and cold, respectively; bundling up in warm clothes, eating "hot" foods.

(continued)

TABLE 10.2 *Continued*

Name in English	Asian Names	Endemic Area	Cultural Explanation	Symptoms
No translation found	*Taijin kyofusho*	Japan	Over-nurturance by maternal figure.	Intense fear of offending or embarrassing others with one's body, body parts, or bodily functions; hypersensitivity of one's appearance, odor, facial expressions, and movements.
Soul Loss	*Imu Latah* *Amurakh, Irkunii, Ikota, Olan, Myriachit, and Menkeiti* *Bah-tschi, Bah-tsi , & Baah-ji Mali-mali & Silok*	Japan (Ainu, & Sakhalin), Malaysia, Siberia, Thailand, Philippines	Soul loss or detachment due to a sudden shocking event.	Hypersensitivity to sudden fright, dissociative or trancelike behavior, command obedience, echolalia, or echopraxia.
Anger Syndrome	*Hwa-byung or wool-hwa-byung*	Korea	Suppression of deep anger.	Insomnia, fatigue, panic, fear of impending death, dysphoric affect, indigestion, anorexia, dyspnea, palpitations, generalized aches and pains, and a feeling of a mass in the epigastrium.
** No translation found **	*Amok*	Malaysia Philippines	Being irreparably wronged.	Brooding, followed by sudden violent frenzy, ending with amnesia.
Semen-loss Syndrome	*Dhat & Jiryan* *Sukra prameha* *Shen kui & Shen k'ui*	India Sri Lanka China	Loss of life energy from too much sexual intercourse, nighttime emission or masturbation; yang energy deficiency.	Dizziness, backache, headaches, mental and physical fatigue, insomnia, frequent dreams, complaints of sexual dysfunction (i.e., impotence, premature ejaculation)

203

point of view). Liu, Pope-Davis, Nevitt, and Toporek (1999) therefore strongly suggest that therapists consider clients' acculturation level and perceptions of mental health. Atkinson and Gim (1989) found that attitudes toward professional psychological help are directly related to acculturation, suggesting that psychological services need to be modified if immigrants are to view such help as legitimate and credible.

In addition to this wariness or skepticism, many Asian American individuals and families simply lack awareness about mental health services and their usefulness. Providers wishing to better serve Asian Americans, particularly the newer immigrants and refugees, may want to focus on alternative means of outreach—innovative arrangements with ESL programs, employers, churches, schools, medical clinics, and civic associations salient to this group, as well as outreach efforts to community elders and indigenous healers. These approaches can help establish culture-consonant and community-endorsed approaches to prevention, early detection and treatment, and community empowerment. Language-appropriate written materials, translators, and support groups are often needed.

Strategies for Counseling and Psychotherapy

The preceding discussion has addressed some of the major East-West differences the mental health practitioner should be aware of in preparing to work with Asian Americans, and it pointed to the enormous heterogeneity in this group. Next we list a number of suggestions for approaching an Asian American client or family. These strategies are tendered in the spirit of working hypotheses that can guide counseling and treatment but should not be considered as specific prescriptive courses of action. Rather, it is suggested the practitioner amend and adapt these strategies as an accurate reading of the clients and their issues may suggest alternative or even opposing approaches.

Establish Credibility and Initial Formality

Most Asian Americans have traditions of scholarship and respect for authority. The practitioner can establish initial credibility by comfortably accepting the "doctor" or "*sensei*" (esteemed teacher for Japanese) expert authority role. Demonstrating capacity for cross-cultural effectiveness and inspiring confidence in one's ability to help are of paramount importance in the critical first encounter. Use of formal names (e.g., Mrs. Huong, Dr. Lee) with correct pronunciations is suggested. It is also advisable to show distinct respect to elders and to acknowledge traditional structures by addressing husband before wife and adults before children initially. If the client bows slightly at the time of handshake or other salutation, it is courteous to reciprocate the gesture. If a business card is offered, it should be treated with the same respect that would be shown the person. If a modest gift is given, the counselor or therapist should accept it humbly to the degree possible (Yang, 1994). Particularly in the first session, decorum, dignity, and respect will be valued. Honoring the client is never inappropriate, regardless of ethnic background, but it becomes exceedingly important with face-conscious Asian American clients. It is easier to become less formal, but much harder to become more so after the initial meeting.

Permit Indirect Contextual Communication and Low Emotional Expressiveness

If clients present with a nonlinear contextual interactional style, the practitioner is advised to respect this form of communication, permit it, and indeed join in it, at least initially. This may appear as initial conversational "small talk" or even "beating around the bush" as both parties search for cues to contextualize the other (e.g., their background, acquaintances in common, familiarity with the client's culture, capacity to help). The counselor or therapist should listen for information and store it for later use, in turn using this style of communication to subtly inform the client of his or her knowledge, experience, and capacity to provide meaningful help. In this initial interaction, one should avoid unnecessarily intrusive questions and demands for high emotional expressiveness and confrontations until it appears appropriate to venture in those directions; it is good to permit silences in conversational turn taking, however difficult this may be. This is all part of high context communication. Contrary to the inscrutable stereotypes, Asian American clients typically communicate a rich amount through metaphors, subtle nonverbal language, choice of words said and not said, and the use of silence, so the counselor's challenge is to slow down, watch for issues of face and dialectic, and for holistic modes of thinking, and learn the codes of communication. This indirect, high context communication and low emotional expressiveness is most likely to be seen with more traditional and less acculturated Asian Americans, at the beginning of sessions and when focusing on particularly difficult issues.

Assess Acculturation and Ethnic Identity

Accurate assessment of acculturation level on different dimensions and of ethnic identity requires that a counselor generate hypotheses from intake information, this should be a dominant activity in the first session. Moreover, this assessment may continue on refined points and issues throughout a treatment episode. Incorrect assessment can lead to grievous albeit unwitting offenses to the client and to inappropriate, ineffective diagnosis, treatment plans, and intervention modalities. The less acculturated the Asian American client, the more salient the following guidelines will be. The more "Americanized" the client, the more the counseling can resemble that of mainstream clients, although cultural issues are still paramount even for very acculturated individuals. Lethal *faux pas* can occur if a practitioner treats an Asian American as less acculturated than the client feels he or she is (invoking "foreign-ness" challenges) or as more acculturated (e.g., requiring intimate disclosures, display of intense emotions, use of confrontational strategies or lapses into informality too early). The practitioner should remember, in assessing acculturation, that (a) it is uneven, and a client may be very American in some areas of functioning and very Asian in others; (b) it continues for at least several generations, and family members may be at different acculturative levels and issues; and (c) people cannot always report accurately on their level of acculturation, so responses to direct queries may not always be accurate and/or may reflect socially desirable biases.

In contrast to acculturation, ethnic identity refers to how individuals think of and present themselves. Referencing oneself as Chinese American, or Asian American, or Chinese, or just

American indicates which group the client identifies with and may inform the therapist about the sociopolitical aspects of the client's worldview. In assessing ethnic identity, the provider will want to assess degree of "Chineseness," "Hmongness," and so on, as well as degree of "Americanness." Many highly acculturated individuals view themselves as strongly bi-cultural, with high proficiency in both cultures. Careful assessment of acculturation and ethnic identity is even more important when clients are racially and ethnoculturally blended individuals and families. The practitioner who is successful in these assessments will be rewarded with clients exploring with them, in time, the dilemmas and conflicts around acculturative or identity issues with which they may be involved.

Use of Interpreters

When the client cannot speak English with sufficient proficiency and an interpreter is needed, trust issues and miscommunication problems can arise. Bilingual interpreters and service providers should have training in working with service providers and vice versa. The interpreter typically sits next to the client (and sometimes just slightly behind), so the client and provider can face one another and address each other directly. This underscores the primary relationship between therapist and client, maximizes nonverbal communication between them, and minimizes the diffusion and distortion in communication and relationship-building inherent in adding a third party. When speaking, the counselor or therapist should address the client: "When did these problems begin, Mr. Lee?" is preferable to "Ask him when these problems began." Interpreters should translate literally, resisting the temptation to impose lay or personal understandings onto the material they translate, thereby introducing an unknown personal bias into the discussion. For example, "I drank lemon grass tea and tried Chi Gung again for a while, but the pains kept getting worse and my son insisted I come here" is more informative than "He hasn't had any psychological treatment before." Accurate interpretation can at least double the time for assessment or a treatment session. Although it is clearly resource intensive, utilizing a professional interpreter is preferred to using a bilingual family member, because of the likely distortions and other dynamics related to family shame and face saving.

Honor Face and Face Saving

Maintenance of face and avoiding loss of face can be an important dynamic in effective relationships between Asian American clients and their practitioners. Face issues are implicated in many different aspects of treatment for Asian Americans. For example, studies have shown that loss of face is negatively related to self-disclosure in treatment situations, especially when the client discloses about his or her most intimate relationships. Moreover, differences in a person's preference for different treatment approaches (i.e., directive vs. nondirective approach) can be better explained by loss of face than by a competing model based on differential treatment expectations between Asians and Whites (Zane & Mak, 2003). Dignifying the client, normalizing rather than pathologizing, positively framing and reframing, emphasizing strengths and skill building rather than deficits, etc., are all useful with face-conscious clients. In addition, in keeping with the social sense of self of many Asian Americans, face presentation and maintenance concerns are common in issues brought to therapy.

How can the newly unemployed immigrant father save face in his community when he is now financially dependent on his daughter? How can the family accept the unorthodox career or marriage choice or sexual orientation of their firstborn son without losing face in their church or neighborhood? In the contextual Asian worldview, actions are judged within a specific situation and as seen from the perspective of salient others. For example, if a couple with marital difficulties presents with a list of the ways in which they cope, this list can be elaborated and commended, using positive frames, postponing the direct focus on undisclosed dysfunctions until the couple becomes more trusting and familiar with the therapist. Perceived denial, minimization, internal inconsistencies, poor role performances, and conflicts within the family can indeed be addressed, but the practitioner is advised to use tact and diplomacy, capitalizing on Asian capacities with metaphors, dialectical thinking, and high context communication where possible, to ensure that face remains honored.

Emphasize Structured, Directive, and Goal-Directed Problem-Solving

Many Asian Americans may respond well to directive, structured, problem-focused approaches, especially at the beginning of treatment (Root, 1985; Tan & Dong, 2000). Worldviews and styles of communication, thinking, and perceiving that are potentially disparate, along with face-related concerns, create an unfamiliar situation for the client who is in therapy in which the stimulus field is potentially too open, with too much room for misunderstanding and miscommunication regarding what is expected and what is acceptable. Firm, goal-directed structure and leadership from the practitioner can reduce the ambiguity and face threat in this situation. For example, Kim (1993) advocates a directive approach emphasizing the practitioner's authority, expertise, and knowledge when working with Korean clients. In addition, for the many Asian American clients who often present with major somatic discomfort (e.g., chest pain, headache, breathing difficulty) rather than more psychological symptoms, framing the therapeutic interaction in a formal medical model and treating somatic complaints directly before addressing the associated situational, emotional, and social problems is recommended (Kinzie & Leung, 1993). While certainly some relatively Westernized Asian Americans will seek out reflective, nondirective, open-ended process-oriented therapies, this will not be the preferred mode of intervention for most of this clientele. Indeed, if psychoanalysis is attempted in a language in which the client is not fully proficient, the analyst should expect significant transference associated with whether the immigrant is idealizing or retreating from the new country, its language, and its providers (Litjmaer, 1999). Practitioners are advised to be explicit, by the end of the first session where possible, in describing the treatment plan—the specific goal and time frame, along with what will be required of the client, what procedures will be like, and what research supports those procedures. Structure, directiveness, and problem-focused approaches enhance the practitioner's credibility and the client's hope and comfort, increasing the chances of return visits.

Emphasize the Family Context

Family treatment should be very carefully implemented when working with Asian American clients. In family-based treatment, it is important to acknowledge traditional authority lines in ways that are sensitive to participating members. When an intergenerational conflict between individualist and collectivist values presents, it is advisable to couch it first from the collectivist stance as a way of recognizing the family as a whole. The more "Westernized" younger clients will likely recognize and respond positively to approaches that assume caring, wisdom, and authority from the older cohort. Reassured elders will then be more comfortable supporting their children's pursuits.

The power of Asian American families when they mobilize to support changes in individual or family functioning cannot be overstated. The practitioner should cast a wide net in determining the family system, since some recently immigrated families have key members still back in the home country, whose presence is still felt in a very immediate sense. Other families may keep a shrine in the home for deceased family members, on which they regularly place offerings—again reflecting the very real referred presence of another's influence on the current family dynamics. Even when the family therapy modality is not used, familial relationships and issues of collective face are still likely to surface in the counseling or treatment transactions.

Employ Spiritual Resources

Cultural consonance and efforts to work within the client's spiritual worldview enhance the credibility, attractiveness, and effectiveness of the treatment plan. For example, a colleague who uses biofeedback successfully for Asian Americans with anxiety disorders sometimes engages them first in a discussion of "*chi*" enhancement and alignment. Christian Asian American clients prefer Christian practitioners (Misumi, 1993; Tan & Dong, 2000), and will likely respond favorably to referencing Christian values and beliefs. American-born contemplative Buddhists may find cognitive behavioral and humanistic approaches which focus on "mindfulness" quite attractive and consonant with their meditation practices; they may actually be disproportionately involved in these forms of therapy (Finn & Rubin, 2000).

Exploration of the religious and spiritual aspects of the Asian American client often yields important material for therapy. Is the Japanese American's "it can't be helped" ("*shi kata ga nai*") attitude using the passive acceptance of Buddhist teachings in a positive or negative way? Is the Asian Indian American using the concept of karma to accept or to avoid personal accountability and responsibility? Does the Chinese American's Taoist perspective suggest treatment goals that are couched in terms of balance, or seem compatible with incorporation of meditation or use of a *tai chi* or *chi gung* group as an adjunct to treatment? Are the behaviors of the recent immigrant from a rural outer island in the Philippines in fact a culture-bound syndrome, not psychiatric but spiritual in etiology and remedy? Many American-born contemplative Buddhists are articulate about their beliefs and choice of spiritual leader (Finn & Rubin, 2000), and it is appropriate to explore these significant resources for growth or problem resolution efforts.

Therapists working with Asian American clients will want to be able to identify and access as needed the rich assortment of monks, priests, ministers, shamans, healers, and spiritual teachers their clients look to—sometimes as consultants, sometimes as referral sources or referrals, sometimes for adjunctive roles in treatment. Therapists will also want to remain alert to the potentially beneficial practices of their Asian American client's spiritual systems (e.g., meditation, yoga, martial arts, and other mental-physical practices) and be able to work alongside these practices synergistically, from a holistic perspective where possible.

Enhance Own Cultural Understandings and Cultural Connections

There is a large and growing body of knowledge available about the many facets of Asian American subpopulations and their experiences and worldviews. Mental health practitioners can increase their understanding of these various sub-groups by mastering not only the professional literature but also the growing body of autobiographies, nonfiction accounts, and fictional novels and stories by Asian American authors or about Asian American subjects. Films, plays, and other lively arts also can enhance cultural understandings for the interested learner. Participating in activities of the local Asian American community and joining community groups that attract Asian Americans are other useful and productive ways of gaining greater insights into (and comfort with) cultural practices, forms of communication, and worldviews. This kind of learning by cultural immersion appears to enhance cultural understandings in qualitatively different ways. Bicultural individuals in a mainstream setting behave in accord with the mainstream norms, but behave quite differently in settings where they are the majority, so immersion in those ethnic community settings usually affords rich new perspectives and enhanced multicultural competencies. Community connections also provide the treatment adjuncts, referral sources, cultural materials, and cultural consultants so important for those who serve the culturally diverse.

Enhance Both Asian and American Connections of Client

Asian Americans experience the mixed blessing of biculturalism, each in his or her own way at any given time. Rarely do they seek treatment for bicultural or ethnic identity issues per se, but rather for managing their problems at work, their relationships and health, and the other problems of living. However, because issues of biculturalism, acculturative dynamics, and ethnic identity evolution seem forever part of the substrate, the practitioner might consider setting ancillary goals regarding improved identity alignment and enhanced empowerment in connections with both the mainstream American culture and organizations and the ethnic Asian ones. Outcomes may be measured as improved self-efficacy, greater comfort in declaring one's identity, greater ease in navigating across cultures, stronger connections with both mainstream and ethnic community organizations and values, or comfort in taking more leadership as a bridge person of sorts. It is our experience that when counseling or psychotherapy with Asian Americans is successful, this is an unsought but nonetheless significant benefit. The following case examples illustrate some of the strategies that have been discussed.

Case Examples

Roles, Obligations, Face, and Grief
David Uyemoto is the hospital liaison to the four grown children of Mrs. Watanabe, a 95-year-old Japanese American who came to the United States as a

picture bride, was long ago widowed, and has recently declined rapidly from Alzheimer's disease. Uyemoto's job is to help the children attend their mother's last days and make necessary decisions. These children are well-educated professionals with a 30-year age spread, acculturated in varying degrees. Only the two eldest speak Japanese; the women have out-married; and the youngest has divorced. Now they are arriving from all corners of the country.

At the family's request, Uyemoto holds several family counseling sessions around issues of who will pay for what expense, when to stop applying unusual life saving means, and what kind of funeral "*Okasan*" would want. In these sessions, the traditional duty of the eldest son clashes with pragmatics—some younger daughters are better informed and more skilled in performing the executive and case managerial duties that are his by tradition. Power issues surface: Should sons, particularly the eldest one, have greater decision-making power, or should the family function as a simple democracy? Japanese family dynamics of guilt and obligation become apparent. The siblings quarrel softly and obtusely about issues of filial piety: Who has done what to support *Okasan* and be there for her, along the way and at the end? The discussion about the funeral centers on what "a good Japanese" funeral would be like, but disagreements of what "Japaneseness" means reflect the acculturative heterogeneity within the sibling group. Mrs. Watanabe was Buddhist for most of her life, but had begun attending services and social events at the nearby Japanese Methodist church, where Japanese was spoken.

Dr. Uyemoto presides over the Watanabe children's decision-making sessions, staying task-focused and directing the group's discussion, while probing the different perspectives of the children. The reunited siblings interact intensely outside of their sessions with Uyemoto, grateful for the privacy to work through, outside of his presence, the intimate family matters of mourning, filial piety, and sibling rivalry, and to define what being "Japanese" and "American" mean to them as they confront the loss of *Okasan,* the most Japanese of them.

For the third anniversary of Mrs. Watanabe's death, the time of ascent to Buddhist heaven, the siblings contract Dr. Uyemoto to preside over their reunion, although none of them is a practicing Buddhist. Here the discussion covers their evolved sense of what being Japanese American means, their mourning and recovery, and their appreciation to Uyemoto for managing their journey together in such a fruitful and healing way.

Cultural Adaptations in Crisis and Mourning

The local Refugee Resettlement program calls Ann Lorenzo to attend a crisis. An eight-year-old Hmong boy has hung himself. Lorenzo drives to the public housing project where the family lives and sits on the floor of the cramped living room with a translator, the parents, and some younger children. The conversation does not much resemble a typical psychotherapy session with mainstream clients. Family members seem transfixed with fear, unable to keep from glancing to the corner where the boy has hung himself with an electric cord. They talk about "ghosts" (per the translator), and want more than anything to change dwellings, to switch to a different unit in the project. The young translator is clearly embarrassed, calls them superstitious, and notes what his supervisor has told him—that this is not possible, given the housing rules.

In this difficult situation, Lorenzo develops the family's trust in three ways. She attends the boy's funeral in the town's Paupers Field. She successfully intervenes with the public housing authority to have the family moved to a different unit. She finds shamans in the local Hmong community and elicits the family's agreement that they be put in touch with each other. Later she learns that several sessions of shamanistic rituals have occurred to banish destructive spirits, and the family is at peace that their young child is safely home in their ancestral spirit world.

Lorenzo later meets with the family three more times. In these sessions, working with the same translator, she helps connect the father with a maintenance job, compliments the younger children for their growing grasp of English and exhorts them to help and obey their parents, and focuses extensively on the mother, who is deteriorating, complaining of incapacitating headaches, refusing to learn English, and remaining very disconnected from the extant Hmong community. Lorenzo recruits a kind and solicitous Hmong woman in the ESL program to serve as a volunteer sponsor, and this volunteer befriends the disconsolate mother, bringing her herbal headache remedies and inducting her to the ESL program. The client becomes a regular member of the Hmong ESL program, developing friendship supports in the community while learning English. Over time her headaches cease.

The typical issues of mourning the boy's death were never part of the therapy directly presided upon by Lorenzo, but instead were addressed by Lorenzo's attendance at the funeral, the introduction of the community shamans, and the recruitment of the outreach volunteers from the Hmong community. This resulted in strengthening the family and enhancing its adaptation to this new country, and it improved relations between the Hmong community and the mental health establishment.

References

Araneta, E. G. (1993). Psychiatric care of Filipino Americans. In A. C. Gaw (Ed.), *Culture, ethnicity, and mental illness* (pp. 377–411). Washington, DC: American Psychiatric Press, Inc.

Armas, G. C. (2001). Asian population jumps across country [Electronic version]. *The Detroit News,* Retrieved August 8, 2001, from http://detnews.com/2001/census/0103/09/197658.htm

Atkinson, D. R., & Gim, R. H. (1989). Asian-American cultural identity and attitudes toward mental health services. *Journal of Counseling Psychology, 36 (2),* 209–212.

Banerjee, N. (2001, May 17–23). Census releases data on Asian subgroups. *Asian Week,* p. 8.

Baytan, R. (2000). Sexuality, ethnicity and language: Exploring Chinese Filipino male homosexual identity. *Culture, Health and Sexuality, 2* (4), 391–404.

Central Intelligence Agency. (2001). *World factbook,* Retrieved August 10, 2001, from http://www.cia.gov/cia/publications/factbook/index.html

Ching, J. W. J., McDermott, J. F., Fukunaga, C., Yanagida, E., Mann, E., & Waldron, J. A. (1995). Perceptions of family values and roles among Japanese Americans: Clinical considerations. *American Journal of Orthopsychiatry, 65* (2), 216–224.

Columbia Encyclopedia, Sixth Edition. (2001). Asia. *Bartleby.com,* Retrieved February 25, 2002, from http://www.bartleby.com/65/as/Asia.html

Espiritu, Y. L. (1999). Gender and labor in Asian immigrant families. *American Behavioral Scientist, 42,* 628–634.

Finn, M., & Rubin, J. B. (2000). Psychotherapy with Buddhists. In P. C. Richards & A. E. Bergin (Eds.), *Handbook of Psychotherapy and Religious Diversity* (pp. 317–340). Washington, D.C.: American Psychological Association.

Hines, P. M., Garcia-Preto, N., McGoldrick, M., Almeida, R., & Weltman, S. (1992). Intergenerational relationships across cultures. *Families in Society, 73*(6), 323–338.

Hong, W, Yamamoto, J, Chang, D. S., & Lee, F. (1993). Sex in a Confucian society. *Journal of the American Academy of Psychoanalysis, 21,* 405–419.

Howard, K. (1998). *Korean shamanism: revivals, survivals, and change.* Seoul, Korea: Royal Asiatic Society, Korea Branch, Seoul Press.

Hsu, J. (1983). Asian family interaction patterns and their therapeutic implications. *International Journal of Family Psychiatry, 4,* 307–320.

Isomura, T., Fine, S., & Lin, T. (1987). Two Japanese families: A cultural perspective. *Canadian Journal of Psychiatry, 32,* 282–286.

Ji, L. J., Peng, K., & Nisbett, R. E. (2000). Culture, control, and perception of relationships in the environment. *Journal of Personality & Social Psychology, 78,* 943–955.

Kibria, N. (2000). Race, ethnic options, and ethnic binds: Identity negations of second-generation Chinese and Korean Americans. *Sociological Perspectives, 43*(1), 77–95.

Kim, K. C., Hurh, W. M., & Kim, S. (1993). Generation differences in Korean immigrants' life conditions in the United States. *Sociological Perspectives, 36*(3), 257–270.

Kim, L. I. C. (1993). Psychiatric care of Korean Americans. In A. C. Gaw (Ed.), *Culture, ethnicity, and mental illness* (pp. 347–375). Washington, DC: American Psychiatric Press, Inc.

Kinzie, J. D., & Leung, P. K. (1993). Psychiatric care of Indochinese Americans. In A. C. Gaw (Ed.), *Culture, ethnicity, and mental illness* (pp. 281–304). Washington DC: American Psychiatric Press.

Kitano, H. H. L., Fujino, D. C., & Sato, J. T. (1998). Interracial marriages: Where are the Asian Americans and where are they going? In L. C. Lee & N. W. S. Zane (Eds.), *Handbook of Asian American psychology* (pp. 233–260). Thousand Oaks, CA: Sage Publications.

KTVU/Fox 2 and Associated Press. (2001). CA's population soars [Electronic version]. *Baysinsider.com.* Retrieved July 26, 2001, from http://www.bayinsider.com/news/2001/05/24/census.html.

Lam, D. H., Chan, N., & Leff, J. (1995). Family work for schizophrenia: Some issues for Chinese immigrant families. *Journal of Family Therapy, 17*(3), 281–297.

Landrine, H. (1992). Clinical implications of cultural differences: The referential versus the indexical self. *Clinical Psychology Review, 12* (4), 401–415.

Lee, E. (1989). Assessment and treatment of Chinese-American immigrant families. *Journal of Psychotherapy and the Family, 6* (1–2), 99–122.

Lee, J., & Cynn, V. (1991). Issues in counseling 1.5 generation Korean Americans. In C. Lee & B. Richardson (Eds.), *Multicultural issues in counseling: New approaches to diversity* (pp. 127–140). Alexandria, VA: American Association for Counseling and Development.

Lin, K. M., Miller, M. H., Poland, R. E., Nuccio, I., & Yamaguchi. (1991). Ethnicity and family involvement in the treatment of schizophrenic patients. *Journal of Nervous & Mental Disease, 179*(10), 631–633.

Lin, M. H., & Fiske, S. T. (in press). Attitudes toward Asian Americans: Developing a prejudice scale.

Litjmaer, R. M. (1999). Language shift and bilinguals: Transference and Counter-transference implications. *Journal of the American Academy of Psychoanalysis, 27,* 611.

Liu, W. M., Pope-Davis, D. B., Nevitt, J., & Toporek, R. L. (1999). Understanding the function of acculturation and prejudicial attitudes among Asian Americans. *Cultural Diversity and Ethnic Minority Psychology, 5*(4), 317–328.

Markus, H. R., & Kitayama, S. (1991). Culture and self: Implications for cognition, emotion, and motivation. *Psychological Review, 98*(2), 224–253.

Marsella, A. J. (1993). Counseling and psychotherapy with Japanese Americans: cross-cultural considerations. *American Journal of Orthopsychiatry, 63*(2), 200–208.

Matsuoka, J. K. (1990). Differential acculturation among Vietnamese refugees. *Social Work, 35*(4), 341–345.

McDermott, J. F., Char, W. F., Robillard, A. B., Hsu, J., Tseng, W.-S., & Ashton, G. C. (1983). Cultural variations in family attitudes and their implications for therapy. *Journal of the American Academy of Child Psychiatry, 22*(5), 454–458.

Merton, R. K. (1957). *Social theory and social structure.* New York, NY: The Free Press.

Misumi, D. (1993). Asian-American Christian attitudes towards counseling. *Journal of Psychology and Christianity, 12,* 214–224.

Morris, M. W., & Peng, K. (1994). Culture and cause: American and Chinese attributions for social and physical events. *Journal of Personality & Social Psychology, 67* (6), 949–971.

Morrow, R. D. (1989). Southeast Asian child rearing practices: Implications for child and youth care workers. *Child & Youth Care Quarterly, 18* (4), 273–287.

Nguyen, N. A., & Williams, H. L. (1989). Transition from East to West: Vietnamese adolescents and their parents. *Journal of the American Academy of Child and Adolescent Psychiatry, 28,* 505–515.

Nguyen, L., & Peterson, C. (1992). Depressive symptoms among Vietnamese-American college students. *Journal of Social Psychology, 133,* 65–71.

Nicholson, B. L., & Kay, D. M. (1999). Group treatment of traumatized Cambodian women: A culture-specific approach. *Social Work, 44*(5), 470–479.

Peng, K., & Nisbett, R. E. (2000). Dialectical responses to questions about dialectical thinking. *American Psychologist, 55* (9), 1067–1068.

Phinney, J. S. (1989). Stages of ethnic identity development in minority group adolescents. *Journal of Early Adolescence, 9*(1–2): 34–49.

Phinney, J. S., Cantu, C., & Kurtz, D. (1997). Ethnic and American identity as predictors of self-esteem among African American, Latino, and White adolescents. *Journal of Youth and Adolescence, 26,* 165–185.

Ratliff, B. W., Moon, H. F., & Bonacci, G. A. (1978). Intercultural marriage: The Korean-American experience. *Social Casework, 59,* 221–226.

Root, M. P. P. (1985). Guidelines for facilitating therapy with Asian American clients. *Psychotherapy, 22,* 349–356.

Sharma, A. R. (2000). Psychotherapy with Hindus. In P. S. Richards & A. E. Bergin (Eds.), *Handbook of religious diversity* (pp. 341–365). Washington, D.C.: American Psychological Association.

Shiang, J. (1998). Does culture make a difference? Racial/ethnic patterns of completed suicide in San Francisco, CA 1987–1996 and clinical applications. *Suicide and Life-Threatening Behavior, 28*(4), 338–354.

Sodowsky, G. R. (1991). Effects of culturally consistent counseling tasks on American and international student observers' perception of counselor credibility: A preliminary investigation. *Journal of Counseling and Development, 69,* 253–256.

Sodowsky, G. R., Kwan, K.-L. K, & Pannu, R. (1995). Ethnic identity of Asians in the United States. In J. G. Ponterotto & J. Casas (Eds.), *Handbook of multicultural counseling* (pp. 123–154). Thousand Oaks, CA: Sage Publications.

Sodowsky, G. R., Lai, E. W. M., & Plake, B. S. (1991). Moderating effects of sociocultural variables on acculturation attitudes of Hispanics and Asian Americans. *Journal of Counseling and Development, 70,* 194–204.

Sue, D. (1999). Asian American masculinity and therapy: The concept of masculinity in Asian American males. In G. R. Brooks & G. E. Good (Eds.), *The new handbook of psychotherapy and counseling with men* (pp. 780–795). San Francisco, CA: Jossey-Bass.

Sue, D. W., & Sue, D. (1990). *Counseling the culturally different: Theory and practice* (2nd ed.). New York, NY: John Wiley & Sons.

Sue, S. (2001). Mental health: Culture, race, and ethnicity. *A supplement to Mental Health: A Report of the Surgeon General.* United States Department of Health and Human Services.

Sue, S., & Okazaki, S. (1990). Asian-American educational achievement: A phenomenon in search of an explanation. *American Psychologist, 45,* 913–920.

Takahashi, K. (1986). Examining the strange-situation procedure with Japanese mothers and 12-month-old infants. *Developmental Psychology, 22*(2), 265–270.

Takeuchi, S., Imahori, T. T., & Matsumoto, D. (2001). Adjustment of criticism styles in Japanese returnees to Japan. *International Journal of Intercultural Relations, 25*(3), 315–327.

Tan, S., & Dong, N.J. (2000). Psychotherapy with members of Asian American churches and spiritual traditions. In P. S. Richards & A. E. Bergin (Eds.), *Handbook of psychotherapy and religious diversity* (pp. 421–444). Washington, DC: American Psychological Association.

Tanaka, J. S., Ebrero, A., Linn, N., & Morera, O. F. (1998). Research methods: The construct validity of self-identity and its psychosocial implications. In N. Zane & L. C. Lee (Eds.), *Handbook of Asian American Psychology* (pp. 21–79). Thousand Oaks, CA: Sage.

Tran, T. V. (1991). Family living arrangement and social adjustment among three ethnic groups of elderly Indochinese refugees. *International Journal of Aging & Human Development, 32*(2), 91–102.

Tsai, J. L. (1999). Culture. In D. Levinson, J. J. Ponzetti, & P. F. Jorgensen (Eds.), *Encyclopedia of human emotions, Vols. 1 & 2* (pp. 159–166). New York, NY: Macmillan Reference.

Tsai, J. L., & Levenson, R. W. (1997). Cultural influences on emotional responding: Chinese American and European American dating couples during interpersonal conflict. *Journal of Cross Cultural Psychology, 28,* 600–625.

Tse, L. (1999). Finding a place to be: Ethnic identity exploration of Asian Americans. *Adolescence, 34*(133): 121–138.

Uba, L. (1994). *Asian Americans: Personality patterns, identity, and mental health.* New York, NY: The Guilford Press.

U.S. Census Bureau (2000). *Profile of General Demographic Statistics: 2000.* Washington, DC: U.S. Government Printing Office.

U.S. Census Bureau (1990). *Summary of General Characteristics of Asian or Pacific Islander Persons and Households: 1990.* Washington, DC: U.S. Government Printing Office.

Unschuld, P. (1985). *Medicine in China: A history of ideas.* Berkeley: University of California Press.

Vitebsky, P. (1995). *The shaman.* 1st American ed. Boston: Little, Brown.

Warikoo, N. (2001). Asian populations leaps 71%: Metro area shops, eateries, churches attest to the influx [Electronic version]. *Detroit Free Press,* Retrieved August 8, 2001, from www.freep.com/news/census/casia29_20010329.htm

Williams, A., Ota, H., Giles, H., Pierson, H. D., Gallois, C., Ng, S. H., Lim, T.-S., Ryan, E. B., Somera, L., Maher, J., Cai, D., & Harwood, J. (1997). Young people's beliefs about intergenerational communcation. *Communication Research, 24*(4), 370–393.

Williams, D. R., Spencer, M. S., & Jackson, J. S. (1999). Race, stress, and physical health. In R. J. Contrada and R. D. Ashmore (Eds.), *Self, social identity, and physical health* (pp. 71–100). NY: Oxford University Press.

Word, R. (2001). Florida's Asian population increases dramatic 77.7%. *Tcpalm.com,* Retrieved July 26, 2001, from www.tcpalm.com/news/florida/23sasian.shtml

Yang, M. M. (1994). *Gifts, favors, and banquets: The art of social relationships in China.* Ithaca, NY: Cornell University Press.

Ying, Y. W., Lee, P. A., & Tsai, J. L. (2000). Cultural orientation and racial discrimination: Predictors of coherence in Chinese American young adults. *Journal of Community Psychology, 28*(4), 427–442.

Zane, N., & Mak, W. (2003). Major approaches to the measurement of acculturation among ethnic minority populations: A content analysis and an alternative empirical strategy. In G. Marin, P. Balls Organista, & K. M. Chun (Eds.), *Acculturation: Advances in theory, measurement, and applied research* (pp. 39–60). Washington, DC: American Psychological Association.

Zane, N., & Sue, S. (1996). Health issues of Asian Pacific American adolescents. In M. Kagawa-Singer & P. A. Katz (Eds.), *Health issues for minority adolescents* (pp. 142–167). Lincoln, NE: University of Nebraska Press.

11

Counseling and Psychotherapy with Native American Clients

Aaron P. Jackson
Brigham Young University

Sherri Turner
University of Minnesota

The purposes of this chapter are (1) to provide relevant information to counseling professionals regarding Native American culture, and (2) to discuss how counseling can be done in a way that is sensitive to the culture. Native American culture is a complex topic. There are many levels at which Native American cultures can be understood. At one end of the spectrum, there is danger in looking at Native American culture too broadly—perpetuating a myth of uniformity and denying geographic, spiritual, and tribal differences. Yet it would be an error to focus too much on the differences among Native American groups and minimize the common issues and traditions that are the essence of Native American culture. Accordingly, any discussion of Native American culture must be limited. All the intriguing subtleties of various tribes and smaller cultural groups cannot be adequately addressed in this chapter. Likewise, the general topics discussed in this chapter, while typical of many Native American cultures will not necessarily be true for all Native American cultures.

This chapter will first introduce Native American cultures in terms of history and demographics. This will be followed by a discussion of aspects of Native American cultures that are particularly relevant to counseling and psychotherapy. Finally, suggestions for working with Native American clients will be outlined.

Contextual Issues

Historical Background

In recent years it has become fashionable to discuss Native American cultures in an idealistic and somewhat romantic way. While there are certainly aspects of Native American cultures that are inspiring and worth incorporating into any culture, and while it is understandable that mainstream culture would idealize Native American culture in an attempt to compensate for years of racism, genocide, and oppression, such idealized conceptualizations may oversimplify and limit our understanding of Native American cultures. In order for counselors or therapists to be able to work effectively with Native American clients, the depth, diversity, and paradoxes of Native American cultures must be incorporated into their conceptualizations.

Many aspects of Native American life have been threatened since Europeans began traveling to the American continent. Historically, these challenges included attempts to (1) exterminate the Native American people, (2) relocate and/or restrict Native Americans from their native land, and (3) eliminate Native American cultures by means of boarding schools or forced religious conversion (Beck & Walters, 1977; Choney, Berryhill-Paapke, & Robbins, 1995; Trujillo, 2000).

It is estimated that from the time that Columbus first came to America in 1492 until about 1900, 75–90 percent of the Native American population was destroyed through the combined effects of war, genocide, disease, and dislocation (Choney et al., 1995; Herring, 1999). Since 1900, when the population of Native Americans dipped below 250,000, this population has grown steadily and recently has grown more rapidly than the rest of the population (Herring, 1999). Despite this resurgence, Native Americans are still struggling to regain their estimated pre-Columbian numbers (Herring, 1999; Snipp, 1989; U.S. Census Bureau, 2000).

Once early efforts to eliminate Native Americans fell out of political favor, the next option was to remove Native Americans to designated areas that became known as "reservations" or "reserves" (Choney et al., 1995). Some tribes were entirely removed from their native homeland and forced to adapt to a new environment. Other tribes were assigned areas that included much of their traditional lands except for areas seen as rich in natural resources. While the local effects of these displacements varied, there were some general effects. First, many Native Americans were isolated from the rest of American society. This isolation had the effects of (a) allowing some Native American groups to more easily maintain their cultural heritage but (b) restricting economic and related social development. Second, these geographic designations, while they had the advantage of preserving permanent homelands for Native Americans, caused the negative "us-them" perspective that has been borne out in chronic disputes about sovereignty in political, educational, and business matters.

After Native Americans were isolated on reservations, systematic efforts to assimilate them into mainstream society included educational and missionary programs. These efforts to destroy Native American culture through education and religion, whether intentional or not, included the outlawing of traditional religion and spirituality in the late 1800s (Swinomish Tribal Mental Health Program, 1991), in addition to less overt practices. Missionaries of various denominations focused on converting Native Americans, with an increased number of missionary schools and religious outposts throughout Native American populations during the early and mid-1900s (Choney et al., 1995). The increasing numbers of American Indian converts created tension within some American Indian communities between Christian and traditional Native American ideologies. This increase in Christianity also led to the development of the Native American Church—an alternative to European forms of worship. However, the increase in native religious activities was accompanied by an increase in negative pressure from non-Indians to discontinue these practices. This drove the spiritual practices underground for a time (Trujillo, 2000). Finally, in 1978, the American Indian Religious Freedom Act provided legal protection for native religions and spiritual practices. This law began to ease pressures on traditional Native American religious and cultural practices. However, the Christianization of Native Americans proved to be a most effective means of assimilation, as it did accomplish with some Native Americans the change in attitude and behavior not achieved by other enculturation efforts (Choney et al., 1995).

The last two decades have seen a decrease in overt pressures to assimilate Native Americans into European American culture, with a corresponding increase in efforts to maintain and develop cultural identity, among young Native Americans in particular. Examples of this include the passage of Title VII, a law that requires that bilingual education be available to students in traditionally bilingual areas, such as reservations (cf. http://www.ncbe.gwu.edu). There has been a corresponding increase in the development of culturally sensitive curriculum and instruction on culture per se in formal academic settings. However, many of these programs are facing different challenges. Many Native Americans are losing their language and culture because the parents of today's children were prohibited from learning their cultural heritage. Many of today's middle-aged Native Americans were not allowed to speak their own language in the boarding schools they attended as children; consequently, they have limited capacity to pass the language and related cultural heritage to their children. In some families, this heritage is passed from grandparents to grandchildren, and many of the "lost generation" are working to relearn their native language and culture. The difficulty comes as grandparents pass away and take with them their knowledge of the culture and language—leaving their descendants to acquire their cultural information and experience through less traditional means. The result is that Native Americans vary considerably in their degree of traditional acculturation. The degree to which one is acculturated to both Native American and mainstream cultures has significant implications for counseling. Before discussing this more subtle aspect of multicultural counseling, it is important to get a general picture of Native American peoples.

Demographics

There are currently about 2.5 million people who identify their race as Native American living in the United States. An additional 1.5 million people identify themselves as biracial or multiracial and list American Indian as part of their racial heritage (U.S. Census Bureau, 2000). Though a relatively small fraction of the total U.S. population, this group is growing rapidly. The Native American population grew 38% between 1980 and 1990, more than any other racial group (U.S. Department of Commerce, 1993; Choney et al., 1995). From 1990 to 2000 the population grew approximately another 32% (U.S. Census Bureau, 2000). In addition to being members of a racially and ethnically diverse group, Native Americans have experiences that are typically different from the experiences of those in the dominant culture in a number of ways. These differences are illustrated in Table 10.1 (cf. U.S. Department of Commerce, 1993).

As illustrated above, the Native American population is significantly younger than the total U.S. population. This is more prevalent for Native Americans living on reservations (U.S. Department of Commerce, 1993). The evidences of limited educational opportunities and related employment and poverty data are also illustrated. It is important to note that though these statistics give an accurate general picture of current issues facing many Native Americans, there is considerable variation across tribes and between rural and urban Native Americans. For example, while the average rate of high school completion among Native Americans in general is 65.5 percent, the average rate of completion for Native Americans living on reservations is 54 percent, with completion rates among individuals living on the ten largest reservations ranging from a low of 37.3 percent to a high of 66.3 percent (U.S. Department of Commerce, 1993).

Other demographics of interest include the fact that there are over 500 federally recognized and over 200 state-recognized tribes. Two-thirds of Native Americans live in ten states (U.S. Department of Commerce, 1993), several of which have significant Native American populations. For example, 15.6 percent of Alaska's population is Native American, and New Mexico, Oklahoma, and Arizona have Native American populations between 6 percent and 8 percent. Despite the large number of tribes in the United States, only four tribes—the Cherokee, Navajo, Chippewa, and Sioux—have more than 100,000 members. Most tribes have fewer than 10,000 members (U.S. Department of Commerce, 1993). About one-third of Native Americans live on reservations or other trust lands. Most reservations have populations of fewer than 10,000 people, with the exception of the Navajo Nation, with a population of near 150,000 (U.S. Department of Commerce, 1993). Recent surveys show that over 60 percent of Native Americans are of mixed racial ancestry (Trimble, 1996).

Social and Family Issues

A Native American's view of mental health and mental health treatment may be influenced by tribe, family, educational background, age, and vocational situation. Whether or not a Native American is living or has lived on a reservation may also affect his or her views. Tribes are often independent in language, traditions, identity, and lifestyle; thus identifying and acknowledging specific tribal norms and customs may be an important part of cross-cultural interventions with Native Americans who are highly acculturated to their tribe. However, there are values and cultural perspectives that are common to most Native Americans.

The historical effect of genocidal practices on Native American cultures and families has been negative. However, many Native Americans enjoy strong extended family support, and many Native American cultures have retained this communal perspective (Choney et al., 1995; Garrett & Garrett, 1994; LaFromboise, 1998). Accordingly, it is common to see Native Americans living with extended family and participating in extended family members' lives. Among some tribes, the roles of extended relatives are elaborately and clearly defined. For example, among the Dine' (Navajo), the mother's brother is responsible for disciplining the children in a family (White, 1998). Another example of this communalism can be seen in the approach some Native Americans take to vocational development. Native Americans are much more likely to see the selection and pursuit of their vocation as a group decision—or at least a process for which one has to account to the group—as opposed to the mainstream European American approach of seeing one's vocational development as an individual, psychological process (Martin, 1995).

The dispossession of heritage, resources, and culture experienced by many Native Americans has led to a cycle of poverty. One consequence of this historical oppression has been the increase in single-parent families. As shown in Table 11.1, a significant fraction of Native American families are led by women with no partner present. It is difficult to identify or predict the cultural and social effects of this relatively recent decline in traditional family structure. However, the involvement of grandparents, aunts, and uncles in the parenting process will likely alleviate some of the typical disadvantages of single parenting.

Another aspect of the cycle of poverty among Native Americans is the relative lack of opportunities for educational achievement. As noted in Table 10.1, Native Americans receive bachelors' degrees at less than 50% of the rate of the total population. Statistics for graduation from high school and for completion of graduate degrees show similar discrepancies (U.S. Census Bureau, 2000). This inequity seems to be based in the historical repression of Native American groups and the difficulty that many Native Americans have in adapting to the European American culture inherent in the education system (Jackson & Smith, 2001; Juntunen et al., 2001). The competitive nature of the American educational system runs counter to the cultural values held by some Native Americans. Likewise the linear, time-bound aspect of the system differs from many Native Americans' belief systems. Native Americans living on reservations also experience a dual message when it comes to academic and vocational achievements. They are encouraged to achieve—to attend college and pursue vocations off the reservation. However, at the same time they get the message that to leave the reservation and pursue these goals within the dominant cultural system is turning their back on their people and culture (Jackson & Smith, 2001).

Spirituality among Native American Cultures

Religion and spirituality are fundamental to all Native American cultures. This common regard for religion and spirituality allows different tribal groups to gather and communicate about common issues affecting their people (Trujillo, 2000). Although each tribe maintains its traditional values, beliefs, and spiritual practices, there are a number of beliefs most tribes have in common (Beck & Walters, 1977; Trujillo, 2000).

1. A belief or knowledge about unseen powers including deities and great mysterious powers.
2. Knowledge that all things in the universe depend on each other—fundamental belief in the ideals of balance and harmony.

TABLE 11.1 *Significant Demographic Differences between the Native American Population and the Total Population in the United States*

	Native American Population	*Total Population*
Poverty rates	31 percent	13 percent
Average income	$21,750	$35,225
Bachelors degree or higher	9.3 percent	20.3 percent
Female householder, no husband present	27.3 percent	16.5 percent
Median age	26 years	33 years

3. Conviction that personal worship creates the bond between individual tribal members and the great powers—that worship is a personal commitment to the source of life.

4. Responsibility of traditional healers or Shaman for teaching and guiding in the Native American way of life, for preserving sacred or secret knowledge and using oral tradition to pass special knowledge, ways, and practices to future generations.

5. A belief that being human is a necessary part of the natural harmony; acknowledgement that human beings make mistakes.

Religion and spirituality have been and continue to be important to many Native Americans (Ruthledge & Robinson, 1992). Recognizing and accepting the role of religion and spirituality are important first steps in understanding Native Americans, individually and collectively. It is important to understand that organized religion as conceptualized in traditional western thought is fundamentally different from traditional Native Americans' view of religion (Trujillo, 2000). Understanding what is meant by religion and spirituality among Native Americans may require a radical reconceptualization of these constructs (Toelken, 1976). Religion and spirituality are regarded as the relationship between the Native American people and the spiritual processes of the world (Toelken, 1976). Guidance through these complex relationships is conducted by tribal shaman or traditional healers (Beck & Walters, 1977), historically the source of knowledge for Native Americans' spiritual practices (Halifax, 1982; Beck & Walters, 1977; Trujillo, 2000). The special knowledge and wisdom of the shaman exceed that which is accessible to ordinary members of the tribe (Trujillo, 2000). A shaman's unique relationship with both nature and unseen powers makes this person an invaluable member of the tribe. Shaman conduct and supervise ceremonies, rituals, and prayers to help people of the tribe maintain harmony in life—a fundamental philosophical tenet in most Native American belief systems.

As described by Trujillo (2000):

> The religion and spirituality of the Native American involves all life and emphasizes the importance of maintaining balance in the order and structure of things. This balance is basic to the Native American's well-being and existence. This life orientation maintains that all that is on the earth has a viable life force. Respect and regard for the order and structure of things applies to the interactions the Native American has with any life force, relationships that are necessary to their life and survival (p. 452).

For example, the importance of harmony is reflected in many Native Americans' approach to hunting. The killing of a wild animal is coupled with an appropriate ceremony or ritual that restores the balance between the loss to nature from the animal's death and the life given to the people through consuming it (Trujillo, 2000).

Native American spiritual practices include both personal rituals and group ceremonies. Most tribes have regular ceremonies and celebrations throughout the year that gather the tribe for specific religious and spiritual observances. In many Native American cultures it is important to experience "sacred moments" (Trujillo, 2000, p. 453), which provide insights into the relationships in the natural world and the unseen world. They may also provide personal guidance and give meaning to one's personal path (Beck & Walters, 1977).

Treatment Issues and Approaches

A number of mental health issues are related to the effects of historic cultural oppression and thus permeate the lives of almost all Native Americans. The interrelated and cyclical nature of these issues will be apparent to anyone familiar with the effects of loss, discrimination, and poverty. Counselors and therapists should be aware of these issues when working with Native American clients.

1. Native Americans are four times more likely to complete suicide than the rest of the population (LaFromboise & Howard-Pitney, 1995). This tendency is likely related to (a) the greater likelihood of having experienced significant losses, (b) feelings of hopelessness associated with poverty and discrimination, and (c) higher rates of substance abuse which are, in turn, likely related to (a) and (b).

2. Native Americans are more likely than most others in the population to have experienced significant personal losses. Native Americans are more likely to have known someone who committed suicide, and more likely to have experienced a loss through the death or chronic illness of a loved one. The infant mortality rate is 10 times greater among Native Americans than it is in the rest of the population (Hill, 1985). The incidence of death from diabetes is 3 times greater (Indian Health Service, 1997). Native Americans are also more likely to have lost someone in an accident or through violence as the rate of mortality associated with alcohol is almost 5 times greater among Native Americans than in the rest of the U.S. population (Indian Health Service, 1997).

3. Native Americans are more likely than others in the population to have dealt with the effects of substance abuse. Fetal alcohol syndrome is the most common birth defect among Native Americans (Clawson, 1990). Motor vehicle accidents and other accidents related to alcohol are 50% more prevalent among Native Americans. Some scholars estimate that as many as 1 in 3 Native Americans drinks to excess. Related research shows that Native Americans appear to be more vulnerable than most racial groups to physiological addictions (Reed, 1985).

While these statistics are important in anticipating and understanding the painful circumstances that may bring Native Americans for treatment, counselors and therapists need to be constantly cautious about their assumptions and stereotypes concerning Native Americans. For example, the racist stereotype that "all Indians are alcoholics" is hardly justifiable when one considers that (1) two out of three Native Americans do not drink to excess, and (2) the one-in-three ratio of those who do drink to excess is comparable to that found on many college campuses (Wechsler et al., 2000).

A Perspective for Working with Native Americans

Native Americans have historically viewed the mental health professions skeptically (Dukepoo, 1980; Manson & Trimble, 1982). Two issues that exacerbate this skepticism are

(1) the fact that many Native Americans have developed a mistrust of non-Indian authority figures, problematic in view of the fact that the vast majority of mental health professionals are non-Indian, and (2) the apparent disparity between the ideologies of Native American cultures and traditional mental health practice. These barriers are magnified because many mental health professionals may not be aware that most Western approaches to treatment may undermine traditional Native American values and beliefs (LaFromboise, 1988). These issues likely contribute to the research finding that Native Americans are twice as likely as the general population to discontinue counseling after the first session (Sue, Allen, & Conaway, 1981). Accordingly, mental health professionals who are working with Native Americans and those who anticipate working with Native Americans have a particular challenge and responsibility to establish a trusting working relationship. We propose three keys to empathizing with Native Americans' experiences and developing a therapeutic alliance.

Harmonic Values.   First, it is important to appreciate the prevalence of harmonic models of health and well-being among Native American cultures (Benally, 1992; Choney et al., 1995; Herring, 1999). Traditional Native Americans may not even distinguish "mental health" issues from other issues of well-being (Locust, 1985). Rather, they may experience a disharmony that includes physical, mental, social, and spiritual aspects but which they perceive as divided into life spheres rather than into aspects of the individual. For example, one Native American tradition divides life into four harmonies: spirituality, work, relationships, and nature (Benally, 1992). Some of the values inherent in a harmonic world view are listed in Table 10.2 (Grubbs, 1993; Herring, 1990, 1999; Sue & Sue, 1999). The contrasting values of traditional European American culture are also listed to give perspective.

Locust (1985) sums up the traditional perspective and its relationship to social-emotional well-being as follows:

> If one stays in harmony, keeps all the tribal laws and all the sacred laws, one's spirit will be so strong that negativity will be unable to affect it. If one chooses to let anger or jealousy or self-pity control him, he has created disharmony for himself. Being in control of one's emo-

TABLE 10.2   *Comparison of Traditional Native American Harmonic Values and Traditional European American Values*

Native American Harmonic Values	European American Values
Sharing	Saving
Cooperation	Competition
Noninterference	Aggression
Harmony with nature	Dominance over nature
Present orientation	Future orientation
Cyclical orientation	Linear orientation
Tribe and extended family	Individual and nuclear family
Supernatural explanations	Scientific explanations
Respect for elderly	Respect for youth

tional responses is necessary if one is to remain in harmony. Once harmony is broken, however, the spiritual self is weakened and one becomes vulnerable to physical illness, and/or emotional upsets, and the disharmony projected by others. (p. 14)

Cultural Discontinuity. A second key to understanding Native Americans' experience is appreciating the degree to which traditional Native American and modern mainstream cultures differ. Most Native Americans are pushed to live and function in both Native American and European American cultures. The ways in which Native Americans adapt to this bicultural expectation may have significant implications for counseling and psychotherapy. Ostensibly, this transition back and forth between cultures adds stress and multiplies barriers (Herring, 1999). One participant in a recent study described her experience attending college:

> You always have to do twice as much…because you have to process everything you think, reprocess it back into a thinking that you know [doesn't] fit with your thinking to make it right for the school. [In an archeology class I had to] touch human bones, when you know that's bad. You know you should never do that. You have to go home and you have to cry for those people. You have to go to ceremony to purify yourself and have to go to the class again the next day and do the same thing. It's a hard thing to do. (quoted in Juntunen et al., 2001, p. 281)

One of the authors of this chapter interviewed a woman with a similar dilemma. She was working as a medical assistant and was occasionally required to touch dead bodies, which is forbidden in her culture. She reported that she experienced considerable stress because of the competing cultural expectations and finally went to her "grandmother" who was a medicine woman. The medicine woman told her that the prohibition did not apply to her because she was working in a helping profession and had the protection that any medicine woman might have because it was her obligation to deal with the dead. The medicine woman gave a blessing to the woman which, she reported, relieved her of any subsequent stress in such situations. Apparently the degree to which this "cultural discontinuity" (Garrett & Garrett, 1984) affects individuals varies considerably and may be influenced by individual levels of acculturation, early experiences, and education (Juntunen et al., 2001).

Acculturation. A third key to establishing relationships with Native American clients is to be aware of the varying degrees of acculturation in both Native and mainstream American cultures, as well as their acculturation to other ethnic cultures such as Latino or African American (Choney et al., 1995; Herring, 1999). In order to effectively assess acculturation, mental health professionals must have a solid working definition of the term and a viable model of how it operates for individuals and groups. We will first discuss a definition of acculturation, particularly as it relates to racial identity. We will then discuss models of acculturation. Finally we will address the implications of various acculturation patterns.

Acculturation has been proposed as an alternative to racial identity (Helms, 1990) in efforts to conceptualize the complex mix of cultural influences common to the experience of many Native Americans. Choney et al. (1995) differentiate the two constructs as follows:

"Whereas racial identity implies a variety of complex processes based on ascription to a particular racial group in conjunction with other personal identity attributes (Helms, 1990), acculturation allows for a variety of personal group-oriented ascriptions" (p. 76). They further define the term acculturation as, "The degree to which the individual (in this case, the American Indian person) accepts and adheres to both majority (White/Euro-American) and tribal cultural values (p. 76).

Herring (1999) also used the term *cultural commitment* (p. 51) to help define the construct of acculturation. The advantages of conceptualizing cultural issues in terms of acculturation rather than in terms of racial identity for Native Americans are as follows:

1. Doing so allows for primary identification with a tribe rather than just as "Native American."
2. Doing so allows for greater heterogeneity in being Native American—incorporating, for example, the diverse spiritual and religious influences present in most tribes and allowing for differences among urban and rural Native Americans.
3. Doing so avoids placing identity along a continuum from Indian on one end to White on the other. This helps to avoid the tendency to pathologize one culture or the other.
4. Doing so avoids the artificial dichotomy between cultures—the idea that a person must be one or the other. Eliminating this dichotomy makes it easier to conceptualize a bicultural or multicultural perspective, in all its complexity (Choney et al., 1995).

One danger in adopting acculturation as a conceptual framework for understanding Native American clients is the possibility of assuming a "deficit model" (Choney et al., 1995, p. 83). Such a model assumes that there is a natural shift over time from a traditional, minority culture toward the mainstream, dominant culture. This model also assumes that this movement occurs because fundamental deficits exist in the traditional minority culture. Needless to say, such models perpetuate racist perspectives and contribute, if only covertly, to the oppression of Native Americans. Choney et al. (1995) have proposed an alternative, based on a health or wellness model of acculturation. They suggested that one's acculturation could be conceptualized as a circumplex of cognitive, behavioral, affective/spiritual, and social/environmental domains onto which concentric circles represent various levels of acculturation, as follows:

1. *Traditional.* The individual observes tribal traditions and spiritual practices, speaks the native language, and may not speak much English or socialize with non-Native Americans.
2. *Transitional.* The individual may not fully observe tribal traditions or spiritual practices, but does not accept the dominant culture; he or she speaks the native language and some English.
3. *Bicultural.* The person who is bicultural participates fully in both tribal and dominant cultures, and speaks both the native language and English.
4. *Assimilated.* The assimilated individual participates primarily in the dominant culture, speaks little or none of the native language, and does not typically associate with other Native Americans.
5. *Marginal.* The person speaks English but does not participate fully in either culture.

These levels of acculturation are evidenced in each of the domains described above. So a given individual might have a traditional level of acculturation in the affective/spiritual domain but be bicultural in the social/environmental domain. Such a person would be comfortable in social situations in both tribal and mainstream social settings. However, the person's spiritual and emotional experiences would be based in traditional tribal understanding and culture. A counselor or therapist might easily assume that because the Native American is comfortable in mainstream cultural settings he or she might respond well to typical treatment approaches. However, because counseling and therapy often deal with emotional and spiritual issues, sensitivity to the person's traditional sensibilities in this area would be critical for meaningful counseling to occur. This example illustrates how the acculturation model accounts for some of the complexity among Native Americans' cultural perspectives. It suggests the importance of a professional being able to effectively assess the client's levels of acculturation across the personality domains suggested by Choney et al. (1995).

Living Biculturally. As Choney's (1995) model suggests, most members of an ethnic minority culture are in the unenviable position of having to live biculturally; there is no choice. Living biculturally means having to move quickly from one complex system of values, behaviors, attitudes, and beliefs to another, often competing, system. People who live biculturally do so with varying degrees of success, depending on how familiar they are with the nuances of the dominant culture. To intentionally live biculturally, the minority person must understand the dominant culture and also understand his or her own cultural system so that logical comparisons can be made. However, no matter how much cognitive understanding the minority person has of his or her own culture and of the dominant culture in which he or she is trying to function, there are still two very real problems. First, most cultural assumptions—for example, what daily activities we give priority to—are held and acted upon subconsciously. Second, people react with negative emotional response when they feel that their own culturally based values are being challenged. Both of these problems are prominent for minority persons who are attempting to live biculturally and for majority persons who encounter a minority person who is demonstrating non-majority cultural ideas, attitudes, and behaviors.

We all live under assumptions that are culturally proscribed (*culture* being that set of values, behaviors, attitudes, and beliefs that are socially accepted). Culture is transmitted to us by others' expectations, communicated both verbally and nonverbally, and by the rewards or punishments that follow when the expectations are either met or not met. One of the more difficult challenges for a person who is attempting to live biculturally is to avoid inadvertently activating the wrong set of internalized cultural assumptions when making decisions or responding in some other way to specific environmental demands. Thus the person who is expecting to be rewarded for his or her actions is instead punished. This causes the minority person to be temporarily disoriented. However, as this scenario inevitably repeats itself over time, the psychological outcome can resemble a dissociative disorder, especially if the punishments from those around the minority person are harsh.

Another problem a person who is attempting to live biculturally has is the vast chasm between sets of values which are emotionally laden concerning right and wrong, good and bad, helpful and not helpful. These values are most often associated with moral and social issues. When a minority person who is attempting to live biculturally continually feels pressured to go against his or her own values and accept the values of the dominant culture, the minority person can become offended. This offense can lead to defensiveness or to acting out behavior. A brief case example illustrates these challenges.

John Flyinghorse, a 14-year-old ninth grader, has just moved from the reservation with his parents into the city where his dad has found a new job. John has spent the last nine years in reservation schools, and he believes that he is a competent student. Although he wants to be bicultural, he is at what Choney et al. (1995) might call a transitional level between traditional and bicultural perspectives. Because he wants to fit in at his new school, he cuts his hair to conform to the current style of his new urban peers. He also goes shopping with his mother, who has found a job in the city as a receptionist. With her first paycheck, she buys him all new, stylish clothes. However, these surface changes belie the impending clash between traditional Native American values and the European American values of his new setting.

John is afraid of going to a new school, but as the first day of school approaches, he becomes more and more excited. He is looking forward to having someone to hang out with and to developing new friendships. However, only a month into the school year, John becomes angry—but is not sure why. His behavior becomes more and more unruly. He is frustrated, feels depressed, and begins to talk about going back home.

Several things have happened to John at his school that disappoint and hurt him. First, John was raised with the belief that no one should succeed unless everyone succeeds (cooperation versus competition). Therefore, John helped another student in class during an assignment and got in trouble with the teacher. This reflects Johns traditional spiritual/ affective perspective (Choney et al., 1995). John was also raised to believe that it is impolite to ask another person a direct question—again reflecting his traditional perspective in the social realm (Choney et al., 1995). Therefore, John was highly offended when his teacher singled him out to answer a question in front of the other students. He was humiliated, angry, and ashamed at being treated in such a manner. Another part of John's cultural and spiritual heritage is the belief that everyone has his or her own path and must find that path individually. Therefore, John felt coerced and manipulated when his teacher "tricked" him into giving this kind of information about himself publicly to the class. For John and many of his Native American peers in similar situations the lack of options would mean that they would soon drop out of school, having found it an unfriendly and hostile place.

Approaches to Intervention

The keys to understanding a Native American worldview suggested in the previous section have implications for approaches to treatment. In making recommendations about what is likely to be valuable or detrimental in working with Native Americans, we return to our caution to not oversimplify the process of understanding a given Native American client's personal construction of these issues.

Addressing Issues of Harmony.   Many Native Americans have a holistic view of health and well-being. Accordingly, they may not conceptualize experiences or symptoms in terms of "mental health." Rather they may see their experience of disharmony in terms of what counselors or therapists may see as unrelated experiences. Traditional DSM diagnoses, based on the western medical model and on ever-evolving culturally sanctioned definitions of mental illness, may not provide sufficient means for classifying client concerns and, in some cases, may prove counterproductive (Trujillo, 2000). Likewise, some experiences identified as "symptoms" in mainstream definitions of mental illness may not be symptomatic within a given Native American culture. For example, dreams, visions, or hallucinations might have profound spiritual significance, as opposed to being considered evidence of poor reality testing. There may also be entire syndromes that are specific to a client's culture (Simons & Hughes, 1993). The verity of client complaints in these areas should be assessed by consulting with tribal experts and with the client's family and friends.

As mentioned, many Native Americans have a more communal perspective than most European Americans. This communal perspective may include family members (nuclear and extended), friends, and even an entire community in one's sense of being. This perspective makes individual approaches to counseling seem counterintuitive at best, countercultural at worst. While individual approaches may be appropriate and effective for Native Americans who are acculturated to mainstream society or to members of religions with traditions of individual interventions, family and group approaches may be more consistent with traditional Native American culture (Edwards & Edwards, 1984; Herring, 1999).

Although group approaches may be more culturally consistent than individual approaches, adaptations are desirable for making these approaches more comfortable for traditional Native Americans. Two aspects of group therapy that are inconsistent with Native American values are the expectations that group members (1) confront one another and (2) be willing to readily disclose personal information. These strategies may be effective for Native Americans acculturated to European American styles, but many traditional Native Americans will have difficulty with the format. One alternative approach is to limit the focus of the group and begin with a more structured format, allowing participants to contribute as they are ready without undue pressure. This approach also allows participants to focus on the topic and the leader(s) rather than on each other.

The "talking circles" have been proposed as one culturally sensitive approach to structuring groups (Herring, 1999, p. 79). A talking circle is a group intervention that includes aspects of traditional rituals and prayers rather than depending primarily on the interaction of group members (Ashby et al., 1987; LaFromboise, Berman, & Sohi, 1994). Such approaches may incorporate traditional healing metaphors such as the "four circles of life" (Herring, 1999, p. 78) or the "four forms of sacred knowledge" (Benally, 1992, p. 19). For example, the four circles of life approach uses one's various circles of relationships—with (1) the creator, (2) spouse or partner, (3) immediate family, and (4) extended family and clan—as the focus and structure of the group. These structures provide a topical focus and can give participants culturally sanctioned avenues for sharing their personal perspectives and experiences. A group approach called "network therapy" also involves members of an individual's family, friends, and clan, along with mental health professionals and traditional healers (Attneave, 1969, 1982; LaFromboise & Fleming, 1990). This large group approach, which takes place in the home of the individual or family, mobilizes the social and spiritual support from the entire social network. Of course, structuring groups in these ways may limit participation to members of specific tribes and may require that leaders be either members of the tribe or informed and sanctioned non-members.

Working with the family may be the treatment format most consistent with traditional Native American values. Herring (1999) argues that "family therapy with Native American clients will have more positive results than will individual counseling sessions," and he recommends "culturally sensitive, nondirective approaches which incorporate the use of storytelling [and] metaphor" (p. 79). He also proposes that "the 'Indian Way' consists of families working together to solve problems" and suggests that "family therapy with its systemic approach and emphasis on relationships is particularly effective in working with Native clients" (Herring, 1999, p. 79; cf. Sutton & Broken Nose, 1996). Unconventional formats that take place in the participant's home and may involve individuals beyond the nuclear family are recommended for consideration (Attneave, 1969, 1982; Choney et al., 1995). As with all efforts at family therapy, the challenge is to get an entire family, or even key members in a family together. This limitation tends to make family interventions more of a rare ideal than a typical practicality.

Appreciating Cultural Differences.   Perhaps the most valuable effort a counselor or therapist can make in appreciating the differences among cultures is to be an avid student of those cultures. This is particularly true for non-Native Americans in their efforts to appreciate the differences between Native American cultures and mainstream European American culture. In order to appreciate the cultural discontinuity experienced by many Native Americans, a non-Native American professional must be willing to immerse him or herself, as much as possible, into Native American culture. While it is not possible to become familiar with all the tribal variety of Native American cultures, it is possible to become familiar with the essentials of Native American culture in general and with some of the unique cultural dimensions of some tribes of interest.

Of course, one of the best ways to learn about a culture is to live in it. Although it is not practical to live among all cultures one may encounter as a mental health professional, it may be possible to vicariously experience a culture through those who have studied it and through its literature. Certain ethnographers employ the method of immersion in a culture; their accounts can provide profound insights. For example, the ethnographer Gladys Reichard (1934) spent several summers living among the Dine' (Navajo) in the 1930s. Her account of the traditional Dine' culture offers an important historical perspective into this tribe and into Native American culture in general. Likewise, Briggs (1970) wrote an account of her experiences among an Inuit tribe.

In addition to non-fiction accounts, fiction may also offer valuable windows into a culture. Though a thorough review of Native American literature is beyond the scope of this chapter, we do offer a couple of examples that are particularly relevant to counselors and therapists. *House Made of Dawn*, by N. Scott Momaday (1968), and *Ceremony*, by Leslie Marmon Silko (1977), are both modern classics in Native American literature that provide moving accounts of adjustment issues facing veterans both on and off the reservation. They also portray modern perspectives on how ceremonies, dreams, and traditional healers may facilitate improvement in "mental health." Other recommendations of Native

American literature are easily available through libraries and Native American studies departments at universities. Herring (1999) has compiled a useful appendix of recommended films, fiction, poetry, and other resources for improving one's understanding of Native American culture (pp. 137–146).

Though reading books and articles cannot provide a sufficient background to assume one has a thorough understanding of a given client's cultural heritage, doing so can provide an effective foundation in understanding Native American culture in general. Reading can provide a working repertoire of cultural insights and perspectives that will facilitate understanding individual clients' cultural backgrounds. Having gained a general appreciation of the differences between Native American culture and European American culture and of the differences among various Native American tribes, the counselor is effectively prepared to make assessments of a client's levels of acculturation.

Assessing Acculturation.   As we have discussed, acculturation is not a linear or unidimensional process for Native Americans. In addition to constructing and blending acceptable levels of acculturation in the tribal culture, general Native American culture, and the dominant culture, Native American clients may also be defining themselves in a Latino culture or an African American culture if they have a multiracial or multiethnic background. There are also issues of rural versus urban culture, as well as the possibility of a Christian or other religious cultural commitment. Accordingly, the assessment of a given client's levels of acculturation is a complex process, and the counselor must take care to insure an accurate sense of the client's commitment and involvement in relevant cultures.

Certainly, the most important means of evaluating acculturation is the assessment interview itself. In particular, a critical part of the clinical agenda in the first session or two should be trying to understand the client's unique acculturation. With some clients, the counselor or therapist may be able to address this issue directly and discuss the client's sense of himself in his various cultures. For other clients, the counselor may need to infer levels of acculturation by addressing issues that provide some indications of cultural commitment. Many of these issues are a part of typical counseling interviews and only require that the counselor be listening for them. For example, questions about the client's language preference, place of residence, and circumstances while growing up are all questions that may reveal aspects of acculturation. Other questions that are more specific to acculturation can easily be incorporated into the interview, possibly including discussions about the client's social support system and her spiritual or religious resources.

Beyond these surface evidences of the client's acculturation, the counselor or therapist must be constantly aware of the implications of other material. A client's references to animals, geography, or nature may shed light on traditional spiritual beliefs. Likewise, any discussions of "god" or spiritual forces should be clarified to determine their cultural roots. The counselor or therapist must be particularly aware of her/his own biases and assumptions around such material. A willingness to suspend one's own cultural assumptions and immerse oneself in the culture of the client's worldview is essential.

A final means of assessing a client's acculturation flows from the mental health professional's attitude in engaging another culture. Counselors and therapists must be sufficiently humble to realize that they likely do not have an adequate understanding of the client's cultural heritage(s) and can only understand the client's acculturation by means of the client's descriptions. The counselor or therapist must be willing to learn as much as possible about the cultures and demonstrate interest in understanding how the client incorporates the various cultures into her/his own life. This combination of (1) demonstrating some knowledge about the client's cultures and (2) openly acknowledging one's ignorance and asking for help in understanding the client's acculturation can establish a rapport that will free the client to more easily discuss the issues relevant to his client's acculturation. For example, in the situation cited above in which the woman was working as a medical assistant and had to reconcile handling dead bodies with her tribal prohibitions, the discussion was facilitated because the author was aware of the fact that such prohibitions exist, and he demonstrated interest in understanding the woman's perspective on the dilemma.

Appropriate Interventions

To conclude this chapter, we have compiled a set of recommended counseling interventions from a variety of sources. All are consistent with our own experiences and the professional literature (cf. Bichsel & Mallinckrodt, 2001; Choney, et al., 1995; Fischer, Jome, & Atkinson, 1998; Grubbs, 1993; Herring, 1999; Lee & Armstrong, 1995).

1. Involve family members either in counseling itself or as consultants or cooperatives in the counseling process. This may include extended family members. Of course, the inclusion of family members should adhere to applicable ethical guidelines.
2. Cooperate with Shaman, traditional healers, or other spiritual leaders. While the non-native counselor should not engage in spiritual or traditional practices per se, the counselor can show sensitivity and support for the value of these interventions.
3. Intervene in social systems. The counselor may be in a position to intervene in systems beyond the family. If institutionalized or systemic racism or other forms of oppression are preventing clients from accomplishing their goals, it may be appropriate for the counselor to intervene at the level of the problem.
4. Address the issue of cultural dissimilarity. Counselors should typically bring up the issue of cultural dissimilarity to initiate a dialogue. As we have mentioned, this can be an important means to establishing trust and a working relationship, and it can help the client discuss issues of acculturation.
5. Make appointments as flexible as possible. Native Americans may have value systems that minimize the importance of rigid time structures. Accordingly, allowing for clients to be "late" or for appointments to go longer than typically scheduled can show respect for the culture.
6. Allow more time for casual conversation prior to focusing on problems than you would with European Americans. It may be helpful to spend time in what may seem to non-Native Americans to be unproductive conversation or resistance. This form of conversation reflects the general cultural preference for cyclical rather than linear approaches.
7. Be sensitive to the issue of eye contact. Some experts suggest that it is still most appropriate to minimize eye contact with Native American clients (Turner, 2001). On

the other hand, Herring (1999) recommends that it is most appropriate for non-Native American counselors to make eye contact because that is what Native Americans expect in such situations. Given this conflicting advice, we suggest that counselors minimize eye contact at first and then follow the client's lead as the counseling relationship develops.

8. Show respect for silence. The counselor should become comfortable with silence during sessions. However, the counselor should avoid using silence as a means of manipulating the client to talk more in the session. A more effective technique to help clients who are reluctant to talk is to model appropriate self-disclosure by sharing a story or talking a little about oneself.

9. Use symbolism and the creative arts to expand the levels of communication. Using stories, dreams, and myths is a comfortable means of addressing sensitive issues. Also incorporating the creative arts into treatment may be valuable, as long as the strategy used is consistent with the counselor's training and expertise.

10. Ask permission and express appreciation, thus communicating empathy for the client's personal privacy and respect for the courage it takes to be open in counseling.

11. Be patient. Non-Native American counselors may initially feel frustrated by clients who have a non-linear style or who use long silences in relating their experiences. Counselors should avoid the tendency to interrupt or guess what the client is trying to say.

12. Use descriptive statements or summaries rather than probing questions. Consistent with many Native Americans' view that confrontation is rude, direct questioning can be seen as insensitive. Skilled counselors can guide and deepen sessions effectively by using statements or summaries that suggest the need for a response rather than demand it.

This last recommendation brings up the question of how directive a counselor or therapist should be with Native American clients. Our experience and the research suggest that this is a difficult question to answer (Bichsel & Mallinckrodt, 2001). Or more exactly, it seems that the question of how directive a client expects a counselor to be is more dependent on variables other than ethnicity. For example, the client's level of psychological-mindedness, language skills, acculturation, and readiness, as well as the therapy setting and presenting issues, all seem to impact the question more than ethnicity. Non-Native counselors working with Native American clients, as well as anyone engaged in multicultural counseling, must remember that many of the fears, pains, and joys of being human are transcultural. Accordingly, the fundamentals of counseling and psychotherapy can be appropriately applied across cultures because human beings share these experiences—provided the counselor is sensitive to the cultural issues that may overshadow the counseling process.

References

Ashby, M. R., Gilchrist, L. D., & Miramontez, A. (1987). Group treatment for sexually abused American Indian adolescents. *Social Work with Groups, 10,* 21–32.

Attneave, C. (1969). Therapy in tribal settings and urban network interventions. *Family Process, 8,* 192–210.

Attneave, C. (1982). America Indian and Alaska Native families: Emigrants in their own homeland. In M.

McGoldrick, J. K. Pearce, & J. Giordana (Eds.), *Ethnicity and family therapy* (pp. 55–83). New York: Guilford.

Beck, P. V., & Walters, A. L. (1977). *The sacred ways of knowledge: Sources of life.* Tsaile (Navajo Nation), AZ: Navajo Community College Press.

Benally, H. J. (1992). Spiritual knowledge for a secular society. *Tribal College, Spring,* pp. 19–22.

Bichsel, R. J., & Mallinckrodt, B. (2001). Cultural commitment and the counseling preferences and counselor perceptions of Native American women. *The Counseling Psychologist, 29* (6), 858–881.

Briggs, J. L. (1970). *Never in anger: Portrait of an Eskimo family.* Cambridge, MA: Harvard University Press.

Choney, S. K., Berryhill-Paapke, E., & Robbins, R. R. (1995). The acculturation of American Indians. Developing frameworks for research and practice. In J. G. Ponterotto, J. M. Casas, L. A. Suzuki, & C. M. Alexander (Eds.), *Handbook of Multicultural Counseling* (pp. 73–91). Thousand Oaks, CA: Sage Publications.

Clawson, R. (1990). Death by drink: An Indian battle. [Butte] *Montana Standard, 7 (January),* p. 5.

Dukepoo, P. C. (1980). *The elder American Indian.* San Diego, CA: Campanile.

Edwards, E. D., & Edwards, M. E. (1984). Group work practice with American Indians. *Social Work With Groups, 7,* 7–21.

Fischer, A. R., Jome, L. M., & Atkinson, D. R. (1998). Reconceptualizing multicultural counseling: Universal healing conditions in a culturally specific context. *The Counseling Psychologist, 26* (4), 525–588.

Garrett, M. W., & Garrett, J. T. (1994). The path of good medicine: Understanding and counseling Native Americans. *Journal of Multicultural Counseling and Development 22,* 134–144.

Grubbs, C. G. (1993). Counseling across Anglo and Navajo cultural differences. *Journal of Navajo Education, 11* (1), 27–32.

Halifax, J. (1982). *Shaman: The wounded healer.* London: Thames & Hudson, Ltd.

Helms, J. E. (1990). *Black and White racial identity: Theory, research, and practice.* Westport, CT: Greenwood Press.

Herring, R. D. (1990). Understanding Native American values: Process and content concerns for counselors. *Counseling and Values, 34,* 134–137.

Herring, R. D. (1999). *Counseling with Native American Indians and Alaska Natives.* Thousand Oaks, CA: Sage.

Hill, A. (1985). Treatment and prevention of alcoholism in the Native American family. In T. E. Batter (Ed.), *Alcoholism and substance abuse in special populations* (pp. 247–272). New York: Free Press.

Indian Health Service. (1997). *Trends in Indian health 1997.* Retrieved November 19, 2001, from http://www. ihs.gov/publicinfo/publications/trends97/trends97.asp

Jackson, A. P., & Smith, S. A. (2001). Postsecondary transitions among Navajo Indians. *Journal of American Indian Education, 40* (2), 28–47.

Juntunen, C. L., Barraclough, D. J., Broneck, C. L., Seibel, G. A., Winrow, S. A., & Morin, P. M. (2001). American Indian perspectives on the career journey. *Journal of Counseling* Psychology, 48 (3), 274–285.

LaFromboise, T. D. (1988). American Indian mental health policy. *American Psychologist, 43,* 388–397.

LaFromboise, T. D. (1998). American Indian mental health policy. In D. R. Atkinson, G. Morten, & D. W. Sue (Eds.), *Counseling American minorities* (5th ed., pp. 137–158). Boston: McGraw-Hill.

LaFromboise, T. D., Berman, J. S., & Sohi, B. K. (1994). American Indian women. In L. Comas-Diaz & B. Greene (Eds.), *Women of color: Integrating ethnic and gender identities in psychotherapy* (pp. 30–71). New York: Guilford.

LaFromboise, T. D., & Fleming, C. (1990). Keeper of the fire: A profile of Carolyn Attneave. *Journal of Counseling and Development, 68,* 537–547.

LaFromboise, T. D., & Howard-Pitney, B. (1995). The Zuni Life Skills Development Curriculum. *Journal of Counseling Psychology, 42,* 479–486.

Lee, C. C., & Armstrong, K. L. (1995). Indigenous models of mental health intervention. In J. G. Ponterotto, J. M. Casas, L. A. Suzuki, & C. M. Alexander (Eds.), *Handbook of Multicultural Counseling* (pp. 441–456). Thousand Oaks, CA: Sage Publications.

Locust, C. L. (1985). *American Indian beliefs concerning health and unwellness* (Native American Research and Training Center Monograph). Tucson, AZ: University of Arizona Press.

Manson, S. M., & Trimble, J. E. (1982). American Indian and Alaska Native communities: Past efforts, future inquiries. In L. R. Snowden (Ed.), *Researching the Underserved: Mental Health Needs of Neglected Populations* (pp. 143–163). Beverly Hills, CA: Sage.

Martin, W. E., Jr. (1995). Career development assessment and intervention strategies with American Indians. In F. T. L. Leong (Ed.), *Career development and vocational behavior of racial and ethnic minorities* (pp. 227–248). Mahwah, NJ: Lawrence Erlbaum.

Momaday, N. S. (1968). *House made of dawn.* New York: Harper & Row.

Reed, T. E. (1985). Ethnic differences in alcohol use. *Social Biology, 32*(304), 195–209.

Reichard, G. A. (1934). *Spider woman.* Albuquerque, NM: University of New Mexico.

Ruthledge, D., & Robinson, R. (1992). *Center of the world: Native American spirituality.* North Hollywood, CA: Newcastle.

Silko, L. M. (1977). *Ceremony.* New York: Penguin.

Simons, R. C., & Hughes, C. C. (1993). Cultural-bound syndromes. In A. C. Gaw (Ed.), *Culture, ethnicity, and mental illness* (pp. 75–93). Washington, DC: American Psychiatric Press.

Snipp, C. M. (1989). *American Indians: The first of this land.* New York, NY: Sage.

Sue, S., Allen, D. B., & Conaway, L. (1981). The responsiveness and equality of mental health care to Chicanos and Native Americans. *American Journal of Community Psychology, 6,* 137–146.

Sue, D. W., & Sue, D. (1999). *Counseling the culturally different: Theory and practice* (3rd ed.). New York: John Wiley.

Sutton, C. T., & Broken Nose, M. A. (1996). American Indian families: An overview. In J. G. Ponterotto, J. M. Casas, L. A. Suzuki, & C. M. Alexander (Eds.), *Handbook of multicultural counseling* (pp. 31–44). Thousand Oaks, CA: Sage.

Swinomish Tribal Mental Health Program (1991). *A gathering of wisdom.* Tacoma, WA: Author.

Toelken, B. (1976). How many sheep will it hold? In W. H. Capps (Ed.), *Seeing with a native eye.* New York: Harper & Row.

Trimble, J. E., Fleming, C. M., Beauvais, F., & Jumper-Thurman, P. (1996). Essential cultural and social strategies for counseling Native American Indians. In P. B. Pedersen, J. G. Draguns, W. J. Lonner, & J. E. Trimble (Eds.), *Counseling across cultures* (4th ed., pp. 177–242). Thousand Oaks, CA: Sage.

Trujillo, A. (2000). Psychotherapy with Native Americans: A view into the role of religion and spirituality. In P. S. Richards & A. Bergin (Eds.), *Handbook of psychotherapy and religious diversity* (pp. 445–466). Washington, DC: American Psychological Association.

Turner, S. (2001, August). *Counseling Native American and Alaskan Native clients.* Symposium presented at the Annual Meeting of the American Psychological Association, San Francisco, CA.

U.S. Census Bureau. (2000). *United States Census 2000.* Retrieved November 7, 2001, from http://www.census.gov

U.S. Department of Commerce. (1993). 1992 Population profile of the United States. Washington, DC: U.S. Government Printing Office.

Wechsler, H., Lee, J., Kuo, M., & Lee, H. (2000). College binge drinking in the 1990's: A continuing problem: Results of the Harvard School of Public Health 1999 College Alcohol Study. *Journal of American College Health, 48*(5), 199–210.

White, K. (1998). *Navajo adolescent cultural identity and depression.* Unpublished doctoral dissertation, University of Utah.

12

Counseling and Psychotherapy with Arab American Clients

Chris D. Erickson
The George Washington University

Nada R. Al-Timimi
Temple University

To date, there is almost no literature on the mental health experiences of Arab Americans (Abudabbeh & Nydell, 1993; Erickson & Al-Timimi, 2001). Arab Americans have rarely been the focus of psychological research and have received little attention in the mental health services literature. Moreover, Arab Americans comprise one of the most misunderstood cultural groups in the United States. Often misrepresented in the press and other media and negatively portrayed as terrorists, "fanatics," or wealthy sheiks, Arab Americans have often been the victims of the resulting stereotypes (Abraham, 1995; Abudabbeh & Nydell, 1993; Jackson, 1997; Shaheen, 1984; Suleiman, 1988). These stereotypes, in the context of the lack of mental health literature, can lead to biases and mistaken assumptions among counselors and mental health professionals, compromising their abilities to provide effective services to Arab Americans. The purpose of this chapter, therefore, is to provide an overview of the background and experiences of Arab Americans, to correct common misconceptions of Arab Americans, and to present recommendations for working with Arab Americans effectively.

An Introduction to Arab Americans

Rather than a precise racial designation, the word *Arab* refers to an ethnically mixed group of individuals and is more often a cultural and linguistic term than an ethnic or racial one. Arab

Portions of this chapter are based on Erickson, C. D., and Al-Timimi, N. R. (2001). Providing mental health services to Arab Americans: Recommendations and considerations. *Cultural Diversity and Ethnic Minority Psychology, 7,* 308–327. Copyright 2001 by the Educational Publishing Foundation. Adapted with permission.

countries are those that share a common culture and speak Arabic as a primary language (Diller, 1991). Arab Americans have originated from a variety of countries with large regional and national differences in language, politics, religion, and culture (Abraham, 1995). They vary widely in their cultural and socioeconomic backgrounds, political beliefs, family structures, and acculturation to Western society (Abraham, 1995; Abudabbeh & Nydell, 1993; Jackson, 1997). Because they are so heterogeneous, it is important to understand the diversity of their experiences. (See Erickson & Al-Timimi, 2001, for a description of the ethnic, linguistic, and religious composition of the Middle East.)

An estimated two to three million Arab Americans live in the United States (Abraham, 1995; Zogby, 1990), including individuals who are ethnically Arab or have emigrated from one of the countries that comprise the Arab world (Abraham, 1995; Jackson, 1997). Approximately two-thirds are U.S. born (Abraham, 1995), and most are Christian (88%) (Power, 1998). Arab Americans tend to have more education than other ethnic minority groups because Arab culture encourages educational and economic advancement (Abraham, 1995), and U.S. immigration policies favor educated professionals (Jackson, 1997).

Because of their heterogeneity, Arab Americans have often been classified according to period of emigration. There have been three distinct waves of Arab immigration to the U.S., each with different demographic characteristics and adjustment experiences. The first wave came mainly from Greater Syria, now Syria and Lebanon, between the late 1800s and World War I (Abraham, 1995). Mostly Christian merchants and farmers, they settled mainly in urban areas in the Northeast and industrialized cities in the Midwest. The second wave of Arab immigration began in 1948, following the creation of Israel; this group included many more professionals and Muslims, including Palestinian refugees (Abraham, 1995). They also settled in urban areas in the Northeast and in midwestern industrial cities. By the 1950s, the Arab world was breaking free of European colonial rule, and there was an increase in Arab consciousness; thus immigrants in the second wave were more likely than early immigrants to retain an Arab identity in the United States (Abraham, 1995; Naff, 1980, 1983). The third wave of Arab immigration began in 1967, after the Arab defeat in the Arab-Israeli war, is still occurring, and is expected to continue for some time. These immigrants are more often Muslim, and they have settled in a broader geographic pattern across the United States, including the West Coast. Immigrants in the third wave have experienced a more negative reception and have assimilated into mainstream society less than those of the previous waves.

Arab Americans' Worldview

Arab Americans often differ dramatically from each other in important ways (Naff, 1983); however, they share some commonalties that can serve as an introduction to Arab American culture, including sociopolitical and civil rights issues, family dynamics and affiliation factors, generational issues, gender issues, and religious and spirituality factors.

Sociopolitical and Civil Rights Issues

Arabs and Arab Americans are frequently portrayed in the media in negative images that promote anti-Arab biases and stereotypes (Ghareeb, 1983; Hudson & Wolfe, 1980; Mansfield, 1990; Said, 1997; Shaheen, 1984; Suleiman, 1988; Terry, 1985). These stereotypes are perhaps the result of efforts to bolster public support for U.S. foreign policies in the Middle East, of fear and anger regarding acts of terrorism committed by a small number of Arabs, and of a lack of information about Arabs' concerns or perspectives. Commonly held stereotypes include the following:

1. All Arabs are terrorists who are irrational and anti-Western (Abraham, 1995; Said, 1997; Suleiman, 1988).
2. Islam is dangerous, oppressive, unsophisticated, overly ritualistic, and based on superstition; Muslims are fanatical, closed minded, and violent (Said, 1979, 1997; Shaheen, 1986; Suleiman, 1988).
3. Arab families are oppressive and uncaring: husbands mistreat their wives and children, women are ignorant, oppressed, and passively accepting of their inferior role (Al-Mughni, 1993; Suleiman, 1988; Terry, 1985).
4. Arabs are greedy, oil-rich sheiks, who hold U.S. energy needs hostage (Said, 1997; Shaheen, 1984, 1986).
5. Arab culture has nothing of value to the West, and Arabs would be better off adopting Western culture (Said, 1979, 1997).

More troubling than the nature of these stereotypes is the fact that the average American is unaware of holding any prejudice toward Arab Americans (Suleiman, 1988). While most understand that it is racist to make derogatory generalizations about Native Americans, many do not recognize their negative stereotypes about Arab Americans. In fact, some bias against Arabs is considered normal in the United States, even among those who believe it unacceptable to hold biases toward other races (Mansfield, 1990). These stereotypes also affect mental health professionals. In fact, in the only known examination of the attitudes of health care workers toward Arab American patients, Lipson, Reizian, and Meleis (1987) found that health care workers had significantly negative attitudes toward Arab American patients, including perceptions of them as noncompliant, unwilling to utilize mental health services, likely to present unclear diagnostic information, difficult to care for, demanding, and overanxious. The authors found little evidence that health care workers recognize the importance of considering Arab culture or religion in evaluating patients' concerns or developing treatment plans.

Since its creation in 1948, Israel has shared strong political and economic alliances with the United States (Abudabbeh, 1996). Many Arab Americans have therefore perceived U.S. foreign policy as taking sides in the Arab-Israeli conflict and as denigrating to their own cultural heritage (Naff, 1983). While Arab Americans tend to identify themselves as Republican and conservative in their political beliefs (Naff, 1980, 1983, 1985), Arab ethnic loyalty regarding U.S. foreign policy has been increasing, as has dissatisfaction with many U.S. actions toward the Middle East (Abraham, 1995). Many Arab Americans resent U.S. economic and political domination in the Middle East and take exception to American insensitivity to Arabs' political plight and aspirations, with the issue of Palestine being the most obvious example (Abudabbeh & Nydell, 1993). Sadly, the recent legislative and military responses to the attacks of September 11, 2001, have led many Arab Americans to feel that it is dangerous to express their political opinions.

Ethnic invisibility has been another important concern for many Arab Americans. Racial classification, which began in the United States as a function of immigration law, has been used to limit the number of non-Europeans, including Arabs, entering the United States. Over time, different classifications have been devised that have often had little to do with regional or racial background. Until 1920, Arab immigrants were classified as Turks, afterward as Syrian, Asian, or African (Naff, 1980). Racial classifications of census data have also differed dramatically over time, with Arab Americans being alternately classified as "Assyrian," "Turk," and "White." In the mid 1970s, the Federal Interagency Committee on Education was asked to develop a set of standard racial and ethnic definitions to be used by government agencies to ensure consistency of classification and the protection of civil rights. The Committee based their determinations on disparities between various ethnic groups (as they were then classified in the U.S. census) and Whites in their exclusion from citizenship, property rights, and immigration. The Committee established five racial/ethnic categories: (1) "Black," (2) "American Indian/Alaska Native," (3) "Hispanic," (4) "Asian or Pacific Islander," which covered persons from east of the Indian subcontinent but was later adjusted when the Association of Indians in America petitioned to have the Indian subcontinent included, and (5) "White," which included persons from Europe, the Middle East, and North Africa (Hatab Samhan, 1999). The benefits of this racial/ethnic classification system have been that census data are more consistently classified and are available to monitor the health and welfare of different ethnic groups. The system has been used to develop policies to protect the civil rights of ethnic minorities and has enabled the measurement of and development of remedies for the socioeconomic gaps between groups. The classification has added to the visibility of ethnic groups, has increased groups' cohesion and unity and has been a source of ethnic pride and political clout (Hatab Samhan, 1999). Thus many Arab Americans are troubled that they have not been recognized as a distinct group.

In 1994, the Arab Anti-Discrimination Committee (ADC) petitioned to add "Arab American" to the official racial/ethnic categories. The Office of Management and Budget denied their request, however, citing a lack of consensus over the definition of "Arab American" and the relatively small size of this population (though currently there are likely more than twice as many Arab Americans as Native Americans). Continuing to classify Arab Americans as "White" produces many problems: (a) confusion, since many people who may not look White, including those from North Africa (Libyans, Algerians, Sudanese, etc.), are classified as White; (b) service providers such as schools and other government funded agencies are ineligible to receive some funding for providing services to these individuals as they are not a protected class; (c) invisibility, because many Arab Americans feel "invisible" when they fill out forms or enroll for services because none of the ethnic or racial categories applies to them; and (d) Arab Americans often view themselves as members of an ethnic minority group and identify with other individuals of color but are not acknowledged as such. Many Arab Americans resent being classified as White because this designation does not reflect their reality, including experiences of racism and discrimination. Helen Hatab Samhan (1999) describes the plight of Arab Americans as the problem of being "not quite White" (p. 1).

It is clear that Arab Americans have frequently experienced difficulties based on their ethnicity. U.S. anti-Arab sentiment and fear of terrorism have resulted in countless violations of the civil liberties of Arab Americans. Beginning in the 1960s, the Immigration and Naturalization Service and other federal and local law enforcement agencies established systematic surveillance programs for the activities of Arab students and communities (Abraham, 1995). During the Gulf War, "Terrorist Hotlines" were established in many cities asking citizens to report suspicious individuals (who were presumably "Arab-looking"). Numerous hate crimes and acts of violence committed toward Arab Americans went unreported because of victims' fear of the authorities. Several of the authors' friends and family were approached in their homes or businesses by law enforcement officials and asked about their political and religious affiliations and about their position on the war. Since the Gulf War, U.S. airlines have implemented "passenger profiling" practices that include singling out individuals who travel frequently to the Middle East.

The terrorist attacks of September 11, 2001, are likely to have additional negative effects on many Arab Americans. Following the attacks there has been a dramatic increase in the expression of anti-Arab bias, along with discrimination and hate crimes against Arab Americans. Between September 11, 2001, and November 20, 2001, the ADC confirmed reports of 520 violent incidents directed against Arab Americans or people believed to be Arab, including dozens of cases of ethnic discrimination in which Arab or "Arab-looking" travelers were prevented from traveling on airplanes because passengers or crew were suspicious of them, hundreds of cases of employment discrimination, and even anti-Arab threats and violence among children in schools. As of November 29, 2001, the Council on American-Islamic Relations (CAIR) had identified 1,452 reported hate crimes, including simple assault, battery, arson, aggravated assault, and at least six murders.

There has also been a disturbing degradation of the personal freedom and civil liberties of Arab Americans. New Jersey Police Departments gained national attention and faced criminal liability in the late 1990s for their unlawful profiling of African Americans. Ironically, since the September 11th attacks they have been asked to locate over 300 Arab individuals for questioning as part of a national effort to detain and question individuals of Arab descent to determine whether they are connected with terrorist activities. Federal investigators have approached Arab Americans in their homes and at work and have canvassed more than 200 U.S. university campuses to interview and investigate students from the Middle East (Steinberg, 2001). Many Arab Americans have reported fear and indignation at being singled out for questioning. One student described the unsettling experience of an unannounced visit by agents from the Federal Bureau of Investigation and Immigration and Naturalization Service at his apartment one evening during which he was questioned extensively about his coursework, activities, and politics (Boal, 2001).

The USA PATRIOT (Uniting and Strengthening America by Providing Appropriate Tools Required to Intercept and Obstruct Terrorism) Act was passed in November 2001. This act enables U.S. law enforcement agencies to use intensive investigation and detainment procedures in probing possible terrorist threats, thus increasing the safety concerns of Arab Americans and heightening concerns for their civil liberties. This act grants the U.S. government the right to detain non-citizens. Immigrants and non-citizens do not have to be guilty or suspected of terrorist activities to be detained for questioning; even immigration status violations such as overstaying a visa could result in an individual's indefinite detention if his or her country refuses acceptance (American Civil Liberties Union, 2001). The act allows for detention and deportation based on "guilt by association." Under this legislation, individuals who provide assistance for the lawful activities of a group that the government deems a terrorist group (even groups that do not identify themselves as such) could face incarceration or deportation. The Act also allows for "reduced standards of cause and levels of judicial review" (ADC, 2001) in relation to surveillance, searches, and seizure in the investigation of Arabs and Arab Americans. (For a detailed analysis of the USA PATRIOT Act, see ACLU, 2001.) To cope with the experiences of backlash, hate crimes, discrimination, racial profiling, and decreased personal freedoms, many Arab Americans have curtailed their social activities, denied their ethnic identity, or withdrawn into ethnic enclaves. In the aftermath of September 11th, many Arab Americans are experiencing a deepened sense of disenfranchisement and alienation from "mainstream" U.S. society, a condition that will likely continue for some time.

Family Dynamics and Affiliation Factors

The central structure of Arab culture is the family, which plays a critical role in Arab social organization and in Arabs' individual and collective identity (Abudabbeh & Nydell, 1993; Naff, 1983; Soliman, 1986). For many Arab Americans, the development of an individual identity separate from that of the family or community is not valued or supported (Abudabbeh, 1996), and many Arab Americans may not even see a need for individual happiness or healthiness separate from the well-being of the family. For some clients, being asked to consider their personal needs in a situation may cause confusion or guilt if they feel that doing so betrays their family (Gorkin, Masalha, & Yatziv, 1985). Thus individuation from family may not be a culturally appropriate goal for treatment.

Many Arab cultures consider family honor and status to be a central goal for each family member, and practicing conformity and placing family interests over individual ones are expected (Nydell, 1987). Magnanimity, generosity, and hospitality are prized values (Naff, 1983); educational achievement, hard work, thrift, and conservatism are encouraged to promote family honor, and individuals are urged to behave in ways that reflect well on others at all times (Nydell, 1987).

Extended families are of central importance in Arab culture, with two or more generations often residing in the same household (Abraham, 1995). Arab parents will often support their eldest child financially through school and early career. The eldest child is then responsible for supporting the next sibling, and so on to the youngest child. As adults, children are expected to take care of their parents and older relatives, taking them into their home if needed (Abudabbeh & Nydell, 1993). Immediate family is expected to take priority over chosen family or partners in both financial support and loyalty, and placing an elderly family member in a nursing home would be considered disgraceful. Arab family networks provide intense loyalty, emotional support, personal guidance, and financial assistance (Nydell, 1987). During times of difficulty, individuals often depend heavily on their family for help in coping (Abraham, 1995; Al-Mughni, 1993). As a result of these extensive family networks, many Arab Americans may be reserved in initial dealings with individuals outside their social networks (Meleis, 1982).

The Arab family's influence on its members is powerful and lifelong (Patai, 1976; Sharabi & Ani, 1977). Family ties and commitments are expected to take precedence over work or career aspirations (Abudabbeh & Nydell, 1993), and parents have a continuing role in the lives and decisions of their adult children. It can be quite disconcerting for immigrant parents if their children choose to follow American norms and settle in different parts of the country or world. Many Arab Americans experience intense loneliness when separated from their family (Jackson, 1997).

Within Arab cultures, arranged marriages are common (Abraham, 1995; Abudabbeh, 1996), although Islam grants women the right to refuse a prospective partner (Abudabbeh, 1996). Family social status and reputation are carefully considered in selecting a prospective partner, because social interaction between sexes is often restricted and community reputation can be an important source of information about an individual's character (Abraham, 1995). In contrast to the Western view of marriage, many Arabs consider the selection of a mate too serious an issue to be decided by the whims of sentimentality (Abudabbeh, 1996). Arab Americans tend to be practical in their expectations, looking for a match in education, religion, social status, and family reputation. Married adults maintain close familial connections, sometimes relying on their family, more than their spouse, for their emotional needs (Abudabbeh & Nydell, 1993).

Generational Issues

Compared to those born in North America, Arab immigrants tend to have the largest task of adjusting to the social and cultural differences between their homeland and the West. Some of the values that may be most in conflict are the Arab preference for conformity, subordination of individual goals, emphasis on the family and community over self, conservative moral practices, and adherence to a collective sense of honor and reputation (Nydell, 1987; Soliman, 1986). Typically, Arab parents expect their children to practice the cultural customs of the family, though children may reject these practices, resulting in a cultural gap. Since Arab child rearing practices are typically authoritarian (Abudabbeh, 1996), this cultural gap has led many Arab American parents to exert considerable effort to instill traditional values in their children (Abudabbeh & Nydell, 1993; Jackson, 1997). Typically Arab American parents will inform their children of their expectations for everything from their children's interpersonal behavior to dating practices and career choices, and the parents may express strong disapproval when their expectations are not met.

Gender Issues

Within Arab families, men are generally the head of the household, responsible for providing for their family's needs. Money or property owned by wives remains theirs entirely, which can be a source of considerable interpersonal influence. Arab women typically have a great deal of authority over family decisions, more than many Americans realize; however, this influence is usually exerted in private, as the women maintain the appearance of a more passive role in public (Abudabbeh & Nydell, 1993; Jackson, 1997). Whereas Western society values direct communication and sees confrontation as evidence of interpersonal power, Arab cultures value indirect methods of decision making and conflict resolution. Arab women's tendency to use less direct styles of influence is commonly misinterpreted as a sign that they are oppressed. Many Americans consider Arab women to be severely dominated by their husbands and fathers. However, though some Arab American women may be unhappy with aspects of their gender role and desire more autonomy or independence in their decisions regarding work, relationships, etc., many have no complaint. As in the culture of the United States (Rice, 1990), Arab women's status varies considerably with socioeconomic background and religious conservatism.

An important example of misinterpretation of a cultural practice is the issue of Muslim women's head covering. Many Americans view this covering as a sign of oppression. But many Muslim women *prefer* to wear the covering out of cultural and religious pride, much like a Jewish man might wear a yarmulke. These women resent the perception that their head covering represents oppression, pointing out that Catholic nuns who cover their heads are not seen as oppressed, but as devout. Some have argued that to view head covering as a sign of oppression is as naïve as assuming that miniskirts are a sign of emancipation. Thus it is important to use caution in attributing meaning to aspects of a culture one does not really understand.

It is also important to consider ways that Arab women do hold power of the sort easily recognized by Western cultures. For example, an estimated 20% of judges in Morocco are female (Fernea, 1998), similar to the estimated 19.6% of judges in U.S. federal courts who are female (Employee Relations Office, U.S. Courts, 1999). While there are a number of Arab countries that do not have any female judges, these disparities illustrate the diversity of experiences among Arab women. Historically, Muslim women were the first to hold property rights, including the right to inherit property, dating back over 1,400 years. In contrast, European women gained these rights less than 200 years ago (Khan, 1997; Roberts, 1984). These points illustrate the need for mental health professionals to challenge their common assumptions about Arab women and instead learn about each client as an individual.

Religious and Spirituality Factors

Religion often plays an integral role in the lives of Arab Americans, and it may be a central component of their identity (Abudabbeh, 1996; Abudabbeh & Nydell, 1993). Among many Arab Americans, religion may be the primary factor by which people identify themselves (Naff, 1980). There is a great deal of confusion in the U.S. between the terms "Arab" and "Muslim" (Suleiman, 1988). Muslims are followers of Islam, found in all parts of the world including Europe, Asia, Africa, and the United States; Muslims are predominantly non-Arab (Diller, 1991). Worldwide, Arabs account for only 18 percent of all Muslims (Jackson, 1997). Furthermore, many Arabs are not Muslim. Additionally, although a vast range of religious beliefs exist within Islam, most Americans incorrectly assume that all Muslims adhere to the most conservative of doctrines.

Many Muslim Arab Americans feel particularly misunderstood by American society. Islam holds a deep reverence for the importance of knowledge, and Muslims consider learning to be the highest religious activity (Hitti, 1970; Jackson, 1997). Ethical behavior is central to Islamic teachings, and compassion toward others, especially those less fortunate, is expected at all times (Jackson, 1997). Muslims are encouraged to exert considerable physical, intellectual, and spiritual efforts for the good of others (Abudabbeh, 1996). These values are in dramatic contrast to the stereotypes commonly held by Americans of Muslims as angry, violent, or dangerous. Thus many Muslim Arab Americans feel they have been maligned in the U.S. media (Abraham, 1995).

Because religion plays such an important role in the lives of many Arab Americans, mental health professionals need to be sure to assess the ways that each client is impacted by his or her religion and to incorporate issues of spirituality into treatment where appropriate. Explicit discussions of religion, especially early in counseling, can signal to the client that the counselor is open to dealing with issues of spirituality in counseling. At a minimum, counselors should demonstrate respect for clients' spirituality and should provide assurances that their religious values will not be subverted.

Treatment Considerations

Arab Americans' Views of Mental Health

Many Arab Americans may be hesitant to seek counseling for emotional concerns because of skepticism regarding mental health services or negative attitudes about mental illness (Abraham, 1995; Abudabbeh, 1996; Hedayat-Diba, 2000). Some see counseling as only for the seriously troubled (Soliman, 1986). For example, Lipson, Reizian, and Meleis (1987) found that Arab American clinic and hospital patients with needs for psychotherapy resisted referrals to mental health services. Arab Americans' hesitation concerning mental health services may be related to some of their culture's prevalent views of Western society: (a) that raising children to be independent and self-supporting is "cold" and uncaring, and represents a lack of love for one's children, (b) that unrestricted association between men and women has led to lowered moral standards, (c) that Western children do not respect their parents, and this has weakened the American family structure, (d) that Western families do not help each other when in need, which accounts for the large numbers of homeless people, and (e) that materialism is overemphasized in the West and obscures the importance of caring for others and contributing to the well-being of society (Abudabbeh & Nydell, 1993). Some Arab Americans may fear that counselors will not respect their values or that counseling will undermine their moral standards, resulting in these types of social ills.

Another potential concern Arab Americans hold with counseling is that modern psychotherapy was developed in the West and is primarily Western in focus; thus many counseling approaches are inconsistent with traditional Arab culture (Dwairy & Van Sickle, 1996). Western counseling sees individualism and self-actualization as the foundation for healthy psychological development (Abudabbeh & Nydell, 1993). In fact, the concept of psychological mindedness requires that individuals see themselves as separate individuals. Arab cultures, in contrast, do not encourage individuation from family, and individuals are seen primarily as part of the unfolding history of the family group (Dwairy & Van Sickle, 1996; Gorkin et al., 1985). Arabs' self-image, self-esteem, self-confidence, and personal identity are measured in terms of their relationships to family (Daneshpour, 1998). Loyalty, closeness, and interdependency are stressed as requirements for healthy emotional development (Hedayat-Diba, 2000), and individuals lacking these are considered selfish or immature. This lack of individuation should not be considered as abnormal, primitive, or pathological, but rather as a cultural style of family relationships (Abudabbeh & Nydell,

1993). In terms of Maslow's hierarchy of needs, Arab families provide all of an individual's needs, including physiological and safety, love and belonging, and self-esteem. As these needs are met, individuals give up the need for self-actualization. Some may even see self-actualization as selfish or self-centered, and individuals who pursue it may do so at the expense of their basic needs. Thus there is a strong incentive for individuals to remain connected to the family and to forego some individual needs (Dwairy & Van Sickle, 1996).

Arab Americans are also likely to be less "psychologically minded" than Westerners (Jackson, 1997). Because of the group focus in Arab culture, there are fewer opportunities than in mainstream American culture for examining oneself or for focusing on inner experiences (Gorkin et al., 1985). Some may even believe that too much introspection is the root of psychological problems rather than a solution for them (Dwairy & Van Sickle, 1996). Traditional Arab culture provides little exposure to psychological constructs, and there is little psychological terminology in Arabic language. Thus some may not recognize connections between their symptoms and psychological experiences, including intrapsychic or interpersonal conflicts (Dwairy & Van Sickle, 1996). Clients may not define depression or anxiety in psychological terms, but instead use physical symptoms to characterize their concerns. This inexperience with psychological terminology may cause some to become distraught when they receive a psychological diagnosis from a professional, attributing a great deal of importance to the diagnosis, especially if its meaning is not carefully explained.

Once in counseling, many Arab Americans might expect a counselor to offer detailed advice or give explicit directions, viewing the counselor as the "expert" (Gorkin et al., 1985; Hedayat-Diba, 2000). They may appear passive in initial counseling sessions, waiting to be asked questions rather than volunteering information. Such behavior may be due to Arabs' hierarchical social structure, the cultural practice of seeking advice from elders, and the need for showing respect for authority by careful listening (Abudabbeh, 1996). This view of counselors, however, may come with high expectations for a quick or simple solution to their problems. When a counselor does not use his or her authority to direct clients, but instead asks them to look within for their own solutions, clients may be confused or lose trust in the counselor and discontinue counseling (Kulwicki, 1996).

Given the communal nature of Arab culture, many Arab Americans prefer indirect approaches to dealing with conflict, only criticizing others in their absence (Dwairy & Van Sickle, 1996). They may conceal their true feelings, especially negative ones, and avoid the direct expression of anger to please others. They may instead express their feelings indirectly through poetry, fantasy, or somatization (Racy, 1980). They may even indicate that they agree with the counselor even if they do not, since to disagree with an authority figure is considered rude (Hedayat-Diba, 2000). Also, clients may work hard to fulfill the counselor's expectations, sometimes inaccurately reporting their circumstances so as not to disappoint the counselor. Thus counselors should carefully explore clients' situations to understand their underlying dynamics.

Other aspects of Arab culture that may impact counseling are its less structured orientation to time and its openness to non-rational problem-solving approaches. Because Arab culture is much less time-bound than Western culture, Arab Americans may focus on events or circumstances in the present rather than those in the future, and they may favor short-term strategies for dealing with difficulties (Dwairy & Van Sickle, 1996). Thus expecting clients to consider future consequences of decisions may be unrealistic. Also meeting times may need to be clearly outlined at the beginning of counseling, and tardiness for a session should not be automatically interpreted as resistance. Rigidly adhering to an appointment schedule without making expectations known to a client may be perceived as inconsiderate or uncaring. Additionally, Arab Americans are more open to non-rational models of problem solving than are Westerners, who tend to rely on empiricist assumptions in assigning value to decisions (Dwairy & Van Sickle, 1996). Many Arabs do not place the same importance on objectivity or rationality, and many do not equate subjectivity with immaturity (Abudabbeh & Nydell, 1993). Therefore, rational approaches to problem solving may not be as important for some Arab American clients as for their European American counterparts, and alternate styles, such as intuitive, or dependent approaches to problem solving might also be considered.

Because of these attitudes toward mental health, clients likely to come for counseling are those who are more educated, more Westernized, more English-speaking, or those who have a clear and severe diagnosis. Clients likely to resist services are those who are more Arabic speaking, more traditionally Arab, or those who see their difficulties as less severe (Abudabbeh, 1996). Clients may have strong fears about being branded "majnun" or crazy, a term that can carry considerable stigma in Arab culture (Gorkin et al., 1985).

Recommendations for Counseling and Psychotherapy

Multicultural theorists explain that in order to be effective in working with multicultural clients, mental health professionals need to be aware of and to challenge the stereotyped images they have of these clients, to be able to interpret clients' behavior within appropriate cultural contexts, and to use culturally appropriate interventions (Arredondo, 1999; Casas, Ponterotto, & Gutierrez, 1986; Ibrahim & Arredondo, 1986; Sue, Arredondo, & McDavis, 1992; Sue & Sue, 1990). Toward this end the following recommendations are offered.

Recommendations for Reducing Practitioner Bias.   Because counselors likely hold some stereotypes of Arab Americans, it is important for them to carefully consider their attitudes and beliefs to decrease potential harm to Arab American clients. To achieve this, the following are recommended:

1. *Examine your attitudes and beliefs about Arab Americans.* Consider how these may impact counseling. Consider the underlying assumptions of these attitudes and ways they may be harmful or non-growth promoting.

2. *Become a critical consumer of media portrayals of Arabs and Arab Americans.* Rather than assuming that everything published or broadcast about Arabs or Arab Americans is true, consider the nature of messages conveyed, including the subtle but powerful messages of pictures in the media, such as a picture of a mosque during a report on terrorism.

3. *Look for information that is discrepant with common stereotypes.* Consider the things Arab culture has to offer Western societies in general and psychological theory in particular, including the value of Arab indigenous ways of helping.

Recommendations for Understanding Arab Americans' Worldview.   Counselors need to increase their general understanding of Arab Americans' worldview. To accomplish this, one might undertake the following:

1. *Increase your awareness of Arab Americans.* This can be achieved through reading, attending cultural events, and interacting with Arab Americans. Many cities have Arab American community organizations, and there are a number of national Arab American magazines and newspapers and on-line communities. (For a listing of Arab American resources, see Erickson & Al-Timimi, 2001.)

2. *Take time to learn about the particular culture of each client.* Let clients provide information about specific aspects of their acculturation, ethnic identity, family relationships, and religious and cultural beliefs that may impact their particular situation.

3. *Consider using a cultural consultant.* A cultural consultant is someone familiar with Arab culture or language who could assist in interpreting clients' symptoms and concerns or serve as a mediator between the client and the counselor (or between the client and the institution in the case of inpatient treatment) to determine whether communication difficulties or cultural incongruities may be impacting treatment.

4. *Seek information regarding your effectiveness.* Ask clients for feedback about your work and for suggestions about ways you might be more helpful to them. Be sure to probe carefully, as they may not be immediately forthcoming with criticism. Reassure clients that their feedback will improve your ability to help others in the future. Refer clients you are unable to effectively assist.

Recommendations for Building Clients' Trust.   Many Arab Americans may be unaware of a distinction between different types of mental health professionals, viewing all of them as researchers or doctors with little regard for their cultural or religious values rather than as a resource for assistance. To counter this, counselors should carefully explain the nature of counseling, stressing that the connection between the counselor and client is a critical part of the counseling process. To facilitate this, the following are recommended:

1. *Be aware of Arab Americans' perceptions of Western culture.* Some Arab Americans view American culture as cold or uncaring, lacking in respect for others, low in moral standards, and overly materialistic (Abudabbeh & Nydell, 1993). They may worry that Western counselors do not understand or appreciate their values. Therefore, be sure to actively demonstrate an awareness of and respect for traditional Arab values. Describing client problems and deficits in the context of their cultural strengths and assets may reassure clients they are not being denigrated or devalued.

2. *Provide a careful orientation to counseling, developing rapport and pre-rapport when possible.* Provide a careful orientation to treatment to explain what clients can and cannot expect from the services being provided. Explain to clients that they will be expected to take an active role in discussing their personal experiences. Work to establish rapport early in counseling, even before beginning counseling (pre-rapport) if possible (Jackson, 1997). Look for ways to interact with Arab Americans in the community. This approach is consistent with Arabs' respect for kinship and for those who make an effort. If a family member is resistant to counseling, call or visit the individual at home to invite him or her to participate. This may also help get around the person's negative reactions to formalized relationships with caregivers.

3. *Pay attention to culturalisms and manners.* Seek to understand clients from within their cultural context, taking care not to pathologize cultural differences such as somatization, intuition, or enmeshment. Be careful in using the phrase "I understand you," as it can be interpreted as threatening, and for some it connotes that you have detected that the client has malicious intentions. Also, avoid "why" questions, as they can be interpreted as argumentative (Dwairy & Van Sickle, 1996). Arabs tend to evaluate others on their manners and grooming; thus sitting or standing casually, such as leaning against a wall, putting hands in pockets, or resting feet on furniture, may be interpreted as indicating a lack of respect, as may sustained direct eye contact, especially by a man toward a woman (Abudabbeh & Nydell, 1993). It is considered polite to demonstrate hospitality and generosity, and it is customary to offer a guest in your office something to drink. It would be considered impolite not to accept food or gifts offered.

4. *Remember that trust may develop slowly, but intense connections are possible.* Arab clients may take time to develop trust, so do not be dissuaded if they are not eager to discuss aspects of their lives, especially early in counseling. Do not expect clients to share "family secrets" with a relative stranger; this type of sharing may be reserved for deeper relationships that evolve over a longer period of time. In addition, Arabs tend to personalize relationships, evaluating people, including professionals, as potential friends. They are not as apt as Westerners to take on roles, such as teacher-student roles, in which people are friendly but do not expect to become close friends (Abudabbeh & Nydell, 1993). Thus spending a great deal of effort developing rapport is important if a therapeutic relationship is to be successful. Further, if a client is eventually brave enough to reveal his or her true feelings, be careful not to react in an impassive or unemotional way, which may be perceived as remote, uncaring, or indifferent (Dwairy & Van Sickle, 1996). Be sure to recognize the deep honor it is for a client to share personal feelings with someone outside his or her family.

Recommendations for Implementing Culturally Relevant Interventions. No research exists on the effectiveness of Western psychological interventions with Arab Americans (Abudabbeh & Nydell, 1993; Dwairy & Van Sickle, 1996; Erickson & Al-Timimi, 2001; Gorkin, Masalha, & Yatziv, 1985; Jackson, 1997). Recent authors have reviewed some of the cultural factors common to Arab Americans and offered suggestions for mental health professionals (Abudabbeh, 1996; Abudabbeh & Nydell, 1993; Erickson & Al-Timimi, 2001; Jackson, 1997; Jalali, 1996; Meleis, 1981, 1982; Simon, 1996). In the absence of efficacy research, counselors are forced to determine appropriate treatment approaches based on individual clients' needs. The following recommendations are intended to assist that process:

1. *Assess clients' level of acculturation early in counseling.* Assess each client's degree of acculturation to Western culture to determine the suitability of different counseling approaches. Dwairy and Van Sickle (1996) suggest assessing the following aspects of acculturation for each client: (1) ego strength, since individuals with a stronger sense of themselves will be better able to tolerate divergent perspectives, (2) cultural self-identity, the extent to which one's thinking, emotions, perceptions, and behavior are tied to his or her ethnicity, and (3) family or community toleration of diverse perspectives, since families or communities that rely on punishment to maintain member loyalty may not support some types of changes in the client or may sabotage therapeutic efforts when threatened. Clients who have more ego strength, a clearer sense of their own ethnic identity, and families or communities that are permissive or open to change are better candidates for insight-oriented therapeutic strategies, including client-centered, cognitive, humanistic or existential approaches. Clients with little ego strength, unclear ethnic identities, and strict families or communities are candidates for short-term, structured, or problem-focused counseling, such as behavioral or psychoeducational interventions.

2. *Be goal directed, directive, and concrete in the beginning.* Many clients will expect some direction or advice and thus will be dissatisfied when a therapist seems to be using mere conversation to solve their problems (Dwairy & Van Sickle, 1996). Client-centered approaches may be useful in establishing rapport and helping clients feel comfortable, but this self-focused approach may be met with apprehension or confusion if the therapist relies on it to effect change, particularly for less acculturated clients. Psychoeducational or cognitive behavioral approaches that involve more formal or didactic interactions are closer to the helping approaches familiar to many Arab American clients and thus may be more easily accepted. Existential approaches may be very different from some Arab Americans' expectations for assistance and may need to be carefully explained to avoid confusion or misunderstandings.

3. *Work with the client's family.* Because families are central in many Arab Americans' lives, it is unlikely that treatment that does not involve the family, or at least gain family support, will be effective. Many Arab Americans may feel uncomfortable discussing personal problems outside of their family (Jackson, 1997) or see taking problems to an outsider as a threat to family honor or a breakdown of family loyalty (Abudabbeh & Nydell, 1993). Involve a client's family in the treatment process, either through conducting formal family therapy or through involving the family in supporting the client's adjustment and growth. In individual counseling, discuss with the client the family's expectations and reactions to the current difficulties, as well as ways in which the family may be involved in, or even be the source of a solution. Meet with the client first, then approach the head of the family and find a way to work together and involve the whole family in finding solutions for the client. Because more traditional families might see therapy as interfering with the parental authority of the family or with religious teachings (Abudabbeh, 1996), demonstrate an understanding of and respect for the family's cultural norms and authority (Abudabbeh & Nydell, 1993), conveying to the family that no real change can occur without their permission or assistance. Avoid encouraging the client to express intensely negative emotions toward family members, such as disappointment or anger, as this may be difficult and cause long-lasting conflict with the family. The use of genograms can provide the counselor with useful information about the structure of the client's family and demonstrate a respect for the importance of family in a client's life.

In working with families, it is not always necessary that every member express his or her opinion or perspective equally; counselors should address the head of the family first, working in order of authority to solicit perspectives and opinions from family members. Work to establish a balance between the needs of children and the needs of parents, being sure to acknowledge the responsibilities and stresses parents are under, since they frequently have a great deal of responsibility for the well-being of a number of people. Do not try to reconfigure the structural hierarchy of the family, since this will usually alienate family members (Hedayat-Diba, 2000) and may lead to sabotaging the therapy or to terminating treatment. Direct communication or open confrontation among Arab family members is typically not valued, and encouraging unaccustomed openness will likely cause distress and confusion. Family members who state directly what they want may be considered selfish or inconsiderate. Since Arab culture values sensitivity to others' feelings and intuitive ways of communicating, a goal for counseling might be to enhance family members' sensitivity to each others' wishes and expectations, along with respect for each others' feelings. Activities that encourage perspective taking between family members might be better received than assertiveness training (Dwairy & Van Sickle, 1996).

4. *Work within the client's cultural context.* Be open to discussing the cultural differences between the counselor and the client in values, beliefs, and attitudes, including the potential influence of gender differences (e.g., some clients may be less comfortable with counselors of the opposite sex, etc.). Avoid using jargon or colloquialisms, and clarify language to avoid miscommunication since many terms may mean different things in other cultures. Words such as "abuse," "enmeshment," or "dysfunctional," for example, can have dramatically different meanings depending on the cultural context. Be cautious in expressing assertiveness, self-expression, self-actualization, or independent decision-making as goals for counseling because these could cause difficulties in the client's cultural context. Arab communication styles include the use of euphemisms when speaking of negative events such as illness or failure: for example referring to someone as "tired" when the individual is ill. Many Arab cultures avoid talking about death altogether and instead express wishes for a good outcome (Hedayat-Diba, 2000). Be careful not to interpret euphemistic language as avoidance or denial, and use caution when considering whether to confront a client's acceptance of a loved one's illness.

In inpatient settings, a careful orientation to treatment may be necessary if clients are to understand and accept treatment (Dwairy & Van Sickle, 1996). Extra effort may be needed to establish rapport and to make clients feel comfortable and supported. A cultural consultant may be useful in facilitating this process. Counselors may need to look for ways to counter clients' negative attitudes toward mental illness, particularly with respect to how these attitudes impact compliance with and confidence in treatment. Provide general explanations about the treatment process or specific information about the etiology and treatment of certain disorders when needed. Help clients cope with their concerns about the stigma of mental illness through psychoeducation and empowerment strategies.

5. *Work within clients' religious contexts.* Pay particular attention to clients' religious beliefs and practices and to ways these religious aspects may relate to clients' presenting concerns or to potential solutions. In the orientation to counseling, explain to each client that counseling takes a holistic approach to problems, focusing on the mind, body, and spirit (Jackson, 1997), thus providing an opening to include spirituality in the counseling. This will acknowledge the importance of spirituality in the clients' lives and reassure them that counseling will not divert them from their religious beliefs. When appropriate, develop a collaborative or consultative relationship with religious leaders for issues related to clients' spirituality.

6. *Pay careful attention to physical and metaphysical complaints.* Rather than pathologizing them, consider client behaviors within a cultural context and consider them as potentially important indicators of underlying emotional experiences. Some clients may see concern with one's mental state as self-absorbed or narcissistic. Thus somatization or philosophical concerns may be more acceptable ways to report cognitive or emotional difficulties. Carefully assess the physiological features of emotional distress, such as sleep disturbance, appetite changes, concentration and motivation, physical sensations, motor function, and energy levels. To help clients monitor their internal experiences, have them keep a journal of their symptoms so that they will begin to see what events correspond with worsened or improved symptoms. Asking clients to increase their exercise regimen is an intervention that may be readily accepted by the client as a "physical" treatment.

7. *Do not expect individuation.* Accept that Arab American clients will likely present as enmeshed or relatively unindividuated from their families. Do not use individuation as an indication of or goal for psychological "health." Instead, assess a client's goals for relationships with his or her family and use these goals to guide treatment. Look for ways in which the client's interactions with family members can be improved on or drawn from in achieving the goals for therapy. Help the client work with his or her family to generate possible solutions that meet both individual *and* family needs and thus provide the client and the family with opportunities to better understand each other.

8. *Pay attention to identity issues.* To help clients feel comfortable and acknowledged, include on intake forms such categories as "Arab American" or "Middle Eastern." Take time to learn from clients how their cultural background may relate to their current difficulties including the extent to which they feel conflicted between Western customs and their traditional values (Abudabbeh, 1996). Explore the possible impact of anti-Arab bias on a client's self-image or ethnic identity, and help clients develop strategies for coping with bias and maintaining a healthy ethnic identity. Feminist therapy may be particularly useful in this task.

9. *Acknowledge the importance of indigenous methods of healing.* Given the absence of efficacy research on counseling Arab Americans, do not dismiss the potential benefit of traditional approaches to helping. Clients' communities are often a rich source of support and assistance to be relied on in times of trouble, and client's comfort with more familiar strategies may offset their interest in pursuing professional counseling. Show respect for clients' beliefs in traditional methods of healing, which can include (a) relying on God to deal with difficulties, (b) seeking the advice of an elder family or community member for psychological difficulties, with men seeking guidance from older men and women from older women (Abudabbeh, 1996; Jackson, 1997), or (c) consulting with a religious leader. The Quran states that closeness to God facilitates coping with psychic problems, and some Arabs view mental distress as a result of a lack of faith in God; thus they may see mental illness as a terrible event since it represents a serious lack of faith in God. Some Arab Americans may consider the cure for mental illness to be a reaffirmation of one's belief in God and thus may seek the guidance of a religious authority or folk healer to assist in this endeavor. Respect clients' beliefs in religious healing, and consider encouraging such healing efforts as an adjunct to counseling.

10. *Make use of outreach opportunities.* Many non-Western clients are more comfortable receiving therapy within their natural environment (Atkinson, Morten, & Sue, 1989); thus relying only on office-based services will likely not meet all of the counseling needs of Arab Americans. Outreach services offer opportunities for counselors to demonstrate their respect for and interest in the clients' culture (Dwairy & Van Sickle, 1996) and to learn more about Arab American social life and customs. Look for creative and culturally relevant ways to interest clients in mental health services, such as explaining the benefits of individual therapy to the overall functioning of a family.

Case Example

Amira is a 20-year-old first generation Arab American who is a first-semester junior at a mid-size university. Her parents emigrated from the United Arab Emirates to a large city on the east coast to attend college, and they chose to stay in the United States after graduation. Amira's oldest sibling was born in UAE and has returned there for graduate study, while she and her younger brothers were born and remain in the United States. Her parents both earned advanced degrees and elevated themselves to upper middle class. Her father is a physician, and her mother teaches in an elementary school at a local mosque. Amira was raised a Muslim, but she and her siblings are not strongly involved in the mosque. Amira's parents maintain their affiliation with the Muslim community and have strict expectations about dating and about the value of education for their children. Her parents reluctantly allowed Amira to move into a residence hall on campus when she began college at an institution located approximately two hours away from her home.

Amira entered counseling at the university's counseling center after being referred by a tutor at the learning center on campus. During her first session, she discussed the conflict she had been experiencing around her choice of major and career objectives. A professor she met with for some additional help after class suggested that she talk to a tutor, advice that was devastating to her. Amira was doing poorly in her classes, and she sought assistance only because she was desperate, concerned that failing grades would result in her parents removing her from college.

Amira had chosen to major in engineering long before entering college. In the past she had been a strong student, typically in the top 5 percent of her class. She admitted that her dropping grades coincided with beginning course work in her major area, but she was reluctant to consider a relationship. She felt her problem was a lack of discipline, and she was unable to explain her sudden loss of motivation or inability to concentrate. She mentioned that she had recently begun having stomach pains about three to four times a week, usually just after eating. She was embarrassed about speaking with a mental health counselor, but even more concerned about disappointing her parents.

As counseling progressed, it became clear that many of Amira's academic difficulties were probably related to her choice of major. Her parents had strongly encouraged her to pursue engineering since she had written a report in middle school stating that engineering was a field that she particularly enjoyed. When the counselor encouraged Amira to explore her desires and interests as separate from her family's, Amira became withdrawn and stated that she did not understand what he was asking of her. When the counselor asked her to discuss her family and upbringing in more detail, Amira wondered if perhaps therapy would not be helpful for her.

In order for counseling to effectively meet Amira's needs, several issues would need to be clarified in treatment. Amira would need an understanding of the structure of therapy, along with an opportunity to explore her beliefs and expectations about counseling. The counselor should also initiate a conversation about cultural and gender differences between himself and Amira, while acknowledging that Amira might have a hard time discussing these areas of difference initially. By raising the issue early, the counselor would create an opening for either of them to return to this discussion in the future. A further assessment of Amira's physical symptoms should be conducted. The counselor should refer Amira for a medical evaluation, while considering the likelihood of these symptoms being directly related to her emotional distress. Obtaining permission to speak with her physician would allow for continuity of care.

After conferring with a cultural consultant on staff at the counseling center, the counselor pulled back from confronting Amira's concerns directly, and instead he spent a few sessions building trust and rapport. These sessions focused on stress and time management, Amira's ability to use university resources to support her studies, and her daily academic activities. Eventually, the counselor revisited the issue of Amira's career goals, this time including the perspective and desires of her parents in the discussion. He took time to learn how she came to be interested in the field of engineering and how she chose to eliminate other areas in which she had shown an early interest or talent. Finally, he explored with Amira her family's investment and interest in her happiness. The counselor asked Amira to discuss the ways that her family supported her and her choices. After the counselor had helped her to see her family's investment in her happiness and success, Amira began to speak for the first time about talking with them about her interest in changing majors. The counselor coached Amira on discussing her career goals with her parents, and he offered to talk with them as well on her behalf.

Eventually, Amira spoke with her mother and father about her concerns regarding her major. Her parents were surprised and disappointed that she had not discussed these issues first with them. Amira was able to represent her interests, and she followed her counselor's advice to ask her family to support her in making important decisions. Opening up with her parents also increased Amira's comfort level in talking with her counselor.

Conclusion

To provide effective services to Arab Americans, counselors must become aware of Arab history, culture, and worldview to counter the stereotypes Americans have been exposed to in the media. Counselors should learn about the cultural values and expectations of Arab Americans and allow clients to educate them about relevant specific cultural contexts.

There is a pressing need for research on the mental health experiences of Arab Americans to explore the following: (1) ways in which they experience mental health services differently than do other groups, (2) their incidence and prevalence of mental disorders and adjustment difficulties, (3) their attitudes toward and utilization of mental health services, (4) the efficacy of various treatment approaches in ameliorating their concerns, (5) their satisfaction with counseling and mental health services, and (6) the prevalence and impact of bias and anti-Arab stereotypes among mental health professionals. This research, combined with counselors' increased understanding of Arab Americans' experiences, will not only ensure the provision of effective services to Arab Americans, but also enable counselors to advocate for the concerns of Arab Americans and promote recognition and appreciation of their distinctive traditions, rich cultural heritage, and valuable contributions to U.S. society.

References

Abou-Hatab, F. A. (1997). Psychology from Egyptian, Arab, and Islamic perspectives: Unfulfilled hopes and hopeful fulfillment. *European Psychologist, 2(4),* 356–365.

Abraham, N. (1995). Arab Americans. In R. J. Vecoli, J. Galens, A. Sheets, and R. V. Young (Eds.), *Gale encyclopedia of multicultural America* (vol. 1, pp. 84–98). New York: Gale Research Inc.

Abudabbeh, N. (1996). Arab families. In M. McGoldrick, J. Giordano, & J. K. Pearce (Eds.). *Ethnicity and family therapy* (2nd ed, pp. 333–346). New York: Guilford.

Abudabbeh, N., & Nydell, M. K. (1993). Transcultural counseling and Arab Americans. In J. McFadden (Ed.), *Transcultural counseling: Bilateral and international perspectives* (pp. 261–284). Alexandria, VA: American Counseling Association.

Al-Mughni, H. (1993). *Women in Kuwait: The politics of gender.* London: Saqi Books.

American Arab Anti Discrimination Committee (November 21, 2001). ADC fact sheet: The condition of Arab Americans post 9/11. *American Arab Anti Discrimination Committee* [On-line]. Retrieved December 22, 2001, from www.adc.org.

American Civil Liberties Union (October 23, 2001). Fact sheets on the USA-Patriot Act: How the USA-Patriot Act permits indefinite detention of immigrants who are not terrorists; How the USA-Patriot Act allows for detention and deportation of people engaging in innocent associational activities. *American Civil Liberties Union* [On-line]. Available: www.aclu.org/safeandfree/index.html.

Arredondo, P. A. (1999). Multicultural counseling competencies as tools to address oppression and racism. *Journal of Counseling and Development 77,* 102–108.

Atkinson, D., Morten, G., & Sue, D. W. (1989). *Counseling American minorities: A cross-cultural perspective* (3rd ed.). Dubuque, IA: William C. Brown Publishers.

Boal, M. (22 November, 2001). Muslim students feel the backlash. *Rolling Stone Magazine, 882,* 41–44.

Casas, J. M., Ponterotto, J. G., & Gutierrez, J. M. (1986). An ethical indictment of counseling research and training: The cross-cultural perspective. *Journal of Counseling and Development, 64,* 347–349.

Daneshpour, M. (1998). Muslim families in family therapy. *Journal of Marital and Family Therapy, 24,* 355–390.

Diller, D. C. (1991). *The Middle East* (7th ed.). Washington, DC: Congressional Quarterly.

Dwairy, M., & Van Sickle, T. (1996). Western psychotherapy in traditional Arabic societies, *Clinical Psychology Review, 16,* 231–249.

Employee Relations Office, U.S. Courts (1999). *The judiciary employment practices report, Fiscal Year 1999.* [www.gendergap.com/governme.htm]

Erickson, C. D., & Al-Timimi, N. R. (2001). Providing mental health services to Arab Americans: Recommendations and considerations. *Cultural Diversity and Ethnic Minority Psychology, 7,* 308–327.

Fernea E. W. (1998). *In search of Islamic feminism.* New York, NY: Bantam Doubleday.

Ghareeb, E. (1983). *Split vision: The portrayal of Arabs in the American media.* Washington, DC: The American-Arab Affairs Council.

Gorkin, M., Masalha, S., & Yatziv, G. (1985). Psychotherapy of Israeli-Arab patients: Some cultural considerations. *The Journal of Psychoanalytic Anthropology, 8,* 215–230.

Hatab Samhan, H. (1999). Not quite White: Race classification and the Arab American experience. In M. W. Suleiman (Ed.), *Arabs in America: Building a new future.* Philadelphia: Temple University Press.

Hedayat-Diba, Z. (2000). Psychotherapy with Muslims. In P. S. Richards & A. Bergin (Eds.), *Handbook of psychotherapy and religious diversity* (pp. 289–314). Washington, DC: American Psychological Association.

Hitti, P. K. (1970). *The Arabs: A short history.* Chicago, IL: Henry Regnery Company.

Hudson, M. C., & Wolfe, R. A. (1980). *The American media and the Arabs.* Washington, DC: The Center for Contemporary Arab Studies, Georgetown University.

Ibrahim, F. A., & Arredondo, P. M. (1986). Ethical standards for cross-cultural counseling: Counselor preparation, practice, assessment, and research. *Journal of Counseling and Development, 64,* 349–352.

Jackson, M. (1997). Counseling Arab Americans. In Courtland Lee (Ed.), *Multicultural issues in counseling: New approaches to diversity* (2nd ed., pp. 333–349). Alexandria, VA: American Counseling Association.

Jalali, B. (1996). Iranian families. In M. McGoldrick, J. Giordano, & J. K. Pearce (Eds.), *Ethnicity and family therapy* (2nd ed., pp. 347–363). New York: Guilford.

Khan, M. W. (1997). *Women between Islam and Western society.* New York: Al-Risala Books.

Kulwicki, A. (1996). Health issues among American Muslim families. In B. Aswad & B. Bilge (Eds.), *Family and gender among American Muslims* (pp. 187–207). Philadelphia, PA: Temple University Press.

Laffin, J. (1975). *The Arab mind considered: A need for understanding.* New York: Taplinger.

Lipson, J. G., Reizian, A. E., & Meleis, A. I. (1987). Arab-American patients: A medical record review. *Social Science Medicine, 24,* 101–107.

Mansfield, P. (1990). *The Arabs.* New York: Penguin.

Meleis, A. I. (1981). The Arab-American in the health care system. *American Journal of Nursing, 81,* 1108.

Meleis, A. I. (1982). Arab students in Western universities. *Journal of Higher Education, 53,* 439–447.

Naff, A. (1980). Arabs. In Stephan Thernstrom (Ed.). *Harvard encyclopedia of American ethnic groups.* Cambridge, MA: Harvard University Press.

Naff, A. (1983). Arabs in America: A historical overview. In S. Y. Abraham & N. Abraham (Eds.), *Arabs in the new world: Studies on Arab-American communities* (pp. 8–43). Detroit, MI: Wayne State University, Center for Urban Studies.

Naff, A. (1985). *Becoming American: The early Arab immigrant experience.* Carbondale, IL: Southern Illinois University Press.

Nydell, M. (1987). *Understanding Arabs: A guide for Westerners.* Yarmouth, ME: Intercultural Press.

Patai, R. (1976). *The Arab mind.* New York: Scribner's.

Power, C. (1998, March 16). The new Islam. *Newsweek Magazine,* 35–37.

Racy, J. (1980). Somatization in Saudi women: A therapeutic challenge. *British Journal of Psychiatry, 13,* 212–216.

Roberts, J. M. (1984). *The pelican history of the world.* New York, NY: Penguin.

Said, E. W. (1979). *Orientalism.* New York: Random House.

Said, E. W. (1997). *Covering Islam.* New York: Pantheon Books.

Shaheen, J. G. (1984). *The TV Arab.* Bowling Green, OH: Bowling Green State University Popular Press.

Shaheen, J. G. (1986). The Hollywood Arab: 1984–86. *Mideast Monitor, 3,* 1–6.

Sharabi, H., & Ani, M. (1977). Impact of class and culture on social behavior. In L. C. Brown & N. Itzkowitz (Eds.), *Psychological dimensions of Near Eastern studies* (p. 248). Princeton, NJ: Darwin.

Simon, J. P. (1996). Lebanese families. In M. McGoldrick, J. Giordano, & J. K. Pearce (Eds.), *Ethnicity and family therapy* (2nd ed., pp. 364–375). New York: Guilford.

Soliman, A. M. (1986). Status, rationale and development of counseling in the Arab countries: Views of participants in a counseling conference. *International Journal for the Advancement of Counseling, 9,* 11–22.

Steinberg, J. (November 12, 2001). In sweeping campus canvasses, U.S. checks on mideast students. *New York Times* (882).

Sue, D. W., Arredondo, P., & McDavis, R. J. (1992). Multicultural counseling competencies and standards: A call to the profession. *Journal of Counseling and Development 70,* 477–486.

Sue, D. W., & Sue, D. (1990). *Counseling the culturally different: Theory and practice.* New York: Wiley.

Suleiman, M. W. (1988). *Arabs in the mind of America.* Brattleboro, VT: Amana Books.

Terry, J. (1985). *Mistaken identity: Arab stereotypes in American popular writing.* Washington, DC: The American-Arab Affairs Council.

Wehrly, B. (1986). Counseling international students: Issues, concerns, and programs. *International Journal for the Advancement of Counseling, 9,* 11–22.

Zogby, J. (1990). *Arab America today: A demographic profile of Arab Americans.* Washington, DC: Arab American Institute.

13

Counseling and Psychotherapy for Acculturation and Ethnic Identity Concerns with Immigrant and International Student Clients

Gargi Roysircar

Antioch New England Graduate School

In therapy, assessing the acculturation process of immigrants and international students helps counselors conceptualize the dynamics of adapting to the host culture. We need to understand the dynamics of adaptation because these impact clients' psychological functioning, including assumptions, values, relationships, identity, distress, and coping responses. As noted by Culler, Arnold, and Maldonado (1995), significant changes occur at the behavioral, affective, and cognitive levels:

> The behavioral level includes…verbal behaviors or language. Language development obviously include[s] aspects beyond the behavioral and is understood to include cognitive aspects.… Also at the behavioral level are customs, foods and such cultural expressions as the music one chooses to listen or dance to. At the affective level are the emotions that have cultural connections. For example, the way a person feels about important aspects of identity, the symbols one loves or hates, and the meaning one attaches to itself [sic] are all culturally based. At the cognitive level are beliefs about male/female roles, ideas about illness, attitudes about illness, and fundamental values. (p. 281)

To understand acculturation adaptations of immigrants and international students, a therapist needs to first understand the definition and scope of the term "culture." Because many people in the United States are socialized within the political and attitudinal framework of the "melting pot," they may not appreciate the all-inclusive and pervasive nature of culture, which has been defined as a "set of people who have common and shared values, customs, habits, and rituals; systems of labeling, explanation, and evaluation; social rules of behavior; perceptions regarding human nature, natural phenomena, interpersonal relationships, time, and activity; symbols, art, and artifacts; and historical developments" (Roysircar, 2003, p. 170). In the United States this definition would include American music, television shows, and all other popular media content; English monolingualism; nuclear families; dating, attraction, and love preceding marriage and opposite feelings leading to divorce; trends in clothing style and fashions; democracy and capitalism, etc. Understanding the broad nature of culture can help the counselor appreciate the complexity of the adaptation process that immigrants and international students experience.

Models of Acculturation

In part because culture itself is so complex, several models for understanding the acculturation process have been proposed. These include unilinear, bilinear, and non-linear models, each of which is explained below.

Unilinear Understanding of Acculturation

Szapocznik and Kurtines (1980) asserted that individual acculturation is a linear function of the amount of time a person has been exposed to the host culture, and that the rate at which the acculturation process takes place is a function of the age of the individual. For example, elementary-age foreign-born children show greater acculturation than their parents who immigrated as adults (Roysircar-Sodowsky & Frey, 2003). The unilinear vision of the process posited that as immigrants adopted host-culture behavior and values, they simultaneously discarded those attributes of their culture of origin. While there is some truth to the concept that acculturation is affected by exposure, continuous contact, and habituation resulting from the length of time spent in the host society, a bilinear model of acculturation (Berry, 1980) is currently more favored.

Bilinear Understanding of Acculturation

The bilinear model accounts for biculturalism: the high adherence to both original and host cultures. Individuals who adopt the bicultural mode of acculturation find value in both their native culture and their new culture. They can utilize elements from both cultures with minimal stress. A two-dimensional model provides a framework for the two-way interaction between a minority group and a majority group to determine the adaptation of an individual living in a bicultural context: an ethnic minority society and the White dominant society. Two key issues must be considered: (1) the value of an individual maintaining cultural identity and characteristics and (2) the value of maintaining relationships within the dominant and other minority groups. An individual's response in aligning these values can result in four types of acculturation attitudes and ways of adaptation: integration, assimilation, sepa-

Are positive relations to be sought with the dominant society?

		Yes	No
Is my cultural identity to be retained?	Yes	INTEGRATION Retain own cultural identity while also connecting with dominant culture	ASSIMILATION Relate/interact only with dominant society, thereby relinquishing own cultural identity
	No	SEPARATION Retain only own cultural identity and avoid contact with dominant culture	MARGINALIZATION Neither connected to dominant nor own culture

FIGURE 13.1 *Acculturation adaptation modes determined by answers to two questions: Is my cultural identity to be retained? Are positive relations to be sought with the dominant society?*

ration, and marginalization (Berry, 1980; see Glossary for definitions). Figure 13.1 explains the four modes.

Nonlinear Understanding of Acculturation

The two-dimensional model allows for a nonlinear understanding of how individuals adapt, including their decisions regarding how much of their cultural identity they will retain and how much of the dominant culture they will incorporate. It allows for variations in acculturation rates within an individual and between individuals based on the differing amounts of situation-specific pressure from the dominant culture to assimilate and on the individual immigrant's responses to this pressure (Sodowsky & Lai, 1997). Responses to pressure are predicated on such personal attributes as one's identifications, affiliations, occupation, gender, sexual orientation, psychological characteristics (ego strength, locus of control, self/collective esteem), and the individual's contextual mediating variables as well (Roysircar-Sodowsky & Maestas, 2000, 2002). Acculturation adaptations are affected by several contextual mediating variables: the nature of the dominant society (e.g., enforcing assimilation or practicing pluralism); the nature of the ethnic group (in terms of voluntary immigrants versus political refugees); religion; first, second, versus third/nth wave of immigrants; movement and permanence of contact; class; color; and level of education.

To illustrate the suggested nonlinear variations, Sodowsky, Kwan, and Pannu (1995) explained how individuals move among the four orientations—integration, assimilation, separation, and marginalization—over time or across situations. This seems to be a particularly useful model because individuals approach the acculturation process with their own uniqueness, family history, cultural expectations, and values, as well as life experiences prior to and after immigration. Individuals utilize a vast number of acculturation adaptations as they function in two cultures, as indicated by the following case study of the author's immigration experience.

The experience of the author's immigration to the United States illustrates a nonlinear acculturation process. The author immigrated by choice after applying for and being granted the green card. She came from India, a country that appreciates professional and economic opportunities and is familiar with Western values, science, and education, having been a British-colonized nation for almost two centuries. The author is proficient in both spoken and written English. She came with goals for higher education and professional status. These circumstances have made her acculturation process easier than the processes for others, such as political refugees, children of war, and indentured laborers and slaves, who have arrived involuntarily. On the other hand, the author has a strong sense of her family integrity, roles, interdependence, and Hindu religion, which point to the retention of her Asian Indian cultural identity. She sought emotional and physical support from siblings who were also in the initial phase of relocation in the United States. In this way, the author has been *bicultural* since her arrival in the United States.

That the author is different from members of the dominant society is reinforced, however, by her feelings of being different and by her perceptions that members of the dominant society and members of other minority societies see her as different. She has experienced attitudes of prejudice and acts of discrimination in her workplace and her profession. Here, she is *separated* from the White society. At the same time, her feminism sets her apart from Asian Indian immigrants of the 1970s and 1980s, who hold traditional views of gender roles. While she shows *assimilation* with regard to gender attitudes and behaviors, she is clearly conscious that she is a feminist of color with a different set of priorities from White feminists or lesbians. Thus certain situations leave the author feeling alone and *marginalized,* while at other times she reaches out to interact with the dominant society and with diverse people to achieve *integration.*

The strategies she uses for insurmountable challenges are to recognize and contain them outside of herself, making meaning with her existential philosophical orientation, predicting and preventing prejudice with a healthy dose of cultural mistrust, and seeking comfort and guidance from her natural support system and multicultural allies (Kuo & Roysircar-Sodowsky, 1999). At other times, she is self-reliant and independent because that is the only coping resource available. This process is similar to how Kawanishi (1995) has described Japanese individuals who cope with stress through "akirame": existential resignation, to endure rather than fight a problematic situation. In sum, the experiences of the author illustrate a nonlinear acculturation model that accommodates the tremendous complexity of culture and cultural adaptation also reflected in the following cases of South Asian immigrants and international students.

Case Studies of South Asian Immigrants and Implications for Therapy

Mrs. Sen, a First-Generation Immigrant from India
Differences in norms regarding gender roles and family interactions between one's culture of origin and the host culture can be difficult and confusing for foreign-born, first-generation immigrants who enter the United States as adults

and show *separation* from the U.S. culture. Mrs. Sen's story, as narrated in a collection of short fiction (Lahiri, 1999), illustrates the cultural dilemmas that affect a recently immigrated woman who was born and raised in India.

Mrs. Sen has come to the United States after her arranged marriage to Mr. Sen, a college professor trying to secure tenure. Upon her arrival, Mrs. Sen feels isolated because she cannot yet drive, and she misses her family in India. She is also isolated in some ways from her husband, who is absorbed in his work. Mrs. Sen's life is centered around preserving the life she knew in India. She cooks Bengali food and maintains her home diligently. She begins providing daycare for Eliot, a 12-year-old White American boy, who is placed for baby-sitting by his working single mother. As Eliot is integrated into the Sen household, he is witness to Mrs. Sen's loneliness and longing for her homeland.

Mrs. Sen asks Eliot, "If I began to scream right now at the top of my lungs, would someone come?" (Lahiri, p. 116). Mrs. Sen proceeds to explain, "At home that is all you have to do...just raise your voice a bit, or express grief or joy of any kind, and one whole neighborhood and half of another has come to share the news, to help with arrangements" (Lahiri, p. 116). Mrs. Sen's loneliness becomes even more apparent when she brings Eliot into her room and shows him myriads of saris, stored away in her closet and drawers, and she says, "Where have I ever worn this one? And this? And this?" (p. 125). Mrs. Sen describes the silence of her U.S. neighborhood as disturbing. On occasion, it prevents her from sleeping. At one point, she looks around and says, "Everything is there" (Lahiri, p. 112), by which she means Calcutta, India. When she says "home," it is never in reference to her apartment, but rather to the India of her nostalgia. It is clear that in the United States Mrs. Sen misses a sense of community.

Issues of primary importance to Mrs. Sen are as basic as needing to obtain fresh whole fish and cook it. The importance of family to Mrs. Sen is shown in many ways: her joy in receiving letters from her family, her sorrow at having missed the death of her grandfather, and her repeated listening to the tape-recorded messages of her loved ones. Eliot is with her when she receives a letter from her family informing her that her sister has had a baby girl. Mrs. Sen laments that her niece will not know her when the time comes for her to visit her country in about three years, when Mr. Sen is expected to get tenure. Mrs. Sen wonders if Eliot misses his mother during the afternoons that he spends with her, and she says, "When I think of you, only a boy, separated from your mother for so much of the day, I am ashamed" (Lahiri, p. 123). Later Mrs. Sen asks Eliot if he will put his mother in a nursing home when she is old. When Eliot admits that he might, Mrs. Sen describes to Elliot how the situation will play out, "And then she will have to drag herself onto a bus just to get herself a bag of lozenges" (Lahiri, p. 132).

Mrs. Sen tries to drive under her husband's instructions, but the task is overwhelming for her. Ultimately she has a car crash as she impetuously gets behind the wheel to get to the fish market. After the car accident, Eliot's mother stops the baby-sitting arrangement with Mrs. Sen. A question that arises is how a therapist can be of benefit to a recent immigrant, like Mrs. Sen, who is having acculturation difficulties. Possible interventions are discussed below.

Therapist Responses to Acculturation Difficulties

Conceptualization.   Conceptually speaking, Mrs. Sen is suspended between two cultures. She does not have social connections in the United States for support. But she cannot discuss her problems with people she left in India. Her family has the expectation that she is living like a queen in a palace, and she has not confided the truth of her situation to them. She may be experiencing shame for not having met her family's high aspirations for her status in the United States. It is helpful to have some understanding about her apparent reluctance to tell her family what her life is really like. Is her reluctance related to her loyalty to her husband, perhaps to her attempt to avoid bringing shame to him and to her family for her unhappiness, or due to some misbelief that everyone is wealthy in the United States?

To leave one's familiar surroundings and venture to a place with many hardships in terms of social customs, language barriers, lack of contact with family or familiar others, and perceived prejudice (Sodowsky, Lai, & Plake, 1991; Sodowsky & Plake, 1991) seems to be a heavy price to pay to better one's life circumstances. An immigrant's struggle to find a way to maintain cultural integrity and to discover appropriate ways to express it in the new surroundings without offending anyone or crossing norms of the new environment must create stress (Sodowsky & Lai, 1997).

This brings to mind the cultural assumptions that therapists must put aside about marriage (Roysircar, 2003b). Therapists in the United States generally do not understand the tradition of arranged marriages. Failure to understand the issue of an arranged marriage, with two persons who are virtually strangers having to live together, particularly in a new environment, certainly complicates the challenge of understanding the experiences of a member of a culturally different group. Therapists need to understand familial and societal expectations and values of marriage in non-Western, non-Christian societies. Therapists may be struck by the apparent lack of intimacy in the relationships of married couples from India. However, it may occur later to them that this reaction is based on their American definition of intimacy and on the value Americans assign to affective, physical, and verbal intimacy. With Mrs. Sen, therapists understand that her marital relationship, along with her system of extended kinship, is very different from significant relationships of Americans and as such needs to be respected and understood in its context.

Intentional Cultural Communications.   Within an acculturation model for therapy, each member of the dyad is enriched by intentional cultural communications (Roysircar et al., 2003). Therapists ask questions that allow them to see the client's world. They provide the client an opportunity to tell her story. Knowing that her story will not be judged, the client begins to heal. To be heard within a cultural framework is therapeutic. At the same time, the therapist's discussion of White American values and behaviors, such as autonomy and assertiveness, would be appropriate as Mrs. Sen is helped to make decisions about her acculturation choices, based on her explorations of her cultural values, expectations, and goals as these interface those of the host society.

Traditional as well as bicultural individuals might find it easier to get in touch with emotional states in their primary language, which may not be English. Different languages may elicit different emotional experiences. Thus a trusted bilingual friend or community member may be asked to help by clarifying problems and providing support (Roysircar et al., 2003).

Advocacy. Therapists realize that the helping relationship with a new immigrant can occur at many levels, such as mentoring, life skills coaching, tutoring, advocacy, and therapy (Roysircar et al., 2003). Adjusting to this framework may be difficult for therapists who are trained primarily in interventions for psychopathology or severe mental disorders. The therapist, an advocate, would want to assist Mrs. Sen in finding an Indian community, perhaps in a cosmopolitan city that might be within a few hours' drive. It is especially important for Mrs. Sen to locate people with a cultural background similar to her own so that she associates with people who come "to share news, to help with arrangements." Perhaps, it would be possible to live in a less remote area of town, if there is one. The type of community is not the only problem: Mrs. Sen's apartment is troublesome also. One could explore the issue of Mr. and Mrs. Sen finding accommodations that would facilitate her mobility and her desire to reach a fresh food market.

When Mrs. Sen drives the car, without a license and without her husband's knowledge, she does appear to have initiative and agency, albeit misguided. She works with Eliot, and both appear happier for the company. Therefore, it may be helpful to engage Mrs. Sen in some type of activity where she can feel like she is contributing to the community around her. Perhaps volunteer activity helping the elderly cook meals or some such altruistic, nurturing service might reduce the tension she is feeling in this individualistic culture into which she has been transported.

Advocacy includes mentoring that is relevant to the client understanding the new culture's norms (Roysircar, Hubbell, & Ortega, 2003). Mrs. Sen definitely needs to be enrolled for driver's education, especially since her husband does not seem to be an effective instructor. She needs to be informed of the relevant laws of this country, such as endangering a child by driving without a license.

Ethnotherapeutic Relationship. Generally speaking, therapists approach immigrants from the position that as therapists they cannot possibly know what it is like to go through the immigration experience. Therefore, therapists' first priority is to convey willingness to understand their immigrant clients in the multiple contexts of their lives (Roysircar, 2003b), such as their culture of origin or ethnic society, the dominant White culture, workplace, family, generation status, gender, sexual orientation, social class, and religion. A culturally sensitive therapist pays attention to these issues, while at the same time recognizing that an immigrant must learn about a new environment, having the freedom to navigate around and through it, make mistakes, and continue to learn. There's a fine line between advocacy and saving, and therapists do not save their clients. The therapist considers how a culturally connected professional relationship might itself ease the process of acculturation for Mrs. Sen.

Therapists accept the fact that their immigrant clients may not feel comfortable with them. Seeking therapy might clash with Mrs. Sen's cultural beliefs. This is an important issue to discuss early in the acculturation model of therapy. Therapists maintain a stance that they are in a helping relationship not to impose their ideas on their immigrant clients, but to try to help them sort out from their culturally different worldview what is right and wrong for them, including how far they feel comfortable revealing themselves (Roysircar et al., 2003). While immigrants feel validated when asked to tell their stories, they may not be quick to reveal what is personal and private. When conceptualizing immigrant cases, it becomes clear to therapists how much their own cultural assumptions need to be known and accounted for, so that they catch themselves from attempting to fix things that may not be broken (Roysircar, 2003b).

Mrs. Sen could benefit from therapy because it appears that she is suffering. As treatment moves forward, respect for her traditional gender role and for the Asian Indian family orientation must be inherent (Sodowsky, 1991). For instance, since Mrs. Sen prefers to go by her married name, it is wise not to address her by her first name, a familiarity not acceptable to Mrs. Sen's social standards. As previous statements indicate, there are paradoxes when the therapist works with dual contexts. The therapist works within the client's cultural framework, but uses Western talk therapy and makes possible the acculturation change process. Rather than combining cultural contexts, the therapist responds to both, using two frameworks, that is, using the bilinear acculturation model. Therapists also understand what they have in common with their immigrant clients because those common areas build the mutual attraction and connection in the relationship.

Shonfeld-Ringel (2001) has presented a reconceptualization of the working alliance in light of Asian cultural dynamics. The construct of working alliance in Western psychotherapy includes the domains of empathy, power, authority, and communication. However, empathy may be viewed differently between Western and Asian cultures, with empathy understood by an Asian client as "part of traditional philosophical and religious systems and considered an essential social structure that reinforces necessary harmony" (Shonfeld-Ringel, 2001, p. 55), in contrast to empathy taught to the therapist as a professional skill or viewed as an aspect of a unique relationship. Similarly, while a goal of many therapy relationships (e.g., feminist therapy or psychotherapy of liberation or empowerment) is to equalize power dynamics to the extent possible, Asian clients may expect a more hierarchical professional relationship which is, however, benign, caring, and giving.

Culture-Specific Assessment. In assessing Mrs. Sen, it is important to remember that her culture has a more sociocentric view of the self than does the White culture. With this in mind, it might be wise to focus on her social status, roles, and obligations rather than on her intrapersonal intensity and spontaneous behaviors (which might be seen as Axis I mental disorders when using the DSM-IV-TR diagnostic system). Doing so would enable the therapist to more accurately assess for possible acculturative stress and adaptation reactions. It appears that Mrs. Sen has experienced a decline in her standard of living. In India, she traveled in her father's chauffeured car, and there were servants who helped in the house. Thus the issue of loss extends interpersonally as well as materially. It is important to have some understanding of her religious/spiritual belief system when discussing issues of loss, in order to recognize culturally normative grief behaviors. Understanding culturally normative-nonnormative responses also prevents underdiagnosis of behaviors that are significant enough to warrant concern, such as Mrs. Sen rushing behind the wheel with Eliot in the car when she does not know how to drive. Such underdiagnosis constitutes Type II error which is using a cultural rationale to minimize the existence of mental health concerns (Roysircar-Sodowsky & Kuo, 2001).

It is important to assess Mrs. Sen's acculturation adaptations and to consider the types of adaptation to which she aspires. These considerations are appropriate because cultural conflicts and consequent acculturative stress lead to feelings of guilt, loneliness, resentment, hopelessness, and finally depression (Sodowsky & Lai, 1997). Equally important is Mrs. Sen's experience of her husband's expectation for her acculturation. For some immigrant couples, the husband might place great value on his wife's traditional manners. If this is true for the Sens, Mrs. Sen's ability to relate to her new culture will be limited. While she is apparently operating in the *separation* mode of acculturation, paradoxically she has sought a babysitting job in White society, bringing Eliot to her home, and she is fluent in English. These behaviors suggest *biculturalism.* However, even though she speaks English well, Mrs. Sen is not acculturated in many ways, so a therapist would need to be extremely cautious about using any psychological tests. If testing is to be considered, the results need to be interpreted within Mrs. Sen's cultural context (Roysircar-Sodowsky & Kuo, 2001).

As a final point, it is also important to know more about why Mr. and Mrs. Sen have come to this town and how long they intend to stay. If they have plans to return to India in the near future, the goals developed will be different than if their plans are to remain for a long time, if not indefinitely, in North America.

Cultural Consultation.   Lastly, to provide an accurate assessment and efficacious intervention, therapists need to consult as much multicultural literature as they can find about Indian women and new Asian Indian immigrants and also to consult with a professional familiar with Indian culture. Preferably the professional would be a mental health specialist, but anthropological professionals, well-traveled individuals, Asian studies experts, and Asian Indian literature references could also provide good information.

The next case, also an Asian Indian woman, shows different acculturation dynamics from Mrs. Sen. Complex are the dynamics of someone *assimilated* to the host culture, such as a U.S.-born, second-generation ethnic person. A therapist's apparent similarities with such a client can make the initial interviews superficial at best and confusing at worst, in that the therapist may slip into assuming that the client holds similar values, meanings, and experiences as herself or himself (Roysircar, 2003b). It is easier to ignore cultural differences when an ethnic client is overtly behaving and speaking the way the therapist does. Therapists may not perceive such a person's real concerns and never know the extent to which the client is divulging information that may be the key to the help needed, thus committing a Type I assessment error. Type I errors occur when the therapist sees no differences caused by cultural issues (Roysircar-Sodowsky & Kuo, 2000).

Mrs. Das, a Second Generation Asian Indian

Take the case of Mrs. Das, a young second generation Asian Indian woman, born and reared in the United States. We are told her story in Lahiri's (1999) book of short fiction. Mrs. Das and her husband, also a second-generation Asian Indian in the United States, are playing tourists in their ancestral land, India. Mr. Kapasi, native to India, is their guide. In the short course of the trip, Mrs. Das and Mr. Kapasi establish a connection based on misunderstandings of their obvious cultural differences (East-West) and apparent phenotypic similarity (color). Mr. Kapasi is enamored with Mrs. Das's informality, her Western looks, and her short summer dress. He imagines her to be sexually freer than his traditional Indian wife. Mrs. Das's young life has been devoted to her children, and she has had few friends with whom to confide. Mrs. Das wants to be heard. When they arrive at a temple displaying avatars (i.e., incarnations) of the God Surya, the setting sun, Mr. Kapasi hopes that Mrs. Das will appreciate the beauty and power of the avatars, but she regards these sculptural wonders briefly. Her husband barely talks to her and is excitedly taking pictures.

For his primary occupation, Mr. Kapasi is an interpreter of patient presentations of maladies to a physician. He wants Mrs. Das's approval and admiration for his medical skills. Mrs. Das, on the other hand, mistakenly seeks him as a guide for her emotional life. Mrs. Das reveals that she was once unfaithful to her husband early in their marriage and thus conceived one of her children by another man. While this situation might not be highly unusual in North American culture, Mrs. Das has not been able to tell this to anyone in the United States, and she has lived in pain for eight years over the secret. Mrs. Das says, "I was hoping you could make me feel better, say the right thing. Suggest some kind of remedy" (p. 59). Their fantasies of connectedness are shattered when Mr. Kapasi asks Mrs. Das whether it is guilt or pain that she feels over the situation. What Mrs. Das needs at this time is to be heard and not to be censored on the basis of Hindu religious myths about pure, guiltless, self-sacrificing women. (For example, Lord Ram's wife Sita had to prove her sexual purity by successfully undergoing the test of fire and yet was rejected by Ram because his kingdom's people disbelieved her.) The distance between Mr. Kapasi and Mrs. Das becomes irreparable, and it is apparent that they go back to their former lives unchanged.

Critique of Difficulties in Establishing an Ethnotherapeutic Relationship

It is apparent that Mrs. Das and Mr. Kapasi view each other from projected images of their own needs for approval. Despite being born and reared in the United States, Mrs. Das does not confide her secret to an American, but confesses to a member of her parents' culture of origin. Yet culturally, Mr. Kapasi cannot empathize with Mrs. Das. Her infidelity would be better understood by a therapist in the United States, where this problem is not rare. In asking if she feels guilty, Mr. Kapasi implies an evaluation that is based on a Hindu belief in the importance of a woman's purity. On some level, Mrs. Das has confessed to her parents vicariously by divulging her secret to someone who has values that are closer to the views that her foreign-born, first-generation Indian immigrant parents might hold. This searching, failing to find a fit, and feeling rejected by both cultures points to Mrs. Das's *margin-*

alization. The gap between two conflicting views, that of the traditional Indian and that of an "Americanized" second-generation Asian Indian woman, is too great for Mrs. Das to have a corrective emotional experience. The situation exemplifies the misunderstanding inherent in a brief relationship that assumes similarity on a superficial basis, such as ethnic similarity (as opposed to cultural similarity) and on a temporary sharing of physical space and time. At a deeper level, the cultural differences of the helper and helpee are extreme, and these are not understood or processed.

For Mrs. Das and Mrs. Sen, isolation, loss, cultural identity, and spousal detachment appear to be major themes. Yet these concerns have a qualitatively different effect on each woman, a contrast from which three conclusions may be made: (1) therapists cannot assume that a person raised in the United States will not experience issues of loneliness related to the minority-majority dynamics of acculturation, (2) clients who have the same cultural or ethnic background may vary greatly in their levels of acculturation, and (3) concomitantly, stereotypical expectations of a given cultural group may impede accurate understanding of clients.

In the next case, an Asian Indian girl, isolation and loss are, however, not the concerns. This girl's story of growing up in the United States is rich with issues of ethnic identity, as a counterpoint to her *assimilation.*

Lilia, Child of Immigrants

Lilia is a ten-year-old U.S.-born, second-generation Asian Indian girl. We read her story in Lahiri's (1999) book of short fiction. Of characters discussed so far, Lilia is least affected by isolation. Appreciating that their struggles of educating and caring for their daughter are easier in the United States than they would have been if the family had remained in India, Lilia's parents, her mother in particular, have kept her somewhat sheltered in what she knows of the parents' previous lives in Calcutta. Thus Lilia has had little understanding of the social, political, and financial troubles that have historically plagued her nation of origin, until Mr. Pirzada comes to dinner.

Lilia starts on the road of cultural self-exploration and self-reflection, spurred by the visits of Mr. Pirzada, an international scholar from Pakistan teaching at a local university, who dines with her parents weekly in the fall and winter of one year. What makes this guest stand out in Lilia's mind are not the sugary treats that he gives her each week, but what she learns about India, about Pakistan, and about herself. Lilia is dealing with ethnic identity issues as she begins to identify with her ethnic culture vicariously through Mr. Pirzada, while she personally remains firmly entrenched in the dominant American culture. Bilinear processes are occurring for Lilia, as she is developing a keener understanding of both her Indian heritage and her niche in U.S. society.

Although young, Lilia is insightful. She is able to appreciate the struggles of a man who is separated from his daughters. She can sense the impact that the war-torn country Pakistan, a neighbor of India, has on her Indian family's dynamics, bringing a non-relative sojourner into their family. Lilia watches her parents act differently, observing customs that are foreign to her.

Lilia is learning a different history in school than she hears during the discussions that her parents and Mr. Pirzada have about nationalistic wars and religious strife in the subcontinent of India, Pakistan, and the newly forming Bangladesh. In short, her worldview has been expanded, and she sees herself differently as a result.

Therapist's Conceptualization

Ethnic Identity Issues.   Several aspects in Lilia's story point to issues of ethnic identity. First, Lilia learns that her parents make a distinction between Mr. Pirzada and themselves. Specifically, despite looking alike, speaking the same Bengali language, and sharing some customs (e.g., removing shoes before entering a room, eating the same types of food, and finding humor in the same jokes), Lilia's parents make clear that Mr. Pirzada is not Indian, and he may be offended if she mistakenly refers to him as such. Therapists may wonder whether Lilia is at a particularly vulnerable age to be learning ideas of difference, whether she can integrate the notion of difference, and whether in instances of difference she sees one side as having to be inferior to the other.

However, as therapists work longer with children of immigrants, they learn that the above outlook on children is an American bias. Being different is a basic schemata for immigrant children (Roysircar-Sodowsky & Frey, 2003). That Lilia is ethnically different is pointed out when she goes trick-or-treating. Her neighbors comment that they have never seen an Indian witch before. Lilia's mother gives Lilia and her friend burlap rice bags to contain their Halloween "loot."

Along with revelations of difference, Lilia displays a newly piqued interest about her parents' home country and Mr. Pirzada's, a curiosity that is plainly discouraged by her grade school teacher, who takes away Lilia's book on India and admonishes her for reading it. Unlike the teacher, therapists find it easily understandable that Lilia is far more compelled by the war being waged in Mr. Pirzada's homeland than she is by the American Revolution. After all, the India-Pakistan war is being played out in front of her eyes via television, and she can feel it emotionally through her relationship with Mr. Pirzada. At her friend's house nobody sits on the edge of the sofa waiting eagerly for the news of India and its people and Pakistan and its people, as they are doing in her living room.

Working within a family context, therapists are interested in the use of language in the household. For example, what exposure does Lilia have to Bengali, the native language of her parents, and in what different contexts do she and her parents use Bengali versus English? When working with a family of different immigrant generations, therapists keep in mind that the members might be adopting different modes of acculturation with regard to language, gender attitudes, customs, child-rearing practices, discipline, family relationships, power hierarchies, obedience to parents, extended kinship, and involvement in ethnic communities versus involvement in social functions in the dominant society. Treatment is designed with this issue of acculturation differences in the family as a central premise (Roysircar-Sodowsky & Frey, 2003).

Recognition and Response to International Trauma.   In the case of Mr. Pirzada, therapists may not be able to imagine what it must be like for this man to be in the United

States while his homeland is under attack and he is cut off from his family. How is it that he can daily go to the university and do his research with the knowledge that his wife and seven daughters, not to mention his extended family, might be killed in the war that started while he was in the United States? What must it be like for him to watch the devastation on television? How does he experience the support and hospitality from Lilia's family whom he comes to know only after his arrival in the United States and with whom he will not retain contact upon return to his country? These are questions that therapists might want to ask of Mr. Pirzada in order to understand his circumstances and observe how he copes. It does seem, based on his frequent visits to Lilia's home, that he takes comfort in spending time with a family from a neighboring South Asian country, who, even though of a different religious faith, might understand his situation of imminent losses and national crises. He projects his seven daughters onto Lilia, and Lilia sees herself as one of them. Possibly a therapist, as an advocate, could help Mr. Pirzada make contact with the U.S. ambassador's office in his country in order to get information about his family.

By way of summary, each of the cases presented—Mrs. Sen, Mrs. Das, and Lilia— demonstrates a nonlinear acculturation process whereby unique factors influence the adaptation experiences of immigrants and their children. Similar patterns can be noted in the experiences of international students, although there are notable differences that also need to be considered.

Case Studies of International Students and Implications for Therapy

Freedom, parties, staying up late, and enjoying being young—these are some things that many American students look forward to in college. They grow up knowing that college is a time to become an individual, to decide who they are and what they want to do with their life. For many international students, however, college holds a different meaning.

International students come to the United States to attend college and embark on a difficult period of living away from family and friends in order "to expand one's mind and learn to think clearly, in a concentrated fashion" (Garrod & Davis, 1999, p. 48). Some leave home for a better education; for some, higher education is not accessible to them in their own country. Others leave because their homeland is being destroyed by war or by a totalitarian regime, and they feel there is no way to survive unless they move. International students come to the United States with a very serious view of late adolescence and of educational opportunities (Sodowsky, 1991). Thus when they come face to face with American college students, they encounter a different culture, different relationships, and different expectations—all challenges far from what they have ever faced before.

Conceptualizing Acculturation Concerns of International Students

Language Barriers. One of the major challenges that almost all of the students face is the language barrier, which is the most important variable of acculturation (Roysircar,

2003a; Roysircar-Sodowsky & Maestas, 2000). For example, Maria Popova of Bulgaria (Garrod & Davis, 1999) and her American roommate stopped talking to each other because Maria does not want to be reminded of how funny she sounds to Americans. Even though Maria knows enough English words to get her point across, it is hard for her to grasp "subtle things such as intonation, slang, and connotations" (p. 82). Similarly, students make fun of Misun Kim of South Korea (Garrod & Davis) because she does not socialize much, and when she does try to speak, they expect her "to speak flawless English" (p. 135). She says, "I was in constant battle with myself because my ability to express myself in English was nowhere near my intellectual capacity" (p. 135). Yu Chen of China (Garrod & Davis) is challenged when studying subjects in a foreign language. Many times in class, she holds back questions or comments because she is worried that she cannot "speak as eloquently as American students" (p. 159). Almin Hodzic of Bosnia (Garrod & Davis) writes about a time when his high school social studies teacher in the United States put him in front of the class and asked him to teach about what was happening in Bosnia. His English was so limited that he had to draw pictures and use his body to try to explain the horrible fighting going on at home. He remembers being extremely frustrated and ready to cry after this experience. Devyani of India (Garrod & Davis) says, "I see students struggle with English here. We so easily forget that they are really saying next to nothing about themselves, that we know nothing about who they are" (p. 58).

Culture Clash.   Most of the international students described by Garrod and Davis (1999) face a college culture that is strange to them. Stephen Kobourov of Bulgaria (Garrod & Davis) writes about the different levels of knowledge that have been acquired by eastern Europeans vs. Americans of the same age. He writes, "Most Bulgarians at my age have some knowledge of art, music, theater and literature, without having taken classes and without having any special interest in those areas" (p. 14). This is a contrast to the American students he meets who do not have knowledge of these things unless they have taken a class in the area. He comments that because Americans have access to almost every book ever printed, they take books for granted, whereas Bulgarians' lack of such free access to books cause them to "hunger for books" (p. 14) and to cherish their libraries. Similarly, Maria Popova of Bulgaria says that what contributed to her happiness was developing the ability to value the minute details of life, "A single banana on a winter day could make me happy.... A letter from an unknown pen pal from Japan was the biggest event of the week. A new stamp from Mexico was a treasure I would brag about" (p. 74). James from Nigeria (Garrod & Davis) is aggravated that he has to listen to American students talking about television, marijuana, and chewing gum. Maria Popova is discouraged by American students' idea of a good time. She does not understand why alcohol and sex are at the center of a party. She views American students as privileged, decadent, and involved in trivialities. Aassia Haroon of Pakistan (Garrod & Davis) feels a lack of honesty among the students, who are afraid of showing their true emotions because they want to be accepted and don't want to be different from other students. Paradoxically, she too hides behind a smile, and this makes her feel even more personally disconnected.

Perhaps because of such negative views, some of these international students resent that the Americans perform better than they do in coursework and criticize them for being overly grade-conscious. Misun Kim says that she has "had to accept the fact that these beer-guzzling airheads got better grades than [she] did" (p. 137).

For many American college students alcohol and sex are rites of passage to adulthood. International students from Europe come from cultures where there is no age limit for drinking, or if there is a limit it is much younger than it is in America. In Europe alcohol use is more accepted and is not as tempting for the younger people. In the Muslim countries, alcohol use is forbidden by religious sanctions. Some students come from Asian cultures that are not as open about sex as Americans are, and some others come from cultures that are more open about it. With all these differences, how are international students to adapt to campus life?

Significance of Family and Community. Misun Kim from South Korea (Garrod & Davis, 1999) struggles with her feelings of obligation to her family versus a more Americanized need for autonomy (see also Sodowsky, 1991). She chooses to pursue a career as a doctor because she wants to fulfill her obligation to support her parents when they become elderly. She makes this choice even though she longs to study philosophy. Misun Kim's decision to become a doctor illustrates the value she places on her family. She has a very special relationship with her father. Having been conflicted with self-image and body image problems since she was a young girl, Misun is guided by her father in the direction of recognizing her intellectual strength. She says, "If it weren't for my father, I would have accomplished nothing; he was my voice and my ears" (p. 135). Devyani similarly shares the importance of her family ties to her sense of well-being. She says, "My most inspiring moments of learning were rarely in school, sometimes in books, but most often while talking to [my father]" (p. 59). Maria Popova says that she is lucky to have grown up in a "family where three generations of women…lived in perfect accord" (p. 77) and that it was a rewarding experience to have "so many people I can trust for everything, to receive understanding, advice, compassion, and help in any situation" (p. 77). Maria goes on to say that her schoolmates for 13 years were her second family, like brothers and sisters, and she felt very close to her teachers.

Applying Interventions within the Nonlinear Acculturation Model

Therapist Responses to the Language Barrier. It is revealing that none of the international students depicted in Garrod and Davis's (1999) book seeks assistance in a college counseling center to work through their circumstances. Rather they write about their experiences in an English seminar that teaches them to write with a process orientation. For international students, therapy on campus is probably an unfamiliar service; it may be seen as not relevant to their academic goals or as the last recourse for the severely mentally ill (Sodowsky, 1991). The language barrier may also have something to do with these students not choosing "talk therapy." Therapists must know ways of putting into words the problems that international students see, without their clients viewing the therapy process as endless talking with no immediate relief. Devyani says, "Sometimes I sit alone in this college and feel very fully what the word 'alone' means.… For that moment, you want neither to 'talk about it'—the American cure for all ills—nor to receive verbalized sympathy from another" (p. 64). A process of creative therapy may provide international students opportunities to share their story. In their preferred language they could write a journal to understand better their acculturation journey, and then for later therapeutic processing they could translate the major domains and underlying themes in their journaling.

Most therapists find it difficult to understand what it is like to move to a country, not know the dominant language, and then receive formal education in that language. Many Americans take it for granted that wherever they go there will probably be someone who can speak in English. For example, when the author was in Nigeria, West Africa, she never had to learn Efik or Yoruba because everyone in the villages, towns, and cities knew English as well as their native languages. Therapists affirm international students' intellectual courage to be taking classes in a language that is not their native tongue and was not the medium of instruction and writing in their earlier schooling. Therapists advocate for proofreading and tutorial services in English on campus.

Therapist Responses to Culture Clash.   Since American students do not understand international students, it is a responsibility of university counseling center staff to reach out to these students and communicate that the counselors do understand international perspectives (Sodowsky & Taffe, 1991). Some international students feel hopeless. Devneesh of India (Garrod & Davis, 1999) contemplated suicide. Suicide in Indian culture does not share the stigma that it does in the United States. Therefore, Devneesh's life may have been at risk. Devneesh reported overt racism, ridicule, and bullying from his roommate. He would benefit from a safe place to vent his despair and disappointments rather than internalizing these experiences. Therapists could show him how to analyze, place, and contain the locus of prejudice outside of himself.

Therapists could frame Devneesh's despair within the normalcy of adolescent identity development. International students are a select, talented group. They are future leaders of nations, industry, academia, and professions. They are idealists who want to do something lasting and productive. They are secretly hoping to make a difference. For instance, Devneesh is involved in an identity development process as he is clarifying his values, "Why should I go on—what is there for me in [this college], or anywhere else.... What was it all for?" (p. 115). These are familiar questions to university therapists. They can facilitate the process of self-discovery. An existential statement of hope to international students might be what Devneesh himself says, "Trying experiences help one see oneself and know oneself better" (p. 131). Perhaps therapists help their clients rediscover some of those "minute details of life that sometimes make it utterly joyful" (p. 74), a coping strategy used by Maria Popova.

Almin Hodzic's interest in sports is a bridge that takes him to a common ground with U.S. students. Being a member of a college sports team provides him with group identification. Almin says, "After losing my closest friends in Bosnia to death and disappearance, crew practice means the stability of being surrounded by teammates, my friends" (p. 189). Therapists could involve international students in watching and, consequently, learning about American college sports, availing themselves of facilities in the college gym and participating in intramural sports activities.

It would be difficult to be in a therapeutic relationship with any of the international students described here. How do therapists explain American adolescents' attitudes towards alcohol? How do they explain why Americans act so artificial and hide their emotions? How do they help someone to acculturate to American college life that might be difficult even for White therapists to acculturate to?

One of the biggest challenges that therapists face is in trying to be prepared for people from so many different cultures around the world. Within this challenge, the point is to remember that just because a person comes from a culture that we feel we know a lot about does not mean that we know that particular person or anything about him or her. The counterpoint to remember is that it is important to know the background of any person with whom we might work, especially one from a different culture, because domestic students at least share a common worldview, socialization process, and cultural background with counseling center therapists. How can we expect individuals to want to learn about American college life and to adapt to it if we don't learn about their culture? What is important for international students? What do they need to learn to be able to understand us? What do we need to learn to be able to understand them? These are questions that determine therapists' treatment repertoire (Sodowsky, 1991). Therapists could begin treatment by distilling the presentations of international students into domains and themes, as has been done in this chapter, so that they feel less overwhelmed by the multicultural knowledge and competencies that seem to be required.

Therapist Responses to Issues of Defensiveness.   The international students' criticisms and strong perception of prejudice on campus may cause therapists to become defensive. They could personalize critical statements as attacks on them. Like their clients, therapists may have nationalistic responses. This countertransference must receive attention before the therapist attends to the cases clinically. The therapist may have a negative reaction because of fear that the international students have accurately analyzed certain aspects of American culture. If this countertransference is not identified, a therapist's international clients may feel doubly victimized, blamed, and rejected.

Therapist Responses to Accommodation and Integration.   Certainly the international students feel defensive about their differences; thus they feel vulnerable. Georgina Gemmill of South Africa (Garrod & Davis) considered American students visiting her parents' home as somewhat lacking in politeness and refinement. But she, like some other international students referred to earlier, found individual American students and faculty to share her interests and dreams. For these individual students, it might be beneficial to discover what they have in common with their American community, rather than to focus solely on differences. As therapists give opportunity to international clients to share their stories, they teach reconciliation skills for dual identities, splits and disconnections, disjunction of past and present, and polarities in experiences. Steven Kobourov says,

> Since I came to study in the United States, two urges have been struggling in me. The first urge is to cast off the past.... The second is the all too human desire to unload what I have

been forced to keep hidden inside me.... Somewhere along the way, I succeeded in reconciling my past and my present, instead of forsaking one for the other. (p. 17)

Therapist Responses to Systemic Issues.   A thorough assessment at the organizational level is needed. Many colleges market themselves in a manner that attracts minority students, but the colleges may fail these students when they arrive. If a school were truly multicultural, there would be extensive structural support for international students, such as tutorial labs that help students to edit their papers. An intervention at the organizational level could include the alumni, especially alumni who are diverse or international. Alumni support of multiculturalism might convince the college's executive administrators to implement a multicultural setting. As alums, they are no longer directly dependent on the school. Therefore, they would not need to fear retribution for their multicultural views, whereas many of the faculty, staff, and students do have such fears. Donors who are supporters of multiculturalism should be solicited. A campaign could be started to include racial, ethnic, and cultural minority individuals on the slate for elections to the board of trustees.

Therapists would be involved at the systems level. They might foster communication on campus that attracts the attention of academic departments. Such a forum could alert the faculty to issues that international students are experiencing in their classes and brainstorm ideas on improving classroom climate. The students in *Crossing Customs* (Garrod & Davis, 1999) explained that much of their self-esteem and identity have developed from their academic achievements back home. Thus therapists should intervene before international students' faltering grades further lower their self-esteem and confidence. Therapists can organize a buddy system, matching each international student who wants such a support system with several American volunteer buddies, mentors, and tutors. The international students may find some commonalities with the American students, who become a social network for them. To connect international students with American students, therapists can organize an international students' speaker series, so that these students can give voice to their countries' history and their current U.S. experiences, and American students can learn about the richness of the lives of international students.

Therapist Responses to Stress and Coping Issues.   The overwhelming amount of personal, intellectual, and political freedoms that American students have on U.S. college campuses may, in many cases, threaten the collectivistic identity of international students. They also experience culture shock, language barriers, and racism. Interventions can be focused on directly bolstering their coping skills in the context of both their collective resources and individual strategies (Roysircar-Sodowsky & Maestas, 2002). Turning to conationals, to similar-others among international students, and to family and friends via letters, telephone calls, and holiday visits comes naturally to many international students. Therapists can encourage international clients to tap into these natural resources, especially those who have lost touch with ties. Therapists can develop international student networks and support groups on campus. The presence of other minority students can be of comfort, especially for an incoming international student. Speaking of a Vietnamese female student and a Puerto Rican male student whom he met on his first day, Devneesh, an Indian, says, "I was happy to have them as my friends with whom I ate my meals, trekked the woods" (p. 111). Misun Kim says, "We talked about our identities as females, Koreans, and minorities at [college]. We are often amazed at the similarities in our experiences and our feelings about our circumstances, our future—even our love of Korean food!" (p. 143).

Surviving in isolation where they cannot find a reference group, international students develop self-reliance. Lai Heng Foong of Malaysia says, "I try to reconcile myself to a new home by relying upon myself, which is a constancy that is needed in an unfamiliar environment. Finding familiarity in the solace of oneself provides a welcome sense of permanence" (p. 208). The therapist needs to confirm to Lai that he is himself a constant survivor, a person with ego integrity and resilience. Therapists familiarize their clients with both types of coping because the degree to which collectivistic and individualistic coping methods are used varies by individual international student and by the stress-producing contexts. Stress management and resiliency could be approached from the goals of offering a sense of empowerment, promoting connectedness to the college community and to American peers, forming networks with other international students, finding meaning in the American education that they are receiving, and hoping for a productive vocational and personal future. All these goals are placed in the context of individual and cultural circumstances.

Therapist Responses to Religious or Spirituality Issues.   Almin Hodzic (Garrod & Davis) had been brutalized by the Serbian military. Given his history, therapists would be concerned about post-traumatic stress disorder. Or they might have conceptualized Almin's positive outlook as denial. However, Almin used his traumatic experience to have a deeper appreciation for his life and for diversity. He gave speeches to schools and church groups in an attempt to master and share his experience in a way that was healthy and productive. If Almin ever requires psychological services, it would be important to interface his religion, which has been a natural support for him. Almin describes the importance of his Muslim culture from the earliest of his childhood memories. A therapist would need to conceptualize Almin's case with an understanding of his Muslim values, connecting this belief system to his worldview that demonstrates trust and empowerment, which, in fact, has been helpful in his transition to American college life. Similar to Almin, Devyani, an Indian, finds a source of strength in spirituality. She says, "My politics, and also my notion of self, stem from a kind of spirituality that has helped me to control recurring moments of panic, isolation, and bewilderment" (p. 60). Therapists explore the meaning of religion and spirituality in the life of some international students, for herein lies a potential source of strength.

Conclusion

The stories of immigrants and international students are filled with emotions: loneliness, pain, joy, longing, alienation, vulnerability, and interpersonal distance. In reality, these emotions are not different from those experienced by everyone, no matter what cultures individuals come from. What is special about the individuals described in this writing is that they originate from cultures steeped in centuries-old traditions and worldview orientations much different from those of the average American who belongs to a fast moving, ever-changing society engaged in modernization transitions. While at an obvious level the emotions can be felt, therapists exert a great deal of thoughtfulness, world-mindedness, and cognitive flexibility to understand the cultural meanings behind the emotions. The overlooked subtle cultural cues lie hidden in reactions that are universal or similar only in appearance. Working with the effects of implicit culture is a therapist competency. The therapist taking a perspective informed by implicit culture breaks down barriers and creates an affective connection with the client. This process is called ethnotherapeutic (Sodowsky, Kuo-Jackson, Richardson, & Corey, 1998).

References

Berry, J. W. (1980). Acculturation as varieties of adaptation. In A. M. Padilla (Ed.), *Acculturation: Theory, models and some new findings* (pp. 9–25). Boulder, CO: Westview Press.

Culler, I., Arnold, B., & Maldonado, R. (1995). Acculturation Rating Scale for Mexican Americans-II: A revision of the original ARSMA scale: *Hispanic Journal of Behavioral Sciences, 17,* 275–304.

Garrod A., & Davis, J. (Eds.) (1999). *Crossing customs: International students write on U.S. college life and culture.* New York: Falmer Press/Taylor & Francis Group.

Kawanishi, Y. (1995). The effects of culture on beliefs about stress and coping: Causal attribution of Anglo-American and Japanese persons. *Journal of Contemporary Psychotherapy, 25,* 49–60.

Kuo P. Y., & Roysircar-Sodowsky, G. (1999). Cultural ethnic identity versus political ethnic identity: Theory and research on Asian Americans. In D. S. Sandhu (Ed.), *Asian and Pacific Islander Americans: Issues and concerns for counseling and psychotherapy* (pp. 78–104). Commack, NY: Nova Science.

Lahiri, J. (1999). *Interpreter of maladies.* Boston, MA: Mariner, Houghton Mifflin.

Roysircar, G. (2003a). Understanding immigrants: Acculturation theory and research. In F. D. Harper & J. McFadden (Eds.), *Culture and counseling: New approaches* (pp. 164–185). Boston, MA: Allyn & Bacon.

Roysircar, G. (2003b). Counselor awareness of own assumptions, values, and biases. In G. Roysircar, P. Arredondo, J. Fuertes, J. G. Ponterotto, & R. Toporek (Eds.), *Multicultural counseling competencies 2003: Association for multicultural counseling and development.* Alexandria, VA: AMCD.

Roysircar, G., & Gard, G. (in press). Research in multicultural counseling: Impact of counselor variables on process and outcome. In C. E. Lee (Ed.), *Multicultural issues in counseling. New approaches to diversity* (3rd ed.). Alexandria, VA: American Counseling Association.

Roysircar, G., Hubbell, R., & Ortega, M. (2003). *Relationships of client evaluations of outcome, observer reports, and self-reports of multicultural competencies: Evaluation of multicultural training.* Manuscript submitted for Publication.

Roysircar, G., Webster, D. R., Germer, J., Campbell, G., Lynne, E., Palensky, J. J., Liu, J., Yang, Y., & Bludgett-McDeavitt, J. (2003). Experiential training in multicultural counseling: Implementation and evaluation of counselor process. In G. Roysircar, D. S. Sandhu, & V. B. Bibbins (Eds.), *Multicultural competencies: A guidebook of practices* (pp. 3–15). Alexandria, VA: American Counseling Association.

Roysircar-Sodowsky, G., & Frey, M. (2003). Children of immigrants: Their worldviews value conflicts. In P. Pedersen & J. C. Carey (Eds.), *Multicultural counseling in the schools: A practical handbook* (2nd ed., pp. 61–83). Boston, MA: Allyn & Bacon.

Roysircar-Sodowsky, G. R., & Kuo, P. Y. (2001). Determining cultural validity of personality assessment. Some guidelines. In D. Pope-Davis & H. Coleman (Eds.), *The intersection of race, class, & gender: Implications for multicultural counseling* (pp. 213–239). Thousand Oaks, CA: Sage.

Roysircar-Sodowsky, G., & Maestas, M. (2000). Acculturation, ethnic identity, and acculturative stress: Theory, research, and measurement. In R. H. Dana (Ed.), *Handbook of cross-cultural and multicultural assessment* (pp. 131–172). Mahwah, NJ: Lawrence Erlbaum.

Roysircar-Sodowsky, G., & Maestas, M. (2002). Assessing acculturation and cultural variables. In K. S. Kurasaki, S. Okazaki, & S. Sue (Eds.), *Asian American mental health: Assessment theories and methods* (pp. 77–94). Dordrecht, The Netherlands. Kluwer Academic Publishers.

Shonfeld-Ringel, S. (2001). A re-conceptualization of the working alliance in cross-cultural practice with non-western clients: Integrating relational perspectives and multicultural theories. *Clinical Social Work Journal, 29,* 53–63.

Sodowsky, G. R. (1991). Effects of culturally consistent counseling tasks on American and international student observers' perception of counselor credibility: A preliminary investigation. *Journal of Counseling and Development, 69,* 253–256.

Sodowsky, G. R., Kuo-Jackson, P. Y., Richardson, M. F., & Corey, A. T. (1998). Correlates of self-reported multicultural competencies: Counselor multicultural social desirability, race, social inadequacy, locus of control, racial ideology, and multicultural training. *Journal of Counseling Psychology, 45,* 256–264.

Sodowsky, G. R., Kwan, K-L. K., & Pannu, R. (1995). Ethnic identity of Asians in the United States: Conceptualization and illustrations. In J. G. Ponterotto, J. M. Casas, L. A. Suzuki, & C. M. Alexander (Eds.), *Handbook of multicultural counseling* (pp. 123–154). Thousand Oaks, CA: Sage.

Sodowsky, G. R., & Lai, E. W. M. (1997). Asian immigrant variables and structural models of cross-cultural distress. In A. Booth, A. C. Crouter, & N. Landale (Eds.), *Immigration and the family: Research and policy on U.S. immigrants* (pp. 221–237). Mahwah, NJ: Lawrence Erlbaum.

Sodowsky, G. R., Lai, E. W. M., & Plake, B. S. (1991). Moderating effects of sociocultural variables on acculturation variables of Hispanics and Asian Americans. *Journal of Counseling and Development, 70,* 194–204.

Sodowsky, G. R., & Plake, B. (1991). Psychometric properties of the American-International Relations Scale. *Educational and Psychological Measurement, 51,* 207–216.

Sodowsky, G. R., & Taffe, R. C. (1991). Counselor trainees' analyses of multicultural counseling videotapes. *Journal of Multicultural Counseling and Development, 19,* 115–129.

Szapocznik, J., & Kurtines, W. (1980). Acculturation, biculturalism, and adjustment among Cuban Americans. In A. M. Padilla (Ed.), *Acculturation: Theory, models and some new findings* (pp. 139–159). Boulder, CO: Westview Press.

14

Religious and Spiritual Diversity in Counseling and Psychotherapy

P. Scott Richards, Roger R. Keller, and Timothy B. Smith

Brigham Young University

Addressing Religious and Spiritual Diversity in Counseling and Psychotherapy

No book on human diversity and the practice of multicultural counseling and psychotherapy would be complete without a chapter on religious and spiritual aspects of diversity. Shafranske and Malony (1996) have argued that religious affiliation and beliefs "may be a far more potent social glue than the color of one's skin, cultural heritage, or gender." They claim, "Religious identification for some may be the thread that unites individuals into a social unit.... religion must be taken account of as a factor in any appreciation of individual difference and cultural diversity" (p. 564). We agree that an understanding of religious and spiritual diversity is essential for true multicultural competency.

Although human diversity is broad and rich when gender, race, ethnicity, sexual orientation, language, and age are considered, it becomes even more astonishing when religious differences are included (Richards & Bergin, 2000). In North America, 97 percent of

Portions of this chapter were based on P. S. Richards and A. E. Bergin (2000), Toward religious and spiritual competency for mental health professionals, In P. S. Richards and A. E. Bergin (Eds.), (2000). *Handbook of psychotherapy and religious diversity* (pp. 3–26), Washington, DC: American Psychological Association; and R. R. Keller (2000), Religious diversity in North America, In P. S. Richards and A. E. Bergin (Eds.), (2000). *Handbook of psychotherapy and religious diversity* (pp. 27–55), Washington, DC: American Psychological Association. Copyright 2000 by the American Psychological Association. Adapted with permission.

the people profess to have some form of spiritual beliefs, and 65 percent report that those beliefs are central to their life (Gallup, 1995). In the *Encyclopedia of American Religions,* J. Gordon Melton (1996) listed over 1,200 different Christian groups. In addition to the Christian denominations, there are over 700 non-Christian traditions in the United States and Canada, including Eastern, Middle Eastern, Spiritualist, Psychic, New Age, Ancient Wisdom, and Magick groups. According to Hoge (1996), the religious diversity of North America will continue to increase due to the effects of higher education, the media, world consciousness, individualism, and immigration.

Currently in North America, 85.2 percent of the population is Christian (Barrett & Johnson, 1998). The largest Christian denominations are Roman Catholic, Southern Baptist, United Methodist, National Baptist, Church of God in Christ, Church of Jesus Christ of Latter-day Saints, and Evangelical Lutheran (Bedell, 1997). The largest non-Christian groups are Jews, Muslims, Buddhists, and Hindus (Barrett & Johnson, 1998).

In this chapter we first define our use of the terms *religious* and *spiritual*. We then discuss some of the benefits for therapists of seeking competency in religious and spiritual aspects of diversity. We describe some of the basic attitudes and skills of mental health professionals who are competent in religious issues and practices. We then provide a brief introduction to the history and beliefs of the five largest world religions with adherents in North America: Christianity, Judaism, Islam, Buddhism, and Hinduism. Finally, we offer some denomination-specific guidelines for professionals who work with members of these religious traditions.

Definitions of Religious *and* Spiritual

There has been much discussion and some controversy regarding the meaning of the terms *religious* and *spiritual*. Without claiming to resolve the disagreements, we wish to make it clear at the outset of this chapter how we will use these terms. We view *religious* and *spiritual* as highly overlapping and interrelated. Both religious and spiritual beliefs and practices may involve a search for and worship of the divine, transcendent, or sacred (Larson, Swyers, & McCullough, 1998). Many people who are members of a particular religious denomination or tradition view themselves as both religious and spiritual, making little distinction between the terms. In fact, in most cultures and throughout much of recorded history, the terms *religious* and *spiritual* have not been conceptually separated (Wulff, 1991).

Nevertheless, we recognize that many people who regard themselves as spiritual are not affiliated with a particular religious tradition. In addition, some people who are affiliated with a religious denomination have no interest in a relationship with the divine or other spiritual matters. Thus while we do not think it is helpful to make attempts to completely polarize or separate the terms *religious* and *spiritual* because they are often so intricately intertwined, we use both in this chapter to acknowledge that it "is possible to be religious without being spiritual and spiritual without being religious" (Richards & Bergin, 1997, p. 13). This distinction is potentially important to many clients, and it also has implications regarding the manner and degree to which spiritual issues may appropriately become a focus of treatment.

Potential Benefits of Competency in Issues of Religious Diversity

Religious Clients and Leaders May Trust Therapists More.   Many religious and spiritual people distrust mental health professionals and avoid the process of counseling and psychotherapy because they fear that secular therapists will misunderstand or seek to undermine their beliefs (Richards & Bergin, 1997, 2000; Worthington, 1986; Worthington, Kurusu, McCullough, & Sanders, 1996). Furthermore, many religious leaders are reluctant to refer members of their congregations to mental health professionals who are not of their own faith. As a result, religiously devout people often underutilize mental health services (Richards & Bergin, 2000). When they do seek professional help, religious people often seek out those who share or at least openly respect their values (e.g., Worthington, 1986; Worthington et al., 1996). Counselors and therapists who acquire competency in religious and spiritual aspects of diversity will enjoy more credibility with religious clients and leaders. Such therapists will receive more referrals from within religious communities, and their opportunities to assist this underserved population will increase.

Therapists May More Fully Understand Their Religious Clients.   A goal of multicultural counseling and psychology is to accurately understand individuals within their cultural context (Sue & Sue, 1999). Because the religious traditions of the world have such a major influence on culture (Smart, 1983), understanding a client's religious and spiritual background is central to understanding his or her cultural context.

It is also widely accepted that in order to work effectively with clients, it is important for counselors and therapists to understand and empathize with each client's unique phenomenological view of the world (Rogers, 1961). Ibrahim (1985) stated:

> Lack of understanding of one's own and one's clients' world views results in frustration and anxiety for both the helper and the client. Goals and processes considered appropriate by the helper may be antithetical and meaningless for the client. In such an instance, the appropriate course for the helper is to establish clearly how the client views the world. (pp. 629–630)

For the majority of people in the world, their religious and spiritual beliefs have a profound influence on their phenomenological worldview. People's beliefs about the big questions of life—such as the origin and purpose of life, nature of deity, morality and ethics, death and life after death, and ways of knowing—are often heavily influenced by the teachings of their religious tradition (Richards & Bergin, 1997; Smart, 1983). Mental health professionals who acquire competency in religious and spiritual aspects of diversity are more likely to understand and empathize with their religious clients and to work with them in a sensitive and ethical manner.

Treatment Interventions May Be More Effective.   As widely acknowledged, professionals should tailor their treatment interventions whenever possible to the unique problems, personality, and preferences of individual clients. Not all secular treatment interventions are appropriate for devout members of some religious traditions (Richards & Bergin, 2000). For example, some techniques of sex therapy, gay affirmative therapy, or feminist therapy may offend and lead to premature termination with religiously orthodox clients (Richards & Bergin, 2000). Counselors and therapists who have acquired competency in religious and spiritual aspects of diversity will be less likely to offend and alienate religious clients by prescribing interventions that conflict with their religious beliefs.

There is also increasing evidence that some time-honored religious practices, such as praying, meditating, reading sacred writings, forgiving, repenting, and worshipping, may promote coping and healing (Benson, 1996). Many contemporary therapists are accessing the healing potential of these practices by prescribing them as interventions during treatment (Richards & Bergin, 1997; Worthington et al., 1996). Therapists who are competent in religious areas will be more capable of using spiritual interventions when appropriate to assist their clients.

Finally, as widely recognized, counselors and therapists who fail to draw upon the external resources available to their clients will only be partially effective (Sue & Sue, 1999). For religious and spiritual clients, external resources may include worship services, opportunities to give and receive meaningful service, consultation with spiritual leaders, and certain religious rituals (Richards & Bergin, 2000; Fukuyama & Sevig, 1999). Counselors and therapists who are competent in dealing with religious matters will be more capable of recognizing the availability of these healing resources and using them to facilitate their clients' progress.

Attitudes and Skills of Religiously Competent Professionals

The capacity to adopt an ecumenical therapeutic stance is essential for therapists who work with religious and spiritual clients. The word *ecumenical* means "of worldwide scope or applicability" (*American Heritage Dictionary of the English Language,* 1992, p. 584). Richards and Bergin (1997) defined an ecumenical therapeutic stance as "an attitude and approach to therapy which is suitable for clients of diverse religious affiliations and backgrounds" (p. 118). The foundations of an ecumenical therapeutic stance are the attitudes and skills of an effective multicultural therapist. Multicultural therapeutic attitudes and skills have been described earlier in this book (Chapter 1) and in other publications (e.g., Sue et al., 1982; Sue & Sue, 1999; Sue, Zane, & Young, 1994). Effective ecumenical therapists are able to generalize multicultural attitudes and skills to the religious and spiritual domains.

Therapists with good ecumenical skills are aware of their own religious heritage and values and are sensitive to how these factors could impact their work with clients from different spiritual traditions. They communicate understanding and respect to clients who have spiritual beliefs that are different from their own. They learn more about the spiritual beliefs and cultures of clients with whom they work. They make efforts to establish trusting relationships with leaders in religious communities and draw upon these sources of social support when appropriate. They use spiritual interventions that are in harmony with their clients' beliefs when doing so could help their clients. All psychologists and counselors, regardless of their religious and spiritual beliefs, have an ethical obligation to acquire these ecumenical attitudes and skills (ACA, 1995; APA, 1992).

The capacity to adopt a denominational therapeutic stance, when appropriate, can also enhance therapists' effectiveness with some clients. Richards and Bergin (1997) defined a denominational therapeutic stance as "an approach to therapy that is tailored for clients who are members of a specific religious denomination" (p. 121). When using a denominational approach, therapists may use language, assessment tools, and spiritual interventions that are uniquely suited to the client's particular denominational beliefs and practices. They may also become more directive, challenging, and educational in their style than they would when using an ecumenical approach. Counselors and therapists who use a denominational approach should do so only with clients of their own religious faith or with clients from other spiritual traditions who view them as able to understand and respect their culture and beliefs.

In order to gain both ecumenical and denominational expertise, mental health professionals may find it helpful to explore and examine their own religious and spiritual heritage, assumptions, biases, and values (Lovinger, 1984; Kelly, 1995). They could also seek to increase their knowledge, understanding, and empathy for religious and spiritual traditions, cultures, and beliefs that are different from their own. Studying books on world religions, taking classes on world religions, and attending religious services of faiths other than their own could all be helpful in this regard. Reading professional literature and taking either classes or continuing education seminars in the psychology of religion and in spiritual issues in psychotherapy, which are offered at some universities and professional conventions, would also be valuable. In order to gain true denominational expertise, therapists will also find it necessary to experience the religious culture firsthand over a significant period of time.

Five Major Religious Groups in North America

Because of the dangers in making generalizations about members of a group, counselors and therapists working with an individual from a specific religious group should assess rather than assume certain characteristics, perceptions, or experiences (Sue & Sue, 1999). The following information about Christianity, Judaism, Islam, Hinduism, and Buddhism will not apply to all individuals in these groups. However, these generalizations may be useful in beginning to understand the unique historical, social, and doctrinal influences within each group.

Christianity

Christianity is the predominant religion in North America. Of those who are religiously affiliated in the United States, 95 percent are Christians, with Catholics (Roman Catholic, Orthodox, and Roman Rite) constituting 42 percent of the religiously affiliated and Protestants constituting 53.7 percent of the religious total. The remaining 4.3 percent of religiously affiliated people include of Jews, Muslims, Buddhists, and persons of other religions (Wright, 1997).

The founder of Christianity was Jesus, the carpenter of Nazareth who lived approximately 6 BCE to 27 CE. What Christians believe about Jesus is encapsulated in the Apostles'

Creed, which states that Jesus was the Son of God, "born of the Virgin Mary, suffered under Pontius Pilate, was crucified, died, and buried; the third day he rose from the dead; he ascended into heaven and sitteth at the right hand of God the Father Almighty. From thence he shall come to judge the quick and the dead."[1] Thus Jesus is believed to be the second of three members of the Godhead; he became incarnate, taught, suffered, died, and was resurrected, working a substitutionary atonement whereby the sins of all humanity were taken upon him. Those who believe in him and his work will be able to enter the presence of his Heavenly Father after death.

Following the resurrection of Jesus Christ, the Christian Church began to spread across the world. At first there was only one church, the Catholic or universal church, but as time went by the church began to split along political lines with the Eastern Orthodox Church established around Constantinople and the Roman Catholic Church focused on leadership in Rome. For a time the two groups worked together, but tensions developed leading to a split between them. The final division occurred when crusaders from Europe sacked Constantinople in 1204. In 1517 an Augustinian monk by the name of Martin Luther nailed 95 theses to the church door in Wittenberg, Germany, challenging the sale of indulgences authorized by the Pope for the forgiveness of sins. In the context of a rising nationalism, this challenge to papal authority led to the Reformation and to the creation of the Lutheran Church. The Reformation quickly spread across Europe with a major center in Switzerland. In Geneva, John Calvin became the leading theologian of the Reformation, and from his work is derived the Reformed tradition, which has a strong emphasis on God's sovereignty or control over all things. Churches arising from this tradition are the Dutch Reformed Church, the Christian Reformed Church, and the Presbyterian Church via Scotland.

While the continent was undergoing changes, so was England. Between 1533 and 1535 Henry VIII effectively separated the English Church from Rome and placed himself at its head. In essence, he was returning the English Church to a time prior to the arrival of Roman authorities. The resulting Church, the Anglican Church, retains many similarities in worship to the Roman Catholic Church. Some groups were dissatisfied with the Anglican Church and either wanted to purify it (Puritans) by bringing in elements of the Reformation or wanted to separate (Separatists) from it. It was Separatists who landed at Plymouth in 1620 and Puritans who a few years later established Massachusetts Bay Colony. From these came the Congregational Church. The Baptists broke off from the Church of England, as did the Methodists.

Some uniquely American churches arose in the nineteenth century, coming from groups known as restorationists who were seeking a return to New Testament Christianity or had a concern about the anticipated return of Jesus Christ. The most visible of these today are The Church of Jesus Christ of Latter-day Saints (Mormons), Seventh Day Adventists, and Jehovah's Witnesses. Arising about the same time came the Christian Scientists.

There is a great deal of variety in both organization and worship patterns among these traditions. Some organizations are highly structured: the Roman Catholic, Episcopalian,

---

[1]*The book of worship for church and home: With orders of worship, services for the administration of Sacraments, and aids to worship according to the usages of The United Methodist Church* (Nashville, TN: The United Methodist Publishing House, 1964), 179.

Lutheran, Methodist, Presbyterian, and Church of Jesus Christ of Latter-day Saints. Others are loosely organized, with the local congregations being the focal point—Baptists, Congregationalists (or United Church of Christ), and Jehovah's Witnesses. Worship is just as varied, with high liturgical (structured) services in the Roman Catholic, Eastern Orthodox, Episcopalian, Methodist, Lutheran and Presbyterian traditions. Having said this, however, it is necessary to add that one is very likely to find highly unstructured services in all of the above traditions, especially in relation to the youth. Church services with limited formality are found in the Baptist, Latter-day Saint, and Pentecostal traditions (those that believe in all the gifts of the Spirit, especially the gift of tongues). In a very real sense, there is great diversity in the beliefs and practices of contemporary Christian traditions, which sometimes leads to tensions within and between groups.

Judaism

Judaism in America is marked by three major groupings. The most conservative are the Orthodox Jews, who were the first Jews to arrive in the colonies. In the 1800s two other forms of Judaism appeared—Reform and Conservative. Today Jews live in most areas of the United States, with large concentrations in the northeast. In 1991 there were 5,944,000 Jews in the United States (Wright, 1997), 50 percent of those practicing their religion being Conservative, 25 percent being Orthodox, and 25 percent being Reform (Eck, 1997a; World Almanac and Book of Facts, 1998).

Judaism normally traces its beginnings to Abraham, the father of the faith, who was called by God to leave his polytheistic homeland and to travel at God's direction to a promised land. Abraham was promised three things: (1) numerous posterity, (2) a choice land, and (3) a blessing of posterity that would bless all nations—which defines what it means for Jews to regard themselves as chosen by God. In the calling of Abraham, all his descendants were given a vocation: i.e., the vocation of proclaiming the one God of the universe. The people became known as Israelites, named after the patriarch Jacob to whom God gave the name Israel. The election of the Israelites was ratified by God at Sinai when, as an act of graciousness, he gave them the Law through Moses. From thenceforth, Israel would remember God and be a peculiar people among the nations through obedience to the ethical and ritual precepts found in the Law of God, a law that was not static but applicable to every new situation that would face the people.

Traditionally, the Jewish people have held that God is not above history, but involved in it. He guides and directs His people and even punishes them when necessary. Jewish identity is tied to their heritage as the people of Israel. Apart from the community within which God works, there is no religion and no identity. Most of the religious festivals around which Jewish life is centered celebrate and remember God's acts in history on behalf of his people. The most regular festival is the weekly Sabbath, which celebrates two of God's creative acts—the creation of the world and the creation of Israel as a people. Like virtually all Jewish festivals, the center of the Sabbath is the home and the family table. Its symbols are two loaves of bread and wine. The Sabbath, which begins at sundown Friday and lasts until an hour after sundown on Saturday, is a day of rest, reflection, worship, and family. Sabbath is the festival that has enabled Jews to continue their lives despite persecution and hardship, for persons look forward to the Sabbath toward the end of the week and back on it at the beginning. Jewish lives are oriented around the Sabbath.

Other critical festivals are the ten Days of Awe and Succoth, in the fall, and Passover, in the spring. The Days of Awe are ushered in by Rosh Hashanah, the new year, and culminate ten days later in Yom Kippur, the day of atonement. This is a solemn period of self-examination and repentance, for at the end of it God determines how people will be affected for good or ill in the coming year. Succoth, the Festival of Booths, follows five days after Yom Kippur to celebrate God's care of Israel in the 40 years of wandering in the wilderness. The central symbol for this festival is the booth, built by the family with at least three sides and a roof through which the stars may be seen. Children decorate the booth, and the family's meals are taken in it. Succoth is a joyous festival. Passover remembers the angel of death passing over the Israelite people when they were slaves in Egypt. Once again, the center of the festival is the family table, which contains various symbols reminding the people of the slavery in Egypt and of God's deliverance. Children ask four questions around which the Passover story is told. The ritual is both serious and enjoyable.

Most Americans are aware of the Jewish festival of Hanukkah. Like other festivals, Hanukkah celebrates a historical event: the rededication of the temple in Jerusalem in 165 BCE after it had been polluted by the Syrians. Hanukkah is known as the feast of lights, for at the time of the temple dedication, there was only enough oil for the lamps to burn one day, but miraculously the lights continued to burn for eight days until a supply of oil could be secured. The central symbol of Hanukkah is the nine branched menorah, or candlestick.

Judaism maintains many rituals and laws of purity, all designed to keep the people aware of God's constant presence and claim upon their lives. The rituals may include the morning prayers, the wearing of the kippah (round head covering), celebration of bar and bat mitzvahs (transition to adulthood), scrolls on doorposts, and circumcision of infant males. Laws of purity include dietary and sexual regulations. Very strict Jews may only eat certain foods which are Kosher (fit). They may not eat meat and drink milk at the same meal, which means that two sets of dishes must be kept by fully observant Jews. They may not eat pork, shellfish, or sea life without fins and scales. They may eat the meat only of animals that both have a cloven hoof and chew the cud. The complex rules of diet keep persons constantly aware that they stand before God. In rituals concerning sexuality, in the Orthodox and Ultra-Orthodox communities women are considered impure for 14 days from the beginning of their menstrual period. At the end of that time, they immerse themselves in the mikveh (pool of water) before resuming conjugal relations.

The range of groups within the Jewish community orient themselves between the poles of tradition and modernity. The Ultra-Orthodox Jews try to avoid the modern world and focus solely on tradition. In contrast, assimilated Jews want nothing to do with tradition and see themselves as purely secular. However, most Jewish persons try to deal with both tradition and modernity. Those who live and work in the modern world but try to keep the Law closely are Orthodox Jews. Those who try to keep most of the Law, but see some of it as being time bound are Conservative Jews. Those who feel that much of the Law is not relevant to modern life but still see themselves within the Jewish worshiping community are Reform Jews. These three divisions occur predominantly in the United States. In summary, Judaism encompasses all aspects of life: Nothing is outside God's Lordship.

Islam

Islam is a rapidly growing religion in North America. The first Muslims arrived in the colonies as slaves during the seventeenth century, but they had no hope of practicing their religion. Most simply became absorbed into the Christian community. Along with many of the Eastern religions, Islam received attention at the Parliament of the World's Religions held in Chicago in 1893, when Mohammed Alexander Russell Webb, one of the first American converts to Islam, gave lectures on the faith (Eck, 1997b).

From that time, Islam has grown slowly but steadily in the United States. The first mosque was built by Albanian Muslims in Biddeford, Maine, in 1915. Today mosques are being built in all parts of North America. Other indications of the acceptance of Islam into American culture have been the rise of The Nation of Islam among African Americans (1933), the recognition of the right of persons in the military to identify themselves as Muslims (1952), President Eisenhower's dedication of the Islamic Center in Washington, DC (1957), and the offering of a Muslim prayer at the opening of the U.S. House of Representatives in 1991 (Eck, 1997b). According to one estimate, there are 5,100,000 Muslims in the country (The World Almanac and Book of Facts, 1998), and that number is steadily increasing.

Of the five faiths that we will examine, Islam is the newest and probably the least understood by most Americans. The name *Islam* means submission (to God), and a Muslim (the practitioner) is one who submits. Islam was founded by Muhammad (570–632 CE) in what is now Saudi Arabia.

Muhammad was poor but respected. He was orphaned early in his life and cared for by his uncle, a caravaner who traveled widely through the Middle East. Muhammad traveled with his uncle, encountering persons of various religions including Christians and Jews. In his early twenties Muhammad worked for a wealthy widow named Khadijah, who was so impressed with his integrity that she proposed marriage. Even though she was 15 years older than Muhammad, the union was happy, and Khadijah was Muhammad's strongest supporter. Following marriage, Muhammad was able to spend more time in searching for the one God. While Muhammad was on a spiritual retreat to the mountains north of Mecca during the year 610 CE, the angel Gabriel appeared to him and called him to be a prophet of Allah (which means "the God"). After accepting the call, Muhammad would periodically go into a trance or dreamlike state in which he would receive revelation in the form of beautiful Arabic poetry which, when collected, became the Qur'an, the incarnate word of God. Thus the Qur'an is for Muslims what the Bible is for Christians.

Worldwide, Islamic life is oriented around the Five Pillars of Islam. The first of these is the Confession of Faith: "There is no God but God (Allah), and Muhammad is his messenger. Thus, God is eternal, supreme, all powerful, and all knowing. All things were and are created by him. There are no other Gods besides him, for God has no partners according to the Qur'an" (Sura 6:63). Muhammad was the one who delivered God's incarnate word (the Qur'an) to the world, and this was his great miracle. He is considered not merely a prophet, but a messenger: for example, one who delivers text or holy scripture. Muhammad is not, however, considered divine; he is regarded as a human being, as are all.

The second pillar is prayer, or perhaps a better English word would be *praise*. Five times a day (just before sunrise, midday, mid-afternoon, evening, and nightfall), Muslims stop to praise God. They are summoned by a call to prayer. Some go to a nearby mosque to pray, while others pray at home (most often women and children), or at their places of employment. Five times a day they stop to reorient their lives and thoughts toward God. These times of reflection include both praise and personal prayer for the various things concerning their lives and families.

The third pillar is almsgiving. Muslims feel an obligation to their neighbors, especially to the poor. They contribute annually 2.5 percent of their wealth for the maintenance of the mosques and for the assistance of the poor. In addition, they are expected to provide direct assistance to those less fortunate through personal contributions and other forms of support.

The fourth pillar is the fast during the month of Ramadan. Ramadan was the month in which the angel Gabriel appeared to and called Muhammad. The fast is carried out during the daylight hours for 30 days, and persons may not eat, drink, smoke, or have sexual relations during those hours. At sundown each day, families gather together to break the fast. This fast breaking is a time of enjoyment, as well as service, for the poor are to be invited to join in these meals. Ramadan is a period of introspection, self-examination, and rededication, much like Lent in the Christian calendar. It is not possible to locate Ramadan in the western calendar, because the Islamic calendar is lunar. Thus Ramadan, as well as the pilgrimage to Mecca, move through the entire solar calendar every 13 years.

The fifth pillar is the pilgrimage to Mecca, which Muslims are expected to make once in a lifetime if they are physically able and do not have to go into debt to do so. The pilgrimage occurs in the last month of the Islamic calendar year. While people may visit Mecca at other times during the year, unless they go during the month of the pilgrimage they may not assume the title of *pilgrim*. The pilgrimage involves various ceremonial activities both in and out of Mecca. All of these ceremonies are rooted in the Abrahamic history, which includes the stories of Ishmael's near sacrifice by his father, Abraham; the banishing of Hagar and Ishmael; God's providential care of them; and the necessity of facing temptations in one's own life. The high point of the pilgrimage is the "standing ceremony" at the mount and plain of Arafat on the ninth day of the month from noon to sundown. Here one symbolically stands alone before God, although in the midst of two million others. It is at Arafat that God is most ready to forgive the faithful. It is at Arafat that he is most near and present.

Islam is a faith of high moral principles, a faith that respects and values human life. It is a faith that believes that the self-evident truths of Islam are so powerful that there needs to be no compulsion in religion (Sura 10:99).

Hinduism

There are reported to be over 900,000 Hindus in the United States (World Almanac and Book of Facts, 1998). Hindu influence was felt in the United States through trade and literature before there was an actual Hindu presence in the country. Trade with India began in the 1780s, and writers such as Ralph Waldo Emerson and Henry David Thoreau were influenced by such Hindu classics as the *Rig Veda* and the *Upanishads*. In 1851 the Hindu presence became visible as a small group of Hindus marched with the East India Society in Salem, MA, in the Fourth of July parade. Hindu teachings were presented at the

World's Parliament of Religion in 1893. In 1894 the first Vedanta Society was founded in New York, with another established in San Francisco in 1899. In 1906 the first major Hindu temple was built in San Francisco by the Vedanta Society. Hindu migration, along with all other Asian migration, was brought to a halt by the Asian Exclusion Act of 1917, but this did not stop Hindu teachers such as Paramahansa Yogananda from touring and teaching. Yogananda founded the International Headquarters of the Self-Realization Fellowship in Los Angeles in 1925. The organization has attracted many Americans (Eck, 1997c).

The Immigration Act of 1965 lifted restrictions against Asian immigration and placed the Asian quotas on a par with those from other parts of the world. Thus immigration from India grew, with many of the immigrants being well educated and affluent. With these people came the desire for temples, and Hindu temples now dot the United States in a variety of places. The most visible and well-known Hindu movement is that of the International Society for Krishna Consciousness (ISKCON), known to most Americans as the Hare Krishna movement. Hinduism is becoming prominent among the religions of America, and while the largest populations may still be on the west coast, their presence is being felt across the country (Eck, 1997c).

The origins of Hinduism have not been recorded. There was no one founder, and Hinduism as it exists today is probably a blend of the Dravidian religion, which was indigenous to India, and the Aryan religion, which was brought to India by a conquering Caucasoid people from the north. The former was a fertility cult, and the latter was a nature-based religion. Today Hinduism is extremely broad, encompassing a wide range of traditions— polytheistic, monotheistic, and even non-theistic. It is not a missionary religion, and it is highly tolerant of religious diversity. For the Hindu, all paths lead to ultimate reality, for the paths are appropriate to the individuals who follow them.

There are three concepts which all Hindus support: Karma, Reincarnation, and Dharma. Karma is the law of cause and effect. Sooner or later what persons do will have either positive or negative effects. Essentially, Karma is the cosmic balance between all of one's good and bad deeds from all past lives. Karma is negative, thus something of which people want to be free. It is Karma that holds persons on the cycle of death and rebirth that constitutes reincarnation. Until Karma is dissipated through merit, persons return again and again to the mortal realm. Thus Hindu religious tradition offers ways to break out of the round of rebirths.

Historically, there have been three ways to break the cycle of reincarnation. The first, known as the Way of Works, required that persons live out the lives they had created for themselves over many lifetimes. They had to follow their Dharma, their way, living within their caste and its boundaries. This might have meant living as a Brahmin (the priestly caste), a Kshatriya (the noble/warrior caste), a Vaisya (the farmer/merchant caste), or a Sudra (the servant caste). The rules, limitations, and privileges differed from caste to caste. The Brahmins were at the top of the hierarchy and the Sudras at the bottom. The castes included numerous sub-castes, many oriented around vocations. In addition, there were outcastes or untouchables who were completely outside the caste system. Intermarriage or social intercourse across caste lines was forbidden. Today the basic rules are still observed, although discrimination on the basis of caste is forbidden by law in India. Hindus in India still take caste seriously, although in the rest of the world the caste system has less influence. In the Way of Works, persons simply lived out their Dharma, hoping that in future lives they would improve their lot.

The Way of Knowledge was reserved for Brahmin males, for it presumed that a certain level of spiritual maturity had to be attained, meaning that Karma had been drastically reduced. Brahmin men had the possibility of gaining release from the rounds of rebirth. While study of Brahmin philosophy was a part of the Way of Knowledge, knowledge was not intellectual but experiential. The real path to knowledge was meditation, leading to an enlightenment experience. This enlightenment was the experience of ultimate reality that ended the rounds of rebirth at death, releasing the individual to Nirvana, the state of non-individuality and non-identity.

The third way of gaining release was known as the Way of Devotion. The Ways of Works and Knowledge were individual undertakings. No divine beings could provide help to release a person from the rounds of rebirth. However, in the Way of Devotion, Gods could help remove the effects of Karma for men and women of all castes. The two most influential deities were Shiva, the God of meditation and destruction, who was predominantly evil, and Vishnu, the restorer God, who visited earth in a number of incarnations to preserve its proper order.

Today virtually all Hindus follow some form of devotion. They may mix their devotions with the Way of Works (living out their caste obligations) and with Knowledge (practicing meditation and seeking enlightenment). Through this way, men and women of all castes or non-caste have hope for release at the end of this life. Worship is characterized by a wide range of practices. Perhaps the most visible form of devotional Hinduism in America is the Hari Krishna movement, which denies caste distinctions and seeks a life after death with Krishna. The Hari Krishna see themselves as a restoration of true Hinduism.

Buddhism

Today there are approximately 780,000 Buddhists in the United States (World Almanac and Book of Facts, 1998). Buddhism was brought to the United States by the Chinese who came to work on the railroads and in the mines. The first Buddhist temple was constructed in San Francisco's Chinatown in 1852, and by 1875 eight more temples had been built. In 1882 the Chinese Exclusion Act was passed, banning any Chinese migration for ten years. This diminished somewhat the spread of Buddhism. However, the World's Parliament of Religion made Americans aware of Buddhism, and one American, Charles T. Strauss of New York, became the first American to become a member of the Buddhist order (Eck, 1997d).

Japanese Buddhism entered the United States initially through Hawaii, where the first Buddhist temple of the Jodo Shinshu lineage was built in 1889. By 1898 this form of Buddhism was established in San Francisco, and temples were soon after built in Sacramento (1899), Fresno (1900), Seattle (1901), Oakland (1901), San Jose (1902), Portland (1903), and Stockton (1906). In 1944 the Jodo Shinshu Buddhists incorporated as the Buddhist Churches of America, and today this group has 60 temples and approximately 19,000 members (Eck, 1997d).

Buddhism developed from Hinduism and thus shares the beliefs of reincarnation and karma. Its founder, Siddhartha Gautama, lived in the sixth century BCE. He was from a noble family, was married, and had a son, but he was discontent with his life of luxury. Thus he decided to see how persons lived outside his sheltered environment. As he explored, he encountered persons who were ill and aged, and he saw a deceased person for the first time. In a word, he encountered human suffering. But he also met a holy man who seemed to have found peace in the midst of suffering. Siddhartha decided that he wanted to be like this monk, so he left his family and station in life to embark upon a spiritual search. That search ended six years later when he received the enlightenment which included the Four Noble Truths: (1) life is suffering; (2) suffering is caused by desire; (3) suffering will cease when desire ceases; and (4) desire may cease by following the eight-fold path, which includes right thought, behavior, and meditation. Now as the Buddha, or the "one who is fully awake," he began to share his insights. From these beginnings, Buddhism in its various forms spread across Asia, eventually reaching Mongolia, its final outpost, in about 1200 CE.

Within Buddhism, there are three major divisions. The first is the Theravada form, or "the religion of the Elders." This form, found in south Asia—Sri Lanka, Burma, Thailand, etc.—is an individual way: i.e., there are no deities who can help people. Persons progress along the eight-fold path until they are ready to live as monks, focusing on meditation and on the search for enlightenment. On attaining enlightenment, one is believed to go beyond the rounds of rebirth to Nirvana, the nature of which is not explained in Buddhism.

In the Mahayana tradition, which is found in southeast and east Asia, heavenly helping beings can assist persons off the rounds of rebirth. These are fully enlightened beings. It is believed that when persons do attain release, they choose to turn away from Nirvana to help other persons gain release. Mahayana is a devotional tradition in which prayers are said, mystical relations are sought, and meditation may still be used.

Vajrayana Buddhism, the Buddhism of Tibet and Mongolia, is the Mahayana devotional tradition with the addition of mystical—almost magical—practices, mantras (repeated phrases), mudras (hand positions), and the practice of passing down traditions from a mentor (a Lama) to disciples.

Perhaps the most unique doctrine of Buddhism is the belief that human beings have nothing permanent about them—including no permanent soul. Rather, human beings are made up of five Skandhas—body, perception, feelings, subconscious, and reasoning. These Skandhas are impermanent and fall apart at death. However, as long as persons remain on the rounds of rebirth, new Skandhas are "stamped" by individual Karma, causing persons to return to this life.

The most popular form of Buddhism for non-westerners in the United States is Zen Buddhism, a meditative form. Sitting meditation (Zazen) is its focus, with the goal of quieting the "monkey mind." Growing in popularity is the Tibetan Buddhist form, perhaps largely due to the moral influence of the Dalai Lama, head of the Tibetan Buddhists, now in exile, who is a visible world figure speaking for peace. With the arrival of refugees from various parts of Asia, all Buddhist forms are well represented in the United States.

Summary of Similarities and Differences between Western and Eastern Religions

Although there is much variation between and within the three theistic religions (Christianity, Judaism, and Islam) concerning specific religious doctrines and practices, at a more general level there is considerable agreement among them concerning their metaphysical beliefs and worldviews. All three of these world religions teach that there is a God who created the world and human beings. There is a divine purpose to life. God will someday judge human beings for how they lived their lives. Humans' rewards in the afterlife will be influenced by their obedience to God's teachings and by their spiritual progression in this life. Human beings can communicate spiritually with God through prayer, and they can receive guidance and strength from God (Richards & Bergin, 1997).

Hinduism and Buddhism have fewer similarities with the theistic traditions. Hinduism and Buddhism are less clear about the question of whether there is a Supreme God or Creator, although followers are free to believe in a Supreme Being if they wish. Hinduism and Buddhism teach that there are many gods or deities, some of whom can help human beings. These religions are also less definite about whether personal identity continues in an afterlife, teaching that personal identity eventually ceases, either in extinction or in unity with the impersonal and eternal divine essence, or One. Hinduism and Buddhism agree with the theistic traditions in their affirmation that (1) spiritual growth and enlightenment are possible and desirable, (2) human beings have moral agency, (3) there are moral laws and principles that human beings should seek to live in harmony with, and (4) there are spiritual paths or ways that lead to personal and social harmony, enlightenment, and peace (Richards & Bergin, 1997).

Implications for Counseling and Psychotherapy

In terms of counseling and psychotherapy, Christians, Jews, and Buddhists may be fairly open to seeking assistance from mental health professionals. Muslims and Hindus are more likely to seek assistance from family members; adherents of these faiths tend to eschew mental health professionals. But there are many exceptions. In general, it appears that the level to which a person is devout or orthodox is a stronger predictor of whether or not he or she will seek out professional mental health services than is specific religious affiliation. Religiously devout or orthodox individuals tend to distrust secular mental health professionals and underutilize their services (Worthington, 1986, 1988).

Table 14.1 provides some general insights and guidelines for working with clients from the five world religious traditions that have been discussed. Therapists should keep in mind that these guidelines may not apply to all religious clients. Often spiritual and religious beliefs and practices interact with other aspects of diversity. Indeed, it is sometimes difficult to distinguish spiritual from cultural influences because religious traditions and spiritual beliefs have shaped many aspects of culture across the globe (Inglehart & Baker, 2000). Furthermore, many world cultures integrate religion across most aspects of their society, including politics, education, and health treatment. As with all good multicultural counseling and therapy, the unique beliefs and characteristics of each individual client must be assessed and kept in mind during treatment. For more detailed information about how the beliefs and traditions of specific religious denominations may influence the process of psychotherapy, we encourage readers to consult the following sources: *Handbook of Psychotherapy and Religious Diversity* (Richards & Bergin, 2000), *Handbook of Religion and Mental Health* (Koenig, 1998), *Working with Religious Issues in Counseling* (Lovinger, 1984), and *Religion and Counseling: The Psychological Impact of Religious Belief* (Lovinger, 1990). Many other recent books, book chapters, and articles about the interface of psychotherapy and spirituality

TABLE 14.1 *Clinical Issues and Guidelines for Working with Religious Clients*

1. Devout or orthodox members of most religious traditions tend to have negative perceptions of the mental health professions, distrust therapists, and underutilize mental health services. Building trust may be an added therapeutic challenge for such clients.

2. Learning about a client's religious tradition is essential to building a trusting therapeutic relationship. Immersing oneself experientially in the religious culture will help therapists better understand their clients and may increase their credibility with clients and religious leaders.

3. A wide variety of clinical issues may be intertwined or connected in some way with clients' religious and spiritual beliefs (e.g., sexuality, divorce and remarriage, authority figure issues, guilt and shame, perfectionism, alcohol and drug use, abortion, gender roles). To most effectively help religious clients work through such issues, considerable acumen in clients' religious beliefs and cultures may be needed.

4. It is important for therapists to assess the degree of clients' identification and involvement with their religious tradition and to determine whether clients' religious beliefs and practices are normative for that faith and are being used in healthy or unhealthy ways.

5. Therapists must be careful to avoid pathologizing cultural-religious differences and to avoid using psychological or spiritual assessment measures that do so.

6. A variety of psychological and spiritual interventions may be appropriate with religious clients, depending on the client, the nature of the problem, and the therapist's religious affiliation. It is essential for therapists to avoid interventions that conflict with normative religious beliefs.

7. All religious and spiritual traditions encourage their members to engage in a variety of spiritual practices and traditions that presume to have health benefits (e.g., prayer, meditation, forgiveness, worship and ritual, fasting, service, abstinence from alcohol and illegal drugs). Therapists may find that such practices can serve as therapeutic resources or interventions during therapy to promote coping and healing.

8. When working with religious clients, it can be beneficial to consult with their religious leaders, as long as this is done appropriately and with the client's permission.

These guidelines were distilled from the following source: Richards, P. S., & Bergin, A. E. Religious diversity and psychotherapy: Conclusions, recommendations, and future directions (pp. 469–489). In P. S. Richards & A. E. Bergin (Eds.) (2000). *Handbook of psychotherapy and religious diversity,* Washington, DC: American Psychological Association.

are also available (e.g., Elkins, 1995; Epstein, 1995; Faiver, Ingersoll, O'Brien, & McNally, 2001; Griffith & Griffith, 2002; Hedayat-Diba, 2000; Helminiak, 1996; Kelly, 1995; Miller, 1999; Rabinowitz, 2001; Rubin, 1996; Shafranske, 1996; Sharma, 2000; Sperry, 2001; Swinton, 2001; Vaughan, Wittine, & Walsh, 1996; West, 2000).

Conclusion

We recognize that it is impossible to do justice to the topic of religious and spiritual diversity in just one chapter, or even an entire volume. We have given just a brief general introduction to this topic. We hope that counselors and therapists will seek out additional information and training to enhance their competency in religious and spiritual aspects of diversity. The references at the end of this chapter provide a good foundation for further reading. We hope that readers will also look for opportunities to attend classes on world religions, along with continuing education workshops on religious and spiritual issues in counseling and psychotherapy. Seeking out instructors and supervisors who have interest and competency in this domain can also be extremely valuable. The *Psychology of Religion* Division (Division 36) of the American Psychological Association and the *Association for Spiritual, Ethical and Values Issues in Counseling* of the American Counseling Association are two professional associations that can provide resources for students and professionals who are newly acquainted with this domain of practice and scholarship.

Professional journals dedicated to the interface of religion and spirituality with psychology which can be helpful to scholars and practitioners include the *International Journal for the Psychology of Religion, Journal of Psychology and Theology, Counseling and Values, Journal for the Scientific Study of Religion, Mental Health, Religion and Culture,* and the *Review of Religious Research.* Several organizations are dedicated to research and education regarding the interface of religion, spirituality, science, and health, including the International Center for the Integration of Health and Spirituality (ICIHS: *www.icihs.org*) (formerly National Institute for Healthcare Research) and the John Templeton Foundation (*www.templeton.org*). The Center for the Study of World Religions at Harvard University (*www.hds.harvard.edu/cswr*) is also an important resource for professionals wishing to increase their understanding of religious aspects of diversity.

Finally, and perhaps most importantly, we hope that counselors and therapists will let their clients teach them about religious and spiritual aspects of diversity. As a mental health professional sincerely communicates a willingness to humbly listen and learn about their clients' spiritual beliefs, the clients will teach them much. In learning from clients, counselors will often gain insight into how clients' their religious beliefs and their community influence them, in both positive and negative ways. Counselors may also better understand how clients' faith and spirituality can be used as a therapeutic resource to assist them in coping and healing.

References

American Counseling Association (ACA) (1995). *Code of ethics and standards of practice.* Alexandria, VA: Author.

American Psychological Association (APA) (1992). Ethical principles of psychologists and code of conduct. *American Psychologist, 47,* 1597–1611.

Barrett, D. B., & Johnson, T. M. (1998). Religion: World religious statistics. In *Encyclopedia Britannica book of the year* (p. 314). Chicago: Encyclopedia Britannica, Inc.

Bedell, K. B. (1997). *Yearbook of American and Canadian churches.* Nashville, TN: Abingdon Press.

Benson, H. (1996). *Timeless healing: The power and biology of belief.* New York: Scribner.

Eck, D. L. (Ed.) (1997a). Judaism: U.S. timeline [CD-ROM]. In *On common ground: world religions in America.* New York: Columbia University Press.

Eck, D. L. (Ed.) (1997b). Islam: U.S. timeline [CD-ROM]. In *On common ground: world religions in America.* New York: Columbia University Press.

Eck, D. L. (Ed.) (1997c). Hinduism: U.S. timeline [CD-ROM]. In *On common ground: world religions in America.* New York: Columbia University Press.

Eck, D. L. (Ed.) (1997d). Buddhism: U.S. timeline [CD-ROM]. In *On common ground: world religions in America.* New York: Columbia University Press.

Elkins, D. N. (1995). Psychotherapy and spirituality: Toward a theory of the soul. *Journal of Humanistic Psychology, 35,* 78–98.

Epstein, M. (1995). *Thoughts without a thinker: Psychotherapy from a Buddhist perspective.* New York: Basis Books.

Faiver, C., Ingersoll, R. E., O'Brien, E., McNally, C. (2001). *Explorations in counseling and spirituality.* Belmont, CA: Wadsworth Group.

Fukuyama, M., & Sevig, T. (1999). *Integrating spirituality into multicultural counseling.* Thousand Oaks, CA: Sage.

Gallup, G. (1995). *The Gallup poll: Public opinion in 1995.* Wilmington, DE: Scholarly Resources.

Griffith, J. L., & Griffith, M. E. (2002). *Encountering the sacred in psychotherapy: How to talk with people about their spiritual lives.* New York: Guilford Press.

Helminiak, D. A. (1996). *The human core of spirituality: Mind as psyche and spirit.* Albany: State University of New York Press.

Hedayat-Diba, Z. (2000). Psychotherapy with Muslims. (pp. 289–314) In P. S. Richards & A. E. Bergin (Eds.), *Handbook of psychotherapy and religious diversity* (pp. 289–314). Washington, DC: American Psychological Association.

Hoge, D. R. (1996). Religion in America: The demographics of belief and affiliation. In E. P. Shafranske (Ed.), *Religion and the clinical practice of psychology* (pp. 21–41). Washington, DC: American Psychological Association.

Ibrahim, F. A. (1985). Effective cross-cultural counseling and psychotherapy: A framework. *The Counseling Psychologist, 13,* 625–683.

Kelly, E. W. (1995). *Religion and spirituality in counseling and psychotherapy.* Richmond, VA: American Counseling Association.

Larson, D. B., Swyers, J. P., & McCullough, M. E. (1997). *Scientific research on spirituality and health: A consensus report.* Rockville, MD: National Insitute for Healthcare Research.

Lovinger, R. J. (1984). *Working with religious issues in therapy.* Northwale, NJ: Jason Aronson.

Lovinger, R. J. (1990). *Religion and counseling: The psychological impact of religious belief.* New York: Continuum.

Melton, J. G. (1996). *Encyclopedia of American religions.* Detroit, MI: Gale Research.

Miller, W. R. (1999). *Integrating spirituality into treatment: Resources for practitioners.* Washington, DC: American Psychological Association.

Rabinowitz, A. (2001). *Judasim and psychology: Meeting points.* New York: Jason Aronson.

Richards, P. S., & Bergin, A. E. (1997). *A spiritual strategy for counseling and psychotherapy.* Washington, DC: American Psychological Association.

Richards, P. S., & Bergin, A. E. (Eds.) (2000). *Handbook of psychotherapy and religious diversity.* Washington, DC: American Psychological Association.

Richards, P. S., & Bergin, A. E. (Eds.) (In press). *Spiritual strategy case studies.* Washington, D.C.: American Psychological Association.

Rogers, C. R. (1961). *On becoming a person.* Boston: Houghton Mifflin.

Rubin, J. B. (1996). *Psychotherapy and Buddhism: Toward an integration.* New York: Plenum Press.

Shafranske, E. P. (Ed.) (1996). *Religion and the clinical practice of psychology.* Washington, DC: American Psychological Association.

Shafranske, E. P., & Malony, H. N. (1996). Religion and the clinical practice of psychology: A case for inclusion. In E. P. Shafranske (Ed.), *Religion and the clinical practice of psychology* (pp. 561–586). Washington, DC: American Psychological Association.

Sharma, A. R. (2000). Psychotherapy with Hindus. In P. S. Richards & A. E. Bergin (Eds.), *Handbook of psychotherapy and religious diversity* (pp. 341–365). Washington, DC: American Psychological Association.

Smart, N. (1994). *Religions of the west.* Englewood Cliffs, NJ: Prentice Hall.

Smart, N. (1983). *Worldviews: Cross-cultural explorations of human beliefs.* New York: Charles Scribner's Sons.

Sperry, L. (2001). *Spirituality in clinical practice: Incorporating the spiritual dimension in psychotherapy and counseling.* Philadelphia, PA: Runner-Routledge.

Sue, D. W., & Sue, D. (1999). *Counseling the culturally different: Theory and practice* (3rd ed.). New York: Wiley.

Sue, D. W., Bergnier, J. E., Duran, A., Feinberg, L., Pedersen, P., Smith, E., & Vasquez-Nuttall, E. (1982). Position paper: Cross-cultural counseling competencies. *The Counseling Psychologist, 10,* 45–52.

Sue, S., Zane, N., & Young, K. (1994). Research on psychotherapy with culturally diverse populations. In A. E. Bergin & S. L. Garfield (Eds.), *Handbook of psychotherapy and behavior change* (pp. 783–817). New York: Wiley.

Swinton, J. (2001). *Spirituality and mental health care.* London, England: Jessica Kingsley Publishers.

The World Almanac and Book of Facts 1998. (1998). Manwah, NJ: World Almanac Books.

Wright, J. W. (Ed.). (1997). *The universal almanac.* Kansas City: Andrews and McMeel.

Vaughan, F., Wittine, B., & Walsh, R. (1996). Transpersonal psychology and the religious person. In E. Shafranske (Ed.), *Religion and the clinical practice of psychology* (pp. 483–509). Washington, DC: American Psychological Association.

West, W. (2000). *Psychotherapy and spirituality: Crossing the line between therapy and religion.* London, England: Sage Publications.

Worthington, E. L. Jr. (1986). Religious counseling: A review of published empirical research. *Journal of Counseling and Development, 64,* 421–431.

Worthington, E. L. Jr. (1988). Understanding the religious values of clients: A model and its application to counseling. *Journal of Counseling Psychology, 35,* 166–174.

Worthington, E. L. Jr., Kurusu, T. A., McCullough, M. E., & Sanders, S. J. (1996). Empirical research on religion and psychotherapeutic processes and outcomes: A ten-year review and research prospectus. *Psychological Bulletin, 119,* 448–487.

Wulf, D. M. (1991). *Psychology of religion: Classic and contemporary views.* New York: Wiley.

15

Understanding Classism to Effect Personal Change

William M. Liu
University of Iowa

Donald B. Pope-Davis
University of Notre Dame

When Sue, Arredondo, and McDavis (1992) delineated the multicultural counseling competencies, they intended for mental health professionals to examine and explore their own biases and worldviews. Particularly important was an understanding of worldviews, assumptions, and biases that could potentially conflict with those of clients from different cultural groups. Typically we understand cultural groups as based upon race, gender, sexual orientation, and age (Ponterotto, Casas, Suzuki, & Alexander, 1995). Consequently, much of the current literature on multicultural competency focuses on examining, for instance, one's racist, sexist, homophobic, and ableistic worldview in preparation for working with a diverse clientele (Pope-Davis, Liu, Toporek, & Brittan-Powell, 2001).

While issues of race and gender diversification provide compelling reasons to become culturally aware, one area of diversity has not been fully developed. Social class, although recognized as pervasive in many people's experience, seems to be the least understood and examined (Helms & Cook, 1999; Frable, 1997; Sue & Sue, 1999). As mental health professionals, we see issues of social class, and we describe these phenomena as poverty, inequality, and economic stratification. We even use social classes as descriptors for our clients: for example, "the client was from a middle-class family" or "she was a working-class woman." But what do we really mean when we describe someone as middle or working class? What do we communicate when we talk about poverty and inequality? How do our own experiences and socialization affect our interpretation and biases related to social class?

In order to understand social class and classism as they affect counseling, we will first discuss the need for a counselor to understand social class as a subjective cultural variable rather than a demographic descriptor. Next, the chapter will provide definitions of important constructs and introduce the Social Class Worldview Model (SCWM) (Liu, 2002; Liu, 2001a, 2001b; Liu, Soleck, Hopps, Dunston, & Pickett, 2001a, 2001b). Following the model, the authors will discuss the Modern Classism Theory (MCT) (Liu et al., 2001a) and the types and functions of classism (Liu, 2001a). Case examples and a training case will be used to illustrate all the theories.

Social Class in Counseling and Therapy

Social class is connected to many aspects of our practice and research. But the way social class operates in our profession is often skewed by a persistent "middle-class" bias that may distort our understanding of people who are not "middle-class" (Carter, 1991; Katz, 1985; Liu, 2001a, 2001b; Liu et al., 2001a, 2001b; Sue & Sue, 1999). One way research is biased, for example, is its frequent use of college samples (Buboltz, Miller, & Williams, 1999; Fitzgerald & Betz, 1994), even though 81 percent of the population in the United States have only a high school educational (Census Bureau, 2001). Further complicating our understanding of social class is the infrequent connection of social class with classism, even though the two are intimately connected (Liu et al., 2001b). Hence social class and classism remain confusing and elusive as therapy issues (Frable, 1997).

Although the professional discourse regarding social class is limited, attempts have been made to understand people of various social class groups. Typically, our attempts center on classifying people and discussing issues we believe salient for a particular group. But as we discuss social class, what does it mean to talk about clients as "middle class" or "lower class?" Usually when we describe another person as being from a particular social class, we are communicating a number of assumptions. First, we assume that everyone agrees on what makes up each social class and that everyone can identify the same or similar characteristics of "middle" or "lower class." Second, we imply that people who are part of a social class tend to see the world similarly. For example, all middle-class people have the same values about lifestyles, politics, and religion. Third, we assume that these social class groups are similar, regardless of geography or context (Liu, 2001b; Liu et al., in press, 2001b). Adding to this confusion is the use of a social class framework that sometimes focuses on class exploitation, other times on lifestyles and life chances (e.g., McLoyd, 1998).

But the most salient problem in our understanding of social class is the use of stratification. Essentially, stratification entails measuring a person's income, education, and occupational type and level and from these indices placing the person into a corresponding social class group. From here, people are assumed to be similar to others in their social class group, and variation within the group is seldom explored. When within-group variation is explored, the stratification approach is employed again, but the result is usually additional striations within a social class group, such as upper-middle-class, lower-working-middle-class, and so on. But the problems of the stratification approach persist.

This stratification approach is problematic because it cannot fully explain classism and stratification behaviors that occur in environments where income, education, and occupation are not relevant (Liu, 2001a, 2001b; Liu et al., in press). For instance, children can exhibit stratification behaviors and strategies and can practice classism by ostracizing other children based on style of shoes or brand of shirt (Liu, 2001b; Liu et al., 2001a). Adult prison inmates often create their own stratification and status system based on small material objects (e.g., cigarettes) or privileges (Phillips, 2001). Consequently, a stratification approach based on indices relevant to unincarcerated individuals cannot explain the classism and stratification that exists in these environments.

Health psychology literature suggests that the way people cope with their environment has much to do with their eventual recovery from life stressors (e.g., homelessness or poor health) (Crespo, Smit, Andersen, Carter-Pokras, & Ainsworth, 2000; Ostrove, Adler, Kuppermann, & Washington, 2000). For example, a study by Ingram, Corning, and Schmidt (1996) that examined homeless and low-income women found that 14 percent of these women did not consider themselves to be homeless because they were not living on the streets, even though they were in homeless shelters. Thus, even though they were considered impoverished, the different worldviews of their condition led to different conceptualizations of their resources and different ways of coping with their environmental stress. In a study which examined 157 White women, subjective social class status was "consistently and strongly related to psychological functioning and health-related factors (self-rated health, heart rate, sleep latency, body fat distribution, and cortisol habituation to repeated stress)" (Adler, Epel, Castellazzo, & Ickovics, 2000, p. 586).

Finally, stratification cannot explain relationships people seek out as part of their social class, cannot explain the feelings that arise from social class situations or relationships, and cannot explain classism. Hence, a subjective worldview of social class may be able to account for within-group variation and to explain how people within a "social class" cope with their environment. As an example of the implications of the principles mentioned in this section, consider the following:

Typical intake notes and descriptive information about clients include the client's current job or educational status and his or her parents' and siblings' job and educational status. What does this information tell a counselor aside from job type and educational attainment? Does a counselor understand better the social class pressures of a client? Does the counselor comprehend how the client copes with internalized classism? What about the client's debt and credit history? How would all this information be used to understand the client better?

The Need for a Subjective Approach to Understanding Social Class

In response to the need for a theoretical model to understand subjective social class experiences and explore within-group variability, Liu (2002, 2001a, 2001b; Liu et al., in press) has developed the Social Class Worldview Model (SCWM). Social class, in this theory, is defined as the inequalities that arise between people when individuals understand the economic expectations of their environment and behave to meet these demands. The premise of the SCWM is that people construct their social class environments based on their worldview and that this social class worldview in turn allows an individual to successfully live in his/her social class environment. Essentially, people's perceptions are their reality, and people respond accordingly. A major assumption of the SCWM is that people, because of their socialization experiences, will usually give different descriptions and criteria for what constitutes a particular class group. Furthermore, the SCWM is an attempt to theoretically link subjective social class with classism because the two are interdependent concepts, much like race and racism.

What Motivates People in Social Classes

One of the major limitations of the stratification approach is that people's reasons for behaving or thinking a certain way are not fully explored. Why do some people focus so much on achievement or on living in a big home while others seem to want a bohemian lifestyle? Why do some people who are from a wealthy background choose to live an impoverished lifestyle? Why do some people focus on buying the "right" clothes, and on speaking and acting a "certain way," and avoid people who may not fit their "upper-class image"? These multifaceted ways people behave are socially classed, but focusing on demographic indicators is insufficient.

One possible way to understand social class behaviors and attitudes is to first situate the person within a context. Different contexts place different social class expectations and demands upon people. Thus a perceived "middle-class" person from Manhattan, New York, will want a certain lifestyle, clothes, and attitude to remain like other middle-class New Yorkers. But a "middle-class" person from Los Angeles, California, may have different priorities, along with different choices in clothing and lifestyle. Even though these two individuals may be similar in income, education, and occupation, they exist within different "middle-class" contexts that place different demands and expectations upon them.

Case Example

Joe is a 37-year-old African American man who just received a job offer from a prestigious company that is headquartered in a rural area of the Midwest. He has spent much of his life in Boston, but is looking forward to his new job and position. But when he tells his friends of his upcoming move, they remark, "really?" His friends start questioning what his lifestyle will be without the conveniences and "excitement" of the city and what he will do without other middle-class African Americans around him. Rather than remain excited about the new position, Joe starts to question his decision, feels pressure to remain in Boston, and experiences increased distress over his upcoming move.

These various contexts can be considered economic cultures (Liu et al., in press). Economic cultures represent the "customs, values, traditions, products, and sociopolitical histories of the social group" (Helms, 1994, p. 292). These social class groups may exist in micro-environments such as neighborhoods, boroughs, towns, and smaller communities that exist within a larger *economic culture,* or macro-environment, such as a state or nation. For those in the United States, the value espoused by the *economic culture* that surrounds us is capitalism. In capitalism, people are constantly compelled to "keep up"—to find various ways to remain congruent with others in the "social class."

One way to "keep up" is through constantly accumulating resources that can be used in one's economic culture to maintain one's social class. In the SCWM, these resources do not correspond simply to money, but extend to the symbols of social class aside from "income." People cannot walk around with money attached to them to signify their "social class." They have to reflect their social class in other ways: clothing, lifestyle choices, work behavior, chosen associates, and social behavior. Moreover, in the world of credit cards income may not be a sufficient measure of one's monied status; hence, other ways to "perform" one's social class are employed.

According to the SCWM, because people seek symbols of social class that they can use within an economic culture to remain congruent, people may search out intangible resources that are linked to objective indices such as income. Resources that people look for can be defined as *capital.* In this theory, capital can be conceptualized as the resources an individual has access to use in achieving another stated goal (Liu, 2001b; Rose, 2000; Schmid, 2000). Capital is constantly sought after since the demands and expectations of an economic culture are always fluid. Hence Liu (2001a) suggests that capital is constantly being sought out and nurtured, to eventually be used within an individual's environment.

There are three types of capital that people possess and work to accrue and refine. First is social capital: the social connections, relationships, and human networks people have (Lin, 1999). This is the "who-you-know" factor. Second is human capital: the physical and intellectual capacities of people (Lin, 1999). This is the "what-you-know" factor. As some people quickly discover, finding good jobs sometimes depends more on "who you know" than "what you know." And third, cultural capital is the aesthetics or "taste" of people (Lin, 1999). For instance, when one is a part of an "upper-class" group, and within a certain economic culture, one should know what "good art" is and be able to critique other people's poorer tastes for their "lack of refinement." Because people live within these economic cultures and with these capital demands and expectations, they develop a certain way of seeing the world that helps them rationalize these demands and meet these expectations.

The Social Class Worldview

The social class worldview is essentially a lens people develop within an economic culture that helps them understand and negotiate their social class world. In general, the worldview is defined as a "pattern of beliefs, behaviors, and perceptions that are shared by a population based on similar socialization and life experiences" (Watts, 1994, p. 52–53). Within the SCWM, there are six domains, grouped into two dimensions. The first dimension is focused on what is expressed, the second dimension on social class socialization messages attended to by the individual. The domain of *Social Class Saliency, Consciousness, and Attitudes* represents an individual's capacity to articulate the relevance and significance of social class in his or her environment, to be aware of social class in his or her life, and to understand his or her feelings about social class. This domain serves to determine the saliency of the other domains in the SCWM.

This first dimension features the socialization messages attended to by the individual. This domain is called *Social Class Referent Groups.* The referent groups refer to the people (past, present, and future) in an individual's life who help guide the development of a Social Class Worldview, as well as steer behavior. Referent groups are (1) *Group of Origin,* which is the family environment that operated as an early social class socialization influence; (2) *Cohort or Peer Group,* the group that is similar to the individual in class-demographic characteristics, the group that helps the individual feel "average" or "middle"; and (3) *Group of Aspiration,* the social class group of which the individual wants to be a part, which may be "above" or "below" the individual.

This next dimension has three domains focused upon social class as expressed by the individual. First is *Social Class Lifestyle,* defined as how one chooses to organize time and resources, to remain congruent within one's economic culture. For instance, a social class lifestyle can reflect the choice in vacation destinations, the value of working at home, and potentially the choice of having children.

The second domain is *Social Class Behaviors,* or the instrumental actions that reinforce an individual's SCW. These are behaviors that a person participates in to perform "normally" within a particular socially classed environment. This may entail losing accents that are deemed lower class (i.e., southern accents), or this may mean acquiring and performing behaviors that one believes are congruent with a particular environment (e.g., table manners). Social class behaviors sometimes refer to the acquisition of behaviors that allow the person to exist within an environment without divulging his or her social class background (e.g., etiquette, table manners, social conversation). Racially, this is referred to as "passing": the capacity of an individual to exist and be treated within an environment as one of the "hosts" (i.e., White or middle-class) because the individual is externally valid (i.e., knows how to act and dress as other middle-class individuals) in that environment and is not perceived as an interloper (i.e., Black and lower-class).

Case Example of Social Class Behaviors

One of the most popular events held each semester through a minority student support office at a large east coast, predominantly White university was a program focused on etiquette. Racial minority students often reported after the event that having the knowledge about dining etiquette and accepted behavior for formal functions eased their anxieties about job interviews and other events requiring social protocol. Prior to this event, many of the students stated that they often avoided "formal" events and situations for fear of looking "foolish."

The third domain is *Property Relationships.* This domain is defined as the instrumental use of material objects as external representation of an individual's real or aspired social class. In this domain, material objects serve to "perform" the individual's social class worldview. For instance, some people choose an expensive pair of dress shoes to reflect their perceived social class, while others may opt for simple athletic shoes (e.g., Derber, 2000; Dittmar & Drury, 2000; Flouri, 1999; Fournier & Richins, 1991).

This SCWM is suggested as an alternative to the objective measures of social class and the problematic subjective measures of social class (e.g., asking participants what social class they are) (Liu, 2001b). The SCWM is a "snap-shot" of a person's perception of his/her economic culture, his/her social class worldview, and the strategies the individual uses to meet the demands of his/her economic culture. The intent was to provide researchers and clinicians an ability to assess the subjective experiences of social class and to describe the ways that people eventually create stratification and classism around them. Now with this heuristic model to understand the subjective experiences of social class and the ways that people construct social class around them, classism may be better understood.

What Is Classism?

Why would people act in classist ways? Why do we sometimes feel awkward and uneasy when we are not properly dressed for an event or situation? Why do we feel anxiety over which fork to use at a formal dinner? How are these thoughts and feelings related to classism?

Our position is that classism, within the SCWM, is essentially a social class strategy people use sometimes to maximize their opportunities to accumulate the valued capital within their economic culture. When an individual senses competition, feels threatened, or recognizes that his/her attempts to accumulate capital are frustrated, that person will exhibit classist behaviors as a means to make the demands of his/her economic culture more distinct and to rationalize (i.e., make sense of) these demands. However, if a person's social class strategies do not work within a situation and his/her attempts to accumulate capital are constantly frustrated, rather than continue with the strategy, that individual may start to feel failure and frustration. It is our position that people constantly fluctuate between homeostasis and feelings of classism (feelings of inadequacies). These feelings of "not-doing-enough" compel people to buy, spend, and act in various ways to meet the demands of their economic culture until they feel a state of homeostasis.

Because classism can exist in many ways, we do not assume that only elite or "wealthy" people can be classist. Rather, within the SCWM, classism can be manifested from "lower class," from "upper class," and among those of the same social class. Because there are other forms of classism that have not been explored, Liu et al. (in press) defined these various aspects of classism as part of a Modern Classism Theory (MCT). We are not arguing that all classism is similar or that everyone has the same power and ability to have their needs met. We recognize that people have different power in our society. However, if the full network of potential "classisms" is not examined, classism will continue to perpetuate itself.

In this theory, it is important to understand that people do not express and experience every type of classism. Instead, depending upon the saliency of a person's social class domains within his/her social class worldview, classism is experienced and expressed primarily through the most salient domains. Hence, the social class worldview may be considered a lens through which people understand and act upon their economic environment. The domains may be perceived as apertures on this lens from which people experience and perpetuate classism. Depending on our economic context, these apertures become wider or smaller and work to filter classism experiences.

Within the SCWM, there are four types of classism (Liu et al., 2001a): upward, downward, lateral, and internalized. We retain the notion of hierarchy (i.e., upward, downward, and lateral) only to reflect the sense that classism reinforces people's perception that there are others who are above, below, and like them in perceived class position.

Downward Classism

Downward classism consists of prejudicial attitudes and discriminatory behavior against people and groups that are perceived to be "below." An example of this type of classism may occur when one enters an upscale department store inappropriately dressed and is treated by the salespeople as unwanted or "invisible." For children, downward classism may occur if they attend school in worn-out shoes or faded clothing and are treated by other children as inferior.

For mental health professionals, one type of pernicious classism is that we may view clients who have little or no education or who hold menial jobs in a patronizing way. We may feel bad that they have to work "so hard" and in such "terrible" jobs. Sympathy is a form of downward classism in this theory. Similarly, Helms and Cook (1999) suggest that these feelings and attitudes are a form of *affluence guilt.* Counselors, especially in university settings, may be prone to reduce their feelings of guilt by over-engaging the custodial staff, initiating discussions with them as a way to allay anxieties stirred by feelings of guilt. Thus we may subtly reinforce the idea of class distinctions by trying to pretend that there are no class distinctions (Langston, 1995). As a "privileged" group, we can pretend that we do not accept class distinctions, which only serves to reinforce our privilege. We also may communicate the assumption that "good" occupations are white collar and do not involve physical tasks.

Upward Classism

Upward classism is defined as prejudice and discrimination directed toward those who are believed to be of a "higher social class." Describing someone as a "snob," "elitist," "spoiled," "wasteful," or "hedonistic" are typical examples of upward classist remarks. The upward classist may speculate that someone's achievement is based on a background of privilege and thus the person's accomplishments have not been earned by hard work and effort (Cherulnik & Bayless, 1986; Crocker & Blanten, 1999; Loch, Humberman, & Stout, 2000; Mudrack, 1997).

In mental health professionals, upward classism may be triggered when working with clients who are perceived to be from an upper-class environment. We may tend to minimize, distort, or de-legitimize their issues and concerns. This may be especially salient for counselors who are first-generation college graduates or who had financial difficulty completing their post-secondary and graduate degrees. Counselors who perceive themselves as having had to struggle harder than their clients may minimize the saliency of those clients' issues.

Lateral Classism

Lateral classism may be more difficult to interpret and understand if one retains the notion of classism as only a dichotomous use of power (up and down). Lateral classism can be defined as classist attitudes and behaviors among people perceived to be of a similar social class. This is often an attempt to render divergent individuals' SCW back into alignment with that of others in the perceived social class group. If an individual does not have a SCW that is congruent with that of others who are perceived to be in the group, classism can produce behaviors and attitudes that seek to re-mold and reshape the SCW into congruency with others of that economic culture.

For mental health professionals, lateral classism may appear subtly as reinforcing a particular worldview without challenging the assumptions behind that worldview. For instance, if a White middle-class man were to talk about needing to do things on his own (i.e., autonomy and independence), a counselor or therapist might not challenge this idea since it might fit readily into his/her own social class worldview. Another form of lateral classism may be a counselor who uses certain phrases or words, and when the client says that he/she is unfamiliar with a particular term or phrase, the counselor will retort, "You mean you don't know that?" These attitudes and behaviors reinforce a particular SCW within a certain economic culture.

Internalized Classism

Internalized classism erupts when an individual is unable to meet the demands and expectations of his or her economic culture (Liu et al., in press). The person's social class strategies may continually fail to produce the necessary capital for the economic culture, and he or she may eventually internalize feelings of depression, sadness, anger, frustration, and despair. Or the individual may be fearful that he or she will be exposed as "not really a part" of a particular economic culture (e.g., middle class) and be marginalized, thereby frustrating the person's attempts at accumulating the valued capital.

For instance, Granfield's (1991) study of lower and working-class law students at a prestigious law school highlighted the feelings of inadequacy, alienation, and anxiety students had in this privileged environment. While they typically were able to "pass" as "middle and upper class," the underlying realization that this fantasy could be shattered created feelings of anxiety as well as resentment. Internalized classism can be elicited by the most innocuous of questions. Croizet and Claire (1998) conducted a study of social class-based stereotype threats. That is people who fit into a widely known stereotype and are fearful of fulfilling this stereotype, when activated, tend to fulfill the stereotypes (e.g., Steele, & Aronson, 1995). Participants in the stereotype threat condition were asked about their parents' occupation and educational level, while those in the non-social class threat condition were asked to provide some detail about their town (Croizet & Claire, 1998). This simple manipulation of asking about parents' occupation and educational level activated for some their own notions of shame based on internalized classism, which worked to depress their scores when compared to the higher scores of the non-social class threat participants. Hence in research endeavors where they attempt to assess for social class status, researchers may instead be inviting social class stereotype threat into the study.

The Operation of the Social Class Worldview
and Modern Classism Theory

With all three parts of the social class theory in place, we will describe the hypothetical operation of these constructs. Essentially there are three levels of social class that operate together (see Figure 15.1). First, the individual operates within a context or economic culture. Second, from the economic culture, with its demands and expectations, people create a social class worldview that is congruent with those expectations. This social class worldview helps individuals make sense of their economic culture and accumulate the valued capital to use within their economic culture. The third level of social class is the individual's strategies to accumulate capital. When the individual feels threatened or in competition, classism is used to maximize his or her capital accumulation. If capital is successfully accumulated, then homeostasis is achieved; however, if capital accumulation is frustrated repeatedly, then internalized classism may erupt.

What to Do about Classism in Training

Now that we have a basic sense of how social class and classism function together, our discussion turns toward training issues for mental health professionals. Some counselors' experiences with classism can result in deep injuries that have yet to be articulated. Contributing to the difficulty in exploring classist experiences is the fact that we have little language that can illuminate these injuries. Damaging classist experiences could have been childhood or adolescent taunts about clothing, hairstyle, or summer vacation. In adults, classism can appear as feelings of shame and inadequacy over high debt and credit card bills, the type of car one drives, an inability to eat at a formal dining setting, or limited knowledge about stocks and investing.

Classism is sometimes objectively identifiable: for instance, when someone who is "rich" or "wealthy" denies or discriminates against someone in poverty. While these situations should be identified and fought by multiculturalists interested in social justice, there are other forms of classism that may appear as racism or sexism. Without an understanding of how classism functions, focusing only on the racist or sexist aspects of oppression leaves much of the problem unidentified.

Already we have discussed the various forms of classism that can exist among people. To take this understanding one step further, we would like to explore the complexities of classism interrelated with other "isms": "White-Trashism" will be explored as one example of this intersection.

The Intersection of Class and Race—"White-Trashism"

For some White counselors, classism and shame may be an issue with which they are struggling and which they need to articulate. In some training situations, we have heard the seemingly automatic use of the term "White-trash" to denote certain White clients and their lifestyle. The laughter that sometimes follows is confusing since we are not sure if this laughter is specifically a statement of classism or is a deflection by students who may identify with that term and feel anxious. Challenging the use of the term typically is met with defensive statements such as "I didn't mean it that way" or "You know what I mean." When the speaker is asked to identify what makes someone "White-trash," "trailer-park trash," "a hillbilly," or a "red-neck," his or her social class worldview is revealed. Interestingly, in our experience students who subscribe to this stereotype focus on different aspects of what makes up "White-trash." It could be lifestyle, choice of clothing, choice of music,

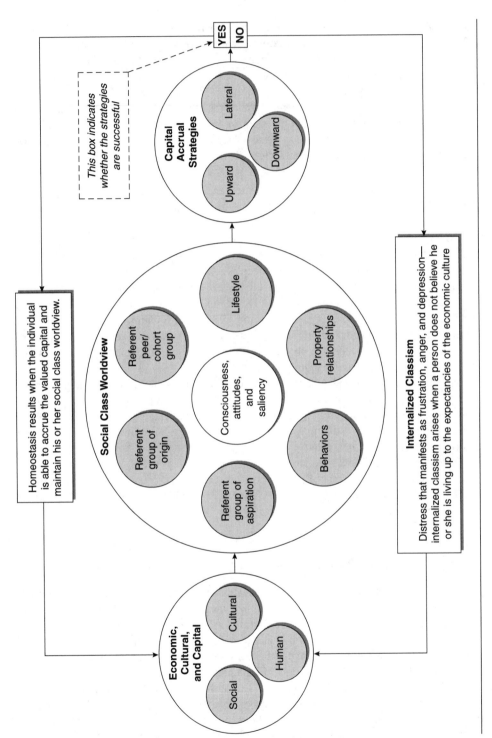

FIGURE 15.1

taste in art, criminal behavior, leisure activities, educational level, or language, to name a few. Also "White-trashism" may be manifest in physical ways, such as obesity (which is considered by some to be a form of gluttony or an anathema to the Protestant Work Ethic) or the "farmer's tan" (which is a partial tan acquired through labor as compared to an all-body tan which is a symbol of leisure). Yet what is unrecognized by those who use the term and imply these identifying features, along with this scornful attitude, is the deep hurt some students have when labeled as "White-trash" (hooks, 2000; Wray & Newitz, 1997), as well as the deleterious and offensive nature of such stereotypes and language.

Typically, "White-trashism" is a stereotype perpetuated by "middle-class" individuals, regardless of race. The use of this term is directed towards those who are unlike the speaker. Sometimes it is used as a form of downward classism, but sometimes it is used as a form of lateral classism. The stereotype is used as a threat to force realignment of a social class worldview held by an individual who may be exhibiting "non-middle-class" attitudes or behaviors. Hence saying to someone "that's so White-trashy" is a reminder that the given behavior, taste, or attitude is incongruent with that of others of the same economic culture. Even though most students have a sense that this descriptor is derogatory, they are unsure of how to decipher the multiple "isms" involved.

One final example of classism is found in the use of language. Language can be a way of differentiating between those who are perceived to be of a lower class and those of a higher class (Argyle, 1994; Giles & Copeland, 1991; Tyler, 1989). One particular way class may be distinguished is by accents. We have encountered, in our classes and in other settings, individuals who will mimic a "southern" accent or drawl to connote "backwardness" or "stupidity." The automaticity of such behavior for some reveals the separation that may exist between racist and classist behavior. It is our speculation that in any other setting, it is unlikely that individuals would mimic an "African American" language style, since it is easily identifiable and labeled as racist. However, it seems that when it comes to "whiteness" and classism, mimicking "southern drawl" is sometimes acceptable and, unfortunately, unchallenged. In these incidences, it is important to stop conversations and call the offensiveness to the attention of the speaker. The discourse then can focus on the covert assumptions and biases the individual may harbor. Connecting these behaviors to other forms of racism may help individuals understand how these unconscious attitudes may be transmitted in counseling and psychotherapy.

Case Example

In an introduction to a multicultural counseling course, racial minority students discussed their experiences with racism. In their discussion, they often referred to White perpetrators as "White-trash." Because the instructor had presented early in the semester about "White-trashism" as a form of racism, other students were willing to challenge the speakers' inferences and explore the speakers' own racism.

Implications for Training

When a framework is provided to understand how classism and other forms of oppression intersect, students can often start to explore their own biases and the history of these behaviors with others. In training, students can be encouraged to examine their own social class worldview and their perceptions of others. A teacher should encourage dialogue among students to help them understand various socialization experiences and the criteria by which they identify different social class groups. Explore the social class fears that students have: Are they anxious about describing their "working-class background;" their lack of knowledge about art, culture, or investment; or the shame they harbor about "being found out"?

One could also focus on understanding how social class, financial issues, and money were discussed and negotiated in families. What types of messages did the students receive about investment, education, money, and trusting other people with their money? Was money always a matter of contention in their family of origin? What are some key moments that they remember connecting money and social class in their upbringing? Have they ever experienced upward, downward, lateral, and internalized classism? The answers to all these questions are just as important as understanding one's racist and sexist experiences and socialization. Connecting all three potentially can provide counselors and therapists a framework to understand what their social class worldview is and what they bring into therapy. To illustrate how social class can be used in training, a brief case study will be used.

How to Help Clients Experiencing Classism

Liu and Rasheed (2002) suggest that in helping clients understand their classism, it is imperative that a common language be developed between the client and counselor. For some clients who feel distress, anxiety, frustration, or anger about their economic situation, it may be difficult to explore how these feelings are connected to their experiences. Additionally, as Croizet and Claire (1998) have identified, clients may be very reluctant or ashamed to discuss income and education levels. Thus it is important that counselors and clients develop a language that minimizes the client's potential social-class-based stereotype threat and anxieties. To start the client's exploration and understanding, counselors and therapists should use the theory in a three-step process. The first step is to explore the client's perceptions about his/her economic context and the various demands expected of him or her. The second step is to explore the client's social class worldview and help the client identify which domain is the most salient to him or her. Finally, the third step is to explore the client's experiences with classism.

Throughout the discussions with the client, it is important for the counselor or therapist to start the discussions around economic issues such as debt and the feelings surrounding the client's debt (e.g., credit card debt, student loans, etc.). Counselors should recognize that shame is a large part of classism and help the client connect experiences with affect. Finally, work with the client to develop a plan of action to change one aspect of his/her current situation.

Case Example

Lauren is a 27-year-old White woman, currently in the second year of her counseling doctoral program. She has been working with a female White college student who is struggling with issues of transition to the university. During the fourth session, the client starts to talk about her problems making friends, her feelings of awkwardness in social situations, and her sense of "not fitting in." Lauren, normally a humanistic-Rogerian counselor, even with the most difficult of clients, suddenly tells the client what she should do to overcome her "transition" problems. The supervisor, recognizing that this advice is atypical of Lauren's usual supportive stance, focuses on this issue in supervision. Using the SCWM and MCT, the supervisor is able to understand Lauren's issues in therapy.

Exploring Lauren's perception of her economic culture, in this case the university and the graduate program, the supervisor learns that Lauren has always felt somewhat marginal in this context. Lauren grew up in a lower-working-class environment, was the first and only child in her family to attend college, and constantly struggles between developing professional relationships (social capital) and studying for her classes (human capital). She is "nervous" in social situations because she does not know how to act or what to talk about (cultural capital). In understanding Lauren's social class worldview, the supervisor comes to understand that Lauren's worldview is oriented toward being a licensed therapist (group of aspiration) and toward her classmates (peer/cohort group), since her family is unfamiliar with collegiate demands and expectations. She also focuses on doing research activities and on teaching, things she enjoys and visualizes as part of her future career (lifestyle). She pays little attention to social class behaviors and property relationships, and she has some awareness that her experiences are much different from those of her family (consciousness, attitudes, and saliency). She sees herself as a "self-starter" who relies on no one else for her successes. Her peers see her as ambitious and tenacious in regards to her career goals.

When probed about her atypical behavior with the client, Lauren says that she feels sympathy (i.e., downward classism) for the client, since she has had many of the same experiences. Because many of her undergraduate peer group were from a middle-class background, while she was from a lower working class, she had internalized the stereotype of "White-trash" and was always afraid people would find out about her real background. In fact, she wore only long-sleeved blouses for a year and a half for fear that others would tease her about her "farmer's tan"—a "dead giveaway" about her rural and working class background. She "over-identified" with the client's situation and knew that no one else would provide this client with the strategies necessary to survive in college. Consequently, Lauren has taken it upon herself to dictate specific behaviors and attitudes the client needs to have to survive and succeed in college.

Once Lauren is able to see that her sympathy, pity, and over-identification with the client manifests as "maternal" behavior, she is able to discuss some of the social class injuries she has endured throughout her life and to identify how these shaming events have shaped her current ambition. Lauren can also identify her mix of feelings and thoughts in session as protective rather than supportive. Practicing with the supervisor and developing a plan of action, Lauren develops some statements that she can use to help the client frame her social class experiences and understand the classist pressures around her. Lauren also feels supported in describing some of her own classist and social class experiences and in acknowledging how she successfully negotiated college.

Conclusion

As we discuss the importance of internalizing the principles and ideology of multiculturalism, it is imperative that we also understand all of the biases and distortions we may harbor. Much has been written about the need to explore our racist, sexist, and homophobic biases, to name a few, but not much has been provided that helps us understand our classism. Because social class is such a pervasive construct in people's lives, classism is an important form of oppression to understand.

While the extant literature in counseling and psychology is relatively vacant of social class theories and of ways to understand classism, this chapter attempted to provide readers with (1) an understanding of why we need to explore the subjective experiences of social class and (2) a way of illuminating how classism functions. The intent has been to provide counselors and therapists a means to discover how classism has shaped their own social class worldview and how counselors may unconsciously create classism and stratification around them. Because classism experiences can often be painful and shaming, it is important that mental health professionals have a tool to articulate these experiences. With such a tool, it is hoped that counselors and therapists will in turn help clients to explore their own classism experiences as well.

References

Adler, N. E., Epel, E. S., Castellazzo, G., & Ickovics, J. R. (2000). Relationship of subjective and objective social status with psychological and physiological functioning: Preliminary data in healthy white women. *Health Psychology, 19,* 586–592.

Argyle, M. (1994). *The psychology of class.* New York: Routledge Press.

Buboltz, W. C., Jr., Miller, M., & Williams, D. J. (1999). Content analysis of research in the *Journal of Counseling Psychology* (1973–1998). *Journal of Counseling Psychology, 46,* 496–503.

Carter, R. T. (1991). Cultural values: A review of empirical research and implications for counseling. *Journal of Counseling and Development, 70,* 164–173.

Census Bureau (2001). *Census 2000 supplementary survey profile for the United States* [On-line]. Available: www.census.gov/c2s/www/Products/Profiles/2000/Tabular/C2SSTable2/01000US.htm.

Cherulnik, P. D., & Bayless, J. K. (1986). Person perception in environmental context: The influence of residential settings on impressions of their occupants. *The Journal of Social Psychology, 126,* 667–673.

Crespo, C. J., Smit, E., Andersen, R. E., Carter-Pokras, O., & Ainsworth, B. E. (2000). Race/ethnicity, social class and their relation to physical inactivity during leisure time: Results from the Third National Health and Nutrition Examination Survey, 1988–1994. *American Journal of Preventive Medicine, 18* (1), 46–53.

Crocker, J., & Blanten, H. (1999). Social inequality and self-esteem: The moderating effects of social comparison, legitimacy, and contingencies of self-esteem. In T. R. Tyler, R. M. Kramer, & O. P. John (Eds.), *The Psychology of the social self* (pp. 171–191). New Jersey: Lawrence Earlbaum Associates.

Croizet, J. C., & Claire, T. (1998). Extending the concept of stereotype threat to social class: The intellectual underperformance of students from low socioeconomic backgrounds. *Personality and Social Psychology Bulletin, 24,* 588–594.

Derber, C. (2000). *The pursuit of attention: Power and ego in everyday life.* New York: Oxford University Press.

Dittmar, H., & Drury, J. (2000). Self-image—is it in the bag? A qualitative comparison between "ordinary" and "excessive" consumers. *Journal of Economic Psychology, 21,* 109–142.

Fitzgerald, L. F., & Betz, N. E. (1994). Career development in a cultural context: The role of gender, race, class, and sexual orientation. In M. L. Savikas & R. W. Lent (Eds.), *Convergence in career development theories* (pp. 103–117). Palo Alto, CA: CPP Books.

Flouri, E. (1999). An integrated model of consumer materialism: Can economic socialization and maternal values predict materialistic attitudes in adolescents? *Journal of Socio-Economics, 28,* 707–724.

Fournier, S., & Richins, M. L. (1991). Some theoretical and popular notions concerning materialism. *Journal of Social Behavior and Personality, 6,* 403–414.

Frable, D. E. S. (1997). Gender, racial, ethnic, sexual, and class identities. *Annual Review of Psychology, 48,* 139–162.

Giles, H., & Copeland, N. (1991). *Language contexts and consequences.* Milton Keynes, UK: Open University Press.

Granfield, R. (1991). Making it by faking it: Working-class students in an elite academic environment. *Journal of Contemporary Ethnography, 20,* 331–351.

Helms, J. E. (1994). The conceptualization of racial identity and other "racial" constructs. In E. J. Trickett, R. J. Watts, & D. Birman (Eds.), *Human diversity: Perspectives of people in context* (pp. 185–311). San Francisco: Jossey-Bass.

Helms, J. E., & Cook, D. A. (1999). *Using race and culture in counseling and psychotherapy: Theory and process.* Boston, MA: Allyn and Bacon.

hooks, b. (2000). *Where we stand: Class matters.* New York: Routledge Press.

Ingram, K. M., Corning, A. F., & Schmidt, L. D. (1996). The relationship of victimization experiences to psychological well-being among homeless women and low-income housed women. *Journal of Counseling Psychology, 43,* 218–227.

Katz, J. H. (1985). The sociopolitical nature of counseling. *The Counseling Psychologist, 13,* 615–624.

Langston, D. (1995). Tired of playing monopoly? In M. L. Andersen & P. H. Collins (Eds.), *Race, class, and gender: An anthology* (2nd ed.) (pp. 100–109). New York: Wadsworth Publishing.

Lin, N. (1999). Social networks and status attainment. *Annual Review of Sociology, 25,* 467–487.

Liu, W. M. (2002). The socially classed experiences of men: Integrating theory and practice. *Professional Psychology: Research and Practice, 33,* pp. 355–360.

Liu, W. M. (2001a). Expanding our understanding of multiculturalism: Developing a social class worldview model. In D. B. Pope-Davis & H. L. K. Coleman (Eds.), *The intersection of race, class, and gender in counseling psychology* (pp. 127–170). Thousand Oaks, CA: Sage Publications.

Liu, W. M. (2001b, February). *The intersection of race, class, and gender among Asian American men: The theoretical application of the social class worldview model.* Paper presented at the 18th Annual Teachers College Winter Roundtable on Cross-Cultural Psychology and Education, Teachers College, Columbia University, New York, New York.

Liu, W. M., Soleck, G., Hopps, J., Dunston, K., & Pickett, T. (in press). *A new framework to understand social class in counseling: The social class worldview and modern classism theory.* Journal of Multicultural Counseling & Development.

Liu, W. M., Soleck, G., Hopps, J., Dunston, K., & Pickett, T. (2001b). *A review of social class in counseling research: A meta-analysis of the Journal of Counseling Psychology, Journal of Counseling and Development, and the Journal of Multicultural Counseling and Development 1981–2001.* Manuscript in preparation, University of Iowa.

Liu, W. M., & Rasheed, S. (2002, February). Creating new dialogues: Applying the social class worldview model and modern classism theory. Paper presented at the 19th Annual Teachers College Winter Roundtable on Cross-Cultural Psychology and Education. Teachers College, Columbia University, New York.

Loch, C. H., Humberman, B. A., & Stout, S. (2000). Status competition and performance in work groups. *Journal of Economic Behavior and Organization, 43,* 35–55.

McLoyd, V. C. (1998). Socioeconomic disadvantage and child development. *American Psychologist, 53,* 185–204.

Mudrack, P. E. (1997). Protestant work ethic dimensions and work orientations. *Personality and Individual Differences, 23,* 217–225.

Ostrove, J. M., Adler, N. E., Kuppermann, M., & Washington, A. E. (2000). Objective and subjective assessments of socioeconomic status and their relationship to self-rated health in an ethnically diverse sample of pregnant women. *Health Psychology, 19,* 613–618.

Phillips, J. (2001). Cultural construction of manhood in prison. *Psychology of Men and Masculinity, 2,* 13–23.

Pope-Davis, D. B., Liu, W. M., Toporek, R. L., & Brittan-Powell, C. S. (2001). What's missing from multicultural competency research: Review, introspection, and recommendations. *Cultural Diversity and Ethnic Minority Psychology, 7,* 121–138.

Ponterotto, J. G., Casas, J. M., Suzuki, L. A., & Alexander, C. M. (Eds.) (1995). *Handbook of multicultural counseling.* Thousand Oaks, CA: Sage.

Rose, R. (2000). How much does social capital add to individual health? A survey study of Russians. *Social Science and Medicine, 51,* 1421–1435.

Schmid, A. A. (2000). Affinity as social capital: Its role in development. *Journal of Socio-Economics, 29,* 159–171.

Steele, C. M., & Aronson, J. (1995). Stereotype threat and the intellectual test performance of African Americans. *Journal of Personality and Social Psychology, 69,* 797–811.

Sue, D. W., Arredondo, P., & McDavis, R. J. (1992). Multicultural counseling competencies and standards: A call to the profession. *Journal of Counseling and Development, 70,* 477–486.

Sue, D. W., & Sue, D. (1999). *Counseling the culturally different: Theory and practice* (3rd ed.). New York: John Wiley and Sons.

Tyler, B. M. (1989). Black jive and white repression. *The Journal of Ethnic Studies, 16* (4), 31–66.

Watts, R. J. (1994). Paradigms of diversity. In E. J. Trickett, R. J. Watts, & D. Birman (Eds.), *Human diversity: Perspectives on people in context* (pp. 49–80). San Francisco: Jossey-Bass.

Wray, M., & Newitz, A. (Eds.) (1997). *White trash: Race and class in America.* New York: Routledge.

Part IV

Conclusion

16

Understanding Individuals in Their Context

A Relational Perspective of Multicultural Counseling and Psychotherapy

Timothy B. Smith and Matthew Draper

Brigham Young University

Who are you?

—I am a White male. I am also Jewish and gay.

—I know who I am. I am a Black woman—I am Black, I am a woman, I am strong.

—In our family we share a common identity, the heritage of our ancestors. We do not need to ask who we are as individuals because we know who we are to each other.

—My Italian American mother has taught me to respect my father's Albanian culture—and I love them both.

—I am pursuing a career helping others.

—I am an American. My parents were both born in India, but they were Muslim and moved to Pakistan, then Canada, then here. My brother's best friend died September 11, 2001.

—There are too many people asking superficial questions—who's to say who I am? Do you know that I play tennis or hate American food? Sure, on the outside I am White. Is that what you wanted to know?!

—I am an artist.

—My therapist says I need to ask that question more often!

—I get so tired of people asking me what's it like being blind that in the past I have refused to label myself visually impaired—everyone else does that automatically. There is nothing more frustrating than having people put a label on you and then treat you that way without giving you a chance to be yourself. To them, *I* am invisible. So when you ask "who are you?" I only feel defensive and ticked off that you would expect some sort of answer. If you really want to know who I am, then get to know me!

We live in a multicultural world. Multiple contexts of diversity such as gender, sexual orientation, abilities, resources, opportunities, etc., all interact continuously. The resulting complexity is astounding, with each individual completely unique, understood best through relationships that go beyond obvious external characteristics and simplistic generalizations. Knowing basic differences across race, gender, sexual orientation, etc., can help in understanding an individual, but there is simply no substitute for knowing the individual. In a multicultural world the challenge is to establish mutually beneficial relationships that go beyond the superficial and view differences as opportunities. "If you really want to know who I am, then get to know me."

This chapter addresses the importance of a complex contextual understanding of each individual through *a relational perspective.* From this perspective, the focus of mental health treatment is not the individual client but the individual client in his or her many contexts. The concluding section presents arguments against individualism and describes an alternative paradigm: a relational perspective that affirms a contextual approach to multicultural counseling and psychology.

Need to Identify and Challenge Individualism in Counseling and Psychology

All of the chapters of this book have described various ways in which mental health professionals tend to minimize context and over-emphasize the individual in approaching assessment and treatment. Unfortunately, the biases and errors described in each chapter often remain, even after counselors and therapists receive multicultural training, *because individualism and the accompanying attribution errors, reductionism, self-interest, etc., remain interwoven in society and in traditional approaches to counseling and psychology* (see Chapter 6 and also Miller, 1999; Richardson, Fowers, & Guignon, 1999).

Individualism is "the modern notion that the basic unit of human reality is the individual person, who is assumed to exist and have determinate characteristics prior to, and independent of, his or her social existence" (Richardson & Zeddies, 2000, p. 5). Individualism pervades contemporary society, particularly Western societies but increasingly all societies as Western influences become widespread. From a multicultural perspective, a clear advantage of individualism is that it gives primacy to individual autonomy, personal liberties, and freedom from dogmatism and oppression (Richardson, Fowers, & Guignon, 1999). However, as has been illustrated throughout this book, individualism (1) obscures the interactive nature of multiple contexts and (2) enables self-interest potentially at the expense of others (Bellah, et. al., 1985; Etzioni, 1996). (Even though self-interest and the subsequent abuse of power are common human tendencies, individualistic values tend to cloak self-interest as a desirable virtue ["self-appreciation/self-fulfillment," "second place is the first loser," etc.], reify social norms of self-interest [Miller, 1999], and thereby justify individuals' abuse of privileges and power in a climate that favors competition and individual success over cooperation and mutual enrichment.) Thus individualistic values underlie much of the bias and error that multiculturalism attempts to correct (see Chapter 6). And although the multicultural movement has generally succeeded in raising awareness of important issues of racism, sexism, classism, ageism, and homophobia, it has inadequately addressed the roots of those problems, including pervasive individualistic values that promote self-interest and that emphasize individual autonomy in isolation from external contexts. Practicing multiculturalism requires not only awareness of bias and error but a fundamental shift of values.

A Relational Foundation for Counseling and Psychology

Practicing multiculturalism necessitates a perspective that not only affirms individual autonomy, liberty, and worth but also explicitly addresses context and tempers self-interest. A *relational perspective* may provide exactly that combination. A relational perspective of counseling and psychology emphasizes individual autonomy and freedom but also emphasizes responsibility and external contexts. The following paragraphs present the basic ideas behind a relational perspective, which is offered as an alternative to individualism as a foundation for multicultural counseling and psychology.

Rationale

What elements are foundational to counseling and therapy? If we took away all the terms, techniques, and theories, what would be apparent to the external observer? To an observer, the most obvious fact is that counseling and psychotherapy involve relationships: interactions within dyads or groups.

Moreover, if we were to take a step back and observe human behavior in general, what factors would be most obvious? We would see parents caring for and struggling with children, students interacting with teachers, lovers quarrelling and making up, employees complaining about delegated tasks, and a host of other behaviors that have relational foundations (except, of course, physiological needs and functions such as eating or sleeping and reactions to environmental conditions such as weather or topography). Furthermore, if we were to take another step back, we would perhaps notice how each interaction influences subsequent interactions. For example, we might notice that a child who received a scolding at home in the morning gives her teacher a hard time, eventually producing a headache by the end of the day so that when the teacher gets home she pays little attention to her partner, who then complains that he has to cook meals. If we were to track the effects of relationships over time, we would perhaps see children whose parents generally demonstrated affection and self-sacrifice subsequently raising their own children in the same way, students whose teachers instilled a sense of enjoyment for a given subject matter passing on that same enjoyment to others 57 years later, and employees who received fair treatment from their employers becoming respected employers themselves. Relationships weave the fabric of life, one interaction at a time.

The Basics of a Relational Perspective

A relational perspective of counseling and psychology assumes that humans are not only physical/biological but innately social beings. It draws heavily from the tenets of interpersonal social-cognitive theory (Andersen & Chen, 2002), symbolic interactionism (Hewitt, 1991), feminism (Miller, 1976), interpersonal psychotherapy (Mitchell, 1988), object relational psychoanalysis (Hoffman, 1991), and philosophies advanced by Levinas (1985) and Bakhtin (1981, 1995). The basic idea behind a relational perspective is that individuals are best understood *not as individuals* but as interactive agents in the context of multiple relationships, past, present, and potential.

The basics of a relational perspective may be roughly but adequately represented by an analogy to a spider in the process of constructing a web, with the web symbolizing a person's life and well-being and each line of the web symbolizing a relationship with another person. The first foundational lines influence the size, shape, and strength of the web, as they support subsequent lines which intersect directly or indirectly with one another yet can be modified by the spider at any time. In that sense, the web is never finished but is an ongoing project. Repairs and improvements to the web are inevitable as external forces exert themselves and as strands weaken and dissipate, yet the previous structure influences subsequent modifications, and the basic pattern of the web usually remains consistent over time.

Metaphorically, a relational perspective indicates that individuals are best represented and understood according to their web of relationships. This perspective assumes that individuals' interactions with others form the structure, process, and content of their lives. Every human has a unique pattern of relationships that is constantly changing, yet there are clear similarities across people because they share similar contexts, most notably physiology, but to varying degrees social, historical, economic, and cultural-linguistic contexts as well. Primary relationships (childhood and current) influence other relationships, which vary in importance across time and across contexts. New relationships and repaired relationships alter individuals' perceptions, emotions, cognitions, and behaviors, which all influence other relationships in an ongoing interactive process.

Interactive Volition.   A fundamental assertion of a relational perspective is that individuals possess an innate will and volition. But individual volition is interactive with the environment. In the analogy of the web, the spider is buffeted by external forces yet retains the power to act and adapt to circumstances. External forces, such as sociopolitical oppression, clearly shape the course and pattern of our lives. Past relationships, particularly primary relationships, greatly influence subsequent relationships. Yet we retain the power to work to modify external environments or adapt to them, repair damaged/damaging relationships, and form new relationships. Thus although we cannot be free from external influences, including our own relationship history and culture, we are free to change our perspective, strengthen our own abilities, modify the environment, and create new opportunities. We are restricted but not determined by circumstances. Unlike individualistic perspectives, which tend to emphasize the need for freedom to escape external influences (e.g., to escape or avoid oppression), a relational perspective posits that the only freedom we possess is the freedom to interact with our circumstances (e.g., to combat oppression), creating new opportunities and possibilities as we act to shape the web of our lives.

Becoming. Individualism implies that people are already complete (e.g., "be yourself"). A relational perspective emphasizes that development is ongoing. Identity evolves and stabilizes as relationships evolve and fall into predictable patterns, but every individual will have new experiences and relationships that may change his or her perspectives, emotions, cognitions, and behaviors. A relational perspective therefore emphasizes what the person may become, whereas an individualistic perspective ironically limits human potential as it emphasizes and reifies what the person currently is. Hence, the "self" is not seen as a fixed entity, separate and independent, but as a highly complex and fluid pattern, a "self-in-relation" (Adams & LaFromboise, 2001; Richardson et al., 1999; Warnke, 1987).

Self-in-Relation. According to a relational perspective, people can only understand themselves in terms of their interactions with others. The "self" is co-created "in relation" with others. We are never self-sufficient. We depend upon others for our own identity. A simplistic example is that counselors depend on clients for their identity as a counselor, depend on friends for their identity as a friend, depend on ancestors for their identity as a Jew, etc. We learn about ourselves as we interact with others, who serve as points of comparison and contrast across circumstances and across time. We can even learn about ourselves across a single conversation, in a sudden epiphany that somewhat alters our perceptions of the world and of ourselves. In brief, a relational perspective assumes that after accounting for physiology (e.g., nervous system functioning, genetic predispositions), who we believe ourselves to be is the sum total of all of our interactions with others. That is why our identity is so complex! And that is why responsibility is so fundamental to a relational perspective.

Responsibility to Others. As just illustrated, whenever two or more people interact, they affect one another. Thus the participants are responsible to one another for shared meanings and for mutual impact (Morson & Emerson, 1990). This innate responsibility to others is implicit in the interaction, rarely recognized overtly, but purposefully made explicit by a relational perspective (Levinas, 1985).

Given each individual's responsibility to others, a relational perspective advocates an *other-focus* and a *we-consciousness,* meaning that the focus of individuals' attention during any interaction should be on the other person and on the relationship, not on the fulfillment of self-interest (Levinas, 1985; Morson & Emerson, 1990). Self-interest is reduced by an other-focus and a we-consciousness (Stapel & Koomen, 2001), which help to keep power in the interaction benign rather than oppressive. This perspective is particularly useful and pertinent to the therapeutic relationship, in which therapists maintain a focus on the client and a constant vigilance for how their own actions and assumptions may impact their work with a client (Richardson et al., 1999). Therapists' power is explicitly acknowledged and directed toward the benefit of the client. Therapists working from within a relational perspective openly acknowledge their responsibility to remain aware of their own assumptions and privileges, knowledgeable about diverse influences upon the client, and skillful in their communication and interventions. And complete responsibility to the client is the very essence of practicing multiculturalism.

Implications of a Relational Perspective for Multicultural Counseling and Psychotherapy

There are many opinions about what multiculturalism entails (e.g., Pedersen, 1999). If the aim of multiculturalism is mutual enrichment (Chapter 1), then a relational perspective can perhaps inform practitioners of ways to bring that to pass. Rather than seeing people as radically separated selves who approach each other from across a chasm of difference, a relational perspective suggests that people are codependent on one another for a sense of their identity (Fay, 1996). From this perspective, the basis for effective multicultural practice is a positive relationship with the client.

Although we cannot readily step outside of our own culture as we try to relate positively to persons with backgrounds different from our own, we can recognize how our own expectations and assumptions limit our ability to interact effectively. We can also assume the responsibility to learn about and learn from the other person, creating common ground and common understanding. Therapists who adopt a relational perspective challenge themselves to minimize their own self-interest and adapt themselves to meet the needs of the other person, finding mutual enrichment in the interaction.

Although there are many implications of a relational perspective for multicultural counseling and psychotherapy, the following paragraphs will list only a few. The reader is encouraged to consider others.

First, a rather basic yet exceedingly difficult implication of a relational perspective is that therapists have a responsibility to remain open and learn from clients. Psychological dismissal of others happens often in contemporary society. Whenever someone fails to meet our expectations, we write her off. A person raises her voice at us in public, and we vow to never speak with her again. A person unfairly criticizes our work, and we return the favor. A person sneezes in our direction, and we privately mutter some curse back in her direction. Ridiculous as these examples may seem, you may want to start to notice how often you implicitly dismiss another person from your circle of relationships, isolating her and denying yourself the opportunity to learn from the interaction. And although it is relatively rare for therapists to abandon clients, there are more than a few occasions when clients' actions evoke critical, judgmental responses in therapists. For example, if a therapist finds himself feeling uncomfortable with a client who is dressed in dirty clothes or nervous with a client who has recently been released from prison, it is highly likely that the therapist is focusing on the differences between him and these clients—rather than on the relationship he is attempting to build with the clients. Undoubtedly, clients pick up on the cool reception we give them at such times, and the relationship fails to become enriching for either person. But the outcome could be improved if the therapist first internally acknowledged his own expectations and assumptions about people in prison or people in dirty clothes and then re-focused his attention on the person in front of him, challenging his own personal discomfort with the evidence that this client has much to teach him about circumstances that he has never had to face, rather than being judgmental.

An *other-focus* can aid therapists in minimizing their criticisms and in judging a client more accurately by considering the client's worldview and experiences, rather than by imposing their own or by assuming similarity with the client. A *we-consciousness* minimizes self-serving social comparisons (such as the fundamental attribution error), defensiveness, and competition (Gardner, Gabriel, & Hochschild, 2002) and increases social inclusion and integration (Stapel & Koomen, 2001) (see also Chapter 6). Thus a relational perspective helps us to critically examine and challenge our own assumptions and to maintain a respectful and open approach in which we not only learn *about* our clients but also learn *from* our clients. A relational perspective therefore strongly supports the aim of multiculturalism, which is mutual enrichment. Thus the first implication of a relational perspective is that combating racism, sexism, classism, ageism, and homophobia is important because we have a responsibility to remain open and be taught in our interactions with *all* others.

A second implication is that the basic way that people truly differ is in the patterns of their interactions. To return to the earlier analogy, spider webs come in many, many shapes, sizes, and strengths. Although all webs serve essentially the same function, the differences can be as striking as the similarities. Sometimes, people are so different in their relationship patterns, and consequently in their perceptions and assumptions, that misunderstanding in interactions is likely (e.g., Thompson, Neville, Weathers, & Poston, 1990). Misunderstandings most often occur when one or both parties are too inflexible to accommodate the perceptions and assumptions of the other person (i.e., when people fail to have an *other-focus*). However, misunderstandings also occur when real differences in the experiences/abilities/values of others are taken for granted or are assumed to be irrelevant to therapy. For example, a recent immigrant who inaccurately used a strong word in English was accidentally misdiagnosed by a therapist who took the statement at face value without conducting additional assessment. The discrepancy was found only after the client had been interviewed by a police interpreter. If therapists do not account for differences, their attempts to help others may be ineffective and may even perpetuate self-interest.

A third implication of a relational perspective is that even though identity development is extremely complex, it is generally linear *because* it parallels social development. Thus, children's identity is a reflection of their primary relationships (e.g., with family members). As they increase their scope of interaction with others and as their social development and cognitive development progress, their sense of identity undergoes challenges and redefinitions as they establish more and more relationships outside the family, notably in adolescence. As an individual's interactions with others become more predictable, the individual's identity stabilizes. For example, a person's complex identity as a bisexual Catholic female accountant with a learning disability depends on her interactions with other women, bisexuals, Catholics, accountants, and individuals with learning disabilities, who provide essential modeling and sources of comparison, and on her interactions with people who share none of those attributes, who serve as sources of contrast. If the woman has had positive key interactions with others concerning her gender, she will likely strongly affirm her identity as a woman. But if she has had negative interactions with others concerning her learning disability and has failed to meet a positive role model who also has a learning disability, she may likely minimize or avoid openly acknowledging that aspect of her experience. Identity parallels social interactions. Models of racial identity, gender identity, spiritual identity, etc., may therefore be stronger if they incorporate inter-personal-level variables such as socialization and predictability of interactions.

A fourth implication of a relational perspective is that well-being and mental health are functions of positive interpersonal interactions and a *we-consciousness*. A *we-consciousness* reduces perceived threats and enhances self-esteem (Gardner et al., 2002). Interpersonal relationships that enhance opportunity, trust, responsibility, and intimacy lead to positive self-perceptions and happiness (e.g., Corey, 1986; Myers, 2000). The more secure our relationships, the more willing we are to help others and to respond to others' needs rather than focusing only our own (e.g., Mikulincer et al., 2001). In contrast, self-focused attention is associated with negative mood and decreased well-being (Flory, Raikkonen, Matthews, & Owens, 2000), and self-absorption is a common denominator for nearly all mental illness (Ingram, 1990). *Counselors and psychologists can therefore best assist clients first by establishing a positive relationship with them and then by facilitating clients' positive relationships with others.* This assertion is indirectly supported by a large body of research evidence that indicates that the therapeutic alliance (relationship) is among the most notable predictors of client outcome (Martin, Garske, & Davis, 2000) and that social functioning is among the best predictors of mental health and well-being (Lee & Robbins, 1998; Lee, Draper, & Lee, 2001).

A fifth implication is that values and worldviews do make a large difference in therapy, even when they are not recognized. Sometimes, the values built into the foundations of counseling and psychotherapy conflict with the values of those needing help (Fancher, 1995; Comas-Diaz & Jacobsen, 1991, 1995). For example, two values that are common across psychotherapy theories are personal autonomy and self-actualization (Richardson et al., 1999). Much of counseling and psychotherapy, in fact, can be seen in terms of helping people to become free from constraint and distress and helping them know themselves better (Fancher, 1995). Despite the worthiness of these values, adhering to them uncritically can be problematic. In some contexts, the highest value of the individual is not her own personal happiness, or even her individual freedoms to pursue whatever she wishes in life. Rather, some cultures emphasize the good of the society or culture, holding the health, welfare, and security of others in far more regard than individual freedom or happiness (Ferguson, Gever, Min-Ha, & West, 1990). At other times, the very things that may define joy in some cultural groups may be interpreted as overly enmeshed or excessively dependent by those strictly adhering to many psychological theories (Richardson et al., 1999). For example, a client from China sought counseling from one of the authors (M.D.) not because she was depressed or anxious but because she wanted to be a contributing member of her family thousands of miles away. Being a member of an impoverished family and working to support herself (and family members) while pursuing a graduate degree was very stressful and caused her to work long hours. But she did not necessarily want to reduce personal stress and further her own happiness; she wanted to find new and creative ways to enhance the welfare of her family. Had the author approached this case from a monocultural/

individualistic perspective and tried to free her from familial "constraints" to become more of her own individual, he might have alienated the client and potentially done more harm than good. In brief, values and worldviews are inextricably linked with the practice of counseling and psychotherapy. And although this chapter has specifically targeted limitations of individualistic values in multicultural contexts, a relational perspective requires critical thinking about all values (materialism, relativism, hedonism, etc.) and about ways these values may influence our interactions with others.

Finally, a sixth implication of a relational perspective is that because we learn about ourselves as we interact with others, we can learn more about ourselves from diverse relationships than from those we have typically experienced in the past. Without diversity, identity remains artificially restricted. Multiculturalism therefore offers truly incredible opportunities for personal growth. Similarities draw us closer together perfunctorily, but diversity offers the potential for mutual enrichment. Each new relationship we form has something unique to offer if we can receive it. Each new relationship can assist us in *becoming* more than we now are, increasing our capacity and our potential.

In sum, although there are several limitations to a relational perspective, it has the potential to reduce some of the biases implicit in counseling and psychology. In that sense, it is particularly well suited to multicultural practice (Fay, 1996).

Conclusion

Many mental health professionals receive training in multicultural counseling and psychotherapy and subsequently attempt to act according to the training they have received. However, few therapists become multiculturally proficient, in part because of implicit biases in society and in the traditional practice of counseling and psychotherapy perpetuate misunderstanding, self-interest, and abuse of power. Most notably, therapists often fail to adequately consider the multiple contexts of the client.

A relational perspective on counseling and psychotherapy offers an approach useful in combating tendencies based on individualistic perspectives (e.g., attribution errors, defensiveness, reductionism, and self-interest). This perspective emphasizes that relationships weave the fabric of life and that individuals are best understood in the context of their multiple relationships. We each have relationships that challenge our perceptions of who we are and relationships that confirm who we believe ourselves to be. It is through these constant challenges and confirmations that we learn about ourselves and about our potentials. In sum, "who we are" is a reflection of the diversity that surrounds us.

The chapters in this book have covered many aspects of diversity, but in reality they have only scratched the surface. Diversity comes in so many forms and in so many complex patterns that presenting information, often generalizations, about counseling processes and about groups of people is not altogether unlike asking the question "Who are you?" and then expecting something more than a superficial answer. Yet the value in asking the question is not in the initial response. The value in asking is found in the subsequent interaction, a dialogue which creates a space for mutual understanding and ultimately for mutual enrichment. Similarly, the value of this book is not so much in the information it presents as in the process that it potentially facilitates.

References

Adams, V. L., & LaFromboise, T. D. (2001). Self-in-relation theory and African American female development. In D. Pope-Davis & H. Coleman (Eds), *The intersection of race, class, and gender in multicultural counseling.* (pp. 25–48). Thousand Oaks, CA: Sage.

Andersen, S. M., & Chen, S. (2002). The relational self: An interpersonal social-cognitive theory. *Psychological Review, 109,* 619–645.

Bakhtin, M. M. (1995). *Toward a philosophy of the act.* (V. Liapunov, Trans.). Austin, TX: University of Texas Press.

Bakhtin, M. M. (1981). *The dialogic imagination: Four essays by M. M. Bakhtin.* (C. Emerson & M. Holquist, Trans.) Austin, TX: University of Texas Press.

Bellah, R. N., Madsen, R., Sullivan, W. M., Swidler, A., & Tipton, S. M. (1985). *Habits of the heart: Individualism and commitment in American life.* Los Angeles, CA: University of California Press.

Comas-Diaz L., & Jacobsen, F. M. (1991). Ethnocultural transference and counter transference in the therapeutic dyad. *American Journal of Orthopsychiatry, 61,* 392–402.

Comas-Diaz, L., & Jacobsen, F. M. (1995). The therapist of color and the White patient dyad: Contradictions and recognitions. *Cultural Diversity & Ethnic Minority Psychology, 2,* 93–106.

Corey, G. (1986). *Theory and practice of counseling and psychotherapy.* Pacific Grove, CA: Brooks/Cole Publishing Company.

Etzioni, A. (1996). *The new golden rule: Community and morality in a democratic society.* New York: Basic Books.

Fancher, R. (1995). *Cultures of healing: Correcting the image of American mental health care.* New York: Freeman.

Fay, B. (1996). *Contemporary philosophy of social science: A multicultural approach.* Malden, MA: Blackwell Publishers.

Ferguson, R., Gever, M., Minh-Ha, T., & West, C. (1990). *Out there: Marginalization and contemporary cultures.* Cambridge, MA: MIT Press.

Flory, J., Raikkonen, K., Matthews, K., & Owens, J. (2000). Self-focused attention and mood during everyday social interactions. *Journal of Personality and Social Psychology Bulletin, 26,* 875–883.

Gardner, W. L., Gabriel, S., & Hochschild, L. (2002). When you and I are "we," you are not threatening: The role of self-expansion in social comparison. *Journal of Personality and Social Psychology, 82,* 239–251.

Hewitt, J. P. (1991). *Self and society: A symbolic interactionist social psychology.* Needham Heights, MA: Allyn and Bacon.

Hoffman, I. Z. (1991). Discussion: Toward a social-constructivist view of the psychoanalytic situation. *Psychoanalytic Dialogues, 1,* 74–105.

Ingram, R. E. (1990). Self-focused attention in clinical disorders: Review and conceptual model. *Psychological Bulletin, 107,* 156–176.

Lee, R. M., Draper, M. R., & Lee, S. (2001). The counseling implications of belongingness. *Journal of Counseling Psychology, 48,* 310–318.

Lee, R. M., & Robbins, S. B. (1998). The relationship between social connectedness and anxiety, self-esteem, and social identity. *Journal of Counseling Psychology, 45,* 1–8.

Levinas, E. (1985). *Ethics and infinity: Conversations with Philippe Nemo.* Pittsburgh, PA: Duquense University Press.

Martin, D. J., Garske, J., Davis, M. K. (2000). Relation of the therapeutic alliance with outcome and other variables: A meta-analytic review. *Journal of Consulting and Clinical Psychology, 68,* 438–450.

Mikulincer, M., Gillath, O., Halevy, V., Avihou, N., Avidan, S., & Eshkolo, N. (2001). Attachment theory and reactions to others' needs: Evidence that activation of the sense of attachment security promotes empathic responses. *Journal of Personality and Social Psychology, 81,* 1205–1224.

Miller, D. T. (1999). The norm of self-interest. *American Psychologist, 54,* 1053–1060.

Miller, J. B. (1976). *Toward a new psychology of women.* Boston: Beacon.

Mitchell, S. (1988). The intrapsychic and the interpersonal: Different theories, different domains, or historical artifacts. *Psychoanalytic Inquiry, 8,* 472–496.

Myers, D. G. (2000). The funds, friends, and faith of happy people. *American Psychologist, 55,* 56–67.

Pedersen, P. (Ed.) (1999). *Multiculturalism as a fourth force.* Philadelphia, PA: Brunner/Mazel.

Richardson, F. C., Fowers, B. J., & Guignon, C. B. (1999). *Re-envisioning psychology: Moral dimensions of theory and practice.* San Francisco, CA: Jossey-Bass Publishers.

Richardson, F. C., & Zeddies, T. J. (2000). Individualism and modern psychotherapy. In B. Slife & R. Williams (Eds.), *Critical issues in psychotherapy* (pp. 147–164). Thousand Oaks, CA: Sage.

Stapel, D. A., & Koomen, W. (2001). I, we, and the effects of others on me: How self-construal level moderates social comparison effects. *Journal of Personality and Social Psychology, 80,* 766–781.

Thompson, C. E., Neville, H., Weathers, P. L., & Poston, W. C. (1990). Cultural mistrust and racism reactions among African-American students. *Journal of College Student Development, 31,* 162–168.

Warnke, G. (1987). *Gadamer: Hermeneutics, tradition, and reason.* Stanford, CA: Stanford University Press.

Glossary

Judith V. Kehe

Community College of Baltimore County–Essex Campus and Loyola College in Maryland

Timothy B. Smith

Brigham Young University

ableism   Discriminatory beliefs and actions that are directed against people with disabilities. Often based on implicit assumptions that a particular condition is undesirable, ableism manifests itself in a variety of ways, ranging from overt condemnation or patronization to covert causing of social discomfort or failure to accommodate the needs of those with disabilities.

aborigine   A person indigenous to a particular region as far back as historical records exist. Because the term is often used to refer to the native peoples of Australia (Koori, Murrie, Nunga, Nyungar, Anangu, Yolgnu, etc.), ethnicity should be specified.

absolutism   An ethical principle affirming that the same evaluative process can be applied across cultures/situations in the same fashion and without regard to differences in context.

accommodation   The process of changing one's own understanding to incorporate concepts that conflict with pre-existing ideas and thoughts. The term also refers to the adjustment of environmental, curricular, and direct services to meet the particular needs of clients.

acculturation   The process of adapting to another culture and acquiring knowledge and skills specific to that culture.

action research (also participatory action research)   A form of activism and empowerment that uses qualitative research methods in collaboration with a community or group to determine that group's needs, assess viable solutions, and advocate for optimal outcomes.

activism   Public work to promote recognition of a condition and to improve that condition. Activism is often political, but it is not confined to the national level—it concerns any promotion of change, even in small organizations or academic departments.

325

affirmative action   Policies in hiring and admission processes meant to establish equal opportunities.

afrocentric   Perspective emphasizing the ideas, behaviors, traditions, etc., of African cultures.

ageism   Prejudicial beliefs and discriminatory behaviors directed against persons because of their age.

ALANA   Abbreviation for African-, Latino/a-, Asian-, and Native-American (see also people of color).

alien   Legal term for an individual who is not a citizen or national of a given country.

allocentrism   The tendency for an individual to describe him- or herself from a collectivist framework (see collectivism). Within this framework the needs of the group or family take precedence over personal needs. There is also a tendency to see oneself in relationship to others.

American Personnel and Guidance Association (APGA)   Founded in 1952, this organization changed its name first in 1983 to the American Association for Counseling and Development (AACD) and again in 1992 to the American Counseling Association (ACA), as it is currently known.

American Psychological Association (APA)   Governing and accrediting body that provides guidelines and standards for the training and practice of psychology.

Americans with Disabilities Act (ADA)   Implemented on July 26, 1990, this legislative action supports access to various opportunities to persons with disabilities in the United States.

androgyny   Display of both masculine and feminine traits, rather than the predominance of one or the other.

Anglo conformity   Social norms that reinforce the values, behaviors, customs, etc., associated with European American culture.

anti-miscegenation laws   Laws that prohibited interracial marriage.

anti-semitism   Discriminatory behaviors or prejudicial beliefs directed towards those who are of Jewish faith or heritage.

Asian American   Broad term referring to Americans of Asian ancestry. Given that Asia comprises dozens of nations and hundreds of ethnic groups, it is important to clearly distinguish the nationality and ethnic group being discussed.

assimilation   Adopting the practices, behaviors, etc., of another culture and simultaneously diminishing the salience and expression of one's original culture.

Association for Non-White Concerns (ANWC)   Established in 1972, with the goal of advancing equitable treatment of all clients, the name of this organization was changed to the Association for Multicultural Counseling and Development (AMCD) in 1985.

assumptions   Beliefs grounded in previous experience or vicarious learning that channel subsequent perceptions and interpretations along the same lines as previous experience—rendering different experiences susceptible to misinterpretation.

asylee   Legal term referring to a person in a country or at a port of entry who is unable or unwilling to return to his or her own country of national origin.

attributions   The inferences that one makes about the causes of events and behaviors for both self and others.

becoming   The concept that human beings are optimally in a state of perpetual development.

bias   A preference or an inclination that is partial or prejudicial, typically not readily accommodated to other perspectives.

bicultural   Condition in which individuals share attributes and/or behaviors of two distinct cultures. The term can refer to offspring of interracial unions (see biracial) or to those who adapt their behavior to match different cultural settings. For example, individuals from an underrepresented group may act and speak like members of the predominant group at their workplace and in other settings where there are perceived negative consequences for lack of cultural conformity.

bilingual   The ability to communicate fluently in two languages.

biracial   An individual whose parents are of different races (see multiracial).

buffer   In a multicultural context, research findings that certain cultural beliefs, traditions, or practices which can minimize the harmful experiences of external stigmatization, prejudice, discrimination, etc.

cajun   A native of Louisiana believed to be descended from natives of Acadia.

carpentered world theory   The notion that Westerners tend to perceive things as having square corners, since they are used to seeing rectangular shapes.

caste   Any social class that is clearly separated from others by distinctive features such as rank, profession, language, marriage, etc.,—a hereditary system in certain societies.

chicanos/chicanas   Persons of Mexican descent.

classism   Discriminatory beliefs and behaviors based on socioeconomic class differences such as social networks, wealth, education, access to power, and group values. Classism can be directed against those of similar status, higher status, or lower status.

cognitive flexibility   Ability to acquire and modify perceptions based on new or conflicting information: In a multicultural context, the ability to adapt to real and perceived differences with others.

collectivism   A worldview and a dimension of culture that emphasizes group needs via harmony and cooperation over individual needs and desires.

colonialism   Foreign rule (including customs and ideas) imposed upon a people. In this process, members of the ruling nation settle and govern the lands of native peoples.

color blind   When a person is not aware of or minimizes racial differences.

color obsession   When an individual or group overemphasizes the salience of skin color and race to the point of obscuring related factors such as socioeconomic status.

coming of age   Nearing or surpassing a certain developmental milestone (usually adulthood) within a particular culture.

coming out   Process whereby an individual with homosexual orientation openly declares that orientation.

communal perspective   A worldview that considers the needs and desires of the community over and above the needs and desires of the individual (see also Collectivism).

community psychology (community counseling)   A branch of mental health services that takes a contextual perspective to intervention. Arising out of social activism during the 1960s, community psychology emphasizes wellness and prevention as well as principles of social justice.

compassionate communication   Respectful and honest expression and reception of content through a process characterized by "I statements" and empathy.

contextualism   A perspective that views human beings in relation to their multiple environments, including biological, economic, historic, linguistic, etc.

cross-cultural   An approach that compares one culture against another. Because such comparisons have often been based on measures that lack validity across both cultures, abuses of such comparisons have been noted in the literature, such that some scholars are wary to use this term.

cultural blindness   Assumption that all people are so fundamentally similar that any differences in external appearance, perception, experience, and ability are of little consequence (see also color blind).

cultural display rules   Social norms regarding how emotions are expressed and modified based on the context. For example, although sadness may be a universal emotion, how sadness is expressed varies from culture to culture and is governed by what is deemed socially appropriate.

cultural inversion   The tendency for oppressed groups to resist the values and behaviors of a dominant group.

cultural mismatch   A condition in which the values, expectations, and behaviors of one cultural group conflict with those of another cultural group.

cultural mistrust   A coping skill of skepticism towards the designs and behaviors of members of a dominant cultural group.

cultural paranoia (healthy)   A coping skill of increased vigilance and mistrust of those from dominant cultural groups (see also cultural mistrust).

cultural pluralism   Tenet that multiple cultures can and should be affirmed in a given society. In opposition to the metaphor of the "melting pot," cultural pluralism suggests a metaphor of the "tossed salad," "stir fry," or "mosaic," where each component retains its unique characteristics yet contributes to the balance, flavor, and beauty of the whole.

cultural relativism   An ethical position that the unique characteristics, perceptions, and mores of a particular culture must be considered in understanding the behaviors of persons from that culture.

cultural value deficit   A perception that one culture is "deficient" because it does not place the same value on a particular behavior, trait, or ambition, as another (more dominant) culture.

culturally encapsulated   A condition wherein a group or society acts as if its culture is the only real and valid perspective. In the context of mental health treatment, the term refers to the fact that many of the assumptions of traditional counseling and psychotherapy stem from European and European American worldviews that minimize the value of other perspectives and mask complexities associated with mental health treatment.

culture   The characteristic values, behaviors, products, and worldviews of a group of people with a distinct sociohistorical context. In part because the term is so broad, definitions of culture vary in the literature, sometimes used interchangeably with ethnicity and sometimes confused with race (see ethnicity and race).

culture affiliation hypothesis   The hypothesis that immigrants who are bilingual will affiliate themselves with the values or beliefs of the culture associated with the language that they are currently using.

culture bound syndromes   A list of syndromes that can be found in the Diagnostic and Statistical Manual (DSM-IV-TR) that are described as patterns of aberrant behaviors observed in certain cultures.

culture shock   A term used to describe the psychological and emotional difficulties that occur when individuals interact with a culture that is different from their own.

culture specific   Traits, behaviors, conditions, etc. unique to a given culture; also a form of assessment or a school of thought emphasizing that a culture is best understood from its own unique vantage point.

culture-fair tests   Assessments that acknowledge the influence of certain aspects of a person's culture on the outcome of assessment. For example, tests of non-verbal intelligence have typically been used when there is a concern that a client's level of language may interfere with obtaining accurate results. However, there is currently debate as to whether "culture-fair" tests truly reduce bias.

curanderos   Spanish word for "healers," meaning traditional folk healers.

curriculum infusion   In academe, addressing multicultural issues across many courses and activities, rather than allocating one specific course to carry the burden of covering a myriad of diversity issues.

deficit model (also deficit theory)   Any perspective or approach that negatively contrasts one culture or group against another, with differences labeled as deficiencies rather than merely as differences. For example, group differences on tests of intelligence have been used to posit a hierarchy of genetic endowment. Such models typically assume that other groups should adopt the values and practices of the dominant group.

discrimination (racial)   Adverse or unequal treatment based solely on racial attributes.

diversity (social)   Aspects of difference among individuals and groups.

dominant culture   The culture that has the greatest influence on a given society, usually by comprising the majority of the population or having a disproportionate amount of socioeconomic power. Members of the dominant group have unique privileges compared to other groups, and they often assume that other groups should adapt to their folkways.

ebonics   English dialect spoken in some African American communities, sometimes also referred to as Black English or African American English.

ecological systems theory   A model of human behavior that explicitly considers multiple layers of influence from the micro level (personality, past experience, etc.) to the macro systems level (national economy, social trends, etc.).

egalitarian   Belief that all people, irrespective of differences, have rights to the same privileges, treatment, and opportunities.

emic   A perspective that emphasizes the attributes and traits of the specific case, such as those of a single individual. In multicultural psychology, an emic perspective focuses on unique human experiences and differences across groups (see also etic).

émigré   An emigrant who has fled a country, especially during a conflict.

empowerment   Enabling others by instilling self-confidence and providing opportunities for them to act more freely.

enculturation   The process of socialization wherein individuals learn and internalize the particular values, behaviors, and worldviews of their native culture.

equivalence   A concept in multicultural education and research emphasizing that in order for comparisons among various cultures to be meaningful, the constructs measured and the research methods used must be similar across groups.

ESL   Abbreviation for English as a Second Language, a comprehensive approach to teaching English to non-native speakers. A similar but more contemporary term is English Language Learners (ELL).

espiritismo   Spanish word for "spiritualism," describing various practices such as ritual healing and divination, this term being particularly associated with Puerto Rican culture.

espiritistas   Spanish word for "spiritualists," describing those who use spiritual forms of divination and/or healing.

ethnicity   Identity with or membership in a particular culture. Although *ethnicity* is often used interchangeably with *culture*, ethnicity is more closely linked with one's identity or perception of group membership. Culture, on the other hand, is a broader construct that can include material aspects (such as food, clothing, technology, music, etc.) as well as non-material aspects (citizenship, language, beliefs, etc.). Some equate ethnicity with nationality (Moroccan, Samoan, etc.). Ethnicity often overlaps with race, but it is distinct from race (e.g., Brazilians may be of Japanese ancestry) because race is defined by externally imposed social criteria and perceptions of physical features (see race).

ethnocentrism   The belief that one's own culture is the standard against which other cultures can be judged.

ethnography   Qualitative research method informed by anthropological fieldwork and interviewing used to gain an in-depth understanding/description of the topic studied. This method typically necessitates cultural immersion over time to effectively interpret the data collected.

ethnology   The study of contemporary cultures in an attempt to understand their unique patterns.

ethnotherapeutic   Healing in culturally appropriate ways (see also multicultural proficiency).

etic   A perspective that emphasizes the attributes and traits common to all cases, such as to citizens of a nation. In multicultural psychology, an etic perspective focuses on universal aspects of human experience and similarities across groups (see also emic).

eurocentric   A worldview that values the ideas, behaviors, traditions, etc. that have their roots in European or European American cultures over those of other cultures.

exclusion   At a broad level, implicit or explicit limitations imposed by those in power that reduce access to power for others. At the social level, separation, segregation, and disassociation are all results of exclusion.

exploitation   Use of power for one's own benefit (or the benefit of one's group) at the expense of others. Typically this occurs when one person or group deceives another or does not allow them access to the same power or opportunities.

false uniqueness effect   The tendency to underestimate the commonality of one's desirable traits and to overestimate the uniqueness of these traits. This is one way that individuals boost their self-esteem.

familismo   Spanish word signifying the pervasive influence and importance of the family.

feminist theory   A perspective affirming the values, experiences, and contributions of women. Although there are several branches of feminist theory (liberal, Marxist, postmodern, etc.), the common emphasis is on gender and gender power differences, with an understanding that patriarchy has been oppressive to women and that social action is needed to create a more egalitarian society.

filial piety   Ethic of respect and duty to family members, particularly parents, characteristic of collectivistic cultures.

fourth force   A designation of multiculturalism as a major influence upon the mental health professions, following the three earlier "forces:" (1) Psychodynamic (e.g., Freud, Jung), (2) Behaviorism (e.g., Skinner, Watson), and (3) Humanistic (e.g., Maslow, Rogers).

functional paranoia   The attitude of suspicion that a client may exhibit towards a clinician because of the client's previous experiences with persons of the same background as the clinician. Functional paranoia can be distinguished from mental health conditions such as interpersonal anxiety, social skills deficits, etc. because it is displayed only in the presence of those affiliated with a dominant group (see cultural paranoia).

fundamental attribution error   The tendency to attribute others' behaviors to disposition characteristics, such as those that indicate a personality flaw (e.g., "lazy"), but to attribute one's own behavior to external or situational factors (e.g., "the work was too hard").

gender identity   The sex that a person identifies as his or her own. This term may also refer to the degree to which individuals recognize or adhere to particular gender roles.

gender roles   The gender-specific behaviors that are adopted by males and females as ascribed by a particular culture.

gender-sensitive therapy   Treatment approach informed by feminist theory that addresses gender issues for both men and women.

glass ceiling   The imposition of upper limits on personal advancement in terms of profession, salary, promotion, etc. by institutional or cultural discrimination (e.g., ageism, classism, racism, sexism). Like glass, the metaphorical ceiling is transparent because the individuals or groups so treated can see those with different backgrounds advance above them, yet it is also solid because they are denied advancement regardless of their own achievement or merit.

great divide theories   Theories that suggest that the cognitive development of Westerners is superior to that of persons from other societies deemed less advanced.

heterosexism   Belief that heterosexuality is preferable to homosexuality, used to justify prejudicial beliefs and discriminatory behaviors directed against gays, lesbians, or bisexuals.

homophobia   A fear of contact with individuals who are of a homosexual orientation.

idiocentric   The tendency towards describing and promoting one's own personal needs. The term is equivalent to *individualistic,* which is used to describe groups.

illusory correlation   The erroneous belief that when an unusual behavior occurs together with a distinct group, the behavior and group are related; hence, an incorrect connection is made which can result in stereotypes.

immigrant   A person not born in a country who lawfully resides there on a permanent visa received through the Immigration and Naturalization Service (INS) or an equivalent governmental agency.

indigenous personalities   Personality traits and characteristics found only in a particular culture.

individualism   A value that encourages, promotes, and advocates for individual autonomy and for fulfillment of individual needs and desires over the needs of the group.

institutional racism   Policies, procedures, or programs at the organizational level that maintain privileges for races in power at the expense of those with less power.

integration   During acculturation, the process of incorporating aspects of a new culture while maintaining aspects of one's native culture.

interactive volition   An assumption that humans possess an innate ability to choose (e.g., agency, free will) that interacts with the limitations imposed by their environment and physiological makeup. This perspective asserts that even though external behaviors may be limited and influenced by a variety of factors, human beings can choose their own internal responses.

intergenerational pain   Pain passed on from those who have directly suffered to successive generations. The term is frequently used to describe the lingering effects of slavery and oppression: Offspring have received a legacy of both suffering and resilience passed on through stories and on occasion are revived and reinforced by ongoing experiences.

Kwanzaa   A celebration of family, community, and culture among African Americans from December 26 to January 1. Seven principles (Nguzo Saba) are celebrated each day over this seven-day period: Unity (Umoja), Self-determination (Kujichagulia), Collective Work and Responsibility (Ujima), Cooperative Economics (Ujamaa), Purpose (Nia), Creativity (Kuumba), and Faith (Imani). The word Kwanzaa is derived from a Kiswahili phrase that is translated to mean "first fruits of the harvest."

linguistic relativity   Theory emphasizing the unique role that language plays in shaping people's thoughts and worldviews (see Sapir-Whorf hypothesis).

marginalization   Term used to refer either to a form of social exclusion wherein those with privilege and power tacitly disregard or fail to recognize others, or to an outcome of acculturation wherein individuals not only lose cultural and psychological contact with their traditional culture but do not adopt the ways of the new culture (see also integration, separation, and acculturation).

matriarchal   A family or society in which authority and power are held by women.

matrilineal   The custom of tracing kinship, descent, and inheritance through women.

melting pot   Metaphor for the idea that immigrants of different backgrounds should assimilate into an amalgam of people sharing similar national values, behaviors, traditions, etc. In the United States, this idea has at its core the principle of E Pluribus Unum (Out of many, One).

mindfulness   A state of being in tune to the present moment, including self-awareness and self-control. When acting mindfully, a person focuses on process rather than outcome, on appreciating rather than resolving.

misogynist   A person who has negative feelings toward women.

monocultural   A worldview informed by a single culture, characteristically the predominant culture in a given society. In North America, it would refer to a European American middle class perspective.

mulatto   A person of both Black and White heritage. This term can be used in a derogatory way; thus *biracial* or *multiracial* is often preferred.

multicultural competence   Sufficient awareness, knowledge, and skills to relate effectively with those who differ in race, gender, sexual orientation, age, ability, language, residency, nationality, faith, socioeconomic status, etc.

multicultural proficiency   Ability to consistently interact positively with those who differ in race, gender, sexual orientation, age, ability, language, residency, nationality, faith, and socioeconomic status. This ability is accompanied by an internalized commitment to challenge oppression and continually improve in cultural self-awareness, knowledge, and skills.

multiracial   Individuals whose ancestry includes different races (see also Biracial).

naikan therapy   A culture-specific approach to therapy used among Japanese peoples that includes meditation, self-reflection, and self-observation.

NAME   Abbreviation for the National Association for Multicultural Education.

native   Broadly, any person born in his or her country of residence or citizenship. More specifically, the original inhabitants of a region or nation prior to colonization.

naturalization   The process of conferring citizenship upon a person after birth. There is, typically, a specific number of years in residence required to attain this status.

nemawashi   An inclusive, consensus-building approach that is common among Japanese cultures (see Ringi).

network therapy   A treatment approach that recognizes and values the collaboration between the client, therapist, and outside persons (the client's network). In this approach, the roles of extended and intergenerational family members, as well as the roles of personnel within certain systems (such as school or church) are underscored in treatment outcome.

nigrescence   The process of internalizing a Black identity, typically associated with William Cross's model of racial identity development of Blacks, also referred to as the Psychology of Being Black.

orthogonal cultural self-identity   An assertion that individual identity is multifaceted, complicated by simultaneous group membership and the resulting interactions.

other-focus   A perspective that considers the needs, desires, perceptions, and abilities of the person with whom one is interacting with the purpose of adapting one's own behaviors to optimize the benefit for the other person.

outgroup homogeneity effect   The tendency to think and believe that members of an outgroup are all alike and that members of one's own group, or ingroup, are unique individuals.

pan-ethnicity   Use of a single term to label members of several ethnic groups as if they belonged to a single group, such as labeling Korean Americans, filipino Americans, and Sri Lankan Americans all as "Asian Americans."

patriarchy   A system or society where authority and power are vested in males.

patrilineal   The custom of tracing kinship, descent, and inheritance through males.

pecking order   A hierarchy within a social group in which the members at each tier assume leadership, power, and authority over those who are below them.

people of color   Contemporary term referring to individuals of African, Latin American, Asian, Pacific Islander, or Native (American Indian, Australian Aboriginal, etc.) descent.

personalismo   Spanish word that describes the mindset that values human relationships over formal rules and regulations.

postmodernism   A philosophy reacting against modernism that emphasizes the dialectical and narrative aspects of human experience. Social constructivism is a postmodern theory of psychology.

power (social power)   Ability to expand or diminish opportunities for oneself and/or others.

power distance   Signifies the degree to which cultures emphasize and maintain status and hierarchical differences among individuals.

powerful questions   Questions that invite consideration of core issues (without sarcasm or prejudice). Such questions can diffuse combative communication, invite dialogue where there was monologue, or encourage a shift away from the superficial or speculative.

prejudice   Judgments and attitudes (usually negative) about others based solely on their group affiliations or differences.

privileges   Unearned resources, opportunities, or advantages (typically taken for granted or not considered when judging oneself or others).

process (social process)   Refers to *how* interactions occur, particularly the emotional overtones and messages that underlie overt content.

psychosociocultural   A holistic, context-specific, culturally focused approach to social science (see also contextualism).

race   Social categorization of human beings based on geographic ancestry, as well as skin color and other physical attributes, as determined by the perceptions of the dominant group. Race is a political construct that reinforces divisions and hierarchies benefiting the dominant group.

racial identity development   The process of acquiring awareness and appreciation of one's own race and acceptance of the racial differences of others.

racial coping skills   Methods developed within a racial group for overcoming harmful effects of racial bias and discrimination (for example, see cultural mistrust).

racial-cultural psychology   In contrast to the generic term *multicultural psychology,* which denotes a host of human characteristics (race, gender, sexual orientation, etc.) and contains an implicit bias for an etic perspective, *racial-cultural psychology* emphasizes the salience of race and culture over other aspects of human diversity and leans toward an emic perspective.

racial profiling   The practice of targeting members of a particular racial or ethnic group for investigation of illegal behavior.

racism   A system whereby a group maintains power and privileges by disadvantaging others or failing to recognize others based on race or ethnicity.

reductionism   An approach to analysis that seeks to break down a phenomenon into smaller and smaller components.

refugee   Any person who is outside his or her country and is unable to return to that country because of persecution or the fear of persecution.

relational perspective   A framework for the social sciences that emphasizes the salience of interpersonal relationships for mental health and well-being.

ringi   A process of decision making found in Japanese cultures whereby members who will be influenced by a proposal are given the opportunity to address their concerns so that a consensus may be reached prior to formalization.

santería   Traditional form of healing and divination among Latin American cultures of the Caribbean.

sapir-whorf hypothesis   Proposition that people who speak different languages may in fact think in different ways and that bilinguals may have thought processes that differ from those of monolinguals (see also linguistic relativity).

self-in-relation   The perspective of considering the individual person in the context of his or her relationships with others and with the environment.

sexism   Any system, ideology, or action that fails to recognize women or accord them the same rights and freedoms as men.

social class (also socioeconomic status)   The relative standing of an individual in his or her larger society with regards to education, social networks, employment, and economic power and potential.

social constructivism (also social constructionism)   A theory that assumes that reality is a social construction. Social forces shape human perceptions, and those perceptions vary from one group and one individual to another. Thus reality is relative to the social experiences of the individual or group.

socialization   The process of learning and internalizing norms, attitudes, values, and beliefs of a given culture.

social mobility   The ability of an individual or group to move upward or downward in status. This movement can be based on wealth, occupation, education, or some other variable related to power and privilege.

stereotype   A generalized (and therefore oversimplified) belief about a group that is often used to distinguish that group from others and to interpret actions of that group's members.

system of multicultural pluralistic assessment (SOMPA)   An assessment procedure that attempts to adjust scores on the Wecshler Scale for Children-Revised (WISC-R) by taking into consideration various demographic, social, cultural, and linguistic variables, as well as medical assessments and parental input.

tightness   A measure of cultural variability that indicates the homogeneity of a particular culture.

triad training model   A training model for multicultural mental health delivery that makes internal dialogue explicit as two other professionals assume roles during a session: a procounselor, who points out effective practice, and an anticounselor, who calls attention to potential assumptions and biases in the counseling situation.

umoja One of the seven principles that are celebrated at Kwanzaa. Symbolizing unity, this principle emphasizes the need to strive for and maintain unity in the family, community, and nation.

uncertainty avoidance The process by which groups develop rituals and other mechanisms to deal with anxiety that arises from uncontrollable circumstances.

universalism Perspective affirming the fundamental similarities in human perception and experience, minimizing differences between people and groups.

worldview Conceptual framework from which to interpret and make sense of the world. Worldview is in essence the internalized culture of an individual, reflecting and reinforcing the previous observational learning and personal experience of the individual.

xenophobia An unreasonable fear or distrust of strangers, foreigners, or anything perceived as being different.

YAVIS Abbreviation describing people who are young, attractive, verbal, intelligent, and successful, who may be best suited for therapy within a Eurocentric framework.

Index